Student, Parent, Teacher
Internet Resources

Science Online   glencoe.com

Access your Student Edition on the Internet so you don't need to bring your textbook home every night. You can link to features and get additional practice with these Online Study Tools.

Check out the following features on your Online Learning Center:

Study Tools

- Animated Illustrations
- Section Self-Check Quizzes
- Chapter Test Practice
- Intermediate-Level Science Examination Practice

- Vocabulary PuzzleMaker
- Interactive Tutor
- Multilingual Science Glossary
- Online Student Edition
- BrainPOP Movies

Extensions

- Virtual Labs
- Microscopy Links
- Periodic Table Links
- Career Links

- Prescreened Web Links
- WebQuest Project
- Science Fair Ideas
- Internet Labs

For Teachers

- Teacher Bulletin Board
- Teaching Today, and much more!

SAFETY SYMBOLS

	HAZARD	EXAMPLES	PRECAUTION	REMEDY
DISPOSAL	Special disposal procedures need to be followed.	certain chemicals, living organisms	Do not dispose of these materials in the sink or trash can.	Dispose of wastes as directed by your teacher.
BIOLOGICAL	Organisms or other biological materials that might be harmful to humans	bacteria, fungi, blood, unpreserved tissues, plant materials	Avoid skin contact with these materials. Wear mask or gloves.	Notify your teacher if you suspect contact with material. Wash hands thoroughly.
EXTREME TEMPERATURE	Objects that can burn skin by being too cold or too hot	boiling liquids, hot plates, dry ice, liquid nitrogen	Use proper protection when handling.	Go to your teacher for first aid.
SHARP OBJECT	Use of tools or glassware that can easily puncture or slice skin	razor blades, pins, scalpels, pointed tools, dissecting probes, broken glass	Practice common-sense behavior and follow guidelines for use of the tool.	Go to your teacher for first aid.
FUME	Possible danger to respiratory tract from fumes	ammonia, acetone, nail polish remover, heated sulfur, moth balls	Make sure there is good ventilation. Never smell fumes directly. Wear a mask.	Leave foul area and notify your teacher immediately.
ELECTRICAL	Possible danger from electrical shock or burn	improper grounding, liquid spills, short circuits, exposed wires	Double-check setup with teacher. Check condition of wires and apparatus.	Do not attempt to fix electrical problems. Notify your teacher immediately.
IRRITANT	Substances that can irritate the skin or mucous membranes of the respiratory tract	pollen, moth balls, steel wool, fiberglass, potassium permanganate	Wear dust mask and gloves. Practice extra care when handling these materials.	Go to your teacher for first aid.
CHEMICAL	Chemicals can react with and destroy tissue and other materials	bleaches such as hydrogen peroxide; acids such as sulfuric acid, hydrochloric acid; bases such as ammonia, sodium hydroxide	Wear goggles, gloves, and an apron.	Immediately flush the affected area with water and notify your teacher.
TOXIC	Substance may be poisonous if touched, inhaled, or swallowed.	mercury, many metal compounds, iodine, poinsettia plant parts	Follow your teacher's instructions.	Always wash hands thoroughly after use. Go to your teacher for first aid.
FLAMMABLE	Flammable chemicals may be ignited by open flame, spark, or exposed heat.	alcohol, kerosene, potassium permanganate	Avoid open flames and heat when using flammable chemicals.	Notify your teacher immediately. Use fire safety equipment if applicable.
OPEN FLAME	Open flame in use, may cause fire.	hair, clothing, paper, synthetic materials	Tie back hair and loose clothing. Follow teacher's instruction on lighting and extinguishing flames.	Notify your teacher immediately. Use fire safety equipment if applicable.

 Eye Safety Proper eye protection should be worn at all times by anyone performing or observing science activities.

 Clothing Protection This symbol appears when substances could stain or burn clothing.

 Animal Safety This symbol appears when safety of animals and students must be ensured.

 Handwashing After the lab, wash hands with soap and water before removing goggles.

Unit 1 and Unit 2

Glencoe Science

New York Science
Grade 6

NATIONAL GEOGRAPHIC

Unit 1
Simple and Complex/Compound Machines

Unit 2
The Atmosphere, Hydrosphere, and Lithosphere

Mc Graw Hill **Glencoe**

New York, New York   Columbus, Ohio   Chicago, Illinois   Woodland Hills, California

Glencoe Science

New York Grade 6

The cover shows the Brooklyn Bridge spanning the East River between Manhattan and Brooklyn. At the completion of its construction on May 24, 1833, it was the longest suspension bridge in the world. The fossilized *Barosaurus* skeleton is on display at the American Museum of Natural History.

The polar bear, one of the attractions at the Bronx Zoo, is native to the Arctic and the only bear classified as an aquatic animal.

Glencoe Science

New York Science

Grade 6

Unit 1
Simple and Complex/Compound Machines

Unit 2
The Atmosphere, Hydrosphere, and Lithosphere

Unit 1 and Unit 2

NATIONAL GEOGRAPHIC

 Glencoe

The McGraw-Hill Companies

Send all inquiries to:
Glencoe/McGraw-Hill
8787 Orion Place
Columbus, OH 43240-4027

ISBN: 978-0-07-880316-1
MHID: 0-07-880316-0

1 2 3 4 5 6 7 8 9 10 071/055 12 11 10 09 08 07

Contents In Brief

The Glencoe Formula xx

unit 1

Simple and Complex/Compound Machines . . . 2
Chapter 1   The Nature of Science 4
Chapter 2   Energy and Energy Resources 40
Chapter 3   Work and Simple Machines 72

unit 2

**The Atmosphere, Hydrosphere,
and Lithosphere 100**
Chapter 4   States of Matter. 102
Chapter 5   Thermal Energy 134
Chapter 6   Atmosphere 160
Chapter 7   Weather 188

Authors

NATIONAL GEOGRAPHIC
Education Division
Washington, D.C.

Lucy Daniel, PhD
Teacher/Consultant
Rutherford County Schools
Rutherfordton, NC

Peter Rillero, PhD
Associate Professor of Science Education
Arizona State University West
Phoenix, AZ

Susan Leach Snyder
Retired Teacher, Consultant
Jones Middle School
Upper Arlington, OH

Dinah Zike
Educational Consultant
Dinah-Might Activities, Inc.
San Antonio, TX

Series Consultants

CONTENT

Alton J. Banks, PhD
Director of the Faculty Center
for Teaching and Learning
North Carolina State University
Raleigh, NC

Jack Cooper
Ennis High School
Ennis, TX

Sandra K. Enger, PhD
Associate Director,
Associate Professor
UAH Institute for Science Education
Huntsville, AL

David G. Haase, PhD
North Carolina State University
Raleigh, NC

Michael A. Hoggarth, PhD
Department of Life and
Earth Sciences
Otterbein College
Westerville, OH

Jerome A. Jackson, PhD
Whitaker Eminent Scholar in Science
Program Director
Center for Science, Mathematics,
and Technology Education
Florida Gulf Coast University
Fort Meyers, FL

William C. Keel, PhD
Department of Physics
and Astronomy
University of Alabama
Tuscaloosa, AL

Linda McGaw
Science Program Coordinator
Advanced Placement Strategies, Inc.
Dallas, TX

Madelaine Meek
Physics Consultant Editor
Lebanon, OH

Robert Nierste
Science Department Head
Hendrick Middle School, Plano ISD
Plano, TX

Connie Rizzo, MD, PhD
Department of Science/Math
Marymount Manhattan College
New York, NY

Dominic Salinas, PhD
Middle School Science Supervisor
Caddo Parish Schools
Shreveport, LA

Cheryl Wistrom
St. Joseph's College
Rensselaer, IN

Carl Zorn, PhD
Staff Scientist
Jefferson Laboratory
Newport News, VA

MATH

Michael Hopper, DEng
Manager of Aircraft Certification
L-3 Communications
Greenville, TX

Teri Willard, EdD
Mathematics Curriculum Writer
Belgrade, MT

READING

Elizabeth Babich
Special Education Teacher
Mashpee Public Schools
Mashpee, MA

Barry Barto
Special Education Teacher
John F. Kennedy Elementary
Manistee, MI

Carol A. Senf, PhD
School of Literature,
Communication, and Culture
Georgia Institute of Technology
Atlanta, GA

Rachel Swaters-Kissinger
Science Teacher
John Boise Middle School
Warsaw, MO

SAFETY

Aileen Duc, PhD
Science 8 Teacher
Hendrick Middle School, Plano ISD
Plano, TX

Sandra West, PhD
Department of Biology
Texas State University-San Marcos
San Marcos, TX

ACTIVITY TESTERS

Nerma Coats Henderson
Pickerington Lakeview Jr. High
School
Pickerington, OH

Mary Helen Mariscal-Cholka
William D. Slider Middle School
El Paso, TX

**Science Kit and Boreal
Laboratories**
Tonawanda, NY

Reviewers

Deidre Adams
West Vigo Middle School
West Terre Haute, IN

Sharla Adams
IPC Teacher
Allen High School
Allen, TX

Maureen Barrett
Thomas E. Harrington Middle School
Mt. Laurel, NJ

John Barry
Seeger Jr.-Sr. High School
West Lebanon, IN

Desiree Bishop
Environmental Studies Center
Mobile County Public Schools
Mobile, AL

William Blair
Retired Teacher
J. Marshall Middle School
Billerica, MA

Tom Bright
Concord High School
Charlotte, NC

Lois Burdette
Green Bank Elementary-Middle
School
Green Bank, WV

Marcia Chackan
Pine Crest School
Boca Raton, FL

Obioma Chukwu
J.H. Rose High School
Greenville, NC

Karen Curry
East Wake Middle School
Raleigh, NC
Merrilville, IN

Joanne Davis
Murphy High School
Murphy, NC

Robin Dillon
Hanover Central High School
Cedar Lake, IN

Teacher Advisory Board

The Teacher Advisory Board gave the authors, editorial staff, and design team feedback on the content and design of the Student Edition. They provided valuable input in its development.

John Gonzales
Challenger Middle School
Tucson, AZ

Rachel Shively
Aptakisic Jr. High School
Buffalo Grove, IL

Roger Pratt
Manistique High School
Manistique, MI

Kirtina Hile
Northmor Jr. High/High School
Galion, OH

Marie Renner
Diley Middle School
Pickerington, OH

Nelson Farrier
Hamlin Middle School
Springfield, OR

Jeff Remington
Palmyra Middle School
Palmyra, PA

Erin Peters
Williamsburg Middle School
Arlington, VA

Rubidel Peoples
Meacham Middle School
Fort Worth, TX

Kristi Ramsey
Navasota Jr. High School
Navasota, TX

Student Advisory Board

The Student Advisory Board gave the authors, editorial staff, and design team feedback on the design of the Student Edition. We thank these students for their hard work and creative suggestions.

Jack Andrews
Reynoldsburg Jr. High School
Reynoldsburg, OH

Peter Arnold
Hastings Middle School
Upper Arlington, OH

Emily Barbe
Perry Middle School
Worthington, OH

Kirsty Bateman
Hilliard Heritage Middle School
Hilliard, OH

Andre Brown
Spanish Emersion Academy
Columbus, OH

Chris Dundon
Heritage Middle School
Westerville, OH

Ryan Manafee
Monroe Middle School
Columbus, OH

Addison Owen
Davis Middle School
Dublin, OH

Teriana Patrick
Eastmoor Middle School
Columbus, OH

Ashley Ruz
Karrar Middle School
Dublin, OH

The Glencoe middle school science Student Advisory Board taking a timeout at COSI, a science museum in Columbus, Ohio.

Contents

unit 1

Simple and Complex/ Compound Machines—2

chapter 1

The Nature of Science—4

Section 1 What is science? 6
Section 2 Science in Action 12
Section 3 Models in Science .21
Section 4 Evaluating Scientific Explanation 27
      Lab What is the right answer? 31
      Lab Identifying Parts of an Investigation 32

chapter 2

Energy and Energy Resources—40

Section 1 What is energy? 42
Section 2 Energy Transformations 47
      Lab Hearing with Your Jaw 54
Section 3 Sources of Energy 55
      Lab: Use the Internet
      Energy to Power Your Life 64

chapter 3

Work and Simple Machines—72

Section 1 Work and Power 74
      Lab Building the Pyramids 79
Section 2 Using Machines 80
Section 3 Simple Machines 85
      Lab Pulley Power 92

In each chapter, look for these opportunities for review and assessment:
- Reading Checks
- Caption Questions
- Section Review
- Chapter Study Guide
- Chapter Review
- Intermediate-Level Science Examination Practice
- Online practice at glencoe.com

unit 2 The Atmosphere, Hydrosphere, and Lithosphere—100

chapter 4 States of Matter—102

Section 1 Matter 104
Section 2 Changes of State 109
           Lab The Water Cycle 117
Section 3 Behavior of Fluids .118
           Lab: Design Your Own
           Design Your Own Ship 126

chapter 5 Thermal Energy—134

Section 1 Temperature and Thermal Energy 136
Section 2 Heat 140
           Lab Heating Up and Cooling Down 146
Section 3 Engines and Refrigerators 147
           Lab: Design Your Own
           Comparing Thermal Insulators 152

chapter 6 Atmosphere—160

Section 1 Earth's Atmosphere .162
           Lab Evaluating Sunscreens 170
Section 2 Energy Transfer in the Atmosphere 171
Section 3 Air Movement 175
           Lab: Design Your Own
           The Heat is On 180

chapter 7 Weather—188

Section 1 What is weather? 190
Section 2 Weather Patterns 198
Section 3 Weather Forecasts 206
           Lab Reading a Weather Map 209
           Lab: Model and Invent
           Measuring Wind Speed 210

Contents

Student Resources—340

▪ Science Skill Handbook—342
Scientific Methods 342
Safety Symbols 351
Safety in the Science Laboratory 352

▪ Extra Try at Home Labs—354

▪ Technology Skill Handbook—360
Computer Skills 360

▪ Math Skill Handbook—364
Math Review 364
Science Applications 374

▪ Reference Handbooks—379
Use and Care of a Microscope 379
Topographic Map Symbols 380
Weather Map Symbols 381
Diversity of Life: Classification of
     Living Organisms 382
Periodic Table of Elements 386

▪ English/Spanish Glossary—388

▪ Index—402

▪ Credits—413

NATIONAL GEOGRAPHIC Unit Openers

Unit 1 How are Train Schedules and Oil Pumps Connected? 2
Unit 2 How are Bats and Tornadoes Connected? 100

NATIONAL GEOGRAPHIC VISUALIZING

1 Visualizing the Modeling of King Tut 24
2 Visualizing Energy Transformations. 50
3 Visualizing Levers 89
4 Visualizing States of Matter. 112
5 Visualizing the Four-Stroke Cycle. 149
6 Visualizing Global Winds 177
7 Visualizing Tornadoes 203

Content Details

Content Details

TIME SCIENCE AND Society

1 Women in Science 34
5 The Heat is On 154
7 Rainmakers 212

TIME SCIENCE AND HISTORY

3 Bionic People. 94

4 The Incredible Stretching Goo 128

Science and Language Arts

6 "Song of the Sky Loom" 182

SCIENCE Stats

2 Energy to Burn 66

LABS

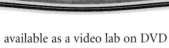 available as a video lab on DVD

Launch LAB

1 Observe How Gravity Accelerates Objects 5
2 Marbles and Energy 41
3 Compare Forces 73
4 Experiment with a Freezing Liquid 103
5 Measuring Temperature 135
6 Observe Air Pressure 161
7 What causes rain? 189

Mini LAB

1 Thinking Like a Scientist 23
2 Building a Solar Collector 59
3 Observing Pulleys 90
4 Observing Vaporization 114
5 Observing Convection 143
6 Determining if Air Has Mass 167
7 Determining Dew Point 192

Content Details

 available as a video lab on DVD

1 Classifying Parts of a System 8
1 Forming a Hypothesis 14
2 Analyzing Energy Transformations. 49
3 Work and Power 77
4 Predicting a Waterfall 121
5 Comparing Rates of Melting 142
6 Modeling Heat Transfer 173
7 Measuring Rain. 207

One-Page Labs

1 What is the right answer?. 31
2 Hearing with Your Jaw 54
3 Building the Pyramids 79
4 The Water Cycle 117
5 Heating Up and Cooling Down 146
6 Evaluating Sunscreens 170
7 Reading a Weather Map. 209

Two-Page Labs

1 Identifying Parts of an Investigation. 32
3 Pulley Power 92

Design Your Own Labs

(DVD) **4** Design Your Own Ship. 126
5 Comparing Thermal Insulators. 152
6 The Heat is On 180

Model and Invent Lab

(DVD) **7** Measuring Wind Speed 210

Use the Internet Lab

2 Energy to Power Your Life 64

Content Details

Activities

Applying Math

1 Seasonal Temperatures 17
3 Calculating Work 76
3 Calculating Power 77
3 Calculating Mechanical Advantage 81
3 Calculating Efficiency 83
4 Calculating Density 123
5 Converting to Celsius 138
7 Dew Point 193

Applying Science

2 Is energy consumption outpacing production? 58
4 How can ice save oranges? 113
6 How does altitude affect air pressure 166

Career: 13, 150
Earth Science: 56
Environment: 204
Health: 9, 169
History: 76, 77, 106
Life Science: 49, 51, 83, 87, 125, 144, 145, 168, 191
Physics: 110, 172, 199

18, 22, 48, 58, 78, 81, 107, 113, 115, 125, 148, 164, 176, 199, 202

Intermediate-Level Science Examination Practice

38-39, 70-71, 98-99, 132-133, 158-159, 186-187, 216-217

The Glencoe Formula

for successfully mastering the New York Intermediate Level Science Core Curriculum.

Learning + Practicing = *Success!*

Content Details

Learning

chapter 11

Ecosystems

LE 7.1a: A population consists of all individuals of a species that are found together at a given place and time. Populations living in one place form a community. The community and the physical factors with which it interacts compose an ecosystem. 7.1c: In all environments, organisms interact with one another in many ways. **Also covered:** 7.2a, 7.2b, 7.2c, 7.2d.

Major Understandings
• The beginning of each chapter lists the Major Understandings you'll learn in that chapter.

• The beginning of each section lists the Major Understandings you'll learn in that section.

section 1

LE 7.2b: The environment may be altered through the activities of organisms. Alterations are sometimes abrupt. Some species may replace others over time, resulting in long-term gradual changes (ecological succession). **Also covered:** 7.1c, 7.2a.

How Ecosystems Change

as you read

***What* You'll Learn**

■ Explain how ecosystems change over time.
■ Describe how new communities begin in areas without life.
■ Compare pioneer species and climax communities.

***Why* It's Important**

Understanding ecosystems and your role in them can help you manage your impact on them and predict the changes that may happen in the future.

Review Vocabula

Ecological Succession

What would happen if the lawn at your home were never cut? The grass would get longer, as in **Figure 1,** and soon it would look like a meadow. Later, larger plants would grow from seeds brought to the area by animals or wind. Then, trees might sprout. In fact, in 20 years or less you wouldn't be able to tell that the land was once a mowed lawn. An ecologist can tell you what type of ecosystem your lawn would become. If it would become a forest, they can tell you how long it would take and predict the type of trees that would grow there. **Succession** refers to the normal, gradual changes that occur in the types of species that live in an area. Succession occurs differently in different places around the world.

Primary Succession As lava flows from the mouth of a volcano, it is not that destroys everything in its path

The Glencoe Formula

Practicing

Major Understanding Focus
• Focuses on and assesses Major Understandings presented in that section

 Living Environment

7.2c, 7.2d: Hypothesize how the effects of human activities have resulted in pollution to aquatic ecosystems.

New York Intermediate Level Science Examination Practice
Two Pages Created Specifically for New York covering the New York Intermediate-Level Science Core Curriculum.

Content Details

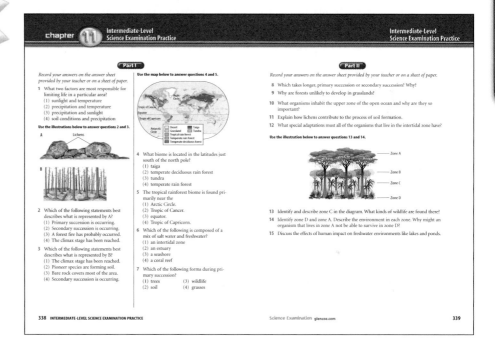

Test–Taking Tips

✓ Go to bed early the night before the test. You will think more clearly after a good night's rest.

✓ Read each problem carefully, underline key words, and think about ways to solve the problem before answering the question.

✓ Relax. It's natural to be nervous when taking a test. Just do your best.

✓ Try to answer each question in order. If you are unsure of an answer, mark your best guess and then mark the question in your test booklet. This will be a reminder to come back to the question at the end of the test.

✓ Think positively. Some problems may seem hard to you, but you may be able to figure out what to do if you read each question carefully.

✓ If no figure is provided, draw one. If one is furnished, mark it up to help you solve the problem.

✓ When you have finished each problem, reread it to make sure your answer is complete and reasonable.

✓ Make sure that the number of the question on the answer sheet matches the number of the question on which you are working in your test booklet.

The Intermediate-Level Science Core Curriculum

The New York State Intermediate Level Science Core Curriculum was written to guide instruction and assessment for Standards 1, 2, 4, 6, and 7 of the New York State Learning Standards for Mathematics, Science, and Technology. The standards have been organized into Key Ideas, Performance Indicators, and Major Understandings.

- **Key Ideas** are broad, unifying, general statements of what students need to know.
- **Performance Indicators** for each Key Idea are statements of what students should be able to do to provide evidence that they understand the Key Idea.
- **Major Understandings** provide specific detail about the concepts underlying each Performance Indicator.

Interpreting Major Understanding Identifiers

Major Understanding identifiers appear at the beginning of each chapter and section and are organized into the following categories:

LE   The Living Environment
PS   The Physical Setting
AID   Analysis Inquiry and Design
IS   Information Systems
ICT   Interconnectedness: Common Themes
IPS   Interdisciplinary Problem Solving

Here is how to interpret the Major Understanding for **LE 7.2c.**

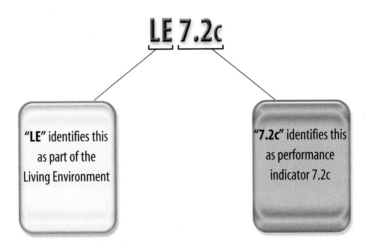

LE 7.2c

"**LE**" identifies this as part of the Living Environment

"**7.2c**" identifies this as performance indicator 7.2c

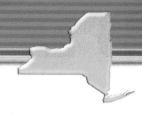

STANDARDS 1, 2, 6, AND 7: EXPANDED PROCESS SKILLS

Science process skills should be based on a series of discoveries. Students learn most effectively when they have a central role in the discovery process. To that end, Standards 1, 2, 6, and 7 incorporate in the Intermediate Core Curriculum *a student centered, problem-solving approach to intermediate science. The following is an expanded version of the skills found in Standards 1, 2, 6, and 7 of the* Learning Standards for Mathematics, Science, and Technology. *This list is not intended to be an all-inclusive list of the content or skills that teachers are expected to incorporate into their curriculum. It should be a goal of the instructor to encourage science process skills that will provide students with background and curiosity sufficient to prompt investigation of important issues in the world around them.*

Standards	Page Numbers
STANDARD 1—Analysis, Inquiry, and Design Students will use mathematical analysis, scientific inquiry, and engineering design, as appropriate, to pose questions, seek answers, and develop solutions.	
MATHEMATICAL ANALYSIS: *Key Idea 1:* Abstraction and symbolic representation are used to communicate mathematically.	
M1.1 Extend mathematical notation and symbolism to include variables and algebraic expressions in order to describe and compare quantities and express mathematical relationships.	
M1.1a identify independent and dependent variables	117
M1.1b identify relationships among variables including: direct, indirect, cyclic, constant; identify non-related material	117, 146
M1.1c apply mathematical equations to describe relationships among variables in the natural world	21, 74, 76, 77, 79, 80, 85, 92–93, 152–153
MATHEMATICAL ANALYSIS: *Key Idea 2:* Deductive and inductive reasoning are used to reach mathematical conclusions.	
M2.1 Use inductive reasoning to construct, evaluate, and validate conjectures and arguments, recognizing that patterns and relationships can assist in explaining and extending mathematical phenomena.	
M2.1a interpolate and extrapolate from data	146, 209
M2.1b quantify patterns and trends	103, 152–153
MATHEMATICAL ANALYSIS: *Key Idea 3:* Critical thinking skills are used in the solution of mathematical problems.	
M3.1 Apply mathematical knowledge to solve real-world problems and problems that arise from the investigation of mathematical ideas, using representations such as pictures, charts, and tables.	
M3.1a use appropriate scientific tools to solve problems about the natural world	126–127, 146, 152–153
SCIENTIFIC INQUIRY: *Key Idea 1:* The central purpose of scientific inquiry is to develop explanations of natural phenomena in a continuing, creative process.	
S1.1 Formulate questions independently with the aid of references appropriate for guiding the search for explanations of everyday observations.	
S1.1a formulate questions about natural phenomena	6, 12, 126–127, 152–153, 170, 180

Standards	Page Numbers
S1.1b identify appropriate references to investigate a question	12, 64–65
S1.1c refine and clarify questions so that they are subject to scientific investigation	5, 6, 12
S1.2 Construct explanations independently for natural phenomena, especially by proposing preliminary visual models of phenomena.	
S1.2a independently formulate a hypothesis	5, 12, 14, 126–127, 152–153, 167, 210–211
S1.2b propose a model of a natural phenomenon	5, 12, 21, 210–211
S1.2c differentiate among observations, inferences, predictions, and explanations	12, 79, 167, 180
S1.3 Represent, present, and defend their proposed explanations of everyday observations so that they can be understood and assessed by others.	103, 142, 143, 145, 152–153, 173, 189, 207, 209, 210–211
SCIENTIFIC INQUIRY: *Key Idea 2:* Beyond the use of reasoning and consensus, scientific inquiry involves the testing of proposed explanations involving the use of conventional techniques and procedures and usually requiring considerable ingenuity.	
S2.1 Use conventional techniques and those of their own design to make further observations and refine their explanations, guided by a need for more information.	
S2.1a demonstrate appropriate safety techniques	12
S2.1b conduct an experiment designed by others	41, 49, 54, 59, 73, 79, 114, 117, 121, 135, 142, 143, 146, 161, 170, 173, 189, 192, 207, 209
S2.1c design and conduct an experiment to test a hypothesis	126–127, 152–153, 180, 210–211
S2.1d use appropriate tools and conventional techniques to solve problems about the natural world, including: • measuring • observing • describing • classifying • sequencing	5, 8, 12, 14, 23, 41, 49, 54, 59, 79, 90, 103, 117, 126–127, 135, 146, 152–153, 210–211

Standards	Page Numbers
S2.2 Develop, present, and defend formal research proposals for testing their own explanations of common phenomena, including ways of obtaining needed observations and ways of conducting simple controlled experiments.	
S2.2a include appropriate safety procedures	12, 19, 92–93, 126–127
S2.2b design scientific investigations (e.g., observing, describing, and comparing; collecting samples; seeking more information, conducting a controlled experiment; discovering new objects or phenomena; making models)	12, 92–93, 152–153
S2.2c design a simple controlled experiment	12, 18, 126–127, 152–153, 180
S2.2d identify independent variables (manipulated), dependent variables (responding), and constants in a simple controlled experiment	12, 18, 32–33
S2.3 Carry out their research proposals, recording observations and measurements (e.g., lab notes, audiotape, computer disk, videotape) to help assess the explanation.	
S2.3a use appropriate safety procedures	92–93, 126–127, 146, 152–153, 210–211
S2.3b conduct a scientific investigation	92–93, 126–127, 146, 152–153
S2.3c collect quantitative and qualitative data	23, 59, 92–93, 126–127, 146, 170, 180
SCIENTIFIC INQUIRY: *Key Idea 3:* The observations made while testing proposed explanations, when analyzed using conventional and invented methods, provide new insights into phenomena.	
S3.1 Design charts, tables, graphs, and other representations of observations in conventional and creative ways to help them address their research question or hypothesis.	
S3.1a organize results, using appropriate graphs, diagrams, data tables, and other models to show relationships	12, 32–33, 54, 59, 117, 126–127, 146, 152–153, 170, 180, 192, 210–211
S3.1b generate and use scales, create legends, and appropriately label axes	32–33
S3.2 Interpret the organized data to answer the research question or hypothesis and to gain insight into the problem.	
S3.2a accurately describe the procedures used and the data gathered	32–33, 126–127, 135, 152–153, 170, 180, 210–211

Standards	Page Numbers
S3.2b identify sources of error and the limitations of data collected	27, 28–29, 32–33, 152–153, 161, 210–211
S3.2c evaluate the original hypothesis in light of the data	14, 32–33, 126–127, 152–153
S3.2d formulate and defend explanations and conclusions as they relate to scientific phenomena	59, 103, 121, 142, 146, 189, 192, 207, 209
S3.2f make predictions based on experimental data	5, 90, 114, 126–127, 152–153
S3.2g suggest improvements and recommendations for further studying	117
S3.2h use and interpret graphs and data tables	32–33, 64–65, 126–127, 146, 152–153, 170, 209
ENGINEERING DESIGN: *Key Idea 1:* Engineering design is an iterative process involving modeling and optimization (finding the best solution within given constraints); this process is used to develop technological solutions to problems within given constraints.	
T1.1 Identify needs and opportunities for technical solutions from an investigation of situations of general or social interest.	
T1.1a identify a scientific or human need that is subject to a technological solution which applies scientific principles	6, 11
T1.4 Develop plans, including drawings with measurements and details of construction, and construct a model of the solution, exhibiting a degree of craftsmanship.	
T1.4b construct a model of the product or process	210–211
T1.5 In a group setting, test their solution against design specifications, present and evaluate results, describe how the solution might have been modified for different or better results, and discuss trade-offs that might have to be made.	
T1.5a test a design	210–211

Standards	Page Numbers
STANDARD 2—Information Systems Students will access, generate, process, and transfer information, using appropriate technologies.	
Key Idea 1: Information technology is used to retrieve, process, and communicate information as a tool to enhance learning.	
1.3 Systematically obtain accurate and relevant information pertaining to a particular topic from a range of sources, including local and national media, libraries, museums, governmental agencies, industries, and individuals.	64–65
1.4 Collect data from probes to measure events and phenomena.	64–65
1.4a collect the data, using the appropriate, available tool	210–211
1.4b organize the data	210–211
1.4c use the collected data to communicate a scientific concept	210–211
1.5 Use simple modeling programs to make predictions.	21
Key Idea 2: Knowledge of the impacts and limitations of information systems is essential to its effectiveness and ethical use.	
2.1 Understand the need to question the accuracy of information displayed on a computer because the results produced by a computer may be affected by incorrect data entry.	
2.1a critically analyze data to exclude erroneous information	170, 180

Standards	Page Numbers

STANDARD 6—Interconnectedness: Common Themes Students will understand the relationships and common themes that connect mathematics, science, and technology and apply the themes to these and other areas of learning.

SYSTEMS THINKING: *Key Idea 1:* Through systems thinking, people can recognize the commonalities that exist among all systems and how parts of a system interrelate and combine to perform specific functions.

1.2 Describe the differences and similarities among engineering systems, natural systems, and social systems.	6, 8
1.4 Describe how the output from one part of a system (which can include material, energy, or information) can become the input to other parts.	8

MODELS: *Key Idea 2:* Models are simplified representations of objects, structures, or systems used in analysis, explanation, interpretation, or design.

2.1 Select an appropriate model to begin the search for answers or solutions to a question or problem.	21, 22, 31
2.2 Use models to study processes that cannot be studied directly (e.g., when the real process is too slow, too fast, or too dangerous for direct observation).	21, 31
2.3 Demonstrate the effectiveness of different models to represent the same thing and the same model to represent different things.	31

PATTERNS OF CHANGE: *Key Idea 5:* Identifying patterns of change is necessary for making predictions about future behavior and conditions.

5.1 Use simple linear equations to represent how a parameter changes with time.	152–153, 180
5.2 Observe patterns of change in trends or cycles and make predictions on what might happen in the future.	152–153

OPTIMIZATION: *Key Idea 6:* In order to arrive at the best solution that meets criteria within constraints, it is often necessary to make trade-offs.

6.2 Use graphs of information for a decision-making problem to determine the optimum solution.	180

Standards	Page Numbers
STANDARD 7—Interdisciplinary Problem Solving Students will apply the knowledge and thinking skills of mathematics, science, and technology to address real-life problems and make informed decisions.	
CONNECTIONS: *Key Idea 1:* The knowledge and skills of mathematics, science, and technology are used together to make informed decisions and solve problems, especially those relating to issues of science/technology/society, consumer decision making, design, and inquiry into phenomena.	
1.2 Make informed consumer decisions by seeking answers to appropriate questions about products, services, and systems; determining the cost/benefit and risk/benefit tradeoffs; and applying this knowledge to a potential purchase.	27, 30, 170
1.3 Design solutions to real-world problems of general social interest related to home, school, or community using scientific experimentation to inform the solution and applying mathematical concepts and reasoning to assist in developing a solution.	170
STRATEGIES: *Key Idea 2:* Solving interdisciplinary problems involves a variety of skills and strategies, including effective work habits; gathering and processing information; generating and analyzing ideas; realizing ideas; making connections among the common themes of mathematics, science, and technology; and presenting results.	
2.1 Students participate in an extended, culminating mathematics, science, and technology project. The project would require students to: • **Working Effectively:** Contributing to the work of a brainstorming group, laboratory partnership, cooperative learning group, or project team; planning procedures; identify and managing responsibilities of team members; and staying on task, whether working alone or as part of a group. • **Gathering and Processing Information:** Accessing information from printed media, electronic data bases, and community resources and using the information to develop a definition of the problem and to research possible solutions. • **Generating and Analyzing Ideas:** Developing ideas for proposed solutions, investigating ideas, collecting data, and showing relationships and patterns in the data. • **Common Themes:** Observing examples of common unifying themes, applying them to the problem, and using them to better understand the dimensions of the problem. • **Realizing Ideas:** Constructing components or models, arriving at a solution, and evaluating the result. • **Presenting Results:** Using a variety of media to present the solution and to communicate the results.	126–127, 152–153, 180, 210–211

Standards	Page Numbers
PROCESS SKILLS BASED ON STANDARD 4	
General Skills	
1. follow safety procedures in the classroom and laboratory	5, 8, 14, 23, 31, 32, ,41, 49, 54, 59, 64, 73, 77, 79, 90, 92, 103, 114, 117, 121, 126, 135, 142, 143, 146, 152, 161, 167, 170, 173, 180, 189, 192, 207, 209, 210, 351–353, 354–359
2. safely and accurately use the following measurement tools:	
• metric ruler	41, 92, 180, 207, 210, 347
• balance	92, 126, 167, 348
• stopwatch	79, 146, 152
• graduated cylinder	126, 152, 348
• thermometer	59, 103, 117, 146, 152, 180, 192, 349, 356
• spring scale	92
3. use appropriate units for measured or calculated values	76, 77, 79, 81, 83, 92, 103, 117, 138, 180, 192, 193, 356
4. recognize and analyze patterns and trends	5, 14, 31, 32, 41, 49, 58, 59, 73, 90, 92, 126, 135, 142, 146, 152, 166, 170, 193, 209, 354, 355, 358
5. classify objects according to an established scheme and a student-generated scheme	349, 355, 357, 382–385

Standards	Page Numbers
7. sequence events	8, 17, 344
8. identify cause-and-effect relationships	23, 41, 49, 54, 59, 73, 92, 113, 114, 121, 126, 142, 143, 146, 152, 161, 173, 189, 209, 354, 356
Living Environment Skills	
1. manipulate a compound microscope to view microscopic objects	379
3. prepare a wet mount slide	379
6. classify living things according to a student-generated scheme and an established scheme	355, 357, 382–385
Physical Setting Skills	
7. generate and interpret field maps including topographic and weather maps	209, 380–381
8. predict the characteristics of an air mass based on the origin of the air mass	209, 381
9. measure weather variables such as wind speed and direction, relative humidity, barometric pressure, etc.	207, 210, 356, 381
11. determine the volume of a regular- and an irregular-shaped solid, using water displacement	126

Standards	Page Numbers

STANDARD 4: The Physical Setting Students will understand and apply scientific concepts, principles, and theories pertaining to the physical setting and living environment and recognize the historical development of ideas in science.

Key Idea 2: Many of the phenomena that we observe on Earth involve interactions among components of air, water, and land.

PERFORMANCE INDICATOR 2.1 *Explain how the atmosphere (air), hydrosphere (water), and lithosphere (land) interact, evolve, and change.*

2.1a Nearly all the atmosphere is confined to a thin shell surrounding Earth. The atmosphere is a mixture of gases, including nitrogen and oxygen with small amounts of water vapor, carbon dioxide, and other trace gases. The atmosphere is stratified into layers, each having distinct properties. Nearly all weather occurs in the lowest layer of the atmosphere.	162–163
2.1b As altitude increases, air pressure decreases.	162
2.1c The rock at Earth's surface forms a nearly continuous shell around Earth called the lithosphere.	162
2.1d The majority of the lithosphere is covered by a relatively thin layer of water called the hydrosphere.	162
2.1j Water circulates through the atmosphere, lithosphere, and hydrosphere in what is known as the water cycle.	171

PERFORMANCE INDICATOR 2.2 *Describe volcano and earthquake patterns, the rock cycle, and weather and climate changes.*

2.2i Weather describes the conditions of the atmosphere at a given location for a short period of time.	190, 192, 206
2.2j Climate is the characteristic weather that prevails from season to season and year to year.	206
2.2k The uneven heating of Earth's surface is the cause of weather.	175, 190
2.2l Air masses form when air remains nearly stationary over a large section of Earth's surface and takes on the conditions of temperature and humidity from that location. Weather conditions at a location are determined primarily by temperature, humidity, and pressure of air masses over that location.	175, 190, 198, 206
2.2m Most local weather condition changes are caused by movement of air masses.	175, 198, 206
2.2n The movement of air masses is determined by prevailing winds and upper air currents.	175, 190, 198
2.2o Fronts are boundaries between air masses. Precipitation is likely to occur at these boundaries.	190, 198, 199
2.2p High-pressure systems generally bring fair weather. Low-pressure systems usually bring cloudy, unstable conditions. The general movement of highs and lows is from west to east across the United States.	198

Standards	Page Numbers
2.2r Substances enter the atmosphere naturally and from human activity. Some of these substances include dust from volcanic eruptions and greenhouse gases such as carbon dioxide, methane, and water vapor. These substances can affect weather, climate, and living things.	55

Key Idea 3: Matter is made up of particles whose properties determine the observable characteristics of matter and its reactivity.

PERFORMANCE INDICATOR 3.1 *Observe and describe properties of materials, such as density, conductivity, and solubility.*

Standards	Page Numbers
3.1a Substances have characteristic properties. Some of these properties include color, odor, phase at room temperature, density, solubility, heat and electrical conductivity, hardness, and boiling and freezing points.	104
3.1c The motion of particles helps to explain the phases (states) of matter as well as changes from one phase to another. The phase in which matter exists depends on the attractive forces among its particles.	104–106, 109, 118
3.1d Gases have neither a determined shape nor a definite volume. Gases assume the shape and volume of a closed container.	104–106
3.1e A liquid has definite volume, but takes the shape of a container.	104–106
3.1f A solid has definite shape and volume. Particles resist a change in position.	104–106
3.1h Density can be described as the amount of matter that is in a given amount of space. If two objects have equal volume, but one has more mass, the one with more mass is denser.	118–119, 122–123
3.1i Buoyancy is determined by comparative densities.	118–119, 122–123

PERFORMANCE INDICATOR 3.2 *Distinguish between chemical and physical changes.*

Standards	Page Numbers
3.2a During a physical change a substance keeps its chemical composition and properties. Examples of physical changes include freezing, melting, condensation, boiling, evaporation, tearing, and crushing.	109, 111, 113–115, 135

PERFORMANCE INDICATOR 3.3 *Develop mental models to explain common chemical reactions and changes in states of matter.*

Standards	Page Numbers
3.3a All matter is made up of atoms. Atoms are far too small to see with a light microscope.	104
3.3b Atoms and molecules are perpetually in motion. The greater the temperature, the greater the motion.	104, 109, 118, 136, 161, 171

Standards	Page Numbers

Key Idea 4: Energy exists in many forms, and when these forms change energy is conserved.

PERFORMANCE INDICATOR 4.1 *Describe the sources and identify the transformations of energy observed in everyday life.*

4.1a The Sun is a major source of energy for Earth. Other sources of energy include nuclear and geothermal energy.	55, 59, 171
4.1b Fossil fuels contain stored solar energy and are considered nonrenewable resources. They are a major source of energy in the United States. Solar energy, wind, moving water, and biomass are some examples of renewable energy resources.	55, 56–63, 64–65, 172
4.1c Most activities in everyday life involve one form of energy being transformed into another. For example, the chemical energy in gasoline is transformed into mechanical energy in an automobile engine. Energy, in the form of heat, is almost always one of the products of energy transformations.	41, 47, 54, 64–65, 109
4.1d Different forms of energy include heat, light, electrical, mechanical, sound, nuclear, and chemical. Energy is transformed in many ways.	42, 44–46, 47, 54, 64–65, 109, 147, 171
4.1e Energy can be considered to be either kinetic energy, which is the energy of motion, or potential energy, which depends on relative position.	42, 43–44, 47, 49, 136, 137

PERFORMANCE INDICATOR 4.2 *Observe and describe heating and cooling events.*

4.2a Heat moves in predictable ways, flowing from warmer objects to cooler ones, until both reach the same temperature.	140, 171
4.2b Heat can be transferred through matter by the collisions of atoms and/or molecules (conduction) or through space (radiation). In a liquid or gas, currents will facilitate the transfer of heat (convection).	140, 141–142, 171
4.2c During a phase change, heat energy is absorbed or released. Energy is absorbed when a solid changes to a liquid and when a liquid changes to a gas. Energy is released when a gas changes to a liquid and when a liquid changes to a solid.	109, 114, 117, 135
4.2d Most substances expand when heated and contract when cooled. Water is an exception, expanding when changing to ice.	103, 117

PERFORMANCE INDICATOR 4.3 *Observe and describe energy changes as related to chemical reactions.*

4.3a In chemical reactions, energy is transferred into or out of a system. Light, electricity, or mechanical motion may be involved in such transfers in addition to heat.	47, 49

Standards	Page Numbers
PERFORMANCE INDICATOR 4.4 *Observe and describe the properties of sound, light, magnetism, and electricity.*	
Key Idea 2: Beyond the use of reasoning and consensus, scientific inquiry involves the testing of proposed explanations involving the use of conventional techniques and procedures and usually requiring considerable ingenuity.	
4.4d Electrical energy can be produced from a variety of energy sources and can be transformed into almost any other form of energy.	47, 52, 55, 64–65
PERFORMANCE INDICATOR 4.5 *Describe situations that support the principle of conservation of energy.*	
4.5a Energy cannot be created or destroyed, but only changed from one form into another.	47, 48, 54, 147
4.5b Energy can change from one form to another, although in the process some energy is always converted to heat. Some systems transform energy with less loss of heat than others.	47, 54
Key Idea 5: Energy and matter interact through forces that result in changes in motion.	
PERFORMANCE INDICATOR 5.1 *Describe different patterns of motion of objects.*	
5.1c An object's motion is the result of the combined effect of all forces acting on the object. A moving object that is not subjected to a force will continue to move at a constant speed in a straight line. An object at rest will remain at rest.	74, 79
5.1d Force is directly related to an object's mass and acceleration. The greater the force, the greater the change in motion.	41, 79
PERFORMANCE INDICATOR 5.2 *Observe, describe, and compare effects of forces (gravity, electric current, and magnetism) on the motion of objects.*	
5.2a Every object exerts gravitational force on every other object. Gravitational force depends on how much mass the objects have and on how far apart they are. Gravity is one of the forces acting on orbiting objects and projectiles.	5
5.2c Machines transfer mechanical energy from one object to another.	73, 80, 147
5.2d Friction is a force that opposes motion.	80, 81
5.2e A machine can be made more efficient by reducing friction. Some common ways of reducing friction include lubricating or waxing surfaces.	80, 81
5.2f Machines can change the direction or amount of force, or the distance or speed of force required to do work.	73, 79, 80
5.2g Simple machines include a lever, a pulley, a wheel and axle, and an inclined plane. A complex machine uses a combination of interacting simple machines, e.g., a bicycle.	73, 79, 85, 90, 92–93

HOW TO...

Use Your Science Book

Before You Read

- **Chapter Opener** Science is occurring all around you, and the opening photo of each chapter will preview the science you will be learning about. The **Chapter Preview** will give you an idea of what you will be learning about, and you can try the **Launch Lab** to help get your brain headed in the right direction. The **Foldables** exercise is a fun way to keep you organized.

- **Section Opener** Chapters are divided into two to four sections. The **As You Read** in the margin of the first page of each section will let you know what is most important in the section. It is divided into four parts. **What You'll Learn** will tell you the major topics you will be covering. **Why It's Important** will remind you why you are studying this in the first place! The **Review Vocabulary** word is a word you already know, either from your science studies or your prior knowledge. The **New Vocabulary** words are words that you need to learn to understand this section. These words will be in **boldfaced** print and highlighted in the section. Make a note to yourself to recognize these words as you are reading the section.

Glencoe Science

New York Science

Grade 6

Unit 1 and Unit 2

NATIONAL GEOGRAPHIC

Unit 1
Simple and Complex/Compound Machines

Unit 2
The Atmosphere, Hydrosphere, and Lithosphere

As You Read

- **Headings** Each section has a title in large red letters, and is further divided into blue titles and small red titles at the beginnings of some paragraphs. To help you study, make an outline of the headings and subheadings.

- **Margins** In the margins of your text, you will find many helpful resources. The **Science Online** exercises and **Integrate** activities help you explore the topics you are studying. **MiniLabs** reinforce the science concepts you have learned.

- **Building Skills** You also will find an **Applying Math** or **Applying Science** activity in each chapter. This gives you extra practice using your new knowledge, and helps prepare you for standardized tests.

- **Student Resources** At the end of the book you will find **Student Resources** to help you throughout your studies. These include **Science, Technology,** and **Math Skill Handbooks,** an **English/Spanish Glossary,** and an **Index.** Also, use your **Foldables** as a resource. It will help you organize information, and review before a test.

- **In Class** Remember, you can always ask your teacher to explain anything you don't understand.

FOLDABLES™ Study Organizer

Science Vocabulary Make the following Foldable to help you understand the vocabulary terms in this chapter.

STEP 1 **Fold** a vertical sheet of notebook paper from side to side.

STEP 2 **Cut** along every third line of only the top layer to form tabs.

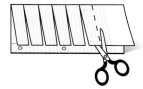

STEP 3 **Label** each tab with a vocabulary word from the chapter.

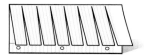

Build Vocabulary As you read the chapter, list the vocabulary words on the tabs. As you learn the definitions, write them under the tab for each vocabulary word.

Look For...

FOLDABLES™

At the beginning of every chapter.

In Lab

Working in the laboratory is one of the best ways to understand the concepts you are studying. Your book will be your guide through your laboratory experiences, and help you begin to think like a scientist. In it, you not only will find the steps necessary to follow the investigations, but you also will find helpful tips to make the most of your time.

- Each lab provides you with a **Real-World Question** to remind you that science is something you use every day, not just in class. This may lead to many more questions about how things happen in your world.

- Remember, experiments do not always produce the result you expect. Scientists have made many discoveries based on investigations with unexpected results. You can try the experiment again to make sure your results were accurate, or perhaps form a new hypothesis to test.

- Keeping a **Science Journal** is how scientists keep accurate records of observations and data. In your journal, you also can write any questions that may arise during your investigation. This is a great method of reminding yourself to find the answers later.

Look For...
- **Launch Labs** start every chapter.
- **MiniLabs** in the margin of each chapter.
- **Two Full-Period Labs** in every chapter.
- **EXTRA Try at Home Labs** at the end of your book.
- the **Web site** with laboratory demonstrations.

Before a Test

Admit it! You don't like to take tests! However, there *are* ways to review that make them less painful. Your book will help you be more successful taking tests if you use the resources provided to you.

- Review all of the **New Vocabulary** words and be sure you understand their definitions.

- Review the notes you've taken on your **Foldables,** in class, and in lab. Write down any question that you still need answered.

- Review the **Summaries** and **Self Check questions** at the end of each section.

- Study the concepts presented in the chapter by reading the **Study Guide** and answering the questions in the **Chapter Review.**

Look For...

- **Reading Checks** and **caption questions** throughout the text.
- the **Summaries** and **Self Check questions** at the end of each section.
- the **Study Guide** and **Review** at the end of each chapter.
- the **Intermediate-Level Exam Practice** after each chapter.

a or b?

?

T or F?

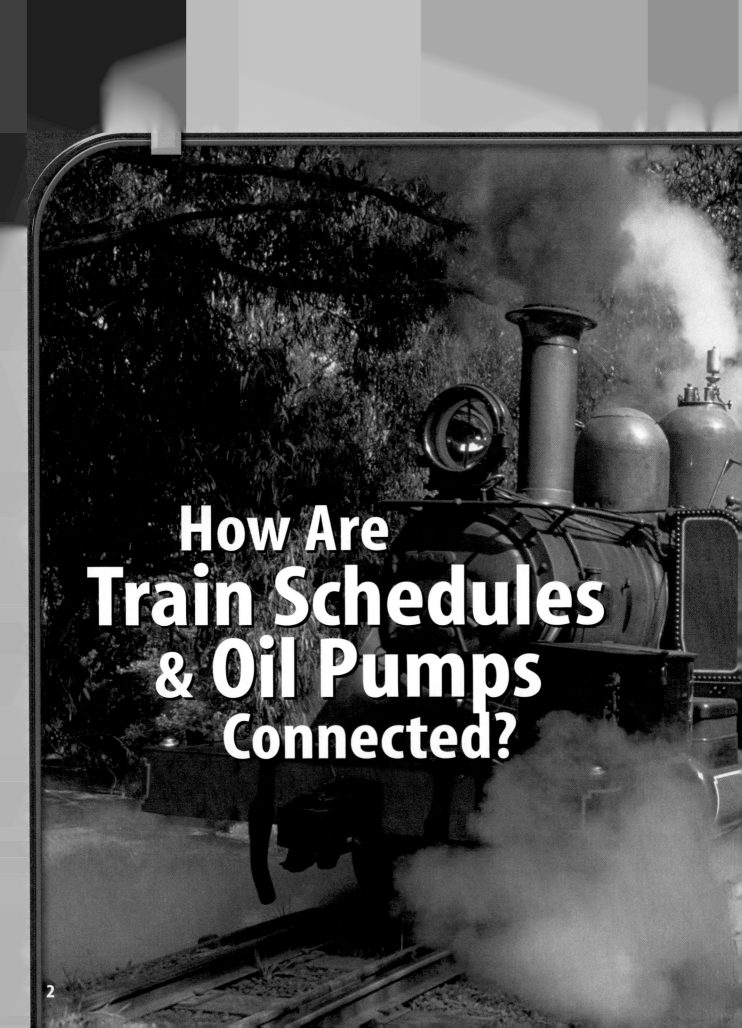

How Are
Train Schedules
& Oil Pumps
Connected?

In the 1800s, trains had to make frequent stops so that their moving parts could be lubricated. Without lubrication, the parts would have worn out due to friction. When the train stopped, a worker had to get out and oil the parts by hand. The process was very time-consuming and made it hard for trains to stay on schedule. Around 1870, an engineer named Elijah McCoy developed the first automatic lubricating device, which oiled the engine while the train was running. (A later version of his automatic lubricator is seen at lower right.) Since then, many kinds of automatic lubricating devices have been developed. Today, automobiles have oil pumps that automatically circulate oil to the moving parts of the engine. When you go for a ride in a car, you can thank Elijah McCoy that you don't have to stop every few miles to oil the engine by hand!

unit ⚡ projects

Visit unit projects at **glencoe.com** to find project ideas and resources. Projects include:

- **Career** As a class, design a chart of the many fields of engineering and how they relate to conserving and protecting the environment.
- **Technology** Design and construct miniature models of energy-producing devices. Explain how your model works.
- **Model** Analyze locations for a future city. Consider what characteristics will make the best location and make a model of a portion of your design.

WebQuest Using virtual programming, *Roller Coaster Physics* provides an opportunity to engineer, test, and evaluate roller coaster design, and then build your own 3-dimensional coaster.

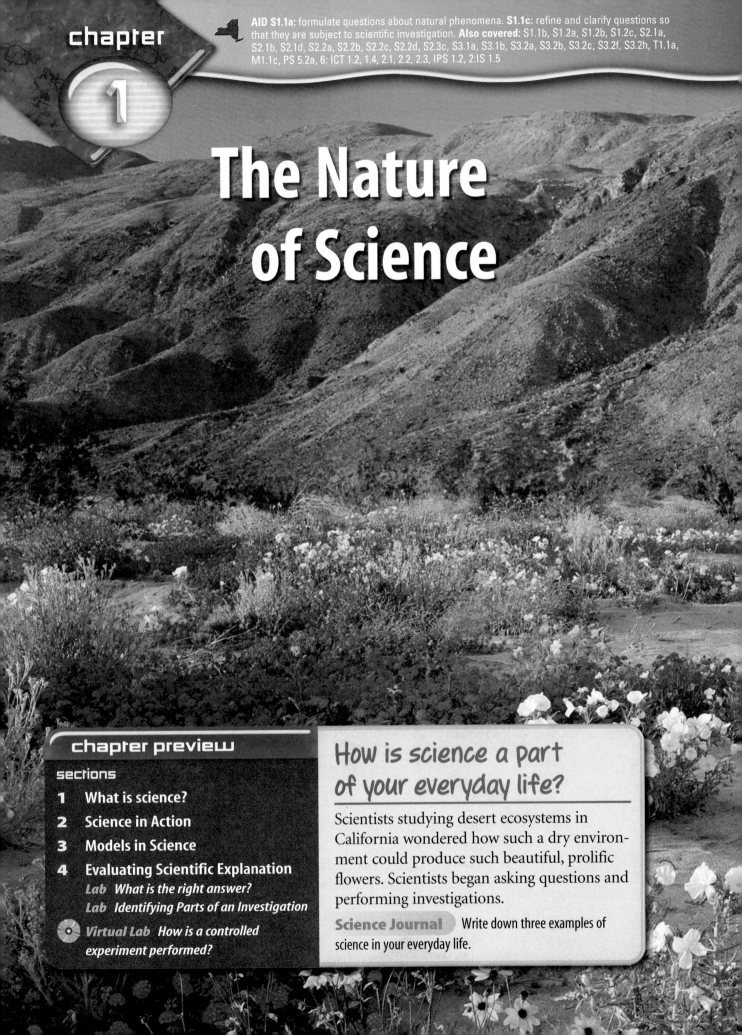

chapter

1

AID **S1.1a:** formulate questions about natural phenomena. **S1.1c:** refine and clarify questions so that they are subject to scientific investigation. **Also covered:** S1.1b, S1.2a, S1.2b, S1.2c, S2.1a, S2.1b, S2.1d, S2.2a, S2.2b, S2.2c, S2.2d, S2.3c, S3.1a, S3.1b, S3.2a, S3.2b, S3.2c, S3.2f, S3.2h, T1.1a, M1.1c, PS 5.2a, 6: ICT 1.2, 1.4, 2.1, 2.2, 2.3, IPS 1.2, 2:IS 1.5

The Nature of Science

chapter preview

sections

1 What is science?

2 Science in Action

3 Models in Science

4 Evaluating Scientific Explanation

Lab What is the right answer?

Lab Identifying Parts of an Investigation

Virtual Lab How is a controlled experiment performed?

How is science a part of your everyday life?

Scientists studying desert ecosystems in California wondered how such a dry environment could produce such beautiful, prolific flowers. Scientists began asking questions and performing investigations.

Science Journal Write down three examples of science in your everyday life.

Start-Up Activities

Observe How Gravity Accelerates Objects

Gravity is a familiar natural force that keeps you anchored on Earth, but how does it work? Scientists learn about gravity and other concepts by asking questions and making observations. By observing things in action scientists can study nature. Perform the lab below to see how gravity affects objects.

1. Collect three identical, unsharpened pencils.
2. Tape two of the pencils together.
3. Hold all the pencils at the same height as high as you can. Drop them together and observe what happens as they fall.
4. **Think Critically** Did the single pencil fall faster or slower than the pair? Predict in your Science Journal what would happen if you taped 30 pencils together and dropped them at the same time as you dropped a single pencil.

Preview this chapter's content and activities at glencoe.com

FOLDABLES Study Organizer

Science Make the following Foldable to help identify what you already know, what you want to know, and what you learned about science.

STEP 1 Fold a vertical sheet of paper from side to side. Make the front edge about 1/2 inch shorter than the back edge.

STEP 2 Turn lengthwise and fold into thirds.

STEP 3 Unfold and cut only the top layer along both folds to make three tabs. Label each tab.

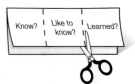

Identify Questions Before you read the chapter, write what you already know about science under the left tab of your Foldable, and write questions about what you'd like to know under the center tab. After you read the chapter, list what you learned under the right tab.

AID S1.1a: formulate questions about natural phenomena. **S1.1c:** refine and clarify questions so that they are subject to scientific investigation. **ICT 1.2:** Describe the differences and similarities among engineering systems, natural systems, and social systems. **Also covered:** AID T1.1a.

section 1

What is science?

as you read

What You'll Learn

- **Define** science and identify questions that science cannot answer.
- **Compare** and contrast theories and laws.
- **Identify** a system and its components.
- **Identify** the three main branches of science.

Why It's Important

Science can be used to learn more about the world you live in.

🔍 Review Vocabulary

theory: explanation of things or events that is based on knowledge gained from many observations and experiments

New Vocabulary

- science
- scientific theory
- scientific law
- system
- life science
- Earth science
- physical science
- technology

Learning About the World

When you think of a scientist, do you imagine a person in a laboratory surrounded by charts, graphs, glass bottles, and bubbling test tubes? It might surprise you to learn that anyone who tries to learn something about the natural world is a scientist. **Science** is a way of learning more about the natural world. Scientists want to know why, how, or when something occurred. This learning process usually begins by keeping your eyes open and asking questions about what you see.

Asking Questions Scientists ask many questions. How do things work? What do things look like? What are they made of? Why does something take place? Science can attempt to answer many questions about the natural world, but some questions cannot be answered by science. Look at the situations in **Figure 1.** Who should you vote for? What does this poem mean? Who is your best friend? Questions about art, politics, personal preference, or morality can't be answered by science. Science can't tell you what is right, wrong, good, or bad.

Figure 1 Questions about politics, literature, and art cannot be answered by science.

Figure 2 As new information becomes available, explanations can be modified or discarded and new explanations can be made.

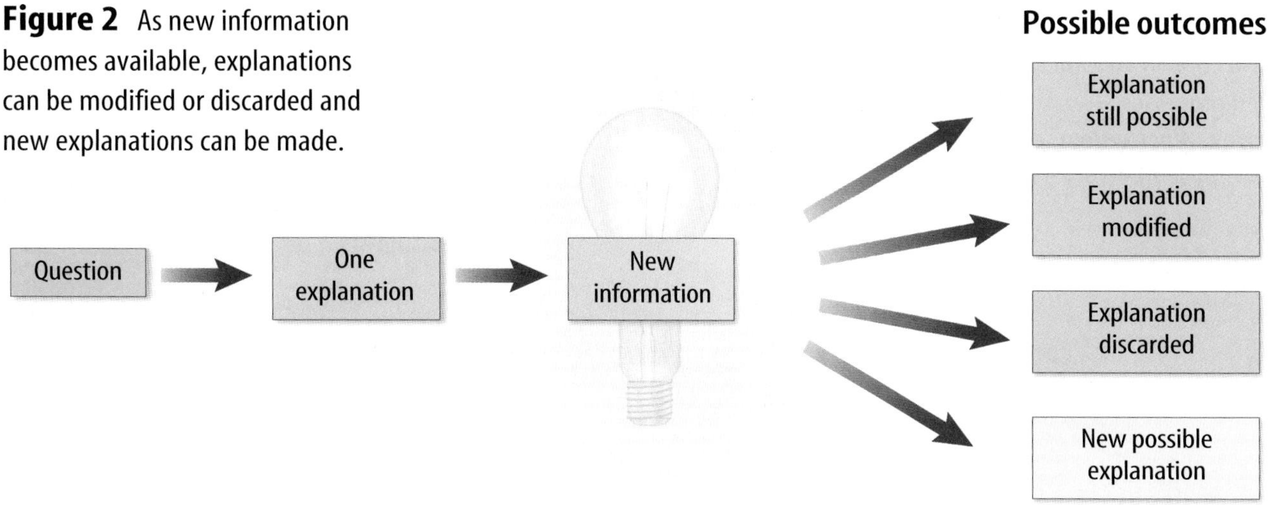

Possible outcomes

Question → One explanation → New information

Explanation still possible

Explanation modified

Explanation discarded

New possible explanation

Possible Explanations If learning about your world begins with asking questions, can science provide answers to these questions? Science can answer a question only with the information available at the time. Any answer is uncertain because people will never know everything about the world around them. With new knowledge, they might realize that some of the old explanations no longer fit the new information. As shown in **Figure 2,** some observations might force scientists to look at old ideas and think of new explanations. Science can only provide possible explanations.

☑ **Reading Check** *Why can't science answer questions with certainty?*

Scientific Theories An attempt to explain a pattern observed repeatedly in the natural world is called a **scientific theory.** Theories are not simply guesses or someone's opinions, nor are theories vague ideas. Theories in science must be supported by observations and results from many investigations. They are the best explanations that have been found so far. However, theories can change. As new data become available, scientists evaluate how the new data fit the theory. If enough new data do not support the theory, the theory can be changed to fit the new observations better.

Scientific Laws A rule that describes a pattern in nature is a **scientific law.** For an observation to become a scientific law, it must be observed repeatedly. The law then stands until someone makes observations that do not follow the law. A law helps you predict that an apple dropped from arm's length will always fall to Earth. The law, however, does not explain why gravity exists or how it works. A law, unlike a theory, does not attempt to explain why something happens. It simply describes a pattern.

Analysis, Inquiry, and Design

S1.1a, S1.1c: Formulate three questions scientists might attempt to answer about the natural world. Rewrite your questions as a hypothesis that could be tested in scientific investigations.

Figure 3 Systems are a collection of structures, cycles, and processes.
Infer *What systems can you identify in this classroom?*

Interconnectedness: Common Themes

1.2: Compare and contrast an engineering system, natural system, and a social system using a three-circle Venn diagram.

Mini LAB

Classifying Parts of a System

Procedure
Think about how your school's cafeteria is run. Consider the physical structure of the cafeteria. How many people run it? Where does the food come from? How is it prepared? Where does it go? What other parts of the cafeteria system are necessary?

Analysis
Classify the parts of your school cafeteria's system as structures, cycles, or processes.

Try at Home

Systems in Science

Scientists can study many different things in nature. Some might study how the human body works or how planets move around the Sun. Others might study the energy carried in a lightning bolt. What do all of these things have in common? All of them are systems. A **system** is a collection of structures, cycles, and processes that relate to and interact with each other. The structures, cycles, and processes are the parts of a system, just like your stomach is one of the structures of your digestive system.

Reading Check *What is a system?*

Systems are not found just in science. Your school is a system with structures such as the school building, the tables and chairs, you, your teacher, the school bell, your pencil, and many other things. **Figure 3** shows some of these structures. Your school day also has cycles. Your daily class schedule and the calendar of holidays are examples of cycles. Many processes are at work during the school day. When you take a test, your teacher has a process. You might be asked to put your books and papers away and get out a pencil before the test is distributed. When the time is over, you are told to put your pencil down and pass your test to the front of the room.

Parts of a System Interact In a system, structures, cycles, and processes interact. Your daily schedule influences where you go and what time you go. The clock shows the teacher when the test is complete, and you couldn't complete the test without a pencil.

Parts of a Whole All systems are made up of other systems. For example, you are part of your school. The human body is a system—within your body are other systems. Your school is part of a system—district, state, and national. You have your regional school district. Your district is part of a statewide school system. Scientists often break down problems by studying just one part of a system. A scientist might want to learn about how construction of buildings affects the ecosystem. Because an ecosystem has many parts, one scientist might study a particular animal, and another might study the effect of construction on plant life.

The Branches of Science

Science often is divided into three main categories, or branches—life science, Earth science, and physical science. Each branch asks questions about different kinds of systems.

Life Science The study of living systems and the ways in which they interact is called **life science.** Life scientists attempt to answer questions like "How do whales navigate the ocean?" and "How do vaccines prevent disease?" Life scientists can study living organisms, where they live, and how they interact. Dian Fossey, **Figure 4,** was a life scientist who studied gorillas, their habitat, and their behaviors.

People who work in the health field know a lot about the life sciences. Physicians, nurses, physical therapists, dietitians, medical researchers, and others focus on the systems of the human body. Some other examples of careers that use life science include biologists, zookeepers, botanists, farmers, and beekeepers.

Health Integration Systems The human body is composed of many different systems that all interact with one another to perform a function. The heart is like the control center. Even though not all systems report directly to the heart, they all interact with its function. If the heart is not working, the other systems fail as well. Research human body systems and explain how one system can affect another.

Figure 4 Over a span of 18 years, life scientist Dian Fossey spent much of her time observing mountain gorillas in Rwanda, Africa. She was able to interact with them as she learned about their behavior.

Figure 5 These volcanologists are studying the temperature of the lava flowing from a volcano.

Figure 6 Physical scientists study a wide range of subjects.

Earth Science The study of Earth systems and the systems in space is **Earth science.** It includes the study of nonliving things such as rocks, soil, clouds, rivers, oceans, planets, stars, meteors, and black holes. Earth science also covers the weather and climate systems that affect Earth. Earth scientists ask questions like "How can an earthquake be detected?" or "Is water found on other planets?" They make maps and investigate how geologic features formed on land and in the oceans. They also use their knowledge to search for fuels and minerals. Meteorologists study weather and climate. Geologists study rocks and geologic features. **Figure 5** shows a volcanologist—a person who studies volcanoes—measuring the temperature of lava.

✔ **Reading Check** *What do Earth scientists study?*

Physical Science The study of matter and energy is **physical science.** Matter is anything that takes up space and has mass. The ability to cause change in matter is energy. Living and nonliving systems are made of matter. Examples include plants, animals, rocks, the atmosphere, and the water in oceans, lakes, and rivers. Physical science can be divided into two general fields—chemistry and physics. Chemistry is the study of matter and the interactions of matter. Physics is the study of energy and its ability to change matter. Figure 6 shows physical scientists at work.

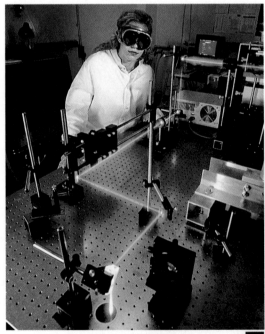

This chemist is studying the light emitted by certain compounds.

This physicist is studying light as it travels through optical fibers.

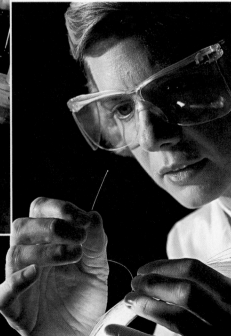

Careers Chemists ask questions such as "How can I make plastic stronger?" or "What can I do to make aspirin more effective?" Physicists might ask other types of questions, such as "How does light travel through glass fibers?" or "How can humans harness the energy of sunlight for their energy needs?"

Many careers are based on the physical sciences. Physicists and chemists are some obvious careers. Ultrasound and X-ray technicians working in the medical field study physical science because they study the energy in ultrasound or X rays and how it affects a living system.

Science and Technology Although learning the answers to scientific questions is important, these answers do not help people directly unless they can be applied in some way. **Technology** is the practical use of science, or applied science, as illustrated in **Figure 7.** Engineers apply science to develop technology. The study of how to use the energy of sunlight is science. Using this knowledge to create solar panels is technology. The study of the behavior of light as it travels through thin, glass, fiber-optic wires is science. The use of optical fibers to transmit information is technology. A scientist uses science to study how the skin of a shark repels water. The application of this knowledge to create a material that helps swimmers slip through the water faster is technology.

Figure 7 Solar-powered cars and the swimsuits worn in the Olympics are examples of technology—the application of science.

Analysis, Inquiry, and Design

1.1a: Identify one scientific or human need that can be solved through the use of technology.

---

section 1 review

Summary

Learning About the World

- Scientists ask questions to learn how, why, or when something occurred.
- A theory is a possible explanation for observations that is supported by many investigations.
- A scientific law describes a pattern but does not explain why things happen.

Systems in Science

- A system is composed of structures, cycles, and processes that interact with each other.

The Branches of Science

- Science is divided into three branches—life science, Earth science, and physical science.
- Technology is the application of science in our everyday lives.

Self Check

1. **Compare and contrast** scientific theory and scientific law. Explain how a scientific theory can change.
2. **Explain** why science can answer some questions, but not others.
3. **Classify** the following statement as a theory or a law: Heating the air in a hot-air balloon causes the balloon to rise.
4. **Think Critically** Describe the importance of technology and how it relates to science.

Applying Skills

5. **Infer** Scientists ask questions and make observations. What types of questions and observations would you make if you were a scientist studying schools of fish in the ocean?

AID **S2.2b:** design scientific investigations, **S2.2c:** design a simple controlled experiment, **S2.2d:** identify independent variables, dependent variables, and constants in a simple controlled experiment. **Also covered:** S1.1a, S1.1b, S1.1c, S1.2a, S1.2b, S1.2c, S2.1a, S2.1d, S2.2a, S3.1a.

Science in Action

as you read

What You'll Learn

- **Identify** some skills scientists use.
- **Define** hypothesis.
- **Recognize** the difference between observation and inference.

Why It's Important

Science can be used to learn more about the world you live in.

🔊 Review Vocabulary

observation: a record or description of an occurrence or pattern in nature

New Vocabulary

- hypothesis
- infer
- controlled experiment
- variable
- independent variable
- dependent variable
- constant

Science Skills

You know that science involves asking questions, but how does asking questions lead to learning? Because no single way to gain knowledge exists, a scientist doesn't start with step one, then go to step two, and so on. Instead, scientists have a huge collection of skills from which to choose. Some of these skills include thinking, observing, predicting, investigating, researching, modeling, measuring, analyzing, and inferring. Science also can advance with luck and creativity.

Science Methods Investigations often follow a general pattern. As illustrated in **Figure 8,** most investigations begin by seeing something and then asking a question about what was observed. Scientists often perform research by talking with other scientists. They read books and scientific magazines to learn as much as they can about what is already known about their question. Usually, scientists state a possible explanation for their observation. To collect more information, scientists almost always make more observations. They might build a model of what they study or they might perform investigations. Often, they do both. How might you combine some of these skills in an investigation?

Figure 8 Although there are different scientific methods for investigating a specific problem, most investigations follow a general pattern.

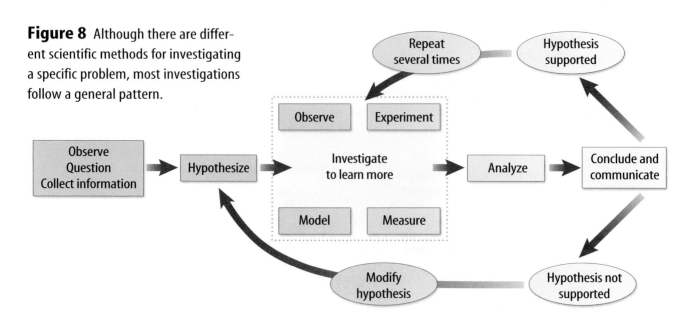

Questioning and Observing Ms. Clark placed a sealed shoe box on the table at the front of the laboratory. Everyone in the class noticed the box. Within seconds the questions flew. "What's in the box?" "Why is it there?"

Ms. Clark said she would like the class to see how they used some science skills without even realizing it.

"I think that she wants us to find out what's in it," Isabelle said to Marcus.

"Can we touch it?" asked Marcus.

"It's up to you," Ms. Clark said.

Marcus picked up the box and turned it over a few times.

"It's not heavy," Marcus observed. "Whatever is inside slides around." He handed the box to Isabelle.

Isabelle shook the box. The class heard the object strike the sides of the box. With every few shakes, the class heard a metallic sound. The box was passed around for each student to make observations and write them in his or her Science Journal. Some observations are shown in **Figure 9.**

Taking a Guess "I think it's a pair of scissors," said Marcus.

"Aren't scissors lighter than this?" asked Isabelle, while shaking the box. "I think it's a stapler."

"What makes you think so?" asked Ms. Clark.

"Well, staplers are small enough to fit inside a shoe box, and it seems to weigh about the same," said Isabelle.

"We can hear metal when we shake it," said Enrique.

"So, you are guessing that a stapler is in the box?"

"Yes," they agreed.

"You just stated a hypothesis," exclaimed Ms. Clark.

"A what?" asked Marcus.

Analysis, Inquiry, and Design

S2.2b: Design a simple scientific investigation using observation, description, comparison, sample collection, or construction of a model.

INTEGRATE
Career

Biologist Some naturalists study the living world, using mostly their observational skills. They observe animals and plants in their natural environment, taking care not to disturb the organisms they are studying. Make observations of organisms in a nearby park or backyard. Record your observations in your Science Journal.

Forming a Hypothesis

Procedure

1. Fill a large **pot** with **water**. Place an **unopened can of diet soda** and an **unopened can of regular soda** into the pot of water and observe what each can does.

2. In your **Science Journal**, make a list of the possible explanations for your observation. Select the best explanation and write a hypothesis.

3. Read the nutritional facts on the back of each can and compare their ingredients.

4. Revise your hypothesis based on this new information.

Analysis

1. What did you observe when you placed the cans in the water?

2. How did the nutritional information on the cans change your hypothesis?

3. Infer why the two cans behaved differently in the water.

Try at Home

The Hypothesis "A **hypothesis** is a reasonable and educated possible answer based on what you know and what you observe."

"We know that a stapler is small, it can be heavy, and it is made of metal," said Isabelle.

"We observed that what is in the box is small, heavier than a pair of scissors, and made of metal," continued Marcus.

Analyzing Hypotheses "What other possible explanations fit with what you observed?" asked Ms. Clark.

"Well, it has to be a stapler," said Enrique.

"What if it isn't?" asked Ms. Clark. "Maybe you're overlooking explanations because your minds are made up. A good scientist keeps an open mind to every idea and explanation. What if you learn new information that doesn't fit with your original hypothesis? What new information could you gather to verify or disprove your hypothesis?"

"Do you mean a test or something?" asked Marcus.

"I know," said Enrique, "We could get an empty shoe box that is the same size as the mystery box and put a stapler in it. Then we could shake it and see whether it feels and sounds the same." Enrique's test is shown in **Figure 10.**

Making a Prediction "If your hypothesis is correct, what would you expect to happen?" asked Ms. Clark.

"Well, it would be about the same weight and it would slide around a little, just like the other box," said Enrique.

"It would have that same metallic sound when we shake it," said Marcus.

"So, you predict that the test box will feel and sound the same as your mystery box. Go ahead and try it," said Ms. Clark.

Figure 10 Comparing the known information with the unknown information can be valuable even though you cannot see what is inside the closed box.

Testing the Hypothesis Ms. Clark gave the class an empty shoe box that appeared to be identical to the mystery box. Isabelle found a metal stapler. Enrique put the stapler in the box and taped the box closed. Marcus shook the box.

"The stapler does slide around but it feels just a little heavier than what's inside the mystery box," said Marcus. "What do you think?" he asked Isabelle as he handed her the box.

"It is heavier," said Isabelle "and as hard as I shake it, I can't get a metallic sound. What if we find the mass of both boxes? Then we'll know the exact mass difference between the two."

Using a balance, as shown in **Figure 11,** the class found that the test box had a mass of 410 g, and the mystery box had a mass of 270 g.

Figure 11 Laboratory balances are used to find the mass of objects.

Organizing Your Findings "Okay. Now you have some new information," said Ms. Clark. "But before you draw any conclusions, let's organize what we know. Then we'll have a summary of our observations and can refer back to them when we are drawing our conclusions."

"We could make a chart of our observations in our Science Journals," said Marcus.

"We could compare the observations of the mystery box with the observations of the test box," said Isabelle. The chart that the class made is shown in **Table 1.**

Table 1 Observation Chart		
Questions	**Mystery Box**	**Our Box**
Does it roll or slide?	It slides and appears to be flat.	It slides and appears to be flat.
Does it make any sounds?	It makes a metallic sound when it strikes the sides of the box.	The stapler makes a thudding sound when it strikes the sides of the box.
Is the mass evenly distributed in the box?	No. The object doesn't completely fill the box.	No. The mass of the stapler is unevenly distributed.
What is the mass of the box?	270 g	410 g

Drawing Conclusions

"What have you learned from your investigation so far?" asked Ms. Clark.

"The first thing that we learned was that our hypothesis wasn't correct," answered Marcus.

"Would you say that your hypothesis was entirely wrong?" asked Ms. Clark.

"The boxes don't weigh the same, and the box with the stapler doesn't make the same sound as the mystery box. But there could be a difference in the kind of stapler in the box. It could be a different size or made of different materials."

"So you infer that the object in the mystery box is not exactly the same type of stapler, right?" asked Ms. Clark.

"What does *infer* mean?" asked Isabelle.

"To **infer** something means to draw a conclusion based on what you observe," answered Ms. Clark.

"So we inferred that the things in the boxes had to be different because our observations of the two boxes are different," said Marcus.

"I guess we're back to where we started," said Enrique. "We still don't know what's in the mystery box."

"Do you know more than you did before you started?" asked Ms. Clark.

"We eliminated one possibility," Isabelle added.

"Yes. We inferred that it's not a stapler, at least not like the one in the test box," said Marcus.

"So even if your observations don't support your hypothesis, you know more than you did when you started," said Ms. Clark.

Continuing to Learn "So when do we get to open the box and see what it is?" asked Marcus.

"Let me ask you this," said Ms. Clark. "Do you think scientists always get a chance to look inside to see if they are right?"

"If they are studying something too big or too small to see, I guess they can't," replied Isabelle. "What do they do in those cases?"

"As you learned, your first hypothesis might not be supported by your investigation. Instead of giving up, you continue to gather information by making more observations, making new hypotheses, and by investigating further. Some scientists have spent lifetimes researching their questions. Science takes patience and persistence," said Ms. Clark.

Figure 12 Observations can be used to draw inferences.

Infer *Looking at both of these photos, what do you infer has taken place?*

Communicating Your Findings It is not unusual for one scientist to continue the work of another or to try to duplicate the work of another scientist. It is important for scientists to communicate to others not only the results of the investigation, but also the methods by which the investigation was done. Scientists often publish reports in journals, books, and on the Internet to show other scientists the work that was completed. They also might attend meetings where they make speeches about their work.

Like the science-fair student in **Figure 13** demonstrates, an important part of doing science is the ability to communicate methods and results to others.

 **Reading Check** *Why do scientists share information?*

Figure 13 Presentations are one way people in science communicate their findings.

Hot Words Hot Topics: Bk 1 pp. 89, 190

Applying Math   Make a Data Table

SEASONAL TEMPERATURES Suppose you were given the average temperatures in a city for the four seasons over a three-year period: spring 1997 was 11°C; summer 1997 was 25°C; fall 1997 was 5°C; winter 1997 was −5°C; spring 1998 was 9°C; summer 1998 was 36°C; fall 1998 was 10°C; winter 1998 was −3°C; spring 1999 was 10°C; summer 1999 was 30°C; fall 1999 was 9°C; and winter 1999 was −2°C. How can you tell in which of the years each season had its coldest average?

Solution

1 *This is what you know:*

Temperatures were: 1997: 11°C, 25°C, 5°C, −5°C

1998: 9°C, 36°C, 10°C, −3°C

1999: 10°C, 30°C, 9°C, −2°C

2 *This is what you need to find out:*

Which of the years each season had its coldest temperature?

3 *This is the procedure you need to use:*

• Create a table with rows for seasons and columns for the years.

• Insert the values you were given.

4 *Check your answer:*

The four coldest seasons were spring 1998, summer 1997, fall 1997, and winter 1997.

Practice Problems

Use your table to find out which season had the greatest difference in temperatures over the three years from 1997 through 1999.

 **Science Online** For more practice, visit glencoe.com

Figure 14 The 400-m race is an example of a controlled experiment. The distance, track material, and wind speed are constants. The runners' abilities and their finish times are varied.

Experiments

Different types of questions call for different types of investigations. Ms. Clark's class made many observations about their mystery box and about their test box. They wanted to know what was inside. To answer their question, building a model—the test box—was an effective way to learn more about the mystery box. Some questions ask about the effects of one factor on another. One way to investigate these kinds of questions is by doing a controlled experiment. A **controlled experiment** involves changing one factor and observing its effect on another while keeping all other factors constant.

Variables and Constants Imagine a race in which the lengths of the lanes vary. Some lanes are 102 m long, some are 98 m long, and a few are 100 m long. When the first runner crosses the finish line, is he or she the fastest? Not necessarily. The lanes in the race have different lengths.

Variables are factors that can be changed in an experiment. Reliable experiments, like the race shown in **Figure 14,** attempt to change one variable and observe the effect of this change on another variable. The variable that is changed in an experiment is called the **independent variable.** The **dependent variable** changes as a result of a change in the independent variable. It usually is the dependent variable that is observed in an experiment. Scientists attempt to keep all other variables constant—or unchanged.

The variables that are not changed in an experiment are called **constants.** Examples of constants in the race include track material, wind speed, and distance. This way it is easier to determine exactly which variable is responsible for the runners' finish times. In this race, the runners' abilities were varied. The runners' finish times were observed.

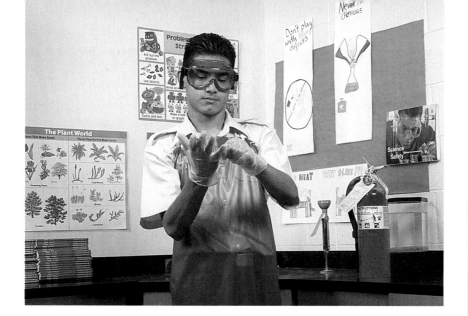

Figure 15 Safety is the most important aspect of any investigation.

Analysis, Inquiry, and Design

S2.2a: Analyze the simple controlled experiment you designed earlier. List all safety precautions and the safety symbol warnings for your experiment.

Laboratory Safety

In your science class, you will perform many types of investigations. However, performing scientific investigations involves more than just following specific steps. You also must learn how to keep yourself and those around you safe by obeying the safety symbol warnings, shown in **Figure 16.**

In a Laboratory When scientists work in a laboratory, as shown in **Figure 15,** they take many safety precautions.

The most important safety advice in a science lab is to think before you act. Always check with your teacher several times in the planning stage of any investigation. Also make sure you know the location of safety equipment in the laboratory room and how to use this equipment, including the eyewashes, thermal mitts, and fire extinguisher.

Good safety habits include the following suggestions. Before conducting any investigation, find and follow all safety symbols listed in your investigation. You always should wear an apron and goggles to protect yourself from chemicals, flames, and pointed objects. Keep goggles on until activity, cleanup, and handwashing are complete. Always slant test tubes away from yourself and others when heating them. Never eat, drink, or apply makeup in the lab. Report all accidents and injuries to your teacher and always wash your hands after working with lab materials.

In the Field Investigations also take place outside the lab, in streams, farm fields, and other places. Scientists must follow safety regulations there, as well, such as wearing eye goggles and any other special safety equipment that is needed. Never reach into holes or under rocks. Always wash your hands after you've finished your field work.

 Eye Safety

 Clothing Protection

 Disposal

 Biological

 Extreme Temperature

 Sharp Object

 Fume

 Irritant

 Toxic

 Animal Safety

 Flammable

 Electrical

 Chemical

 Open Flame

 Handwashing

Figure 16 Safety symbols are present on nearly every investigation you will do this year.
List the safety symbols that should be on the lab the student is preparing to do in **Figure 15.**

Figure 17 Accidents are not planned. Safety precautions must be followed to prevent injury.

Why have safety rules? Doing science in the class laboratory or in the field can be much more interesting than reading about it. However, safety rules must be strictly followed, so that the possibility of an accident greatly decreases. However, you can't predict when something will go wrong.

Think of a person taking a trip in a car. Most of the time when someone drives somewhere in a vehicle, an accident, like the one shown in **Figure 17,** does not occur. But to be safe, drivers and passengers always should wear safety belts. Likewise, you always should wear and use appropriate safety gear in the lab—whether you are conducting an investigation or just observing. The most important aspect of any investigation is to conduct it safely.

section 2 review

Summary

Science Skills

- The scientific method was developed to help scientists investigate their questions.
- Hypotheses are possible explanations for why something occurs.

Drawing Conclusions

- Scientists communicate with one another to share important information.

Experiments

- Controlled experiments test the effect of one factor on another.

Laboratory Safety

- Safety precautions must be followed when conducting any investigation.

Self Check

1. **Explain** the difference between an inference and an observation.
2. **Explain** the differences between independent and dependent variables.
3. **Think Critically** A classroom investigation lists bleach as an ingredient. Bleach can irritate your skin, damage your eyes, and stain your clothes. What safety symbols should be listed with this investigation? Explain.

Applying Skills

4. **Describe** the different types of safety equipment found in a scientific laboratory. From your list, which equipment should you use when working with a flammable liquid in the lab?

More Section Review glencoe.com

section 3

Models in Science

Why are models necessary?

Just as you can take many different paths in an investigation, you can test a hypothesis in many different ways. Ms. Clark's class tested their hypothesis by building a model of the mystery box. A model is one way to test a hypothesis. In science, a **model** is any representation of an object or an event used as a tool for understanding the natural world.

Models can help you visualize, or picture in your mind, something that is difficult to see or understand. Ms. Clark's class made a model because they couldn't see the item inside the box. Models can be of things that are too small or too big to see. They also can be of things that can't be seen because they don't exist anymore or they haven't been created yet. Models also can show events that occur too slowly or too quickly to see. **Figure 18** shows different kinds of models.

Figure 18 Models help scientists visualize and study complex things and things that can't be seen.

Prototype model

Solar system model

Cell model

Dinosaur model

Types of Models

Most models fall into three basic types—physical models, computer models, and idea models. Depending on the reason that a model is needed, scientists can choose to use one or more than one type of model.

Physical Models Models that you can see and touch are called physical models. Examples include things such as a table-top solar system, a globe of Earth, a replica of the inside of a cell, or a gumdrop-toothpick model of a chemical compound. Models show how parts relate to one another. They also can be used to show how things appear when they change position or how they react when an outside force acts on them.

Computer Models Computer models are built using computer software. You can't touch them, but you can view them on a computer screen. Some computer models can model events that take a long time or take place too quickly to see. For example, a computer can model the movement of large plates in the Earth and might help predict earthquakes.

Computers also can model motions and positions of things that would take hours or days to calculate by hand or even using a calculator. They can also predict the effect of different systems or forces. **Figure 19** shows how computer models are used by scientists to help predict the weather based on the motion of air currents in the atmosphere.

Reading Check *What do computer models do?*

Science Online

Topic: Topographic Maps
Visit glencoe.com for Web links to information about topographic maps.

Activity List some of the different features found on topographic maps and explain their importance when reading and interpreting maps.

Interconnectedness: Common Themes

2.1, 2.2: Design a simple experiment that uses a model. Analyze which type of model would be best for the experiment.

Figure 19 A weather map is a computer model showing weather patterns over large areas. Scientists can use this information to predict the weather and to alert people to potentially dangerous weather on the way.

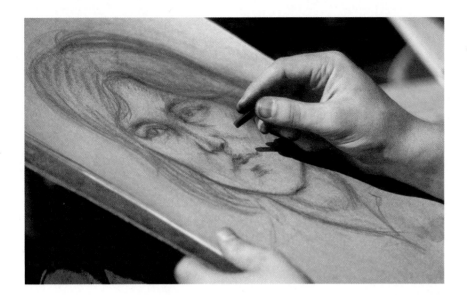

Figure 20 Models can be created using various types of tools.

Idea Models Some models are ideas or concepts that describe how someone thinks about something in the natural world. Albert Einstein is famous for his theory of relativity, which involves the relationship between matter and energy. One of the most famous models Einstein used for this theory is the mathematical equation $E = mc^2$. This explains that mass, m, can be changed into energy, E. Einstein's idea models never could be built as physical models, because they are basically ideas.

Making Models

The process of making a model is something like a sketch artist at work, as shown in **Figure 20.** The sketch artist attempts to draw a picture from the description given by someone. The more detailed the description is, the better the picture will be. Like a scientist who studies data from many sources, the sketch artist can make a sketch based on more than one person's observation. The final sketch isn't a photograph, but if the information is accurate, the sketch should look realistic. Scientific models are made much the same way. The more information a scientist gathers, the more accurate the model will be. The process of constructing a model of King Tutankhamun, who lived more than 3,000 years ago, is shown in **Figure 21.**

Reading Check *How are sketches like specific models?*

Using Models

When you think of a model, you might think of a model airplane or a model of a building. Not all models are for scientific purposes. You use models, and you might not realize it. Drawings, maps, recipes, and globes are all examples of models.

Thinking Like a Scientist

Procedure

1. Pour 15 mL of **water** into a **test tube.**
2. Slowly pour 5 mL of **vegetable oil** into the test tube.
3. Add two drops of **food coloring** and observe the liquid for 5 min.

Analysis

1. Record your observations of the test tube's contents before and after the oil and the food coloring were added to it.
2. Infer a scientific explanation for your observations.

Figure 21

More than 3,000 years ago, King Tutankhamun ruled over Egypt. His reign was a short one, and he died when he was just 18. In 1922, his mummified body was discovered, and in 1983 scientists recreated the face of this most famous of Egyptian kings. Some of the steps in building the model are shown here.

This is the most familiar image of the face of King Tut—the gold funerary mask that was found covering his skeletal face.

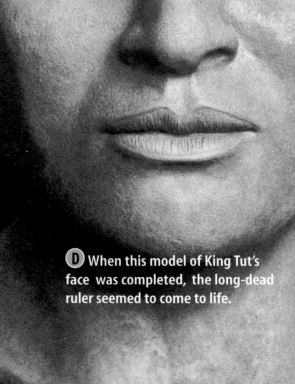

A First, a scientist used measurements and X rays to create a cast of the young king's skull. Depth markers (in red) were then glued onto the skull to indicate the likely thickness of muscle and other tissue.

B Clay was applied to fill in the area between the markers.

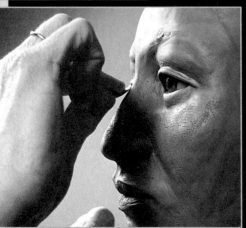

C Next, the features were sculpted. Here, eyelids are fashioned over inlaid prosthetic, or artificial, eyes.

D When this model of King Tut's face was completed, the long-dead ruler seemed to come to life.

Models Communicate Some models are used to communicate observations and ideas to other people. Often, it is easier to communicate ideas you have by making a model instead of writing your ideas in words. This way others can visualize them, too.

Models Test Predictions Some models are used to test predictions. Ms. Clark's class predicted that a box with a stapler in it would have characteristics similar to their mystery box. To test this prediction, the class made a model. Automobile and airplane engineers use wind tunnels to test predictions about how air will interact with their products.

Models Save Time, Money, and Lives Other models are used because working with and testing a model can be safer and less expensive than using the real thing. For example, the crash-test dummies shown in **Figure 22** are used in place of people when testing the effects of automobile crashes. To help train astronauts in the conditions they will encounter in space, NASA has built a special airplane. This airplane flies in an arc that creates the condition of freefall for 20 to 25 seconds. Making several trips in the airplane is easier, safer, and less expensive than making a trip into space.

Figure 22 Models are a safe and relatively inexpensive way to test ideas.

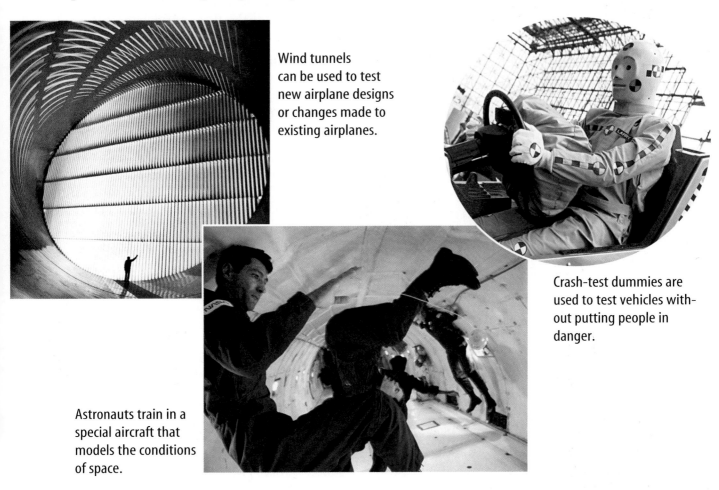

Wind tunnels can be used to test new airplane designs or changes made to existing airplanes.

Crash-test dummies are used to test vehicles without putting people in danger.

Astronauts train in a special aircraft that models the conditions of space.

Figure 23 The model of Earth's solar system changed as new information was gathered.

An early model of the solar system had Earth in the center with everything revolving around it.

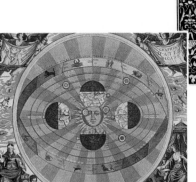

Later on, a new model had the Sun in the center with everything revolving around it.

Limitations of Models

The solar system is too large to be viewed all at once, so models are made to understand it. Many years ago, scientists thought that Earth was the center of the universe and the sky was a blanket that covered the planet.

Later, through observation, it was discovered that the objects you see in the sky are the Sun, the Moon, stars, and other planets. This new model explained the solar system differently. Earth was still the center, but everything else orbited it as shown in **Figure 23.**

Models Change Still later, through more observation, it was discovered that the Sun is the center of the solar system. Earth, along with the other planets, orbits the Sun. In addition, it was discovered that other planets also have moons that orbit them. A new model was developed to show this.

Earlier models of the solar system were not meant to be misleading. Scientists made the best models they could with the information they had. More importantly, their models gave future scientists information to build upon. Models are not necessarily perfect, but they provide a visual tool to learn from.

section 3 review

Summary

Why are models necessary?

- Scientists develop models to help them visualize complex concepts.

Types of Models

- There are three types of models—physical models, computer models, and idea models.

Making Models

- The more information you have when creating a model, the more accurate the model will be.

Using Models

- Models are used to convey important information such as maps and schedules.

Limitations of Models

- Models can be changed over time as new information becomes available.

Self Check

1. **Infer** what types of models can be used to model weather. How are they used to predict weather patterns?
2. **Explain** how models are used in science.
3. **Describe** how consumer product testing services use models to ensure the safety of the final products produced.
4. **Describe** the advantages and limitations of the three types of models.
5. **Think Critically** Explain why some models are better than others for certain situations. Give one example.

Hot Words Hot Topics: Bk 1 pp. 274-276, 369

Applying Math

6. **Use Proportions** On a map of a state, the scale shows that 1 cm is approximately 5 km. If the distance between two cities is 1.7 cm on the map, how many kilometers separate them?

section
4
AID S3.2b: identify sources of error and the limitations of data collected. **IPS 1.2:** Make informed consumer decisions by seeking answers to appropriate questions about products, services, and systems; determining the cost/benefit and risk/benefit tradeoffs; and applying this knowledge to a potential purchase.

Evaluating Scientific Explanation

Believe it or not?

Look at the photo in **Figure 24.** Do you believe what you see? Do you believe everything you read or hear? Think of something that someone told you that you didn't believe. Why didn't you believe it? Chances are you looked at the facts you were given and decided that there wasn't enough proof to make you believe it. What you did was evaluate, or judge the reliability of what you heard. When you hear a statement, you ask the question "How do you know?" If you decide that what you are told is reliable, then you believe it. If it seems unreliable, then you don't believe it.

Critical Thinking When you evaluate something, you use critical thinking. **Critical thinking** means combining what you already know with the new facts that you are given to decide if you should agree with something. You can evaluate an explanation by breaking it down into two parts. First you can look at and evaluate the observations. Based upon what you know, are the observations accurate? Then you can evaluate the inferences—or conclusions made about the observations. Do the conclusions made from the observations make sense?

Figure 24 In science, observations and inferences are not always agreed upon by everyone.
Compare *Do you see the same things your classmates see in this photo?*

Table 2 Favorite Foods

People's Preference	Tally	Frequency
Pepperoni pizza	⳾⳾⳾⳾ ⳾⳾⳾⳾ ⳾⳾⳾⳾ ⳾⳾⳾⳾ ⳾⳾⳾⳾ ⳾⳾⳾⳾ ⳾⳾⳾⳾ II	37
Hamburgers with ketchup	⳾⳾⳾⳾ ⳾⳾⳾⳾ ⳾⳾⳾⳾ ⳾⳾⳾⳾ ⳾⳾⳾⳾ III	28

Analysis, Inquiry, and Design

S3.2b: Discuss why it is important to list specific data that shows multiple trials and whether other scientists have repeated the data.

Figure 25 These scientists are writing down their observations during their investigation rather than waiting until they are back on land.
Draw Conclusions *Do you think this will increase or decrease the reliability of their data?*

Evaluating the Data

A scientific investigation always contains observations—often called **data.** Data are gathered during a scientific investigation and can be recorded in the form of descriptions, tables, graphs, or drawings. When evaluating a scientific claim, you might first look to see whether any data are given. You should be cautious about believing any claim that is not supported by data.

Are the data specific? The data given to back up a claim should be specific. That means they need to be exact. What if your friend tells you that many people like pizza more than they like hamburgers? What else do you need to know before you agree with your friend? You might want to hear about a specific number of people rather than unspecific words like *many* and *more.* You might want to know how many people like pizza more than hamburgers. How many people were asked about which kind of food they liked more? When you are given specific data, a statement is more reliable and you are more likely to believe it. An example of data in the form of a frequency table is shown in **Table 2.** A frequency table shows how many times types of data occur. Scientists must back up their scientific statements with specific data.

Take Good Notes Scientists must take thorough notes at the time of an investigation, as the scientists shown in **Figure 25** are doing. Important details can be forgotten if you wait several hours or days before you write down your observations. It is also important for you to write down every observation, including ones that you don't expect. Often, great discoveries are made when something unexpected happens in an investigation.

Your Science Journal During this course, you will be keeping a science journal. You will write down what you do and see during your investigations. Your observations should be detailed enough that another person could read what you wrote and repeat the investigation exactly as you performed it. Instead of writing "the stuff changed color," you might say "the clear liquid turned to bright red when I added a drop of food coloring." Detailed observations written down during an investigation are more reliable than sketchy observations written from memory. Practice your observation skills by describing what you see in **Figure 26.**

Can the data be repeated? If your friend told you he could hit a baseball 100 m, but couldn't do it when you were around, you probably wouldn't believe him. Scientists also require repeatable evidence. When a scientist describes an investigation, as shown in **Figure 27,** other scientists should be able to do the investigation and get the same results. The results must be repeatable. When evaluating scientific data, look to see whether other scientists have repeated the data. If not, the data might not be reliable.

Evaluating the Conclusions

When you think about a conclusion that someone has made, you can ask yourself two questions. First, does the conclusion make sense? Second, are there any other possible explanations? Suppose you hear on the radio that your school will be running on a two-hour delay in the morning because of snow. You look outside. The roads are clear of snow. Does the conclusion that snow is the cause for the delay make sense? What else could cause the delay? Maybe it is too foggy or icy for the buses to run. Maybe there is a problem with the school building. The original conclusion is not reliable unless the other possible explanations are proven unlikely.

Figure 26 Detailed observations are important in order to get reliable data.
Observe *Use ten descriptive words to describe what you see happening in this photo.*

Interdisciplinary: Problem Solving

1.2: Design a creative advertisement that is intentionally misleading or an exaggeration of data. Supply three examples of how the information is not correct.

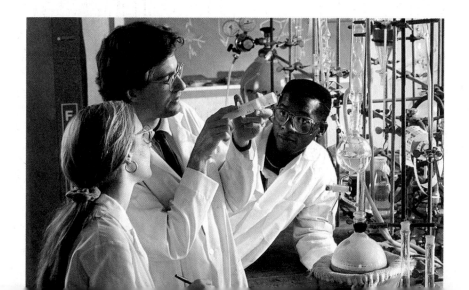

Figure 27 Working together is an important part of science. Several scientists must repeat an experiment and obtain the same results before data are considered reliable.

MIRACLE CREAM
MAKES WRINKLES
DISAPPEAR
OVERNIGHT

With twice daily use you will see
improvement almost immediately,
noticeable change within 30 DAYS...
significant improvement within 60 days
and even greater results after 6 months.

Figure 28 All material should be read with an analytical mind. **Explain** *what this advertisement means.*

Evaluating Promotional Materials

Scientific processes are not used only in the laboratory. Suppose you saw an advertisement in the newspaper like the one in **Figure 28.** What would you think? First, you might ask, "Does this make sense?" It seems unbelievable. You would probably want to hear some of the scientific data supporting the claim before you would believe it. How was this claim tested? How is the amount of wrinkling in skin measured? You might also want to know if an independent laboratory repeated the results. An independent laboratory is one that is not related in any way to the company that is selling the product or service. It has nothing to gain from the sales of the product. Results from an independent laboratory usually are more reliable than results from a laboratory paid by the selling company. Advertising materials are designed to get you to buy a product or service. It is important that you carefully evaluate advertising claims and the data that support them before making a quick decision to spend your money.

section 4 review

Summary

Believe it or not?

- By combining what you already know with new information as it becomes available, you can decide whether something is fact or fiction.
- Explanations should be evaluated by looking at both the observations and the conclusions the explanation is based on.

Evaluating the Data

- It is important to take thorough notes during any investigation.

Evaluating the Conclusions

- In order for a conclusion to be reliable, it must make sense.

Evaluating Promotional Materials

- Independent laboratories test products in order to provide more reliable results.

Self Check

1. **Describe** why it is important that scientific experiments be repeated.
2. **List** what types of scientific claims should be verified.
3. **Explain** how vague claims in advertising can be misleading.
4. **Think Critically** An advertisement on a food package claims it contains Glistain, a safe taste enhancer. Make a list of ten questions you would ask when evaluating this claim.

Applying Skills

5. **Classify** Watch three television commercials and read three magazine advertisements. Record the claims that each advertisement made. Classify each claim as being vague, misleading, reliable, and/or scientific.

More Section Review glencoe.com

What is the right answer?

Scientists sometimes develop more than one explanation for observations. Can more than one explanation be correct? Do scientific explanations depend on judgment?

◉ Real-World Question

Can more than one explanation apply to the same observation?

Goals
- ■ **Make a hypothesis** to explain an observation.
- ■ **Construct** a model to support your hypothesis.
- ■ **Refine** your model based on testing.

Materials
cardboard mailing tubes	length of rope
*empty shoe boxes	scissors

*Alternate materials

Safety Precautions

WARNING: *Be careful when punching holes with sharp tools.*

◉ Procedure

1. You will be shown a cardboard tube with four ropes coming out of it, one longer than the others. Your teacher will show you that when any of the three short ropes—A, C, or D—are pulled, the longer rope, B, gets shorter. Pulling on rope B returns the other ropes to their original lengths.

2. Make a hypothesis as to how the teacher's model works.

3. **Sketch** a model of a tube with ropes based on your hypothesis. Using a cardboard tube and two lengths of rope, build a model

according to your design. Test your model by pulling each of the ropes. If it does not perform as planned, modify your hypothesis and your model to make it work like your teacher's model.

◉ Conclude and Apply

1. **Compare** your model with those made by others in your class.

2. Can more than one design give the same result? Can more than one explanation apply to the same observation? Explain.

3. Without opening the tube, can you tell which model is exactly like your teacher's?

𝒞ommunicating Your Data

Make a display of your working model. Include sketches of your designs. **For more help, refer to the** Science Skill Handbook.

Identifying Parts of an Investigation

Goals

- **Identify** parts of an experiment.
- **Identify** constants, variables, and controls in the experiment.
- **Graph** the results of the experiment and draw appropriate conclusions.

Materials

description of fertilizer experiment

▶ Real-World Question

Science investigations contain many parts. How can you identify the various parts of an investigation? In addition to variables and constants, many experiments contain a control. A control is one test, or trial, where everything is held constant. A scientist compares the control trial to the other trials. What are the various parts of an experiment to test which fertilizer helps a plant grow best?

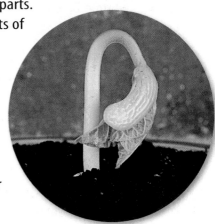

▶ Procedure

1. **Read** the description of the fertilizer experiment.
2. **List** factors that remained constant in the experiment.
3. **Identify** any variables in the experiment.
4. **Identify** the control in the experiment.
5. **Identify** one possible hypothesis that the gardener could have tested in her investigation.
6. **Describe** how the gardener went about testing her hypothesis using different types of fertilizers.

7. **Graph** the data that the gardener collected in a line graph.

A gardener was interested in helping her plants grow faster. When she went to the nursery, she found three fertilizers available for her plants. One of those fertilizers, fertilizer A, was recommended to her. However, she decided to conduct a test to determine which of the three fertilizers, if any, helped her plants grow fastest. The gardener planted four seeds, each in a separate pot. She used the same type of pot and the same type of soil in each pot. She fertilized one seed with fertilizer A, one with fertilizer B, and one with fertilizer C. She did not fertilize the fourth seed. She placed the four pots near one another in her garden. She made sure to give each plant the same amount of water each day. She measured the height of the plants each week and recorded her data. After eight weeks of careful observation and record keeping, she had the following table of data.

Plant Height (cm)				
Week	Fertilizer A	Fertilizer B	Fertilizer C	No Fertilizer
1	0	0	0	0
2	2	4	1	1
3	5	8	5	4
4	9	13	8	7
5	14	18	12	10
6	20	24	15	13
7	27	31	19	16
8	35	39	22	20

Analyze Your Data

1. **Describe** the results indicated by your graph. What part of an investigation have you just done?

2. **Infer** Based on the results in the table and your graph, which fertilizer do you think the gardener should use if she wants her plants to grow the fastest? What part of an investigation have you just done?

3. **Define** Suppose the gardener told a friend who also grows these plants about her results. What is this an example of?

Conclude and Apply

1. **Interpret Data** Suppose fertilizer B is much more expensive than fertilizers A and C. Would this affect which fertilizer you think the gardener should buy? Why or why not?

2. **Explain** Does every researcher need the same hypothesis for an experiment? What is a second possible hypothesis for this experiment (different from the one you wrote in step 5 in the Procedure section)?

3. **Explain** if the gardener conducted an adequate test of her hypothesis.

Communicating Your Data

Compare your conclusions with those of other students in your class. **For more help, refer to the** Science Skill Handbook.

Women in Science

Is your family doctor a man or a woman? To your great-grandparents, such a question would likely have seemed odd. Why? Because 100 years ago, women weren't encouraged to study science as they are today. But that does not mean that there were no female scientists back in your great-grandparents' day. Many women managed to overcome great barriers and made discoveries that changed the world.

Maria Goeppert Mayer

"To my surprise, winning the prize wasn't half as exciting as doing the work itself. That was the fun—seeing it work out." Dr. Maria Goeppert

Mayer won the Nobel Prize in Physics in 1963 for her work on the structure of an atom. Her model greatly increased human understanding of atoms, which make up all forms of matter.

Rita Levi-Montalcini

In 1986, Dr. Rita Levi-Montalcini was awarded the Nobel Prize in Medicine for her discovery of growth factors. Growth factors regulate the growth of cells and organs in the body. Because of her work, doctors are better able to understand why tumors form and wounds heal.

Rosalyn Sussman Yalow

"The world cannot afford the loss of the talents of half its people if we are to solve the many problems which beset us," Dr. Rosalyn Sussman Yalow said upon winning the Nobel Prize in Medicine in 1977 for discovering a way to measure tiny substances in the blood, such as hormones and drugs.

Her discovery made it possible for doctors to diagnose problems that they could not detect before.

Research Visit the link to the right to research some recent female Nobel prizewinners in physics, chemistry, and medicine. Write a short biography about their lives. How did their discoveries impact their scientific fields or people in general?

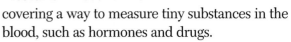

Reviewing Main Ideas

Section 1 What is science?

1. Science is a way of learning more about the natural world. It can provide possible explanations for why and how things happen.

2. Systems are made up of structures, cycles, and processes that interact with one another.

Section 2 Science in Action

1. A hypothesis is a possible explanation based on what you know and what you observe.

2. It is important to always follow laboratory safety symbols and to wear and use appropriate gear during an experiment.

Section 3 Models in Science

1. Models are a graphic representation of an object or an event used to communicate ideas; test predictions; and save time, money, and lives.

Section 4 Evaluating Scientific Explanation

1. Reliable data are specific and repeatable by other scientists.

2. In order for a conclusion to be considered reliable, it must make sense and be the most likely explanation.

Visualizing Main Ideas

Copy and complete the following concept map.

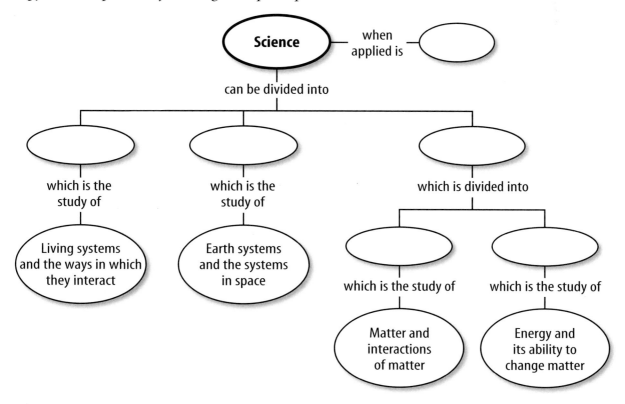

Using Vocabulary

constant p. 18	life science p. 9
controlled experiment p. 18	model p. 21
critical thinking p. 27	physical science p. 10
data p. 28	science p. 6
dependent variable p. 18	scientific law p. 7
Earth science p. 10	scientific theory p. 7
hypothesis p. 14	system p. 8
independent variable p. 18	technology p. 11
infer p. 16	variable p. 18

Explain the relationship between the words in the following sets.

1. hypothesis—scientific theory

2. constant—variable

3. science—technology

4. science—system

5. Earth science—physical science

6. critical thinking—infer

7. scientific law—observation

8. model—system

9. controlled experiment—variable

10. scientific theory—scientific law

Checking Concepts

Choose the word or phrase that best answers the question.

11. What does it mean to make an inference?
    A) make observations
    B) draw a conclusion
    C) replace
    D) test

12. Which of the following CANNOT protect you from splashing acid?
    A) goggles   C) fire extinguisher
    B) apron   D) gloves

13. If the results from your investigation do not support your hypothesis, what should you do?
    A) Should not do anything.
    B) Repeat the investigation until it agrees with the hypothesis.
    C) Modify your hypothesis.
    D) Change your data to fit your hypothesis.

14. Which of the following is NOT an example of a scientific hypothesis?
    A) Earthquakes happen because of stresses along continental plates.
    B) Some animals can detect ultrasound frequencies caused by earthquakes.
    C) Paintings are prettier than sculptures.
    D) Lava takes different forms depending on how it cools.

15. Using a computer to make a three-dimensional picture of a building is a type of which of the following?
    A) model   C) constant
    B) hypothesis   D) variable

16. Which of the following increases the reliability of a scientific explanation?
    A) vague statements
    B) notes taken after an investigation
    C) repeatable data
    D) several likely explanations

17. Which is an example of technology?
    A) a squirt bottle   C) a cat
    B) a poem   D) physical science

18. What explains something that takes place in the natural world?
    A) scientific law   C) scientific theory
    B) technology   D) experiments

19. An airplane model is an example of what type of model?
    A) physical   C) idea
    B) computer   D) mental

Thinking Critically

20. Draw Conclusions When scientists study how well new medicines work, one group of patients receives the medicine while a second group does not. Why?

21. Predict How is using a rock hammer an example of technology?

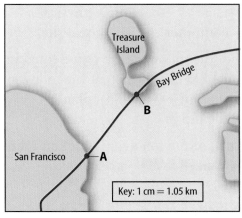

22. Compare and Contrast How are scientific theories and scientific laws similar? How are they different?

Use the table below to answer question 23.

Hardness	
Object	**Mohs Scale**
copper	3.5
diamond	10
fingernail	2.5
glass	5.5
quartz	7
steel file	6.5

23. Use Tables Mohs hardness scale measures how easily an object can be scratched. The higher the number, the harder the material is. Use the table above to identify which material is the hardest and which is the softest.

24. Make Operational Definitions How does a scientific law differ from a state law? Give some examples of both types of laws.

25. Infer Why it is important to record and measure data accurately during an experiment?

26. Predict the quickest way to get to school in the morning. List some ways you could test your prediction.

Performance Activities

27. Hypothesize Using a basketball and a tennis ball, make a hypothesis about the number of times each ball will bounce when it hits the ground. Drop each ball from shoulder height five times, recording the number of bounces in a table. Which ball bounced more? Make a hypothesis to explain why.

28. Observe Pour some water in a small dish and sprinkle some pepper on top. Notice how the pepper floats on the water. Now add a few drops of liquid soap to the water. Write down your observations as you watch what happens to the pepper.

Hot Words Hot Topics: Bk 1 pp. 274-276, 369

Applying Math

Use the illustration below to answer question 29.

Treasure Island

Bay Bridge

B

San Francisco · A

Key: 1 cm = 1.05 km

29. Use Proportions The map above shows the distance between two points. The scale shows that 1 cm is approximately 1.05 km. What is the approximate distance between Point A and Point B?

Record your answers on the answer sheet provided by your teacher or on a sheet of paper.

1 What is a rule describing a pattern in nature called?
(1) possible explanation
(2) scientific law
(3) scientific theory
(4) technology

Use the illustration below to answer questions 2–3.

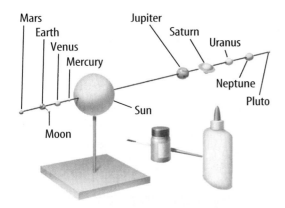

2 The model of the solar system best represents which kind of scientific model?
(1) idea   (3) physical
(2) computer   (4) realistic

3 All of the following are represented in the model EXCEPT which of the following?
(1) the sun   (3) planets
(2) the moon   (4) stars

4 Which of the following is not an example of a model?
(1) CD   (3) recipe
(2) map   (4) drawing

5 Which of the following questions can science NOT answer?
(1) Why do the leaves on trees change colors in the fall?
(2) Why do bears hibernate in the winter?
(3) Where do waves in the ocean form?
(4) What is the most popular book?

6 What is it called when you combine what you already know with new facts?
(1) estimate   (3) inference
(2) hypothesis   (4) critical thinking

7 What are the variables that do not change in an experiment called?
(1) independent variables
(2) dependent variables
(3) constants
(4) inferences

8 An educated guess based on what you know and what you observe is called which of the following?
(1) prediction   (3) conclusion
(2) hypothesis   (4) data

Use the photo below to answer question 9.

9 What type of scientist could the person above be classified as?
(1) life scientist
(2) physical scientist
(3) Earth scientist
(4) medical doctor

Record your answers on the answer sheet provided by your teacher or on a sheet of paper.

Use the photo below to answer questions 10 and 11.

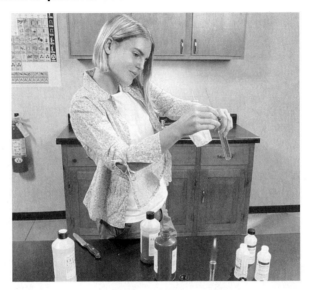

10 Look at the photo above and write down your immediate observations.

11 What safety precautions might this student want to take?

12 Explain why science can only provide possible explanations for occurrences in nature.

13 Explain the relationship between science and technology.

14 List the three branches of science and give examples of questions that they ask.

15 You want to know whether plants grow faster if there is music playing in their environment. How would you conduct this experiment? Be sure to identify the independent and dependent variables, and the constants.

16 Many outdoor clothing products are coated in a special waterproofing agent to protect the material from rain and snow. The manufacturers of the waterproofing agent hire independent field-testers to use their product in the field before marketing it to the public. Why would you want to know the results of the field-testers tests?

17 Body systems interact with one another in order to function. What would happen if one system failed?

18 Make a frequency table from the following data. Make two observations about the data. 15 students prefer cold pizza for lunch; 10 students enjoy peanut butter with jelly; 3 students bring ham and cheese; and 5 students eat hot dogs and chips.

PS 4.1c: Most activities in everyday life involve one form of energy being transformed into another. **4.4d:** Electrical energy can be produced from a variety of energy sources and can be transformed into almost any other form of energy. **Also covered:** AID S1.1b, S2.1b, S2.1d, S2.3c, S3.1a, S3.2d, S3.2h, IS 1.3, 1.4, PS 2.2r, 4.1a, 4.1b, 4.1d, 4.1e, 4.3a, 4.5a, 4.5b, 5.1d.

Energy and Energy Resources

chapter preview

sections

1 What is energy?

2 Energy Transformations
Lab Hearing with Your Jaw

3 Sources of Energy
Lab Energy to Power Your Life

Virtual Lab What are the relationships between kinetic energy and potential energy?

Blowing Off Steam

The electrical energy you used today might have been produced by a coal-burning power plant like this one. Energy contained in coal is transformed into heat, and then into electrical energy. As boiling water heated by the burning coal is cooled, steam rises from these cone-shaped cooling towers.

Science Journal Choose three devices that use electricity, and identify the function of each device.

Start-Up Activities

Marbles and Energy

What's the difference between a moving marble and one at rest? A moving marble can hit something and cause a change to occur. How can a marble acquire energy—the ability to cause change?

1. Make a track on a table by slightly separating two metersticks placed side by side.

2. Using a book, raise one end of the track slightly and measure the height.

3. Roll a marble down the track. Measure the distance from its starting point to where it hits the floor. Repeat. Calculate the average of the two measurements.

4. Repeat steps 2 and 3 for three different heights. Predict what will happen if you use a heavier marble. Test your prediction and record your observations.

5. **Think Critically** In your Science Journal, describe how the distance traveled by the marble is related to the height of the ramp. How is the motion of the marble related to the ramp height?

FOLDABLES
Study Organizer

Energy Make the following Foldable to help identify what you already know, what you want to know, and what you learned about energy.

STEP 1 **Fold** a vertical sheet of paper from side to side. Make the front edge about 1 cm shorter than the back edge.

STEP 2 **Turn** lengthwise and **fold** into thirds

STEP 3 **Unfold, cut, and label** each tab for only the top layer along both folds to make three tabs.

Know? | Like to know? | Learned?

Identify Questions Before you read the chapter, write what you know and what you want to know about the types, sources, and transformation of energy under the appropriate tabs. As you read the chapter, correct what you have written and add more questions under the *Learned* tab.

Science nline | Preview this chapter's content and activities at glencoe.com

PS 4.1d: Different forms of energy include heat, light, electrical, mechanical, sound, nuclear, and chemical. Energy is transformed in many ways. 4.1e: Energy can be considered to be either kinetic energy, which is the energy of motion, or potential energy, which depends on relative position.

What is energy?

What You'll Learn
- **Explain** what energy is.
- **Distinguish** between kinetic energy and potential energy.
- **Identify** the various forms of energy.

Why It's Important
Energy is involved whenever a change occurs.

🔍 Review Vocabulary
mass: a measure of the amount of matter in an object

New Vocabulary
- energy
- kinetic energy
- potential energy
- thermal energy
- chemical energy
- radiant energy
- electrical energy
- nuclear energy

The Nature of Energy

What comes to mind when you hear the word *energy?* Do you picture running, leaping, and spinning like a dancer or a gymnast? How would you define energy? When an object has energy, it can make things happen. In other words, **energy** is the ability to cause change. What do the items shown in **Figure 1** have in common?

Look around and notice the changes that are occurring—someone walking by or a ray of sunshine that is streaming through the window and warming your desk. Maybe you can see the wind moving the leaves on a tree. What changes are occurring?

Transferring Energy You might not realize it, but you have a large amount of energy. In fact, everything around you has energy, but you notice it only when a change takes place. Anytime a change occurs, energy is transferred from one object to another. You hear a footstep because energy is transferred from a foot hitting the ground to your ears. Leaves are put into motion when energy in the moving wind is transferred to them. The spot on the desktop becomes warmer when energy is transferred to it from the sunlight. In fact, all objects, including leaves and desktops, have energy.

Figure 1 Energy is the ability to cause change.
Explain *how these objects cause change.*

Energy of Motion

Things that move can cause change. A bowling ball rolls down the alley and knocks down some pins, as in **Figure 2A.** Is energy involved? A change occurs when the pins fall over. The bowling ball causes this change, so the bowling ball has energy. The energy in the motion of the bowling ball causes the pins to fall. As the ball moves, it has a form of energy called kinetic energy. **Kinetic energy** is the energy an object has due to its motion. If an object isn't moving, it doesn't have kinetic energy.

Kinetic Energy and Speed If you roll the bowling ball so it moves faster, what happens when it hits the pins? It might knock down more pins, or it might cause the pins to go flying farther. A faster ball causes more change to occur than a ball that is moving slowly. Look at **Figure 2B.** The professional bowler rolls a fast-moving bowling ball. When her ball hits the pins, pins go flying faster and farther than for a slower-moving ball. All that action signals that her ball has more energy. The faster the ball goes, the more kinetic energy it has. This is true for all moving objects. Kinetic energy increases as an object moves faster.

Reading Check *How does kinetic energy depend on speed?*

Kinetic Energy and Mass Suppose, as shown in **Figure 2C,** you roll a volleyball down the alley instead of a bowling ball. If the volleyball travels at the same speed as a bowling ball, do you think it will send pins flying as far? The answer is no. The volleyball might not knock down any pins. Does the volleyball have less energy than the bowling ball even though they are traveling at the same speed?

An important difference between the volleyball and the bowling ball is that the volleyball has less mass. Even though the volleyball is moving at the same speed as the bowling ball, the volleyball has less kinetic energy because it has less mass. Kinetic energy also depends on the mass of a moving object. Kinetic energy increases as the mass of the object increases.

Figure 2 The kinetic energy of an object depends on the mass and speed of the object.

A This ball has kinetic energy because it is rolling down the alley.

B This ball has more kinetic energy because it has more speed.

C This ball has less kinetic energy because it has less mass.

Figure 3 The potential energy of an object depends on its mass and height above the ground.
Determine *which vase has more potential energy, the red one or the blue one.*

Energy of Position

An object can have energy even though it is not moving. For example, a glass of water sitting on the kitchen table doesn't have any kinetic energy because it isn't moving. If you accidentally nudge the glass and it falls on the floor, changes occur. Gravity pulls the glass downward, and the glass has energy of motion as it falls. Where did this energy come from?

When the glass was sitting on the table, it had potential (puh TEN chul) energy. **Potential energy** is the energy stored in an object because of its position. In this case, the position is the height of the glass above the floor. The potential energy of the glass changes to kinetic energy as the glass falls. The potential energy of the glass is greater if it is higher above the floor. Potential energy also depends on mass. The more mass an object has, the more potential energy it has. Which object in **Figure 3** has the most potential energy?

Forms of Energy

Food, sunlight, and wind have energy, yet they seem different because they contain different forms of energy. Food and sunlight contain forms of energy different from the kinetic energy in the motion of the wind. The warmth you feel from sunlight is another type of energy that is different from the energy of motion or position.

Thermal Energy The feeling of warmth from sunlight signals that your body is acquiring more thermal energy. All objects have **thermal energy** that increases as its temperature increases. A cup of hot chocolate has more thermal energy than a cup of cold water, as shown in **Figure 4.** Similarly, the cup of water has more thermal energy than a block of ice of the same mass. Your body continually produces thermal energy. Many chemical reactions that take place inside your cells produce thermal energy. Where does this energy come from? Thermal energy released by chemical reactions comes from another form of energy called chemical energy.

Physical Setting

4.1 d, 4.1e: Compare and contrast kinetic energy to potential energy. Include an example of each.

Figure 4 The hotter an object is, the more thermal energy it has. A cup of hot chocolate has more thermal energy than a cup of cold water, which has more thermal energy than a block of ice with the same mass.

Figure 5 Complex chemicals in food store chemical energy. During activity, the chemical energy transforms into kinetic energy.

Sugar

Chemical Energy When you eat a meal, ___ source of energy inside your body. ___ energy that your body uses t___ power your movement ___ food contains chemica___ down in your body. Thes___ bonded together, and en___ atoms. **Chemical energy** is ___ When chemicals are brok___ formed, some of this energy ___ the result of chemical energy ___ burns, chemical energy is trans___ light energy.

✔ **Reading Check** *When is chem___*

___e 6 Electrical energy is ___ned into thermal energy in ___ heating coil. As the ___ metal becomes hotter, it emits more radiant energy.

Light Energy Light from the cand___ flame travels through the air at an incredibly fast speed of 300,000 km/s. This is fast enough to circle Earth almost eight times in 1 s. When light strikes something, it can be absorbed, transmitted, or reflected. When the light is absorbed by an object, the object can become warmer. The object absorbs energy from the light and this energy is transformed into thermal energy. Then energy carried by light is called **radiant energy. Figure 6** shows a coil of wire that produces radiant energy when it is heated. To heat the metal, another type of energy can be used—electrical energy.

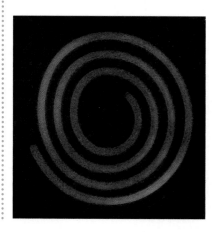

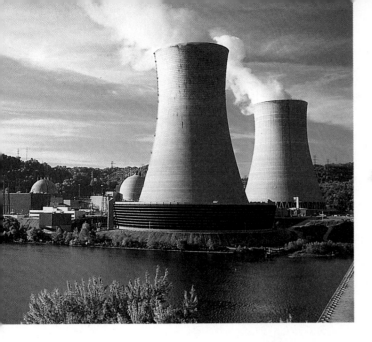

Electrical Energy Electrical lighting is one of the many ways electrical energy is used. Look around at all the devices that use electricity. Electric current flows in these devices when they are connected to batteries or plugged into an electric outlet. **Electrical energy** is the energy that is carried by an electric current. An electric device uses the electrical energy provided by the current flowing in the device. Large electric power plants generate the enormous amounts of electrical energy used each day. About 20 percent of the electrical energy used in the United States is generated by nuclear power plants.

Figure 7 Complex power plants are required to obtain useful energy from the nucleus of an atom.

Nuclear Energy Nuclear power plants use the energy stored in the nucleus of an atom to generate electricity. Every atomic nucleus contains energy—**nuclear energy**—that can be transformed into other forms of energy. However, releasing the nuclear energy is a difficult process. It involves the construction of complex power plants, shown in **Figure 7.** In contrast, all that is needed to release chemical energy from wood is a lighted match.

section 1 review

Summary

The Nature of Energy

- Energy is the ability to cause change.
- Kinetic energy is the energy an object has due to its motion. Kinetic energy depends on an object's speed and mass.
- Potential energy is the energy an object has due to its position. Potential energy depends on an object's height and mass.

Forces of Energy

- Thermal energy increases as temperature increases.
- Chemical energy is the energy stored in chemical bonds in molecules.
- Light energy, also called radiant energy, is the energy contained in light.
- Electrical energy is the energy carried by electric current.
- Nuclear energy is the energy contained in the nucleus of an atom.

Self Check

1. **Explain** why a high-speed collision between two cars would cause more damage than a low-speed collision between the same two cars.

2. **Describe** the energy transformations that occur when a piece of wood is burned.

3. **Identify** the form of energy that is converted into thermal energy by your body.

4. **Explain** how, if two vases are side by side on a shelf, one could have more potential energy.

5. **Think Critically** A golf ball and a bowling ball are moving and both have the same kinetic energy. Which one is moving faster? If they move at the same speed, which one has more kinetic energy?

Applying Skills

6. **Communicate** In your Science Journal, record different ways the word *energy* is used. Which ways of using the word *energy* are closest to the definition of energy given in this section?

PS 4.1c: Most activities in everyday life involve one form of energy being transformed into another. Energy, in the form of heat, is almost always one of the products of energy transformations. 4.4d: Electrical energy can be produced from a variety of energy sources and can be transformed into almost any other form of energy. **Also covered:** 4.1d, 4.1e, 4.3a, 4.5a, 4.5b.

Energy Transformations

Changing Forms of Energy

Chemical, thermal, radiant, and electrical are some of the forms that energy can have. In the world around you, energy is transforming continually between one form and another. You observe some of these transformations by noticing a change in your environment. Forest fires are a dramatic example of an environmental change that can occur naturally as a result of lightning strikes. A number of changes occur that involve energy as the mountain biker in **Figure 8** pedals up a hill. What energy transformations cause these changes to occur?

Tracking Energy Transformations As the mountain biker pedals, his leg muscles transform chemical energy into kinetic energy. The kinetic energy of his leg muscles transforms into kinetic energy of the bicycle as he pedals. Some of this energy transforms into potential energy as he moves up the hill. Also, some energy is transformed into thermal energy. His body is warmer because chemical energy is being released. Because of friction, the mechanical parts of the bicycle are warmer, too. Energy in the form of heat is almost always one of the products of an energy transformation. The energy transformations that occur when people exercise, when cars run, when living things grow and even when stars explode, all produce heat.

as you read

What You'll Learn

- **Apply** the law of conservation of energy to energy transformations.
- **Identify** how energy changes form.
- **Describe** how electric power plants produce energy.

Why It's Important

Changing energy from one form to another is what makes cars run, furnaces heat, telephones work, and plants grow.

Review Vocabulary

transformation: a change in composition or structure

New Vocabulary

- law of conservation of energy
- generator
- turbine

Figure 8 The ability to transform energy allows the biker to climb the hill.
Identify *all the forms of energy that are represented in the photograph.*

The Law of Conservation of Energy

It can be a challenge to track energy as it moves from object to object. However, one extremely important principle can serve as a guide as you trace the flow of energy. According to the **law of conservation of energy,** energy is never created or destroyed. The only thing that changes is the form in which energy appears. When the biker is resting at the summit, all his original energy is still around. Some of the energy is in the form of potential energy, which he will use as he coasts down the hill. Some of this energy was changed to thermal energy by friction in the bike. Chemical energy was also changed to thermal energy in the biker's muscles, making him feel hot. As he rests, this thermal energy moves from his body to the air around him. No energy is missing—it can all be accounted for.

✔ **Reading Check** *Can energy ever be lost? Why or why not?*

Changing Kinetic and Potential Energy

The law of conservation of energy can be used to identify the energy changes in a system. For example, tossing a ball into the air and catching it is a simple system. As shown in **Figure 9,** as the ball leaves your hand, most of its energy is kinetic. As the ball rises, it slows and its kinetic energy decreases. But, the total energy of the ball hasn't changed. The decrease in kinetic energy equals the increase in potential energy as the ball flies higher in the air. The total amount of energy remains constant. Energy moves from place to place and changes form, but it never is created or destroyed.

Science Online

Topic: Energy Transformations

Visit glencoe.com for Web links to information about energy transformations that occur during different activities and processes.

Activity Choose an activity or process and make a graph showing how the kinetic and potential energy change during it.

Physical Setting

4.1c, 4.5a: State the law of conservation of energy. Design a 3-step flowchart to show how energy can change forms.

Figure 9 During the flight of the baseball, energy is transforming between kinetic and potential energy.
Determine *where the ball has the most kinetic energy. Where does the ball have the most total energy?*

Figure 10 Hybrid cars that use an electric motor and a gasoline engine for power are now available. Hybrid cars make energy transformations more efficient.

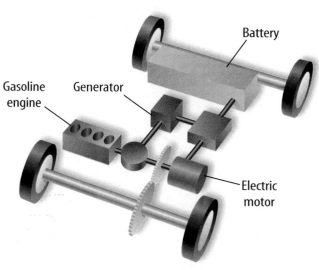

Battery

Gasoline engine   Generator

Electric motor

Energy Changes Form

Energy transformations occur constantly all around you. Many machines are devices that transform energy from one form to another. For example, an automobile engine transforms the chemical energy in gasoline into energy of motion. However, not all of the chemical energy is converted into kinetic energy. Instead, some of the chemical energy is converted into thermal energy, and the engine becomes hot. An engine that converts chemical energy into more kinetic energy is a more efficient engine. New types of cars, like the one shown in **Figure 10,** use an electric motor along with a gasoline engine. These engines are more efficient so the car can travel farther on a gallon of gas.

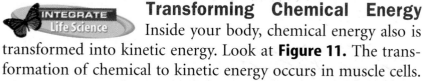

Transforming Chemical Energy Inside your body, chemical energy also is transformed into kinetic energy. Look at **Figure 11.** The transformation of chemical to kinetic energy occurs in muscle cells. There, chemical reactions take place that cause certain molecules to change shape. Your muscle contracts when many of these changes occur, and a part of your body moves.

The matter contained in living organisms, also called biomass, contains chemical energy. When organisms die, chemical compounds in their biomass break down. Bacteria, fungi, and other organisms help convert these chemical compounds to simpler chemicals that can be used by other living things.

Thermal energy also is released as these changes occur. For example, a compost pile can contain plant matter, such as grass clippings and leaves. As the compost pile decomposes, chemical energy is converted into thermal energy. This can cause the temperature of a compost pile to reach 60°C.

Analyzing Energy Transformations

Procedure

1. Place soft **clay** on the floor and smooth out its surface.
2. Hold a **marble** 1.5 m above the clay and drop it. Measure the depth of the crater made by the marble.
3. Repeat this procedure using a **golf ball** and a **plastic golf ball.**

Analysis

1. Compare the depths of the craters to determine which ball had the most kinetic energy as it hit the clay.
2. Explain how potential energy was transformed into kinetic energy during your activity.

Figure 11

Paddling a raft, throwing a baseball, playing the violin — your skeletal muscles make these and countless other body movements possible. Muscles work by pulling, or contracting. At the cellular level, muscle contractions are powered by reactions that transform chemical energy into kinetic energy.

▶ Energy transformations taking place in your muscles provide the power to move.

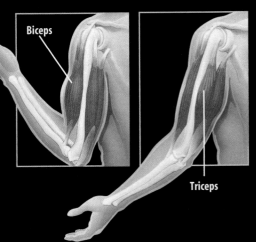

Biceps

Triceps

▲ Many skeletal muscles are arranged in pairs that work in opposition to each other. When you bend your arm, the biceps muscle contracts, while the triceps relaxes. When you extend your arm the triceps contracts, and the biceps relaxes.

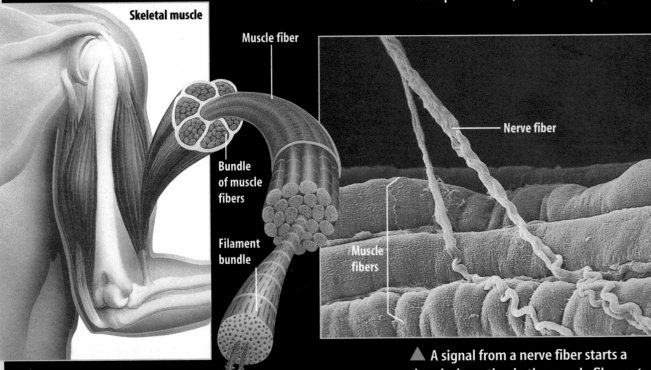

Skeletal muscle

Muscle fiber

Bundle of muscle fibers

Filament bundle

Nerve fiber

Muscle fibers

Muscle filaments

▲ Skeletal muscles are made up of bundles of muscle cells, or fibers. Each fiber is composed of many bundles of muscle filaments.

▲ A signal from a nerve fiber starts a chemical reaction in the muscle filament. This causes molecules in the muscle filament to gain energy and move. Many filaments moving together cause the muscle to contract.

Figure 12 The simple act of listening to a radio involves many energy transformations. A few are diagrammed here.

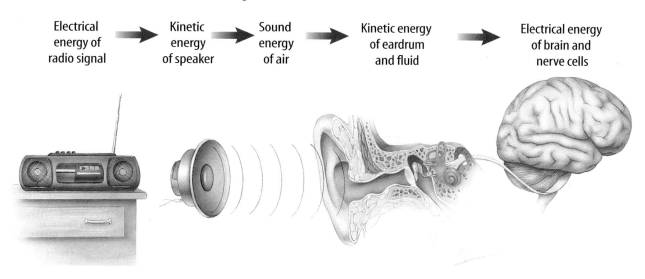

Electrical energy of radio signal → Kinetic energy of speaker → Sound energy of air → Kinetic energy of eardrum and fluid → Electrical energy of brain and nerve cells

Transforming Electrical Energy Every day you use electrical energy. When you flip a light switch, or turn on a radio or television, or use a hair drier, you are transforming electrical energy to other forms of energy. Every time you plug something into a wall outlet, or use a battery, you are using electrical energy. **Figure 12** shows how electrical energy is transformed into other forms of energy when you listen to a radio. A loudspeaker in the radio converts electrical energy into sound waves that travel to your ear—energy in motion. The energy that is carried by the sound waves causes parts of the ear to move also. This energy of motion is transformed again into chemical and electrical energy in nerve cells, which send the energy to your brain. After your brain interprets this energy as a voice or music, where does the energy go? The energy finally is transformed into thermal energy.

Transforming Thermal Energy Different forms of energy can be transformed into thermal energy. For example, chemical energy changes into thermal energy when something burns. Electrical energy changes into thermal energy when a wire that is carrying an electric current gets hot. Thermal energy can be used to heat buildings and keep you warm. Thermal energy also can be used to heat water. If water is heated to its boiling point, it changes to steam. This steam can be used to produce kinetic energy by steam engines, like the steam locomotives that used to pull trains. Thermal energy also can be transformed into radiant energy. For example, when a bar of metal is heated to a high temperature, it glows and gives off light.

Physical Setting

4.3a: Analyze how chemical energy can be transformed into light, electricity, or mechanical motion, as well as heat. Give an example of each transformation.

INTEGRATE Life Science

Controlling Body Temperature Most organisms have some adaptation for controlling the amount of thermal energy in their bodies. Some living in cooler climates have thick fur coats that help prevent thermal energy from escaping, and some living in desert regions have skin that helps keep thermal energy out. Research some of the adaptations different organisms have for controlling the thermal energy in their bodies.

Thermal energy

How Thermal Energy Moves Thermal energy can move from one place to another. Look at **Figure 13.** The hot chocolate has thermal energy that moves from the cup to the cooler air around it, and to the cooler spoon. Thermal energy only moves from something at a higher temperature to something at a lower temperature.

Generating Electrical Energy

The enormous amount of electrical energy that is used every day is too large to be stored in batteries. The electrical energy that is available for use at any wall socket must be generated continually by power plants. Every power plant works on the same principle—energy is used to turn a large generator. A **generator** is a device that transforms kinetic energy into electrical energy. In fossil fuel power plants, coal, oil, or natural gas is burned to boil water. As the hot water boils, the steam rushes through a **turbine,** which contains a set of narrowly spaced fan blades. The steam pushes on the blades and turns the turbine, which in turn rotates a shaft in the generator to produce the electrical energy, as shown in **Figure 14.**

Figure 13 Thermal energy moves from the hot chocolate to the cooler surroundings.
Explain *what happens to the hot chocolate as it loses thermal energy.*

Figure 14 A coal-burning power plant transforms the chemical energy in coal into electrical energy.
List *some of the other energy sources that power plants use.*

Reading Check *What does a generator do?*

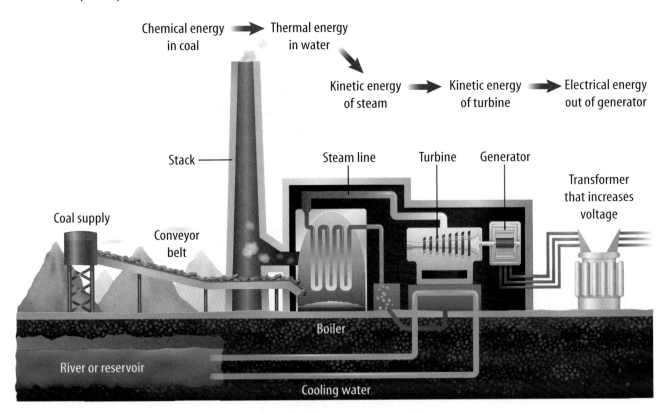

Chemical energy in coal ➡ Thermal energy in water ➡ Kinetic energy of steam ➡ Kinetic energy of turbine ➡ Electrical energy out of generator

Stack

Steam line   Turbine   Generator

Transformer that increases voltage

Coal supply

Conveyor belt

Boiler

River or reservoir

Cooling water

Power Plants Almost 90 percent of the electrical energy generated in the United States is produced by nuclear and fossil fuel power plants, as shown in **Figure 15.** Other types of power plants include hydroelectric (hi droh ih LEK trihk) and wind. Hydroelectric power plants transform the kinetic energy of moving water into electrical energy. Wind power plants transform the kinetic energy of moving air into electrical energy. In these power plants, a generator converts the kinetic energy of moving water or wind to electrical energy.

To analyze the energy transformations in a power plant, you can diagram the energy changes using arrows. A coal-burning power plant generates electrical energy through the following series of energy transformations.

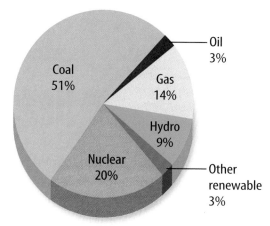

chemical energy of coal	→	thermal energy of water	→	kinetic energy of steam	→	kinetic energy of turbine	→	electrical energy out of generator

Figure 15 The graph shows sources of electrical energy in the United States.
Name *the energy source that you think is being used to provide the electricity for the lights overhead.*

Nuclear power plants use a similar series of transformations. Hydroelectric plants, however, skip the steps that change water into steam because the water strikes the turbine directly.

section 2 review

Summary

Changing Forms of Energy

- Heat usually is one of the forms of energy produced in energy transformations.
- The law of conservation of energy states that energy cannot be created or destroyed; it can only change form.
- The total energy doesn't change when an energy transformation occurs.
- As an object rises and falls, kinetic and potential energy are transformed into each other, but the total energy doesn't change.

Generating Electrical Energy

- A generator converts kinetic energy into electrical energy.
- Burning fossil fuels produces thermal energy that is used to boil water and produce steam.
- In a power plant, steam is used to spin a turbine which then spins an electric generator.

Self Check

1. **Describe** the conversions between potential and kinetic energy that occur when you shoot a basketball at a basket.

2. **Explain** whether your body gains or loses thermal energy if your body temperature is 37°C and the temperature around you is 25°C.

3. **Describe** a process that converts chemical energy to thermal energy.

4. **Think Critically** A lightbulb converts 10 percent of the electrical energy it uses into radiant energy. Make a hypothesis about the other form of energy produced.

   Hot Words Hot Topics: Bk 1 p. 274

Applying Math

5. **Use a Ratio** How many times greater is the amount of electrical energy produced in the United States by coal-burning power plants than the amount produced by nuclear power plants?

Hearing with Your Jaw

You probably have listened to music using speakers or headphones. Have you ever considered how energy is transferred to get the energy from the radio or CD player to your brain? What type of energy is needed to power the radio or CD player? Where does this energy come from? How does that energy become sound? How does the sound get to you? In this activity, the sound from a radio or CD player is going to travel through a motor before entering your body through your jaw instead of your ears.

◉ Real-World Question

How can energy be transferred from a radio or CD player to your brain?

Goals
- **Identify** energy transfers and transformations.
- **Explain** your observations using the law of conservation of energy.

Materials
radio or CD player
small electrical motor
headphone jack

◉ Procedure

1. Go to one of the places in the room with a motor/radio assembly.
2. Turn on the radio or CD player so that you hear the music.
3. Push the headphone jack into the headphone plug on the radio or CD player.
4. Press the axle of the motor against the side of your jaw.

◉ Conclude and Apply

1. **Describe** what you heard in your Science Journal.
2. **Identify** the form of energy produced by the radio or CD player.
3. **Draw** a diagram to show all of the energy transformations taking place.
4. **Evaluate** Did anything get hotter as a result of this activity? Explain.
5. **Explain** your observations using the law of conservation of energy.

Compare your conclusions with those of other students in your class. **For more help, refer to the** Science Skill Handbook.

PS 4.1a: The Sun is a major source of energy for Earth. Other sources of energy include nuclear and geothermal energy. **4.1b:** Fossil fuels contain stored solar energy and are considered nonrenewable resources. **Also covered:** 2.2r, 4.4d.

Sources of Energy

Using Energy

Every day, energy is used to provide light and to heat and cool homes, schools, and workplaces. According to the law of conservation of energy, energy can't be created or destroyed. Energy only can change form. If a car or refrigerator can't create the energy they use, then where does this energy come from?

Energy Resources

Energy cannot be made, but must come from the natural world. As you can see in **Figure 16,** the surface of Earth receives energy from two sources—the Sun and radioactive atoms in Earth's interior. The amount of energy Earth receives from the Sun is far greater than the amount generated in Earth's interior. Nearly all the energy you used today can be traced to the Sun, even the gasoline used to power the car or school bus you came to school in.

as you read

***What* You'll Learn**

- **Explain** what renewable, non-renewable, and alternative resources are.
- **Describe** the advantages and disadvantages of using various energy sources.

***Why* It's Important**

Energy is vital for survival and making life comfortable. Developing new energy sources will improve modern standards of living.

⊙ Review Vocabulary

resource: a natural feature or phenomenon that enhances the quality of life

New Vocabulary

- nonrenewable resource
- renewable resource
- alternative resource
- inexhaustible resource
- photovoltaic

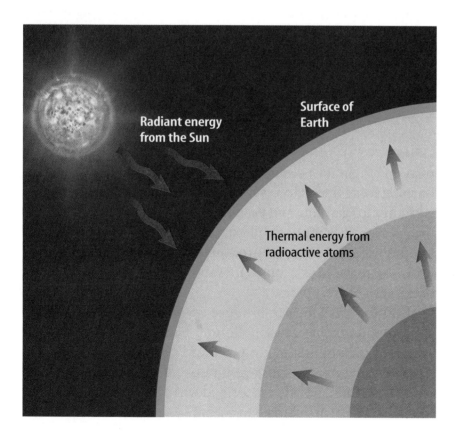

Radiant energy from the Sun

Surface of Earth

Thermal energy from radioactive atoms

Figure 16 All the energy you use can be traced to one of two sources—the Sun or radioactive atoms in Earth's interior.

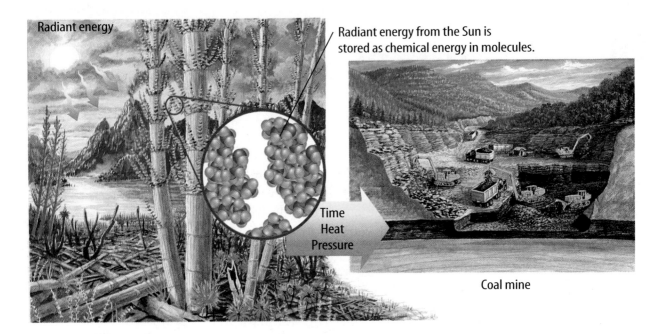

Radiant energy

Radiant energy from the Sun is stored as chemical energy in molecules.

Time
Heat
Pressure

Coal mine

Figure 17 Coal is formed after the molecules in ancient plants are heated under pressure for millions of years. The energy stored by the molecules in coal originally came from the Sun.

INTEGRATE Earth Science

Energy Source Origins The kinds of fossil fuels found in the ground depend on the kinds of organisms (animal or plant) that died and were buried in that spot. Research coal, oil, and natural gas to find out what types of organisms were primarily responsible for producing each.

Fossil Fuels

Fossil fuels are coal, oil, and natural gas. Oil and natural gas were made from the remains of microscopic organisms that lived in Earth's oceans millions of years ago. Heat and pressure gradually turned these ancient organisms into oil and natural gas. Coal was formed by a similar process from the remains of ancient plants that once lived on land, as shown in **Figure 17.**

Through the process of photosynthesis, ancient plants converted the radiant energy in sunlight to chemical energy stored in various types of molecules. Heat and pressure changed these molecules into other types of molecules as fossil fuels formed. Chemical energy stored in these molecules is released when fossil fuels are burned.

Using Fossil Fuels The energy used when you ride in a car, turn on a light, or use an electric appliance usually comes from burning fossil fuels. However, it takes millions of years to replace each drop of gasoline and each lump of coal that is burned. This means that the supply of oil on Earth will continue to decrease as oil is used. An energy source that is used up much faster than it can be replaced is a **nonrenewable resource.** Fossil fuels are nonrenewable resources.

Burning fossil fuels to produce energy also generates chemical compounds that cause pollution. Each year billions of kilograms of air pollutants are produced by burning fossil fuels. These pollutants can cause respiratory illnesses and acid rain. Also, the carbon dioxide gas formed when fossil fuels are burned might cause Earth's climate to warm.

Nuclear Energy

Can you imagine running an automobile on 1 kg of fuel that releases almost 3 million times more energy than 1 L of gas? What could supply so much energy from so little mass? The answer is the nuclei of uranium atoms. Some of these nuclei are unstable and break apart, releasing enormous amounts of energy in the process. This energy can be used to generate electricity by heating water to produce steam that spins an electric generator, as shown in **Figure 18.** Because no fossil fuels are burned, generating electricity using nuclear energy helps make the supply of fossil fuels last longer. Also, unlike fossil fuel power plants, nuclear power plants produce almost no air pollution. In one year, a typical nuclear power plant generates enough energy to supply 600,000 homes with power and produces only 1 m^3 of waste.

Nuclear Wastes Like all energy sources, nuclear energy has its advantages and disadvantages. One disadvantage is the amount of uranium in Earth's crust is nonrenewable. Another is that the waste produced by nuclear power plants is radioactive and can be dangerous to living things. Some of the materials in the nuclear waste will remain radioactive for many thousands of years. As a result the waste must be stored so no radioactivity is released into the environment for a long time. One method is to seal the waste in a ceramic material, place the ceramic in protective containers, and then bury the containers far underground. However, the burial site would have to be chosen carefully so underground water supplies aren't contaminated. Also, the site would have to be safe from earthquakes and other natural disasters that might cause radioactive material to be released.

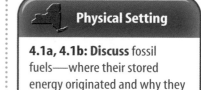

Physical Setting

4.1a, 4.1b: Discuss fossil fuels—where their stored energy originated and why they are considered non-renewable.

Figure 18 To obtain electrical energy from nuclear energy, a series of energy transformations must occur.

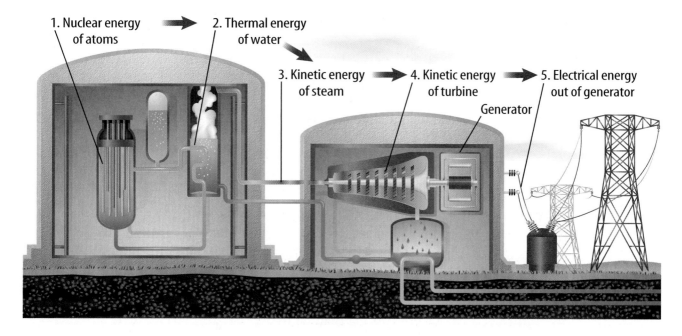

1. Nuclear energy of atoms
2. Thermal energy of water
3. Kinetic energy of steam
4. Kinetic energy of turbine
5. Electrical energy out of generator

Generator

Hydroelectricity

Currently, transforming the potential energy of water that is trapped behind dams supplies the world with almost 20 percent of its electrical energy. Hydroelectricity is the largest renewable source of energy. A **renewable resource** is an energy source that is replenished continually. As long as enough rain and snow fall to keep rivers flowing, hydroelectric power plants can generate electrical energy, as shown in **Figure 19.**

Although production of hydroelectricity is largely pollution free, it has one major problem. It disrupts the life cycle of aquatic animals, especially fish. This is particularly true in the Northwest where salmon spawn and run. Because salmon return to the spot where they were hatched to lay their eggs, the development of dams has hindered a large fraction of salmon from reproducing. This has greatly reduced the salmon population. Efforts to correct the problem have resulted in plans to remove a number of dams. In an attempt to help fish bypass some dams, fish ladders are being installed. Like most energy sources, hydroelectricity has advantages and disadvantages.

Science Online

Topic: Hydroelectricity
Visit glencoe.com for Web links to information about the use of hydroelectricity in various parts of the world.

Activity On a map of the world, show where the use of hydroelectricity is the greatest.

Applying Science

Is energy consumption outpacing production?

You use energy every day—to get to school, to watch TV, and to heat or cool your home. The amount of energy consumed by an average person has increased over time. Consequently, more energy must be produced.

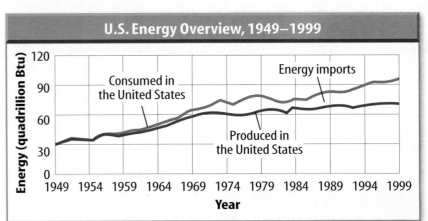

U.S. Energy Overview, 1949–1999

Identifying the Problem

The graph above shows the energy produced and consumed in the United States from 1949 to 1999. How does energy that is consumed by Americans compare with energy that is produced in the United States?

Solving the Problem

1. Determine the approximate amount of energy produced in 1949 and in 1999

and how much it has increased in 50 years. Has it doubled or tripled?

2. Do the same for consumption. Has it doubled or tripled?

3. Using your answers for steps 1 and 2 and the graph, where does the additional energy that is needed come from? Give some examples.

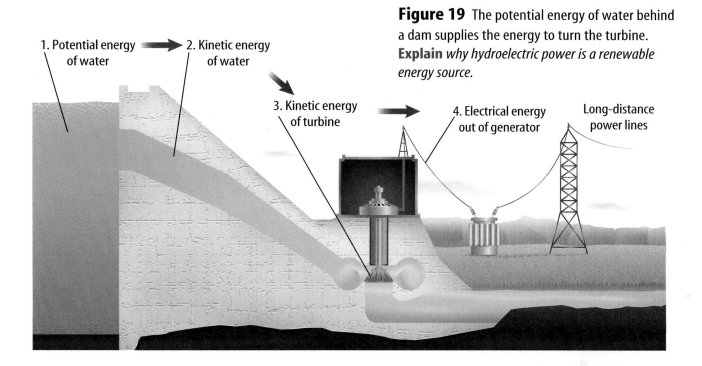

1. Potential energy of water → 2. Kinetic energy of water

3. Kinetic energy of turbine →

4. Electrical energy out of generator

Long-distance power lines

Figure 19 The potential energy of water behind a dam supplies the energy to turn the turbine. **Explain** *why hydroelectric power is a renewable energy source.*

Alternative Sources of Energy

Electrical energy can be generated in several ways. However, each has disadvantages that can affect the environment and the quality of life for humans. Research is being done to develop new sources of energy that are safer and cause less harm to the environment. These sources often are called **alternative resources.** These alternative resources include solar energy, wind, and geothermal energy.

Solar Energy

The Sun is the origin of almost all the energy that is used on Earth. Because the Sun will go on producing an enormous amount of energy for billions of years, the Sun is an inexhaustible source of energy. An **inexhaustible resource** is an energy source that can't be used up by humans.

Each day, on average, the amount of solar energy that strikes the United States is more than the total amount of energy used by the entire country in a year. However, less than 0.1 percent of the energy used in the United States comes directly from the Sun. One reason is that solar energy is more expensive to use than fossil fuels. However, as the supply of fossil fuels decreases, the cost of finding and mining these fuels might increase. Then, it may be cheaper to use solar energy or other energy sources to generate electricity and heat buildings than to use fossil fuels.

 **Reading Check** *What is an inexhaustible energy source?*

Mini LAB

Building a Solar Collector

Procedure
1. Line a **large pot** with **black plastic** and fill with **water.**
2. Stretch **clear-plastic wrap** over the pot and tape it taut.
3. Make a slit in the top and slide a **thermometer** or a **computer probe** into the water.
4. Place your solar collector in direct sunlight and monitor the temperature change every 3 min for 15 min.
5. Repeat your experiment without using any black plastic.

Analysis
1. Graph the temperature changes in both setups.
2. Explain how your solar collector works.

Collecting the Sun's Energy Two types of collectors capture the Sun's rays. If you look around your neighborhood, you might see large, rectangular panels attached to the roofs of buildings or houses. If, as in **Figure 20,** pipes come out of the panel, it is a thermal collector. Using a black surface, a thermal collector heats water by directly absorbing the Sun's radiant energy. Water circulating in this system can be heated to about 70°C. The hot water can be pumped through the house to provide heat. Also, the hot water can be used for washing and bathing. If the panel has no pipes, it is a photovoltaic (foh toh vol TAY ihk) collector, like the one pictured in **Figure 20.** A **photovoltaic** is a device that transforms radiant energy directly into electrical energy. Photovoltaics are used to power calculators and satellites, including the *International Space Station.*

Reading Check *What does a photovoltaic do?*

Figure 20 Solar energy can be collected and utilized by individuals using thermal collectors or photovoltaic collectors.

Geothermal Energy

Imagine you could take a journey to the center of Earth—down to about 6,400 km below the surface. As you went deeper and deeper, you would find the temperature increasing. In fact, after going only about 3 km, the temperature could have increased enough to boil water. At a depth of 100 km, the temperature could be over 900°C. The heat generated inside Earth is called geothermal energy. Some of this heat is produced when unstable radioactive atoms inside Earth decay, converting nuclear energy to thermal energy.

At some places deep within Earth the temperature is hot enough to melt rock. This molten rock, or magma, can rise up close to the surface through cracks in the crust. During a volcanic eruption, magma reaches the surface. In other places, magma gets close to the surface and heats the rock around it.

Geothermal Reservoirs In some regions where magma is close to the surface, rainwater and water from melted snow can seep down to the hot rock through cracks and other openings in Earth's surface. The water then becomes hot and sometimes can form steam. The hot water and steam can be trapped under high pressure in cracks and pockets called geothermal reservoirs. In some places, the hot water and steam are close enough to the surface to form hot springs and geysers.

Geothermal Power Plants In places where the geothermal reservoirs are less than several kilometers deep, wells can be drilled to reach them. The hot water and steam produced by geothermal energy then can be used by geothermal power plants, like the one in **Figure 21,** to generate electricity.

Most geothermal reservoirs contain hot water under high pressure. **Figure 22** shows how these reservoirs can be used to generate electricity. While geothermal power is an inexhaustible source of energy, geothermal power plants can be built only in regions where geothermal reservoirs are close to the surface, such as in the western United States.

Heat Pumps Geothermal heat helps keep the temperature of the ground at a depth of several meters at a nearly constant temperature of about 10° to 20°C. This constant temperature can be used to cool and heat buildings by using a heat pump.

A heat pump contains a water-filled loop of pipe that is buried to a depth where the temperature is nearly constant. In summer the air is warmer than this underground temperature. Warm water from the building is pumped through the pipe down into the ground. The water cools and then is pumped back to the house where it absorbs more heat, and the cycle is repeated. During the winter, the air is cooler than the ground below. Then, cool water absorbs heat from the ground and releases it into the house.

Figure 21 This geothermal power plant in Nevada produces enough electricity to power about 50,000 homes.

Figure 22 The hot water in a geothermal reservoir is used to generate electricity in a geothermal power plant.

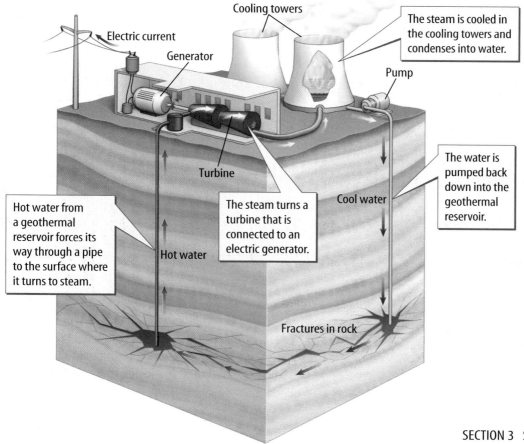

Cooling towers

Electric current

Generator

The steam is cooled in the cooling towers and condenses into water.

Pump

Turbine

The steam turns a turbine that is connected to an electric generator.

Cool water

The water is pumped back down into the geothermal reservoir.

Hot water from a geothermal reservoir forces its way through a pipe to the surface where it turns to steam.

Hot water

Fractures in rock

Energy from the Oceans

The ocean is in constant motion. If you've been to the seashore you've seen waves roll in. You may have seen the level of the ocean rise and fall over a period of about a half day. This rise and fall in the ocean level is called a tide. The constant movement of the ocean is an inexhaustible source of mechanical energy that can be converted into electric energy. While methods are still being developed to convert the motion in ocean waves to electric energy, several electric power plants using tidal motion have been built.

Figure 23 This tidal power plant in Annapolis Royal, Nova Scotia, is the only operating tidal power plant in North America.

Using Tidal Energy A high tide and a low tide each occur about twice a day. In most places the level of the ocean changes by less than a few meters. However, in some places the change is much greater. In the Bay of Fundy in Eastern Canada, the ocean level changes by 16 m between high tide and low tide. Almost 14 trillion kg of water move into or out of the bay between high and low tide.

Figure 23 shows an electric power plant that has been built along the Bay of Fundy. This power plant generates enough electric energy to power about 12,000 homes. The power plant is constructed so that as the tide rises, water flows through a turbine that causes an electric generator to spin, as shown in **Figure 24A.** The water is then trapped behind a dam. When the tide goes out, the trapped water behind the dam is released through the turbine to generate more electricity, as shown in **Figure 24B.** Each day electric power is generated for about ten hours when the tide is rising and falling.

While tidal energy is a nonpolluting, inexhaustible energy source, its use is limited. Only in a few places is the difference between high and low tide large enough to enable a large electric power plant to be built.

Figure 24 A tidal power plant can generate electricity when the tide is coming in and going out.

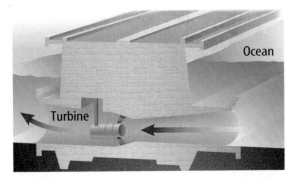

A As the tide comes in, it turns a turbine connected to a generator. When high tide occurs, gates are closed that trap water behind a dam.

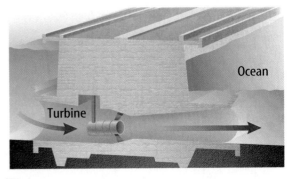

B As the tide goes out and the ocean level drops, the gates are opened and water from behind the dam flows through the turbine, causing it to spin and turn a generator.

Wind

Wind is another inexhaustible supply of energy. Modern windmills, like the ones in **Figure 25,** convert the kinetic energy of the wind to electrical energy. The propeller is connected to a generator so that electrical energy is generated when wind spins the propeller. These windmills produce almost no pollution. Some disadvantages are that windmills produce noise and that large areas of land are needed. Also, studies have shown that birds sometimes are killed by windmills.

Conserving Energy

Fossil fuels are a valuable resource. Not only are they burned to provide energy, but oil and coal also are used to make plastics and other materials. One way to make the supply of fossil fuels last longer is to use less energy. Reducing the use of energy is called conserving energy.

You can conserve energy and also save money by turning off lights and appliances such as televisions when you are not using them. Also keep doors and windows closed tightly when it's cold or hot to keep heat from leaking out of or into your house. Energy could also be conserved if buildings are properly insulated, especially around windows. The use of oil could be reduced if cars were used less and made more efficient, so they went farther on a liter of gas. Recycling materials such as aluminum cans and glass also helps conserve energy.

Figure 25 Windmills work on the same basic principles as a power plant. Instead of steam turning a turbine, wind turns the rotors. **Describe** *some of the advantages and disadvantages of using windmills.*

section 3 review

Summary

Nonrenewable Resources

- All energy resources have advantages and disadvantages.
- Nonrenewable energy resources are used faster than they are replaced.
- Fossil fuels include oil, coal, and natural gas and are nonrenewable resources. Nuclear energy is a nonrenewable resource.

Renewable and Alternative Resources

- Renewable energy resources, such as hydroelectricity, are resources that are replenished continually.
- Alternative energy sources include solar energy, wind energy, and geothermal energy.

Self Check

1. **Diagram** the energy conversions that occur when coal is formed, and then burned to produce thermal energy.
2. **Explain** why solar energy is considered an inexhaustible source of energy.
3. **Explain** how a heat pump is used to both heat and cool a building.
4. **Think Critically** Identify advantages and disadvantages of using fossil fuels, hydroelectricity, and solar energy as energy sources.
   Hot Words Hot Topics: Bk 1 p. 274

Applying Math

5. **Use a Ratio** Earth's temperature increases with depth. Suppose the temperature increase inside Earth is 500°C at a depth of 50 km. What is the temperature increase at a depth of 10 km?

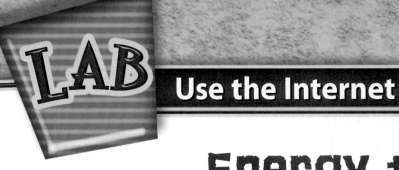

Energy to Power Your Life

Goals

- **Identify** how energy you use is produced and delivered.
- **Investigate** alternative sources for the energy you use.
- **Outline** a plan for how these alternative sources of energy could be used.

Data Source

Science Online

Visit internet lab glencoe.com for more information about sources of energy and for data collected by other students.

▶ *Real-World Question*

Over the past 100 years, the amount of energy used in the United States and elsewhere has greatly increased. Today, a number of energy sources are available, such as coal, oil, natural gas, nuclear energy, hydroelectric power, wind, and solar energy. Some of these energy sources are being used up and are nonrenewable, but others are replaced as fast as they are used and, therefore, are renewable. Some energy sources are so vast that human usage has almost no effect on the amount available. These energy sources are inexhaustible.

Think about the types of energy you use at home and school every day. In this lab, you will investigate how and where energy is produced, and how it gets to you. You will also investigate alternative ways energy can be produced, and whether these sources are renewable, nonrenewable, or inexhaustible. What are the sources of the energy you use every day?

Local Energy Information	
Energy Type	
Where is that energy produced?	
How is that energy produced?	Do not write in this book.
How is that energy delivered to you?	
Is the energy source renewable, nonrenewable, or inexhaustible?	
What type of alternative energy source could you use instead?	

▶ Make a Plan

1. Think about the activities you do every day and the things you use. When you watch television, listen to the radio, ride in a car, use a hair drier, or turn on the air conditioning, you use energy. Select one activity or appliance that uses energy.

2. **Identify** the type of energy that is used.

3. **Investigate** how that energy is produced and delivered to you.

4. **Determine** if the energy source is renewable, nonrenewable, or inexhaustible.

5. If your energy source is nonrenewable, describe how the energy you use could be produced by renewable sources.

▶ Follow Your Plan

1. Make sure your teacher approves your plan before you start.

2. Organize your findings in a data table, similar to the one that is shown.

▶ Analyze Your Data

1. **Describe** the process for producing and delivering the energy source you researched. How is it created, and how does it get to you?

2. How much energy is produced by the energy source you investigated?

3. Is the energy source you researched renewable, nonrenewable, or inexhaustible? Why?

▶ Conclude and Apply

1. **Describe** If the energy source you investigated is nonrenewable, how can the use of this energy source be reduced?

2. **Organize** What alternative sources of energy could you use for everyday energy needs? On the computer, create a plan for using renewable or inexhaustible sources.

𝒞ommunicating Your Data

Find this lab using the link below. Post your data in the table that is provided. **Compare** your data to those of other students. **Combine** your data with those of other students and make inferences using the combined data.

Science⬤nline
internet lab glencoe.com

SCIENCE Stats

Energy to Burn

Did you know...

... The energy released by the average hurricane is equal to about 200 times the total energy produced by all of the world's power plants. Almost all of this energy is released as heat when raindrops form.

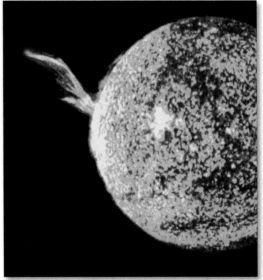

... The energy Earth gets each half hour from the Sun is enough to meet the world's demands for a year. Renewable and inexhaustible resources, including the Sun, account for only 18 percent of the energy that is used worldwide.

... The Calories in one medium apple will give you enough energy to walk for about 15 min, swim for about 10 min, or jog for about 9 min.

Applying Math If walking for 15 min requires 80 Calories of fuel (from food), how many Calories would someone need to consume to walk for 1 h?

Write About It

Where would you place solar collectors in the United States? Why? For more information on solar energy, go to glencoe.com.

Reviewing Main Ideas

Section 1 What is energy?

1. Energy is the ability to cause change.

2. A moving object has kinetic energy that depends on the object's mass and speed.

3. Potential energy is energy due to position and depends on an object's mass and height.

4. Light carries radiant energy, electric current carries electrical energy, and atomic nuclei contain nuclear energy.

Section 2 Energy Transformations

1. Energy can be transformed from one form to another. Thermal energy is usually produced when energy transformations occur.

2. The law of conservation of energy states that energy cannot be created or destroyed.

3. Electric power plants convert a source of energy into electrical energy. Steam spins a turbine which spins an electric generator.

Section 3 Sources of Energy

1. The use of an energy source has advantages and disadvantages.

2. Fossil fuels and nuclear energy are nonrenewable energy sources that are consumed faster than they can be replaced.

3. Hydroelectricity is a renewable energy source that is continually being replaced.

4. Alternative energy sources include solar, wind, and geothermal energy. Solar energy is an inexhaustible energy source.

Visualizing Main Ideas

Copy and complete the concept map using the following terms: fossil fuels, hydroelectric, solar, wind, oil, coal, photovoltaic, *and* nonrenewable resources.

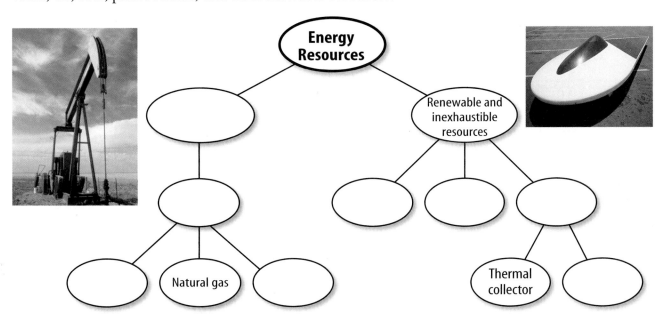

Energy Resources

Renewable and inexhaustible resources

Natural gas

Thermal collector

Using Vocabulary

alternative resource p. 59	nonrenewable
chemical energy p. 45	resource p. 56
electrical energy p. 46	nuclear energy p. 46
energy p. 42	photovoltaic p. 60
generator p. 52	potential energy p. 44
inexhaustible	radiant energy p. 45
resource p. 59	renewable resource p. 58
kinetic energy p. 43	thermal energy p. 44
law of conservation	turbine p. 54
of energy p. 48	

For each of the terms below, explain the relationship that exists.

1. electrical energy—nuclear energy
2. turbine—generator
3. photovoltaic—radiant energy—electrical energy
4. renewable resource—inexhaustible resource
5. potential energy—kinetic energy
6. kinetic energy—electrical energy—generator
7. thermal energy—radiant energy
8. law of conservation of energy—energy transformations
9. nonrenewable resource—chemical energy

Checking Concepts

Choose the word or phrase that best answers the question.

10. Objects that are able to fall have what type of energy?
    A) kinetic
    B) radiant
    C) potential
    D) electrical

11. Which form of energy does light have?
    A) electrical
    B) nuclear
    C) kinetic
    D) radiant

12. Muscles perform what type of energy transformation?
    A) kinetic to potential
    B) kinetic to electrical
    C) thermal to radiant
    D) chemical to kinetic

13. Photovoltaics perform what type of energy transformation?
    A) thermal to radiant
    B) kinetic to electrical
    C) radiant to electrical
    D) electrical to thermal

14. The form of energy that food contains is which of the following?
    A) chemical
    B) potential
    C) radiant
    D) electrical

15. Solar energy, wind, and geothermal are what type of energy resource?
    A) inexhaustible
    B) inexpensive
    C) nonrenewable
    D) chemical

16. Which of the following is a nonrenewable source of energy?
    A) hydroelectricity
    B) nuclear
    C) wind
    D) solar

17. A generator is NOT required to generate electrical energy when which of the following energy sources is used?
    A) solar
    B) wind
    C) hydroelectric
    D) nuclear

18. Which of the following are fossil fuels?
    A) gas
    B) coal
    C) oil
    D) all of these

19. Almost all of the energy that is used on Earth's surface comes from which of the following energy sources?
    A) radioactivity
    B) the Sun
    C) chemicals
    D) wind

Thinking Critically

20. **Explain** how the motion of a swing illustrates the transformation between potential and kinetic energy.

21. **Explain** what happens to the kinetic energy of a skateboard that is coasting along a flat surface, slows down, and comes to a stop.

22. **Describe** the energy transformations that occur in the process of toasting a bagel in an electric toaster.

23. **Compare and contrast** the formation of coal and the formation of oil and natural gas.

24. **Explain** the difference between the law of conservation of energy and conserving energy. How can conserving energy help prevent energy shortages?

25. **Make a Hypothesis** about how spacecraft that travel through the solar system obtain the energy they need to operate. Do research to verify your hypothesis.

26. **Concept Map** Copy and complete this concept map about energy.

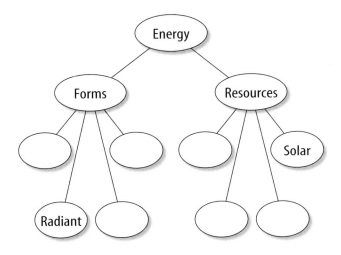

27. **Diagram** the energy transformations that occur when you rub sandpaper on a piece of wood and the wood becomes warm.

Performance Activities

28. **Multimedia Presentation** Alternative sources of energy that weren't discussed include biomass energy, wave energy, and hydrogen fuel cells. Research an alternative energy source and then prepare a digital slide show about the information you found. Use the concepts you learned from this chapter to inform your classmates about the future prospects of using such an energy source on a large scale.

Hot Words Hot Topics: Bk 1 (29) p. 274; (30) p. 89; (31) p. 274

Applying Math

29. **Calculate Number of Power Plants** A certain type of power plant is designed to provide energy for 10,000 homes. How many of these power plants would be needed to provide energy for 300,000 homes?

Use the table below to answer questions 30 and 31.

Energy Sources Used in the United States	
Energy Source	**Percent of Energy Used**
Coal	23%
Oil	39%
Natural gas	23%
Nuclear	8%
Hydroelectric	4%
Other	3%

30. **Use Percentages** According to the data in the table above, what percentage of the energy used in the United States comes from fossil fuels?

31. **Calculate a Ratio** How many times greater is the amount of energy that comes from fossil fuels than the amount of energy from all other energy sources?

Record your answers on the answer sheet provided by your teacher or on a sheet of paper.

1 The kinetic energy of a moving object increases if which of the following occurs?
(1) Its mass decreases.
(2) Its speed increases.
(3) Its height above the ground increases.
(4) Its temperature increases.

Use the graph below to answer questions 2–4.

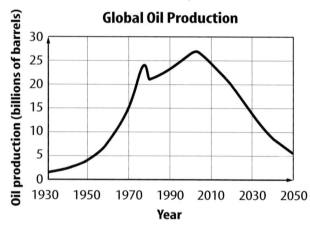

Global Oil Production

Oil production (billions of barrels) vs Year

2 According to the graph above, in which year will global oil production be at a maximum?
(1) 1974   (3) 2010
(2) 2002   (4) 2050

3 Approximately how many times greater was oil production in 1970 than oil production in 1950?
(1) 2 times   (3) 6 times
(2) 10 times   (4) 3 times

4 In which year will the production of oil be equal to the oil production in 1970?
(1) 2010   (3) 2022
(2) 2015   (4) 2028

5 Which of the following energy sources is being used faster than it can be replaced?
(1) tidal   (3) fossil fuels
(2) wind   (4) hydroelectric

Use the circle graph below to answer question 6.

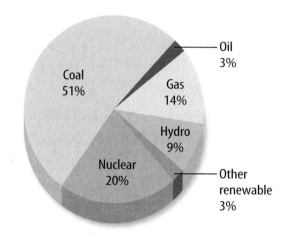

6 The circle graph shows the sources of electrical energy in the United States. In 2002, the total amount of electrical energy produced in the United States was 38.2 quads. How much electrical energy was produced by nuclear power plants?
(1) 3.0 quads   (3) 7.6 quads
(2) 3.8 quads   (4) 35.1 quads

7 When chemical energy is converted into thermal energy, which of the following must be true?
(1) The total amount of thermal energy plus chemical energy changes.
(2) Only the amount of chemical energy changes.
(3) Only the amount of thermal energy changes.
(4) The total amount of thermal energy plus chemical energy doesn't change.

8 A softball player hits a fly ball. Which of the following describes the energy conversion that occurs as it falls from its highest point?
(1) kinetic to potential
(2) potential to kinetic
(3) thermal to potential
(4) thermal to kinetic

Record your answers on the answer sheet provided by your teacher or on a sheet of paper.

9 Why is it impossible to build a machine that produces more energy than it uses?

10 You toss a ball upward and then catch it on the way down. The height of the ball above the ground when it leaves your hand on the way up and when you catch it is the same. Compare the ball's kinetic energy when it leaves your hand and just before you catch it.

11 A basketball is dropped from a height of 2 m and another identical basketball is dropped from a height of 4 m. Which ball has more kinetic energy just before it hits the ground?

12 When you drop a tennis ball, it hits the floor and bounces back up. But it does not reach the same height as released, and each successive upward bounce is smaller than the one previous. However, you notice the tennis ball is slightly warmer after it finishes bouncing. Explain how the law of conservation of energy is obeyed.

Use the graph below to answer questions 13–15.

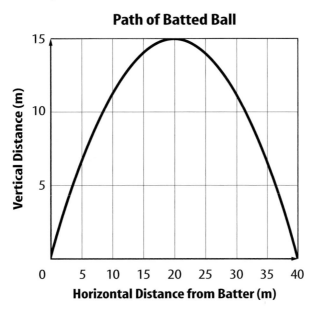

Path of Batted Ball

13 At what horizontal distance from the batter is the height of the ball the greatest?

14 At what horizontal distance from the batter does the ball have the greatest amount of potential energy? The least amount of potential energy?

15 At what horizontal distance from the batter does the ball have the greatest amount of kinetic energy? The least amount of kinetic energy?

16 Compare and contrast the advantages and disadvantages of the following energy sources: fossil fuels, nuclear energy, and geothermal energy.

PS 5.2c: Machines transfer mechanical energy from one object to another. **5.2f:** Machines can change the direction or amount of force, or the distance or speed of force required to do work. **Also covered:** AID S1.2c, S2.1b, S2.1d, S2.2a, S2.2b, S3.2f, M1.1c, M2.3a, M2.3b, M2.3c, PS 5.1c, 5.1d, 5.2d, 5.2e, 5.2g.

Work and Simple Machines

chapter preview

sections

1 Work and Power
Lab Building the Pyramids

2 Using Machines

3 Simple Machines
Lab Pulley Power

⊙ *Virtual Lab What is the relationship between work, force, and distance?*

Heavy Lifting

It took the ancient Egyptians more than 100 years to build the pyramids without machines like these. But now, even tall skyscrapers can be built in a few years. Complex or simple, machines have the same purpose. They make doing work easier.

Science Journal Describe three machines you used today, and how they made doing a task easier.

36

Start-Up Activities

Compare Forces

Two of the world's greatest structures were built using different tools. The Great Pyramid at Giza in Egypt was built nearly 5,000 years ago using blocks of limestone moved into place by hand with ramps and levers. In comparison, the Sears Tower in Chicago was built in 1973 using tons of steel that were hoisted into place by gasoline-powered cranes. How do machines such as ramps, levers, and cranes change the forces needed to do a job?

1. Place a ruler on an eraser. Place a book on one end of the ruler.

2. Using one finger, push down on the free end of the ruler to lift the book.

3. Repeat the experiment, placing the eraser in various positions beneath the ruler. Observe how much force is needed in each instance to lift the book.

4. **Think Critically** In your Science Journal, describe your observations. How did changing the distance between the book and the eraser affect the force needed to lift the book?

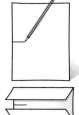

Simple Machines Many of the devices that you use every day are simple machines. Make the following Foldable to help you understand the characteristics of simple machines.

STEP 1 Draw a mark at the midpoint of a sheet of paper along the side edge. Then **fold** the top and bottom edges in to touch the midpoint.

STEP 2 **Fold** in half from side to side.

STEP 3 **Turn** the paper vertically. **Open** and cut along the inside fold lines to form four tabs.

STEP 4 **Label the tabs** *Inclined Plane, Lever, Wheel and Axle,* and *Pulley.*

Read for Main Ideas As you read the chapter, list the characteristics of inclined planes, levers, wheels and axles, and pulleys under the appropriate tab.

Science nline **Preview this chapter's content and activities at** glencoe.com

AID M1.1c: apply mathematical equations to describe relationships among variables in the natural world.
PS 5.1c: An object's motion is the result of the combined effect of all forces acting on the object. A moving object that is not subjected to a force will continue to move at a constant speed in a straight line. An object at rest will remain at rest.

section 1

Work and Power

What is work?

What does the term *work* mean to you? You might think of household chores; a job at an office, a factory, a farm; or the homework you do after school. In science, the definition of work is more specific. **Work** is done when a force causes an object to move in the same direction that the force is applied.

Can you think of a way in which you did work today? Maybe it would help to know that you do work when you lift your books, turn a doorknob, raise window blinds, or write with a pen or pencil. You also do work when you walk up a flight of stairs or open and close your school locker. In what other ways do you do work every day?

Work and Motion Your teacher has asked you to move a box of books to the back of the classroom. Try as you might, though, you just can't budge the box because it is too heavy. Although you exerted a force on the box and you feel tired from it, you have not done any work. In order for you to do work, two things must occur. First, you must apply a force to an object. Second, the object must move in the same direction as your applied force. You do work on an object only when the object moves as a result of the force you exert. The girl in **Figure 1** might think she is working by holding the bags of groceries. However, if she is not moving, she is not doing any work because she is not causing something to move.

✔ Reading Check *To do work, how must a force make an object move?*

Figure 1 This girl is holding bags of groceries, yet she isn't doing any work. **Explain** *what must happen for work to be done.*

Figure 2 To do work, an object must move in the direction a force is applied.

Force

Motion

The boy's arms do work when they exert an upward force on the basket and the basket moves upward.

Force

Motion

The boy's arms still exert an upward force on the basket. But when the boy walks forward, no work is done by his arms.

Applying Force and Doing Work Picture yourself lifting the basket of clothes in **Figure 2.** You can feel your arms exerting a force upward as you lift the basket, and the basket moves upward in the direction of the force your arms applied. Therefore, your arms have done work. Now, suppose you carry the basket forward. You can still feel your arms applying an upward force on the basket to keep it from falling, but now the basket is moving forward instead of upward. Because the direction of motion is not in the same direction of the force applied by your arms, no work is done by your arms.

Force in Two Directions Sometimes only part of the force you exert moves an object. Think about what happens when you push a lawn mower. You push at an angle to the ground as shown in **Figure 3.** Part of the force is to the right and part of the force is downward. Only the part of the force that is in the same direction as the motion of the mower—to the right—does work.

Forward force

Total force

Downward force

Motion

Figure 3 When you exert a force at an angle, only part of your force does work—the part that is in the same direction as the motion of the object.

SECTION 1 Work and Power **75**

INTEGRATE History

James Prescott Joule This English physicist experimentally verified the law of conservation of energy. He showed that various forms of energy—mechanical, electrical, and thermal—are essentially the same and can be converted one into another. The SI unit of energy and work, the joule, is named after him. Research the work of Joule and write what you learn in your Science Journal.

Hot Words Hot Topics: Bk 1 pp. 90, 271

Calculating Work

Work is done when a force makes an object move. More work is done when the force is increased or the object is moved a greater distance. Work can be calculated using the work equation below. In SI units, the unit for work is the joule, named for the nineteenth-century scientist James Prescott Joule.

Work Equation

work (in joules) = **force** (in newtons) × **distance** (in meters)

$$W = Fd$$

Work and Distance Suppose you give a book a push and it slides across a table. To calculate the work you did, the distance in the above equation is not the distance the book moved. The distance in the work equation is the distance an object moves while the force is being applied. So the distance in the work equation is the distance the book moved while you were pushing.

Applying Math   Solve a One-Step Equation

CALCULATING WORK A painter lifts a can of paint that weighs 40 N a distance of 2 m. How much work does she do? *Hint: to lift a can weighing 40 N, the painter must exert a force of 40 N.*

Solution

1 *This is what you know:*
- force: $F = 40$ N
- distance: $d = 2$ m

2 *This is what you need to find out:*
work: $W = ?$ J

3 *This is the procedure you need to use:*
Substitute the known values $F = 40$ N and $d = 2$ m into the work equation:

$W = Fd = (40$ N$)(2$ m$) = 80$ N•m $= 80$ J

4 *Check your answer:*
Check your answer by dividing the work you calculated by the distance given in the problem. The result should be the force given in the problem.

Practice Problems

1. As you push a lawn mower, the horizontal force is 300 N. If you push the mower a distance of 500 m, how much work do you do?

2. A librarian lifts a box of books that weighs 93 N a distance of 1.5 m. How much work does he do?

Science Online

For more practice, visit glencoe.com

What is power?

What does it mean to be powerful? Imagine two weightlifters lifting the same amount of weight the same vertical distance. They both do the same amount of work. However, the amount of power they use depends on how long it took to do the work. **Power** is how quickly work is done. The weightlifter who lifted the weight in less time is more powerful.

Calculating Power Power can be calculated by dividing the amount of work done by the time needed to do the work.

Power Equation

$$\textbf{power (in watts)} = \frac{\textbf{work (in joules)}}{\textbf{time (in seconds)}}$$

$$P = \frac{W}{t}$$

In SI units, the unit of power is the watt, in honor of James Watt, a nineteenth-century British scientist who invented a practical version of the steam engine.

Hot Words Hot Topics: Bk 1 pp. 90, 271

Mini LAB

Work and Power

Procedure
1. Weigh yourself on a **scale**.
2. Multiply your weight in pounds by 4.45 to convert your weight to newtons.
3. Measure the vertical height of a **stairway**. WARNING: *Make sure the stairway is clear of all objects.*
4. Time yourself walking slowly and quickly up the stairway.

Analysis
Calculate and compare the work and power in each case.

Try at Home

Applying Math — Solve a One-Step Equation

CALCULATING POWER You do 200 J of work in 12 s. How much power did you use?

Solution

1️⃣ *This is what you know:*
- work: $W = 200$ J
- time: $t = 12$ s

2️⃣ *This is what you need to find out:*
- power: $P = ?$ watts

3️⃣ *This is the procedure you need to use:*
Substitute the known values $W = 200$ J and $t = 12$ s into the power equation:
$$P = \frac{W}{t} = \frac{200 \text{ J}}{12 \text{ s}} = 17 \text{ watts}$$

4️⃣ *Check your answer:*
Check your answer by multiplying the power you calculated by the time given in the problem. The result should be the work given in the problem.

Practice Problems

1. In the course of a short race, a car does 50,000 J of work in 7 s. What is the power of the car during the race?

2. A teacher does 140 J of work in 20 s. How much power did he use?

Science Online — For more practice, visit glencoe.com

Science nline

Topic: James Watt

Visit glencoe.com for Web links to information about James Watt and his steam engine.

Activity Draw a diagram showing how his steam engine worked.

Work and Energy If you push a chair and make it move, you do work on the chair and change its energy. Recall that when something is moving it has energy of motion, or kinetic energy. By making the chair move, you increase its kinetic energy.

You also change the energy of an object when you do work and lift it higher. An object has potential energy that increases when it is higher above Earth's surface. By lifting an object, you do work and increase its potential energy.

Power and Energy When you do work on an object you increase the energy of the object. Because energy can never be created or destroyed, if the object gains energy then you must lose energy. When you do work on an object you transfer energy to the object, and your energy decreases. The amount of work done is the amount of energy transferred. So power is also equal to the amount of energy transferred in a certain amount of time.

Sometimes energy can be transferred even when no work is done, such as when heat flows from a warm to a cold object. In fact, there are many ways energy can be transferred even if no work is done. Power is always the rate at which energy is transferred, or the amount of energy transferred divided by the time needed.

section 1 review

Summary

What is work?

- Work is done when a force causes an object to move in the same direction that the force is applied.

- If the movement caused by a force is at an angle to the direction the force is applied, only the part of the force in the direction of motion does work.

- Work can be calculated by multiplying the force applied by the distance:

$$W = Fd$$

- The distance in the work equation is the distance an object moves while the force is being applied.

What is power?

- Power is how quickly work is done. Something is more powerful if it can do a given amount of work in less time.

- Power can be calculated by dividing the work done by the time needed to do the work:

$$P = \frac{W}{t}$$

Self Check

1. **Describe** a situation in which work is done on an object.

2. **Evaluate** which of the following situations involves more power: 200 J of work done in 20 s or 50 J of work done in 4 s? Explain your answer.

3. **Determine** two ways power can be increased.

4. **Calculate** how much power, in watts, is needed to cut a lawn in 50 min if the work involved is 100,000 J.

5. **Think Critically** Suppose you are pulling a wagon with the handle at an angle. How can you make your task easier?

Hot Words Hot Topics: Bk 1 pp. 90, 271

Applying Math

6. **Calculate Work** How much work was done to lift a 1,000-kg block to the top of the Great Pyramid, 146 m above ground?

7. **Calculate Work Done by an Engine** An engine is used to lift a beam weighing 9,800 N up to 145 m. How much work must the engine do to lift this beam? How much work must be done to lift it 290 m?

More Section Review glencoe.com

Building the Pyramids

Imagine moving 2.3 million blocks of limestone, each weighing more than 1,000 kg. That is exactly what the builders of the Great Pyramid at Giza did. Although no one knows for sure exactly how they did it, they probably pulled the blocks most of the way.

Work Done Using Different Ramps		
Distance (cm)	Force (N)	Work (J)
Do not write in this book.		

▶ Real-World Question

How is the force needed to lift a block related to the distance it travels?

Goals
- **Compare** the force needed to lift a block with the force needed to pull it up a ramp.

Materials
wood block	thin notebooks
tape	meterstick
spring scale	several books
ruler	

Safety Precautions 🥽 ♨

▶ Procedure

1. Stack several books together on a tabletop to model a half-completed pyramid. Measure the height of the books in centimeters. Record the height on the first row of the data table under *Distance*.

2. Use the wood block as a model for a block of stone. Use tape to attach the block to the spring scale.

3. Place the block on the table and lift it straight up the side of the stack of books until the top of the block is even with the top of the books. Record the force shown on the scale in the data table under *Force*.

4. **Arrange** a notebook so that one end is on the stack of books and the other end is on the table. Measure the length of the notebook and record this length as distance in the second row of the data table under *Distance*.

5. **Measure** the force needed to pull the block up the ramp. Record the force in the data table.

6. Repeat steps 4 and 5 using a longer notebook to make the ramp longer.

7. **Calculate** the work done in each row of the data table.

▶ Conclude and Apply

1. **Evaluate** how much work you did in each instance.

2. **Determine** what happened to the force needed as the length of the ramp increased.

3. **Infer** How could the builders of the pyramids have designed their task to use less force than they would lifting the blocks straight up? Draw a diagram to support your answer.

Add your data to that found by other groups. **For more help, refer to the** Science Skill Handbook.

section 2

Using Machines

as you read

What You'll Learn

- **Explain** how a machine makes work easier.
- **Calculate** the mechanical advantages and efficiency of a machine.
- **Explain** how friction reduces efficiency.

Why It's Important

Machines can't change the amount of work you need to do, but they can make doing work easier.

⊙ Review Vocabulary

friction: force that opposes motion between two touching surfaces

New Vocabulary
- input force
- output force
- mechanical advantage
- efficiency

Physical Setting

5.2c, 5.2f: Interpret how machines transfer mechanical energy from one object to another as they change direction, speed, or amount of force. Give an example of the energy transfers.

What is a machine?

Did you use a machine today? When you think of a machine you might think of a device, such as a car, with many moving parts powered by an engine or an electric motor. But if you used a pair of scissors or a broom, or cut your food with a knife, you used a machine. A machine is simply a device that makes doing work easier. Even a sloping surface can be a machine.

Mechanical Advantage

Even though machines make work easier, they don't decrease the amount of work you need to do. Instead, a machine changes the way in which you do work. When you use a machine, you exert a force over some distance. For example, you exert a force to move a rake or lift the handles of a wheelbarrow. The force that you apply on a machine is the **input force.** The work you do on the machine is equal to the input force times the distance over which your force moves the machine. The work that you do on the machine is the input work.

The machine also does work by exerting a force to move an object over some distance. A rake, for example, exerts a force to move leaves. Sometimes this force is called the resistance force because the machine is trying to overcome some resistance. The force that the machine applies is the **output force.** The work that the machine does is the output work. **Figure 4** shows how a machine transforms input work to output work.

When you use a machine, the output work can never be greater than the input work. So what is the advantage of using a machine? A machine makes work easier by changing the amount of force you need to exert, the distance over which the force is exerted, or the direction in which you exert your force.

Figure 4 No matter what type of machine is used, the output work is never greater than the input work.

Input work   Machine   Output work

Changing Force Some machines make doing work easier by reducing the force you have to apply to do work. This type of machine increases the input force, so that the output force is greater than the input force. The number of times a machine increases the input force is the **mechanical advantage** of the machine. The mechanical advantage of a machine is the ratio of the output force to the input force and can be calculated from this equation:

Mechanical Advantage Equation

$$\text{mechanical advantage} = \frac{\text{output force (in newtons)}}{\text{input force (in newtons)}}$$

$$MA = \frac{F_{out}}{F_{in}}$$

Mechanical advantage does not have any units, because it is the ratio of two numbers with the same units.

 *Hot Words Hot Topics:* Bk 1 pp. 90, 271

Science Online

Topic: Historical Tools
Visit glencoe.com for Web links to information about early types of tools and how they took advantage of simple machines.

Activity Write a paragraph describing how simple machines were used to design early tools.

Applying Math — Solve a One-Step Equation

CALCULATING MECHANICAL ADVANTAGE To pry the lid off a paint can, you apply a force of 50 N to the handle of the screwdriver. What is the mechanical advantage of the screwdriver if it applies a force of 500 N to the lid?

Solution

1 *This is what you know:*
- input force: $F_{in} = 50$ N
- output force: $F_{out} = 500$ N

2 *This is what you need to find out:*
mechanical advantage: $MA = ?$

3 *This is the procedure you need to use:*
Substitute the known values $F_{in} = 50$ N and $F_{out} = 500$ N into the mechanical advantage equation:

$$MA = \frac{F_{out}}{F_{in}} = \frac{500 \text{ N}}{50 \text{ N}} = 10$$

4 *Check your answer:*
Check your answer by multiplying the mechanical advantage you calculated by the input force given in the problem. The result should be the output force given in the problem.

Practice Problems

1. To open a bottle, you apply a force of 50 N to the bottle opener. The bottle opener applies a force of 775 N to the bottle cap. What is the mechanical advantage of the bottle opener?

2. To crack a pecan, you apply a force of 50 N to the nutcracker. The nutcracker applies a force of 750 N to the pecan. What is the mechanical advantage of the nutcracker?

Science Online For more practice, visit glencoe.com

Figure 5 Changing the direction or the distance that a force is applied can make a task easier.

Sometimes it is easier to exert your force in a certain direction. This boy would rather pull down on the rope to lift the flag than to climb to the top of the pole and pull up.

When you rake leaves, you move your hands a short distance, but the end of the rake moves over a longer distance.

Changing Distance
Some machines allow you to exert your force over a shorter distance. In these machines, the output force is less than the input force. The rake in **Figure 5** is this type of machine. You move your hands a small distance at the top of the handle, but the bottom of the rake moves a greater distance as it moves the leaves. The mechanical advantage of this type of machine is less than one because the output force is less than the input force.

Changing Direction
Sometimes it is easier to apply a force in a certain direction. For example, it is easier to pull down on the rope in **Figure 5** than to pull up on it. Some machines enable you to change the direction of the input force. In these machines neither the force nor the distance is changed. The mechanical advantage of this type of machine is equal to one because the output force is equal to the input force. The three ways machines make doing work easier are summarized in **Figure 6.**

Figure 6 Machines are useful because they can increase force, increase distance, or change the direction in which a force is applied.

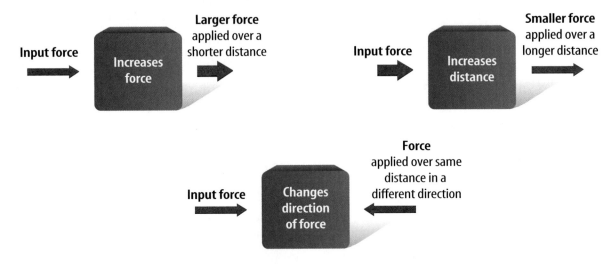

Input force → **Increases force** → Larger force applied over a shorter distance

Input force → **Increases distance** → Smaller force applied over a longer distance

Input force → **Changes direction of force** ← Force applied over same distance in a different direction

Efficiency

A machine doesn't increase the input work. For a real machine, the output work done by the machine is always less than the input work that is done on the machine. In a real machine, there is friction as parts of the machine move. Friction converts some of the input work into heat, so that the output work is reduced. The **efficiency** of a machine is the ratio of the output work to the input work, and can be calculated from this equation:

Efficiency Equation

$$\text{efficiency (in percent)} = \frac{\text{output work (in joules)}}{\text{input work (in joules)}} \times 100\%$$

$$eff = \frac{W_{out}}{W_{in}} \times 100\%$$

If the amount of friction in the machine is reduced, the efficiency of the machine increases.

Hot Words Hot Topics: Bk 1 pp. 90, 140, 271

Body Temperature
Chemical reactions that enable your muscles to move also produce heat that helps maintain your body temperature. When you shiver, rapid contraction and relaxation of muscle fibers produces a large amount of heat that helps raise your body temperature. This causes the efficiency of your muscles to decrease as more energy is converted into heat.

Applying Math — Solve a One-Step Equation

CALCULATING EFFICIENCY Using a pulley system, a crew does 7,500 J of work to load a box that requires 4,500 J of work. What is the efficiency of the pulley system?

Solution

1 *This is what you know:*
- input work: W_{in} = 7,500 J
- output work: W_{out} = 4,500 J

2 *This is what you need to find out:*
efficiency: *eff* = ? %

3 *This is the procedure you need to use:*
Substitute the known values W_{in} = 7,500 J and W_{out} = 4,500 J into the efficiency equation:

$$eff = \frac{W_{out}}{W_{in}} = \frac{4,500 \text{ J}}{7,500 \text{ J}} \times 100\% = 60\%$$

4 *Check your answer:*
Check your answer by dividing the efficiency by 100% and then multiplying your answer times the work input. The product should be the work output given in the problem.

Practice Problems

1. You do 100 J of work in pulling out a nail with a claw hammer. If the hammer does 70 J of work, what is the hammer's efficiency?

2. You do 150 J of work pushing a box up a ramp. If the ramp does 105 J of work, what is the efficiency of the ramp?

Science Online | For more practice, visit glencoe.com

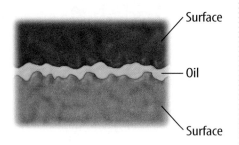

Surface

Oil

Surface

Figure 7 Lubrication can reduce the friction between two surfaces. Two surfaces in contact can stick together where the high spots on each surface come in contact. Adding oil or another lubricant separates the surface so that fewer high spots make contact.

Physical Setting

5.2d, 5.2e: Define friction in your own words. List three ways to reduce friction.

Friction

Friction To help understand friction, imagine pushing a heavy box up a ramp. As the box begins to move, the bottom surface of the box slides across the top surface of the ramp. Neither surface is perfectly smooth—each has high spots and low spots, as shown in **Figure 7.**

As the two surfaces slide past each other, high spots on the two surfaces come in contact. At these contact points, shown in **Figure 7,** atoms and molecules can bond together. This makes the contact points stick together. The attractive forces between all the bonds in the contact points added together is the frictional force that tries to keep the two surfaces from sliding past each other.

To keep the box moving, a force must be applied to break the bonds between the contact points. Even after these bonds are broken and the box moves, new bonds form as different parts of the two surfaces come into contact.

Friction and Efficiency One way to reduce friction between two surfaces is to add oil. **Figure 7** shows how oil fills the gaps between the surfaces, and keeps many of the high spots from making contact. Because there are fewer contact points between the surfaces, the force of friction is reduced. More of the input work then is converted to output work by the machine.

section 2 review

Summary

What is a machine?

- A machine is a device that makes doing work easier.
- A machine can make doing work easier by reducing the force exerted, changing the distance over which the force is exerted, or changing the direction of the force.
- The output work done by a machine can never be greater than the input work done on the machine.

Mechanical Advantage and Efficiency

- The mechanical advantage of a machine is the number of times the machine increases the input force:

$$MA = \frac{F_{out}}{F_{in}}$$

- The efficiency of a machine is the ratio of the output work to the input work:

$$eff = \frac{W_{out}}{W_{in}} \times 100\%$$

Self Check

1. **Identify** three specific situations in which machines make work easier.
2. **Infer** why the output force exerted by a rake must be less than the input force.
3. **Explain** how the efficiency of an ideal machine compares with the efficiency of a real machine.
4. **Explain** how friction reduces the efficiency of machines.
5. **Think Critically** Can a machine be useful even if its mechanical advantage is less than one? Explain and give an example.

Hot Words Hot Topics: Bk 1 pp. 90, 271

Applying Math

6. **Calculate Efficiency** Find the efficiency of a machine if the input work is 150 J and the output work is 90 J.
7. **Calculate Mechanical Advantage** To lift a crate, a pulley system exerts a force of 2,750 N. Find the mechanical advantage of the pulley system if the input force is 250 N.

section
3

AID M1.1c: apply mathematical equations to describe relationships among variables in the natural world.
PS 5.2g: Simple machines include a lever, a pulley, a wheel and axle, and an inclined plane. A complex machine uses a combination of interacting simple machines, e.g., a bicycle.

Simple Machines

What is a simple machine?

What do you think of when you hear the word *machine*? Many people think of machines as complicated devices such as cars, elevators, or computers. However, some machines are as simple as a hammer, shovel, or ramp. A **simple machine** is a machine that does work with only one movement. The six simple machines are the inclined plane, lever, wheel and axle, screw, wedge, and pulley. A machine made up of a combination of simple machines is called a **compound machine.** A can opener is a compound machine. The bicycle in **Figure 8** is a familiar example of another compound machine.

Inclined Plane

Ramps might have enabled the ancient Egyptians to build their pyramids. To move limestone blocks weighing more than 1,000 kg each, archaeologists hypothesize that the Egyptians built enormous ramps. A ramp is a simple machine known as an inclined plane. An **inclined plane** is a flat, sloped surface. Less force is needed to move an object from one height to another using an inclined plane than is needed to lift the object. As the inclined plane becomes longer, the force needed to move the object becomes smaller.

Figure 8 Devices that use combinations of simple machines, such as this bicycle, are called compound machines.

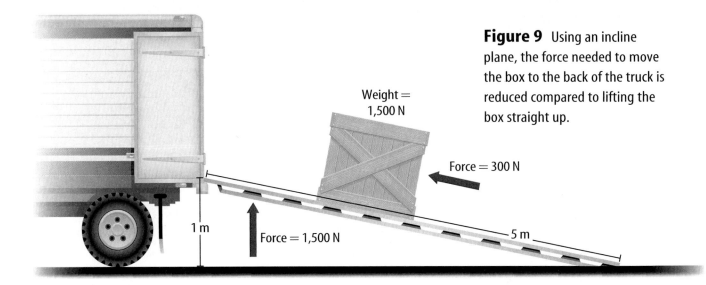

Figure 9 Using an incline plane, the force needed to move the box to the back of the truck is reduced compared to lifting the box straight up.

Weight = 1,500 N

Force = 300 N

1 m

Force = 1,500 N

5 m

Using Inclined Planes Imagine having to lift a box weighing 1,500 N to the back of a truck that is 1 m off the ground. You would have to exert a force of 1,500 N, the weight of the box, over a distance of 1 m, which equals 1,500 J of work. Now suppose that instead you use a 5-m-long ramp, as shown in **Figure 9.** The amount of work you need to do does not change. You still need to do 1,500 J of work. However, the distance over which you exert your force becomes 5 m. You can calculate the force you need to exert by dividing both sides of the equation for work by distance.

$$\text{Force} = \frac{\text{work}}{\text{distance}}$$

If you do 1,500 J of work by exerting a force over 5 m, the force is only 300 N. Because you exert the input force over a distance that is five times as long, you can exert a force that is five times less.

The mechanical advantage of an inclined plane is the length of the inclined plane divided by its height. In this example, the ramp has a mechanical advantage of 5.

Wedge An inclined plane that moves is called a **wedge.** A wedge can have one or two sloping sides. The knife shown in **Figure 10** is an example of a wedge. An axe and certain types of doorstops are also wedges. Just as for an inclined plane, the mechanical advantage of a wedge increases as it becomes longer and thinner.

Figure 10 This chef's knife is a wedge that slices through food.

Figure 11 Wedge-shaped teeth help tear food.

Your front teeth help tear an apple apart.

The wedge-shaped teeth of this *Tyrannosaurus rex* show that it was a carnivore.

Wedges in Your Body You have wedges in your body. The bite marks on the apple in **Figure 11** show how your front teeth are wedge shaped. A wedge changes the direction of the applied effort force. As you push your front teeth into the apple, the downward effort force is changed by your teeth into a sideways force that pushes the skin of the apple apart.

The teeth of meat eaters, or carnivores, are more wedge shaped than the teeth of plant eaters, or herbivores. The teeth of carnivores are used to cut and rip meat, while herbivores' teeth are used for grinding plant material. By examining the teeth of ancient animals, such as the dinosaur in **Figure 11,** scientists can determine what the animal ate when it was living.

The Screw Another form of the inclined plane is a screw. A **screw** is an inclined plane wrapped around a cylinder or post. The inclined plane on a screw forms the screw threads. Just like a wedge changes the direction of the effort force applied to it, a screw also changes the direction of the applied force. When you turn a screw, the force applied is changed by the threads to a force that pulls the screw into the material. Friction between the threads and the material holds the screw tightly in place. The mechanical advantage of the screw is the length of the inclined plane wrapped around the screw divided by the length of the screw. The more tightly wrapped the threads are, the easier it is to turn the screw. Examples of screws are shown in **Figure 12.**

 **Reading Check** *How are screws related to the inclined plane?*

Figure 12 The thread around a screw is an inclined plane. Many familiar devices use screws to make work easier.

Figure 13 The mechanical advantage of a lever changes as the position of the fulcrum changes. The mechanical advantage increases as the fulcrum is moved closer to the output force.

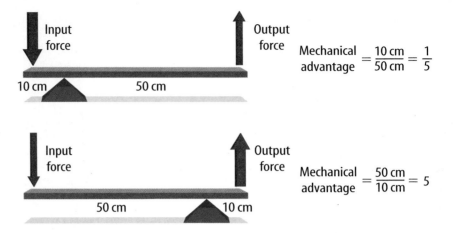

Input force

Output force

$$\text{Mechanical advantage} = \frac{10 \text{ cm}}{50 \text{ cm}} = \frac{1}{5}$$

10 cm   50 cm

Input force

Output force

$$\text{Mechanical advantage} = \frac{50 \text{ cm}}{10 \text{ cm}} = 5$$

50 cm   10 cm

Figure 14 A faucet handle is a wheel and axle. A wheel and axle is similar to a circular lever. The center is the fulcrum, and the wheel and axle turn around it. **Explain** *how you can increase the mechanical advantage of a wheel and axle.*

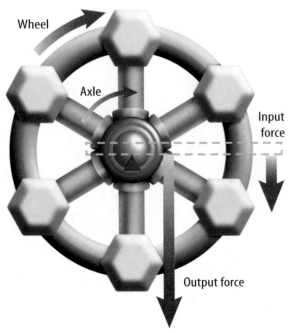

Wheel

Axle

Input force

Output force

Lever

You step up to the plate. The pitcher throws the ball and you swing your lever to hit the ball? That's right! A baseball bat is a type of simple machine called a lever. A **lever** is any rigid rod or plank that pivots, or rotates, about a point. The point about which the lever pivots is called a fulcrum.

The mechanical advantage of a lever is found by dividing the distance from the fulcrum to the input force by the distance from the fulcrum to the output force, as shown in **Figure 13.** When the fulcrum is closer to the output force than the input force, the mechanical advantage is greater than one.

Levers are divided into three classes according to the position of the fulcrum with respect to the input force and output force. **Figure 15** shows examples of three classes of levers.

Wheel and Axle

Do you think you could turn a doorknob easily if it were a narrow rod the size of a pencil? It might be possible, but it would be difficult. A doorknob makes it easier for you to open a door because it is a simple machine called a wheel and axle. A **wheel and axle** consists of two circular objects of different sizes that are attached in such a way that they rotate together. As you can see in **Figure 14,** the larger object is the wheel and the smaller object is the axle.

The mechanical advantage of a wheel and axle is usually greater than one. It is found by dividing the radius of the wheel by the radius of the axle. For example, if the radius of the wheel is 12 cm and the radius of the axle is 4 cm, the mechanical advantage is 3.

NATIONAL GEOGRAPHIC VISUALIZING LEVERS

Figure 15

Levers are among the simplest of machines, and you probably use them often in everyday life without even realizing it. A lever is a bar that pivots around a fixed point called a fulcrum. As shown here, there are three types of levers—first class, second class, and third class. They differ in where two forces—an input force and an output force—are located in relation to the fulcrum.

First-class lever

 Fulcrum

⬇ **Input force**

↟ **Output force**

In a first-class lever, the fulcrum is between the input force and the output force. First-class levers, such as scissors and pliers, multiply force or distance depending on where the fulcrum is placed. They always change the direction of the input force, too.

In a second-class lever, such as a wheelbarrow, the output force is between the input force and the fulcrum. Second-class levers always multiply the input force but don't change its direction.

Second-class lever

Third-class lever

In a third-class lever, such as a baseball bat, the input force is between the output force and the fulcrum. For a third-class lever, the output force is less than the input force, but is in the same direction.

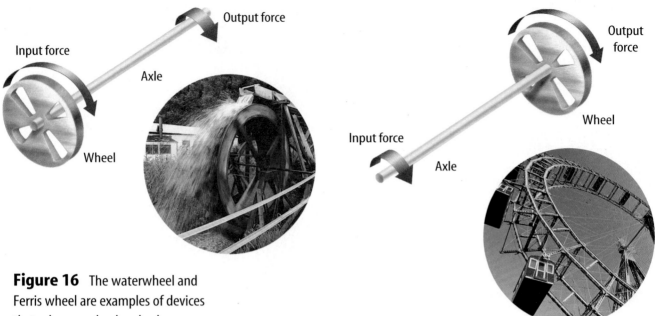

Input force

Output force

Axle

Wheel

Output force

Input force

Axle

Wheel

Figure 16 The waterwheel and Ferris wheel are examples of devices that rely on a wheel and axle. **Compare and contrast** *waterwheels and Ferris wheels in terms of wheels and axles.*

Observing Pulleys

Procedure

1. Obtain two **broomsticks.** Tie a 3-m-long **rope** to the middle of one stick. Wrap the rope around both sticks four times.
2. Have two students pull the broomsticks apart while a third pulls on the rope.
3. Repeat with two wraps of rope.

Analysis

1. Compare the results.
2. Predict whether it will be easier to pull the broomsticks together with ten wraps of rope.

Using Wheels and Axles In some devices, the input force is used to turn the wheel and the output force is exerted by the axle. Because the wheel is larger than the axle, the mechanical advantage is greater than one. So the output force is greater than the input force. A doorknob, a steering wheel, and a screwdriver are examples of this type of wheel and axle.

In other devices, the input force is applied to turn the axle and the output force is exerted by the wheel. Then the mechanical advantage is less than one and the output force is less than the input force. A fan and a ferris wheel are examples of this type of wheel and axle. **Figure 16** shows an example of each type of wheel and axle.

Pulley

To raise a sail, a sailor pulls down on a rope. The rope uses a simple machine called a pulley to change the direction of the force needed. A **pulley** consists of a grooved wheel with a rope or cable wrapped over it.

Fixed Pulleys Some pulleys, such as the one on a sail, a window blind, or a flagpole, are attached to a structure above your head. When you pull down on the rope, you pull something up. This type of pulley, called a fixed pulley, does not change the force you exert or the distance over which you exert it. Instead, it changes the direction in which you exert your force, as shown in **Figure 17.** The mechanical advantage of a fixed pulley is 1.

Reading Check *How does a fixed pulley affect the input force?*

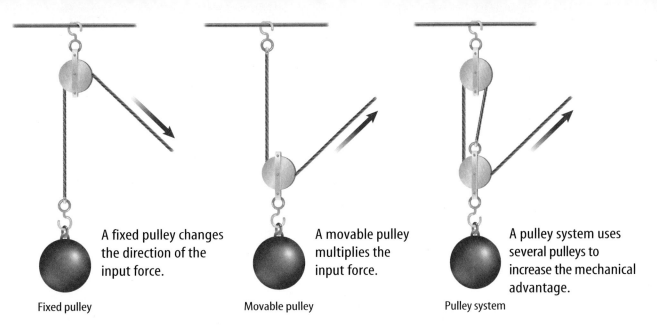

A fixed pulley changes the direction of the input force.

Fixed pulley

A movable pulley multiplies the input force.

Movable pulley

A pulley system uses several pulleys to increase the mechanical advantage.

Pulley system

Movable Pulleys Another way to use a pulley is to attach it to the object you are lifting, as shown in **Figure 17.** This type of pulley, called a movable pulley, allows you to exert a smaller force to lift the object. The mechanical advantage of a movable pulley is always 2.

More often you will see combinations of fixed and movable pulleys. Such a combination is called a pulley system. The mechanical advantage of a pulley system is equal to the number of sections of rope pulling up on the object. For the pulley system shown in **Figure 17** the mechanical advantage is 3.

Figure 17 Pulleys can change force and direction.

section 3 review

Summary

Simple and Compound Machines

- A simple machine is a machine that does work with only one movement.
- A compound machine is made from a combination of simple machines.

Types of Simple Machines

- An inclined plane is a flat, sloped surface.
- A wedge is an inclined plane that moves.
- A screw is an inclined plane that is wrapped around a cylinder or post.
- A lever is a rigid rod that pivots around a fixed point called the fulcrum.
- A wheel and axle consists of two circular objects of different sizes that rotate together.
- A pulley is a grooved wheel with a rope or cable wrapped over it.

Self Check

1. **Determine** how the mechanical advantage of a ramp changes as the ramp becomes longer.
2. **Explain** how a wedge changes an input force.
3. **Identify** the class of lever for which the fulcrum is between the input force and the output force.
4. **Explain** how the mechanical advantage of a wheel and axle change as the size of the wheel increases.
5. **Think Critically** How are a lever and a wheel and axle similar?

Hot Words Hot Topics: Bk 1 pp. 90, 271

Applying Math

6. **Calculate Length** The Great Pyramid is 146 m high. How long is a ramp from the top of the pyramid to the ground that has a mechanical advantage of 4?
7. **Calculate Force** Find the output force exerted by a moveable pulley if the input force is 50 N.

Pulley P⚓wer

Goals

- **Design** a pulley system.
- **Measure** the mechanical advantage and efficiency of the pulley system.

Possible Materials

single- and multiple-
    pulley systems
nylon rope
steel bar to support the
    pulley system
meterstick
*metric tape measure
variety of weights to test
    pulleys
force spring scale
brick
*heavy book
balance
*scale
*Alternate materials

Safety Precautions

WARNING: *The brick could be dangerous if it falls. Keep your hands and feet clear of it.*

⏵ Real-World Question

Imagine how long it might have taken to build the Sears Tower in Chicago without the aid of a pulley system attached to a crane. Hoisting the 1-ton I beams to a maximum height of 110 stories required large lifting forces and precise control of the beam's movement.

Construction workers also use smaller pulleys that are not attached to cranes to lift supplies to where they are needed. Pulleys are not limited to construction sites. They also are used to lift automobile engines out of cars, to help load and unload heavy objects on ships, and to lift heavy appliances and furniture. How can you use a pulley system to reduce the force needed to lift a load?

⏵ Form a Hypothesis

Write a hypothesis about how pulleys can be combined to make a system of pulleys to lift a heavy load, such as a brick. Consider the efficiency of your system.

⏵ Test Your Hypothesis

Make a Plan

1. Decide how you are going to support your pulley system. What materials will you use?

2. How will you measure the effort force and the resistance force? How will you determine the mechanical advantage? How will you measure efficiency?

3. **Experiment** by lifting small weights with a single pulley, double pulley, and so on. How efficient are the pulleys? In what ways can you increase the efficiency of your setup?

4. Use the results of step 3 to design a pulley system to lift the brick. Draw a diagram of your design. Label the different parts of the pulley system and use arrows to indicate the direction of movement for each section of rope.

Follow Your Plan

1. Make sure your teacher approves your plan before you start.

2. Assemble the pulley system you designed. You might want to test it with a smaller weight before attaching the brick.

3. **Measure** the force needed to lift the brick. How much rope must you pull to raise the brick 10 cm?

▶ *Analyze Your Data*

1. **Calculate** the ideal mechanical advantage of your design.

2. **Calculate** the actual mechanical advantage of the pulley system you built.

3. **Calculate** the efficiency of your pulley system.

4. How did the mechanical advantage of your pulley system compare with those of your classmates?

▶ *Conclude and Apply*

1. **Explain** how increasing the number of pulleys increases the mechanical advantage.

2. **Infer** How could you modify the pulley system to lift a weight twice as heavy with the same effort force used here?

3. **Compare** this real machine with an ideal machine.

Communicating
Your Data

Show your design diagram to the class. Review the design and point out good and bad characteristics of your pulley system. **For more help, refer to the** Science Skill Handbook.

Bionic People

Artificial limbs can help people lead normal lives

People in need of transplants usually receive human organs. But many people's medical problems can only be solved by receiving artificial body parts. These synthetic devices, called prostheses, are used to replace anything from a heart valve to a knee joint. Bionics is the science of creating artificial body parts. A major focus of bionics is the replacement of lost limbs. Through accident, birth defect, or disease, people sometimes lack hands or feet, or even whole arms or legs.

For centuries, people have used prostheses to replace limbs. In the past, physically challenged people used devices like peg legs or artificial arms that ended in a pair of hooks. These prostheses didn't do much to replace lost functions of arms and legs.

The knowledge that muscles respond to electricity has helped create more effective prostheses. One such prostheses is the myoelectric arm. This battery-powered device connects muscle nerves in an amputated arm to a sensor.

The sensor detects when the arm tenses, then transmits the signal to an artificial hand, which opens or closes. New prosthetic hands even give a sense of touch, as well as cold and heat.

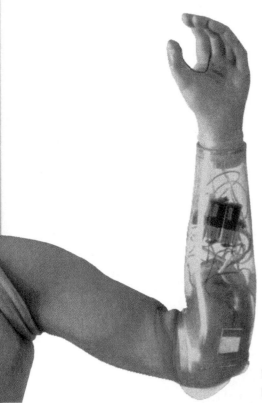

Myoelectric arms make life easier for people who have them.

Research Use your school's media center to find other aspects of robotics such as walking machines or robots that perform planetary exploration. What are they used for? How do they work? You could take it one step further and learn about cyborgs. Report to the class.

Science online

For more information, visit glencoe.com

Reviewing Main Ideas

Section 1 Work and Power

1. Work is done when a force exerted on an object causes the object to move.

2. A force can do work only when it is exerted in the same direction as the object moves.

3. Work is equal to force times distance, and the unit of work is the joule.

4. Power is the rate at which work is done, and the unit of power is the watt.

Section 2 Using Machines

1. A machine can change the size or direction of an input force or the distance over which it is exerted.

2. The mechanical advantage of a machine is its output force divided by its input force.

Section 3 Simple Machines

1. A machine that does work with only one movement is a simple machine. A compound machine is a combination of simple machines.

2. Simple machines include the inclined plane, lever, wheel and axle, screw, wedge, and pulley.

3. Wedges and screws are inclined planes.

4. Pulleys can be used to multiply force and change direction.

Visualizing Main Ideas

Copy and complete the following concept map on simple machines.

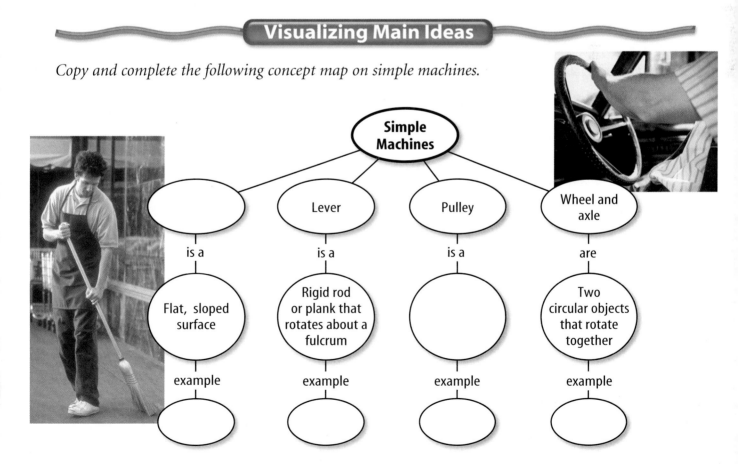

Simple Machines

Lever — is a — Rigid rod or plank that rotates about a fulcrum — example

Pulley — is a — example

Wheel and axle — are — Two circular objects that rotate together — example

is a — Flat, sloped surface — example

Using Vocabulary

compound machine p. 85	output force p. 80
efficiency p. 83	power p. 77
inclined plane p. 85	pulley p. 90
input force p. 80	screw p. 87
lever p. 88	simple machine p. 85
mechanical advantage p. 81	wedge p. 86
	wheel and axle p. 88
	work p. 74

Each phrase below describes a vocabulary word. Write the vocabulary word that matches the phrase describing it.

1. percentage of work in to work out

2. force put into a machine

3. force exerted by a machine

4. two rigidly attached wheels

5. input force divided by output force

6. a machine with only one movement

7. an inclined plane that moves

8. a rigid rod that rotates about a fulcrum

9. a flat, sloped surface

10. amount of work divided by time

Checking Concepts

Choose the word or phrase that best answers the question.

11. Which of the following is a requirement for work to be done?
    A) Force is exerted.
    B) Object is carried.
    C) Force moves an object.
    D) Machine is used.

12. How much work is done when a force of 30 N moves an object a distance of 3 m?
    A) 3 J   **C)** 30 J
    B) 10 J   **D)** 90 J

13. How much power is used when 600 J of work are done in 10 s?
    A) 6 W   **C)** 600 W
    B) 60 W   **D)** 610 W

14. Which is a simple machine?
    A) baseball bat   **C)** can opener
    B) bicycle   **D)** car

15. Mechanical advantage can be calculated by which of the following expressions?
    A) input force/output force
    B) output force/input force
    C) input work/output work
    D) output work/input work

16. What is the ideal mechanical advantage of a machine that changes only the direction of the input force?
    A) less than 1   **C)** 1
    B) zero   **D)** greater than 1

Use the illustration below to answer question 17.

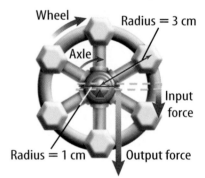

17. What is the output force if the input force on the wheel is 100 N?
    A) 5 N   **C)** 500 N
    B) 200 N   **D)** 2,000 N

18. Which of the following is a form of the inclined plane?
    A) pulley   **C)** wheel and axle
    B) screw   **D)** lever

19. For a given input force, a ramp increases which of the following?
    A) height   **C)** output work
    B) output force   **D)** efficiency

Thinking Critically

Use the illustration below to answer question 20.

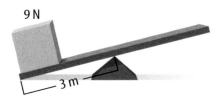

9 N

3 m

20. Evaluate Would a 9-N force applied 2 m from the fulcrum lift the weight? Explain.

21. Explain why the output work for any machine can't be greater than the input work.

22. Explain A doorknob is an example of a wheel and axle. Explain why turning the knob is easier than turning the axle.

23. Infer On the Moon, the force of gravity is less than on Earth. Infer how the mechanical advantage of an inclined plane would change if it were on the Moon, instead of on Earth.

24. Make and Use Graphs A pulley system has a mechanical advantage of 5. Make a graph with the input force on the *x*-axis and the output force on the *y*-axis. Choose five different values of the input force, and plot the resulting output force on your graph.

Use the diagram below to answer question 25.

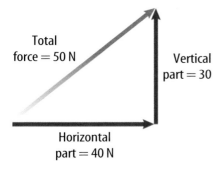

Total force = 50 N

Vertical part = 30

Horizontal part = 40 N

25. Work The diagram above shows a force exerted at an angle to pull a sled. How much work is done if the sled moves 10 m horizontally?

Performance Activities

26. Identify You have levers in your body. Your muscles and tendons provide the input force. Your joints act as fulcrums. The output force is used to move everything from your head to your hands. Describe and draw any human levers you can identify.

27. Display Make a display of everyday devices that are simple and compound machines. For devices that are simple machines, identify which simple machine it is. For compound machines, identify the simple machines that compose it.

Hot Words Hot Topics: Bk 1 pp. 90, 271

Applying Math

28. Mechanical Advantage What is the mechanical advantage of a 6-m long ramp that extends from a ground-level sidewalk to a 2-m high porch?

29. Input Force How much input force is required to lift an 11,000-N beam using a pulley system with a mechanical advantage of 20?

30. Efficiency The input work done on a pulley system is 450 J. What is the efficiency of the pulley system if the output work is 375 J?

Use the table below to answer question 31.

Output Force Exerted by Machines		
Machine	Input Force (N)	Output Force (N)
A	500	750
B	300	200
C	225	225
D	800	1,100
E	75	110

31. Mechanical Advantage According to the table above, which of the machines listed has the largest mechanical advantage?

Record your answers on the answer sheet provided by your teacher or on a sheet of paper.

1 The work done by a boy pulling a snow sled up a hill is 425 J. What is the power expended by the boy if he pulls on the sled for 10.5 s?
(1) 24.7 W   (3) 247 W
(2) 40.5 W   (4) 4460 W

Use the illustration below to answer questions 2 and 3.

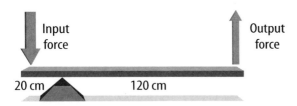

2 What is the mechanical advantage of the lever shown above?
(1) $\frac{1}{6}$ (3) 2

(2) $\frac{1}{2}$ (4) 6

3 What would the mechanical advantage of the lever be if the triangular block were moved to a position 40 cm from the edge of the output force side of the plank?
(1) $\frac{1}{4}$ (3) 2

(2) $\frac{1}{2}$ (4) 4

4 Which of the following causes the efficiency of a machine to be less than 100%?
(1) work
(2) power
(3) mechanical advantage
(4) friction

Use the illustration below to answer questions 5 and 6.

5 The pulley system in the illustration above uses several pulleys to increase the mechanical advantage. What is the mechanical advantage of this system?
(1) 1   (3) 3
(2) 2   (4) 4

6 Suppose the lower pulley was removed so that the object was supported only by the upper pulley. What would the mechanical advantage be?
(1) 0   (3) 2
(2) 1   (4) 3

7 You push a shopping cart with a force of 12 N for a distance of 1.5 m. You stop pushing the cart, but it continues to roll for 1.1 m. How much work did you do?
(1) 8.0 J   (3) 18 J
(2) 13 J   (4) 31 J

8 What is the mechanical advantage of a wheel with a radius of 8.0 cm connected to an axle with a radius of 2.5 cm?
(1) 0.31   (3) 3.2
(2) 2.5   (4) 20

9 You push a 5-kg box across the floor with a force of 25 N. How far do you have to push the box to do 63 J of work?
(1) 0.40 m   (3) 2.5 m
(2) 1.6 m   (4) 13 m

Part II

Record your answers on the answer sheet provided by your teacher or on a sheet of paper.

10 Describe how you can determine the mechanical advantage of a pulley or a pulley system.

Use the figure below to answer questions 11 and 12.

11 What type of simple machine is the tip of the dart in the photo above?

12 Analyze how the mechanical advantage of the dart tip would change if the tip were longer and thinner.

13 The output work of a machine can never be greater than the input work. However, the advantage of using a machine is that it makes work easier. Describe and give an example of the three ways a machine can make work easier.

14 Draw a sketch showing the cause of friction as two surfaces slide past each other. Explain your sketch, and describe how you can reduce the friction between the two surfaces.

Use the figure below to answer question 15.

15 Identify two simple machines in the photo above and describe how they make riding a bicycle easier.

How Are
Bats & Tornadoes
Connected?

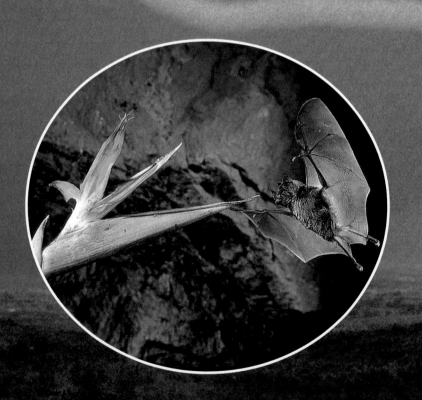

Bats are able to find food and avoid obstacles without using their vision. They do this by producing high-frequency sound waves which bounce off objects and return to the bat. From these echoes, the bat is able to locate obstacles and prey. This process is called echolocation. If the reflected waves have a higher frequency than the emitted waves, the bat senses the object is getting closer. If the reflected waves have a lower frequency, the object is moving away. This change in frequency is called the Doppler effect. Like echolocation, sonar technology uses sound waves and the Doppler effect to determine the position and motion of objects. Doppler radar also uses the Doppler effect, but with radar waves instead of sound waves. Higher frequency waves indicate if an object, such as a storm, is coming closer, while lower frequencies indicate if it is moving away. Meteorologists use frequency shifts indicated by Doppler radar to detect the formation of tornadoes and to predict where they will strike.

unit projects

Visit unit projects at **glencoe.com** to find project ideas and resources. Projects include:

- **Technology** Predict and track the weather of a city in a different part of the world, and compare it to your local weather pattern.
- **Career** Explore weather-related careers while investigating different types of storms. Compare and contrast career characteristics and history.
- **Model** Research animal behavior to discover if animals are able to predict the weather. Present your samples of weather-predicting proverbs as a collection, or use them in a folklore tale.

 Hurricanes! investigates a variety of tropical storms, their source of energy, classifications, and destructive forces.

PS 3.1c: The motion of particles helps to explain the phases (states) of matter as well as changes from one phase to another. The phase in which matter exists depends on the attractive forces among its particles. **3.2a:** During a physical change a substance keeps its chemical composition and properties. **Also covered:** 3.1d, 3.1e, 3.1f, 3.1h, 3.1i, 3.3a, 3.3b, 4.1c, 4.1d, 4.2c, 4.2d.

States of Matter

chapter preview

sections

1 Matter

2 Changes of State
    Lab   The Water Cycle

3 Behavior of Fluids
    Lab   Design Your Own Ship

    Virtual Lab   How does thermal energy affect the state of a substance?

Ahhh!

A long, hot soak on a snowy day! This Asian monkey called a macaque is experiencing the effects of heat—the transfer of thermal energy from a warmer object to a colder object. In this chapter, you will learn about heat and the three common states of matter on Earth.

Science Journal   Write why you think there is snow on the ground but the water is not frozen.

Start-Up Activities

Experiment with a Freezing Liquid

Have you ever thought about how and why you might be able to ice-skate on a pond in the winter but swim in the same pond in the summer? Many substances change form as temperature changes.

1. Make a table to record temperature and appearance. Obtain a test tube containing an unknown liquid from your teacher. Place the test tube in a rack.

2. Insert a thermometer into the liquid. **WARNING:** *Do not allow the thermometer to touch the bottom of the test tube.* Starting immediately, observe and record the substance's temperature and appearance every 30 s.

3. Continue making measurements and observations until you're told to stop.

4. **Think Critically** In your Science Journal, describe your investigation and observations. Did anything unusual happen while you were observing? If so, what?

 **Preview this chapter's content and activities at** glencoe.com

---

 **Changing States of Matter**
Make the following Foldable to help you study the changes in water.

STEP 1 Fold a vertical sheet of paper from left to right two times. Unfold.

STEP 2 Fold the paper in half from top to bottom two times.

STEP 3 Unfold and draw lines along the folds.

STEP 4 Label the top row and first column as shown below.

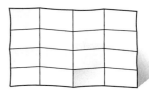

	Define States	+ Heat	– Heat
Liquid water			
Water as a gas			
Water as a solid (ice)			

Read and Write As you read the chapter, define the states of matter as listed on your Foldable in the *Define States* column. Write what happens when heat is added to or lost from the three states of matter.

section 1

Matter

as you read

What You'll Learn

- **Recognize** that matter is made of particles in constant motion.
- **Relate** the three states of matter to the arrangement of particles within them.

Why It's Important

Everything you can see, taste, and touch is matter.

Review Vocabulary

atom: a small particle that makes up most types of matter

New Vocabulary

- matter
- solid
- liquid
- viscosity
- surface tension
- gas

What is matter?

Take a look at the beautiful scene in **Figure 1.** What do you see? Perhaps you notice the water and ice. Maybe you are struck by the Sun in the background. All of these images show examples of matter. **Matter** is anything that takes up space and has mass. Matter doesn't have to be visible—even air is matter.

States of Matter All matter is made up of tiny particles, such as atoms, molecules, or ions. Each particle attracts other particles. In other words, each particle pulls other particles toward itself. These particles also are constantly moving. The motion of the particles and the strength of attraction between the particles determine a material's state of matter.

✔ **Reading Check** *What determines a material's state of matter?*

There are three familiar states of matter—solid, liquid, and gas. A fourth state of matter known as plasma occurs at extremely high temperatures. Plasma is found in stars, lightning, and neon lights. Although plasma is common in the universe, it is not common on Earth. For that reason, this chapter will focus only on the three states of matter that are common on Earth.

Physical Setting

3.1c: Clarify, in your own words, what determines a material's state of matter.

Figure 1 Matter exists in all four states in this scene.
Identify *the solid, liquid, gas, and plasma in this photograph.*

Solids

What makes a substance a solid? Think about some familiar solids. Chairs, floors, rocks, and ice cubes are a few examples of matter in the solid state. What properties do all solids share? A **solid** is matter with a definite shape and volume. For example, when you pick up a rock from the ground and place it in a bucket, it doesn't change shape or size. A solid does not take the shape of a container in which it is placed. This is because the particles of a solid are packed closely together, as shown in **Figure 2.**

Particles in Motion The particles that make up all types of matter are in constant motion. Does this mean that the particles in a solid are moving too? Although you can't see them, a solid's particles are vibrating in place. The particles do not have enough energy to move out of their fixed positions.

Reading Check *What motion do solid particles have?*

Crystalline Solids In some solids, the particles are arranged in a repeating, three-dimensional pattern called a crystal. These solids are called crystalline solids. In **Figure 3** you can see the arrangement of particles in a crystal of sodium chloride, which is table salt. The particles in the crystal are arranged in the shape of a cube. Diamond, another crystalline solid, is made entirely of carbon atoms that form crystals that look more like pyramids. Sugar, sand, and snow are other crystalline solids.

Solid

Figure 2 The particles in a solid vibrate in place while maintaining a constant shape and volume.

Figure 3 The particles in a crystal of sodium chloride (NaCl) are arranged in an orderly pattern.

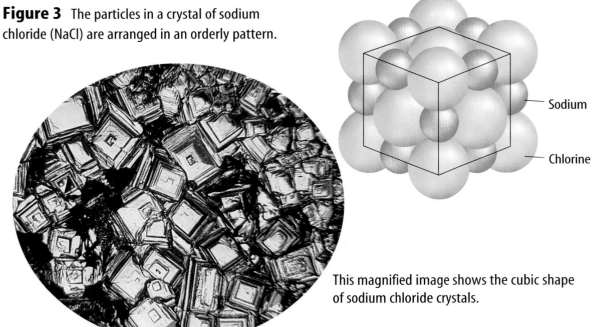

Sodium

Chlorine

This magnified image shows the cubic shape of sodium chloride crystals.

Amorphous Solids Some solids come together without forming crystal structures. These solids often consist of large particles that are not arranged in a repeating pattern. Instead, the particles are found in a random arrangement. These solids are called amorphous (uh MOR fuhs) solids. Rubber, plastic, and glass are examples of amorphous solids.

Reading Check *How is a crystalline solid different from an amorphous solid?*

Liquids

From the orange juice you drink with breakfast to the water you use to brush your teeth at night, matter in the liquid state is familiar to you. How would you describe the characteristics of a liquid? Is it hard like a solid? Does it keep its shape? A **liquid** is matter that has a definite volume but no definite shape. When you pour a liquid from one container to another, the liquid takes the shape of the container. The volume of a liquid, however, is the same no matter what the shape of the container. If you pour 50 mL of juice from a carton into a pitcher, the pitcher will contain 50 mL of juice. If you then pour that same juice into a glass, its shape will change again but its volume will not.

Free to Move The reason that a liquid can have different shapes is because the particles in a liquid move more freely, as shown in **Figure 4,** than the particles in a solid. The particles in a liquid have enough energy to move out of their fixed positions but not enough energy to move far apart.

Fresh Water Early settlers have always decided to build their homes near water. The rivers provided ways for people to travel, drinking water for themselves and their animals, and irrigation for farming. Over time, small communities became larger communities with industry building along the same water.

Physical Setting

3.1d, 3.1e, 3.1f: Design a chart to compare the shape and volume of gases, liquids, and solids.

Figure 4 The particles in a liquid stay close together, although they are free to move past one another.

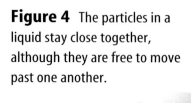
Liquid

Viscosity Do all liquids flow the way water flows? You know that honey flows more slowly than water and you've probably heard the phrase "slow as molasses." Some liquids flow more easily than others. A liquid's resistance to flow is known as the liquid's **viscosity.** Honey has a high viscosity. Water has a lower viscosity. The slower a liquid flows, the higher its viscosity is. The viscosity results from the strength of the attraction between the particles of the liquid. For many liquids, viscosity increases as the liquid becomes colder.

Surface Tension If you're careful, you can float a needle on the surface of water. This is because attractive forces cause the particles on the surface of a liquid to pull themselves together and resist being pushed apart. You can see in **Figure 5** that particles beneath the surface of a liquid are pulled in all directions. Particles at the surface of a liquid are pulled toward the center of the liquid and sideways along the surface. No liquid particles are located above to pull on them. The uneven forces acting on the particles on the surface of a liquid are called **surface tension.** Surface tension causes the liquid to act as if a thin film were stretched across its surface. As a result you can float a needle on the surface of water. For the same reason, the water spider can move around on the surface of a pond or lake. When a liquid is present in small amounts, surface tension causes the liquid to form small droplets.

Science Online

Topic: Plasma
Visit glencoe.com for Web links to information about the states of matter.

Activity List four ways that plasma differs from the other three states of matter

Physical Setting

3.1a: List at least five characteristics of substances.

Figure 5 Surface tension exists because the particles at the surface experience different forces than those at the center of the liquid.

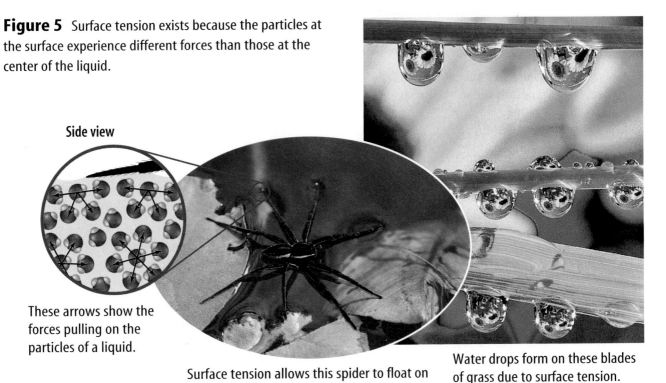

Side view

These arrows show the forces pulling on the particles of a liquid.

Surface tension allows this spider to float on water as if the water had a thin film.

Water drops form on these blades of grass due to surface tension.

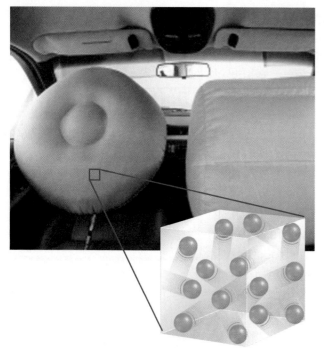

Gases

Unlike solids and liquids, most gases are invisible. The air you breathe is a mixture of gases. The gas in the air bags in **Figure 6** and the helium in some balloons are examples of gases. **Gas** is matter that does not have a definite shape or volume. The particles in gas are much farther apart than those in a liquid or solid. Gas particles move at high speeds in all directions. They will spread out evenly, as far apart as possible. If you poured a small volume of a liquid into a container, the liquid would stay in the bottom of the container. However, if you poured the same volume of a gas into a container, the gas would fill the container completely. A gas can expand or be compressed. Decreasing the volume of the container squeezes the gas particles closer together.

Figure 6 The particles in gas move at high speeds in all directions. The gas inside these air bags spreads out to fill the entire volume of the bag.

Vapor Matter that exists in the gas state but is generally a liquid or solid at room temperature is called vapor. Water, for example, is a liquid at room temperature. Thus, water vapor is the term for the gas state of water.

section 1 review

Summary

What is matter?

- Matter is anything that takes up space and has mass. Solid, liquid, and gas are the three common states of matter.

Solids

- Solids have a definite volume and shape.
- Solids with particles arranged in order are called crystalline solids. The particles in amorphous solids are not in any order.

Liquids

- Liquids have definite volume but no defined shape.
- Viscosity is a measure of how easily liquids flow.

Gases

- Gases have no definite volume or shape.
- Vapor refers to gaseous substances that are normally liquids or solids at room temperature.

Self Check

1. **Define** the two properties of matter that determine its state.
2. **Describe** the movement of particles within solids, liquids, and gases.
3. **Name** the property that liquids and solids share. What property do liquids and gases share?
4. **Infer** A scientist places 25 mL of a yellow substance into a 50-mL container. The substance quickly fills the entire container. Is it a solid, liquid, or gas?
5. **Think Critically** The particles in liquid A have a stronger attraction to each other than the particles in liquid B. If both liquids are at the same temperature, which liquid has a higher viscosity? Explain.

Applying Skills

6. **Concept Map** Draw a Venn diagram in your Science Journal and fill in the characteristics of the states of matter.

PS 3.2a: During a physical change a substance keeps its chemical composition and properties. Examples of physical changes include freezing, melting, condensation, boiling, evaporation, tearing, and crushing. **Also covered:** 3.1c, 3.3b, 4.1c, 4.1d, 4.2c.

section 2

Changes of State

Thermal Energy and Heat

Shards of ice fly from the sculptor's chisel. As the crowd looks on, a swan slowly emerges from a massive block of ice. As the day wears on, however, drops of water begin to fall from the sculpture. Drip by drip, the sculpture is transformed into a puddle of liquid water. What makes matter change from one state to another? To answer this question, you need to think about the particles that make up matter.

Energy Simply stated, energy is the ability to do work or cause change. The energy of motion is called kinetic energy. Particles within matter are in constant motion. The amount of motion of these particles depends on the kinetic energy they possess. Particles with more kinetic energy move faster and farther apart. Particles with less energy move more slowly and stay closer together.

The total kinetic and potential energy of all the particles in a sample of matter is called **thermal energy.** Thermal energy, an extensive property, depends on the number of particles in a substance as well as the amount of energy each particle has. If either the number of particles or the amount of energy in each particle changes, the thermal energy of the sample changes. With identically sized samples, the warmer substance has the greater thermal energy. In **Figure 7,** the particles of hot water from the hot spring have more thermal energy than the particles of snow on the surrounding ground.

as you read

What You'll Learn

- **Define and compare** thermal energy and temperature.
- **Relate** changes in thermal energy to changes of state.
- **Explore** energy and temperature changes on a graph.

Why It's Important

Matter changes state as it heats up or cools down.

Review Vocabulary

energy: the ability to do work or cause change

New Vocabulary

- thermal energy
- temperature
- heat
- melting
- freezing
- vaporization
- condensation

Figure 7 These girls are enjoying the water from the hot spring. **Infer** *why the girls appear to be comfortable in the hot spring while there is snow on the ground.*

Figure 8 The particles in hot tea move faster than those in iced tea. The temperature of hot tea is higher than the temperature of iced tea.
Identify *which tea has the higher kinetic energy.*

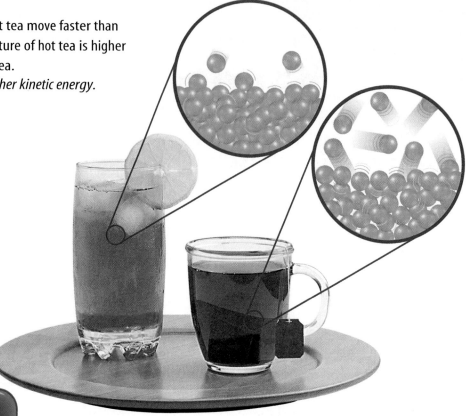

INTEGRATE Physics

Types of Energy Thermal energy is one of several different forms of energy. Other forms include the chemical energy in chemical compounds, the electrical energy used in appliances, the electromagnetic energy of light, and the nuclear energy stored in the nucleus of an atom. Make a list of examples of energy that you are familiar with.

Temperature Not all of the particles in a sample of matter have the same amount of energy. Some have more energy than others. The average kinetic energy of the individual particles is the **temperature,** an intensive property, of the substance. You can find an average by adding up a group of numbers and dividing the total by the number of items in the group. For example, the average of the numbers 2, 4, 8, and 10 is $(2 + 4 + 8 + 10) \div 4 = 6$. Temperature is different from thermal energy because thermal energy is a total and temperature is an average.

You know that the iced tea is colder than the hot tea, as shown in **Figure 8.** Stated differently, the temperature of iced tea is lower than the temperature of hot tea. You also could say that the average kinetic energy of the particles in the iced tea is less than the average kinetic energy of the particles in the hot tea.

Heat When a warm object is brought near a cooler object, thermal energy will be transferred from the warmer object to the cooler one. The movement of thermal energy from a substance at a higher temperature to one at a lower temperature is called **heat.** When a substance is heated, it gains thermal energy. Therefore, its particles move faster and its temperature rises. When a substance is cooled, it loses thermal energy, which causes its particles to move more slowly and its temperature to drop.

✔ **Reading Check** *How is heat related to temperature?*

Specific Heat

As you study more science, you will discover that water has many unique properties. One of those is the amount of heat required to increase the temperature of water as compared to most other substances. The specific heat of a substance is the amount of heat required to raise the temperature of 1 g of a substance 1°C.

Substances that have a low specific heat, such as most metals and the sand in **Figure 9,** heat up and cool down quickly because they require only small amounts of heat to cause their temperatures to rise. A substance with a high specific heat, such as the water in **Figure 9,** heats up and cools down slowly because a much larger quantity of heat is required to cause its temperature to rise or fall by the same amount.

Figure 9 The specific heat of water is greater than that of sand. The energy provided by the Sun raises the temperature of the sand much faster than the water.

Changes Between the Solid and Liquid States

Matter can change from one state to another when thermal energy is absorbed or released. This change is known as change of state. The graph in **Figure 11** shows the changes in temperature as thermal energy is gradually added to a container of ice.

Figure 10 Rather than melting into a liquid, glass gradually softens. Glass blowers use this characteristic to shape glass into beautiful vases while it is hot.

**Melting** As the ice in **Figure 11** is heated, it absorbs thermal energy and its temperature rises. At some point, the temperature stops rising and the ice begins to change into liquid water. The change from the solid state to the liquid state is called **melting.** The temperature at which a substance changes from a solid to a liquid is called the melting point. The melting point of water is 0°C.

Amorphous solids, such as rubber and glass, don't melt in the same way as crystalline solids. Because they don't have crystal structures to break down, these solids get softer and softer as they are heated, as you can see in **Figure 10.**

Figure 11

Like most substances, water can exist in three distinct states—solid, liquid, or gas. At certain temperatures, water changes from one state to another. This diagram shows what changes occur as water is heated or cooled.

MELTING When ice melts, its temperature remains constant until all the ice turns to water. Continued heating of liquid water causes the molecules to vibrate even faster, steadily raising the temperature.

FREEZING When liquid water freezes, it releases thermal energy and turns into the solid state, ice.

VAPORIZATION When water reaches its boiling point of 100°C, water molecules are moving so fast that they break free of the attractions that hold them together in the liquid state. The result is vaporization— the liquid becomes a gas. The temperature of boiling water remains constant until all of the liquid turns to steam.

Gas

100°C

Vaporization

Condensation

Temperature

Liquid

Melting

0°C

Freezing

CONDENSATION When steam is cooled, it releases thermal energy and turns into its liquid state. This process is called condensation.

Solid

Thermal energy

Solid state: ice

Liquid state: water

Gaseous state: steam

Freezing The process of melting a crystalline solid can be reversed if the liquid is cooled. The change from the liquid state to the solid state is called **freezing.** As the liquid cools, it loses thermal energy. As a result, its particles slow down and come closer together. Attractive forces begin to trap particles, and the crystals of a solid begin to form. As you can see in **Figure 11,** freezing and melting are opposite processes.

The temperature at which a substance changes from the liquid state to the solid state is called the freezing point. The freezing point of the liquid state of a substance is the same temperature as the melting point of the solid state. For example, solid water melts at 0°C and liquid water freezes at 0°C.

During freezing, the temperature of a substance remains constant while the particles in the liquid form a crystalline solid. Because particles in a liquid have more energy than particles in a solid, energy is released during freezing. This energy is released into the surroundings. After all of the liquid has become a solid, the temperature begins to decrease again.

Science nline

Topic: Freezing Point Study
Visit glencoe.com for Web links to information about freezing.

Activity Make a list of several substances and the temperatures at which they freeze. Find out how the freezing point affects how the substance is used.

Applying Science

How can ice save oranges?

During the spring, Florida citrus farmers carefully watch the fruit when temperatures drop close to freezing. When the temperatures fall below 0°C, the liquid in the cells of oranges can freeze and expand. This causes the cells to break, making the oranges mushy and the crop useless for sale. To prevent this, farmers spray the oranges with water just before the temperature reaches 0°C. How does spraying oranges with water protect them?

Identifying the Problem
Using the diagram in **Figure 11,** consider what is happening to the water at 0°C. Two things occur. What are they?

Solving the Problem
1. What change of state and what energy changes occur when water freezes?
2. How does the formation of ice on the orange help the orange?

Observing Vaporization

Procedure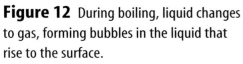

1. Use a **dropper** to place one drop of **rubbing alcohol** on the back of your hand.
2. Describe how your hand feels during the next 2 min.
3. Wash your hands.

Analysis

1. What changes in the appearance of the rubbing alcohol did you notice?
2. What sensation did you feel during the 2 min? How can you explain this sensation?
3. Infer how sweating cools the body.

Changes Between the Liquid and Gas States

After an early morning rain, you and your friends enjoy stomping through the puddles left behind. But later that afternoon when you head out to run through the puddles once more, the puddles are gone. The liquid water in the puddles changed into a gas. Matter changes between the liquid and gas states through vaporization and condensation.

Vaporization As liquid water is heated, its temperature rises until it reaches 100°C. At this point, liquid water changes into water vapor. The change from a liquid to a gas is known as **vaporization** (vay puh ruh ZAY shun). You can see in **Figure 11** that the temperature of the substance does not change during vaporization. However, the substance absorbs thermal energy. The additional energy causes the particles to move faster until they have enough energy to escape the liquid as gas particles.

Two forms of vaporization exist. Vaporization that takes place below the surface of a liquid is called boiling. When a liquid boils, bubbles form within the liquid and rise to the surface, as shown in **Figure 12.** The temperature at which a liquid boils is called the boiling point. The boiling point of water is 100°C.

Vaporization that takes place at the surface of a liquid is called evaporation. Evaporation, which occurs at temperatures below the boiling point, explains how puddles dry up. Imagine that you could watch individual water molecules in a puddle. You would notice that the molecules move at different speeds. Although the temperature of the water is constant, remember that temperature is a measure of the average kinetic energy of the molecules. Some of the fastest-moving molecules overcome the attractive forces of other molecules and escape from the surface of the water.

Figure 12 During boiling, liquid changes to gas, forming bubbles in the liquid that rise to the surface.
Define *the word that describes a liquid changing to the gas.*

Figure 13 The drops of water on these glasses and pitcher of lemonade were formed when water vapor in the air lost enough energy to return to the liquid state. This process is called condensation.

Location of Molecules It takes more than speed for water molecules to escape the liquid state. During evaporation, these faster molecules also must be near the surface, heading in the right direction, and they must avoid hitting other water molecules as they leave. With the faster particles evaporating from the surface of a liquid, the particles that remain are the slower, cooler ones. Evaporation cools the liquid and anything near the liquid. You experience this cooling effect when perspiration evaporates from your skin.

Condensation Pour a nice, cold glass of lemonade and place it on the table for a half hour on a warm day. When you come back to take a drink, the outside of the glass will be covered by drops of water, as shown in **Figure 13.** What happened? As a gas cools, its particles slow down. When particles move slowly enough for their attractions to bring them together, droplets of liquid form. This process, which is the opposite of vaporization, is called **condensation.** As a gas condenses to a liquid, it releases the thermal energy it absorbed to become a gas. During this process, the temperature of the substance does not change. The decrease in energy changes the arrangement of particles. After the change of state is complete, the temperature continues to drop, as you saw in **Figure 11.**

✔ **Reading Check** *What energy change occurs during condensation?*

Condensation formed the droplets of water on the outside of your glass of lemonade. In the same way, water vapor in the atmosphere condenses to form the liquid water droplets in clouds. When the droplets become large enough, they can fall to the ground as rain.

Physical Setting

3.2a: Identify four processes of physical changes in which substances change state.

Topic: Condensation
Visit glencoe.com for Web links to information about how condensation is involved in weather.

Activity Find out how condensation is affected by the temperature as well as the amount of water in the air.

Changes Between the Solid and Gas States

Some substances can change from the solid state to the gas state without ever becoming a liquid. During this process, known as sublimation, the surface particles of the solid gain enough energy to become a gas. One example of a substance that undergoes sublimation is dry ice. Dry ice is the solid form of carbon dioxide. It often is used to keep materials cold and dry. At room temperature and pressure, carbon dioxide does not exist as a liquid. Therefore, as dry ice absorbs thermal energy from the objects around it, it changes directly into a gas. When dry ice becomes a gas, it absorbs thermal energy from water vapor in the air. As a result, the water vapor cools and condenses into liquid water droplets, forming the fog you see in **Figure 14.**

Figure 14 The solid carbon dioxide (dry ice) at the bottom of this beaker of water is changing directly into gaseous carbon dioxide. This process is called sublimation.

section 2 review

Summary

Thermal Energy and Heat

- Thermal energy depends on the amount of the substance and the kinetic energy of particles in the substance.
- Heat is the movement of thermal energy from a warmer substance to a cooler one.

Specific Heat

- Specific heat is a measure of the amount of energy required to raise 1 g of a substance 1°C.

Changes Between Solid and Liquid States

- During all changes of state, the temperature of a substance stays the same.

Changes Between Liquid and Gas States

- Vaporization is the change from the liquid state to a gaseous state.
- Condensation is the change from the gaseous state to the liquid state.

Changes Between Solid and Gas States

- Sublimation is the process of a substance going from the solid state to the gas state without ever being in the liquid state.

Self Check

1. **Describe** how thermal energy and temperature are similar. How are they different?
2. **Explain** how a change in thermal energy causes matter to change from one state to another. Give two examples.
3. **List** the three changes of state during which energy is absorbed.
4. **Describe** the two types of vaporization.
5. **Think Critically** How can the temperature of a substance remain the same even if the substance is absorbing thermal energy?
6. **Write** a paragraph in your Science Journal that explains why you can step out of the shower into a warm bathroom and begin to shiver.

Hot Words Hot Topics: Bk 1 (7) pp. 195, 283-284; (8) pp. 274-276

Applying Math

7. **Make and Use Graphs** Use the data you collected in the Launch Lab to plot a temperature-time graph. At what temperature does the graph level off? What was the liquid doing during this time period?
8. **Use Numbers** If sample A requires 10 calories to raise the temperature of a 1-g sample 1°C, how many calories does it take to raise a 5-g sample 10°C?

The Water Cycle

Water is all around us and you've used water in all three of its common states. This lab will give you the opportunity to observe the three states of matter and to discover for yourself if ice really melts at 0°C and if water boils at 100°C.

⊙ Real-World Question

How does the temperature of water change as it is heated from a solid to a gas?

Goals

- ■ **Measure** the temperature of water as it heats.
- ■ **Observe** what happens as the water changes from one state to another.
- ■ **Graph** the temperature and time data.

Materials

hot plate	*watch with
ice cubes (100 mL)	second hand
Celsius thermometer	stirring rod
*electronic	250-mL beaker
temperature probe	*Alternate materials
wall clock	

Safety Precautions

🧤 🥽 👕 ♨ 🧴 🤚

⊙ Procedure

1. Make a data table similar to the table shown.
2. Put 150 mL of water and 100 mL of ice into the beaker and place the beaker on the hot plate. Do not touch the hot plate.
3. Put the thermometer into the ice/water mixture. Do not stir with the thermometer or allow it to rest on the bottom of the beaker. After 30 s, read and record the temperature in your data table.

Characteristics of Water Sample

Time (min)	Temperature (°C)	Physical State
	Do not write in this book.	

4. Plug in the hot plate and turn the temperature knob to the medium setting.
5. Every 30 s, read and record the temperature and physical state of the water until it begins to boil. Use the stirring rod to stir the contents of the beaker before making each temperature measurement. Stop recording. Allow the water to cool.

⊙ Analyze Your Data

Use your data to make a graph plotting time on the x-axis and temperature on the y-axis. Draw a smooth curve through the data points.

⊙ Conclude and Apply

1. **Describe** how the temperature of the ice/water mixture changed as you heated the beaker.
2. **Describe** the shape of the graph during any changes of state.

Communicating Your Data

Add labels to your graph. Use the detailed graph to explain to your class how water changes state. **For more help, refer to the Science Skill Handbook.**

PS 3.1h: Density can be described as the amount of matter that is in a given amount of space. If two objects have equal volume, but one has more mass, the one with more mass is denser. Also Covered: 3.1c, 3.1i, 3.3b.

Behavior of Fluids

as you read

What You'll Learn

- **Explain** why some things float but others sink.
- **Describe** how pressure is transmitted through fluids.

Why It's Important

Pressure enables you to squeeze toothpaste from a tube, and buoyant force helps you float in water.

Review Vocabulary
force: a push or pull

New Vocabulary
- pressure
- buoyant force
- Archimedes' principle
- density
- Pascal's principle

Pressure

It's a beautiful summer day when you and your friends go outside to play volleyball, much like the kids in **Figure 15.** There's only one problem—the ball is flat. You pump air into the ball until it is firm. The firmness of the ball is the result of the motion of the air particles in the ball. As the air particles in the ball move, they collide with one another and with the inside walls of the ball. As each particle collides with the inside walls, it exerts a force, pushing the surface of the ball outward. A force is a push or a pull. The forces of all the individual particles add together to make up the pressure of the air.

Pressure is equal to the force exerted on a surface divided by the total area over which the force is exerted.

$$\text{pressure} = \frac{\text{force}}{\text{area}}$$

When force is measured in newtons (N) and area is measured in square meters (m²), pressure is measured in newtons per square meter (N/m²). This unit of pressure is called a pascal (Pa). A more useful unit when discussing atmospheric pressure is the kilopascal (kPa), which is 1,000 pascals.

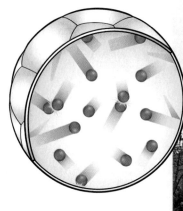

Figure 15 Without the pressure of air inside this volleyball, the ball would be flat.

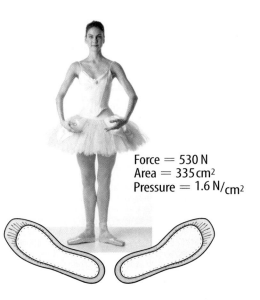

Figure 16 The force of the dancer's weight on pointed toes results in a higher pressure than the same force on flat feet. **Explain** *why the pressure is higher.*

Force = 530 N
Area = 335 cm²
Pressure = 1.6 N/cm²

Force = 530 N
Area = 37 cm²
Pressure = 14 N/cm²

Force and Area You can see from the equation on the opposite page that pressure depends on the quantity of force exerted and the area over which the force is exerted. As the force increases over a given area, pressure increases. If the force decreases, the pressure will decrease. However, if the area changes, the same amount of force can result in different pressure. **Figure 16** shows that if the force of the ballerina's weight is exerted over a smaller area, the pressure increases. If that same force is exerted over a larger area, the pressure will decrease.

☑ Reading Check *What variables does pressure depend on?*

Atmospheric Pressure You can't see it and you usually can't feel it, but the air around you presses on you with tremendous force. The pressure of air also is known as atmospheric pressure because air makes up the atmosphere around Earth. Atmospheric pressure is 101.3 kPa at sea level. This means that air exerts a force of about 101,000 N on every square meter it touches. This is approximately equal to the weight of a large truck.

It might be difficult to think of air as having pressure when you don't notice it. However, you often take advantage of air pressure without even realizing it. Air pressure, for example, enables you to drink from a straw. When you first suck on a straw, you remove the air from it. As you can see in **Figure 17,** air pressure pushes down on the liquid in your glass then forces liquid up into the straw. If you tried to drink through a straw inserted into a sealed, airtight container, you would not have any success because the air would not be able to push down on the surface of the drink.

Figure 17 The downward pressure of air pushes the juice up into the straw.

Air pressure

Figure 18 Atmospheric pressure exerts a force on all surfaces of this dancer's body.
Explain *why she can't feel this pressure.*

Balanced Pressure If air is so forceful, why don't you feel it? The reason is that the pressure exerted outward by the fluids in your body balances the pressure exerted by the atmosphere on the surface of your body. Look at **Figure 18.** The atmosphere exerts a pressure on all surfaces of the dancer's body. She is not crushed by this pressure because the fluids in her body exert a pressure that balances atmospheric pressure.

Variations in Atmospheric Pressure
Atmospheric pressure changes with altitude. Altitude is the height above sea level. As altitude increases atmospheric pressure decreases. This is because fewer air particles are found in a given volume. Fewer particles have fewer collisions, and therefore exert less pressure. This idea was tested in the seventeenth century by a French physician named Blaise Pascal. He designed an experiment in which he filled a balloon only partially with air. He then had the balloon carried to the top of a mountain. **Figure 19** shows that as Pascal predicted, the balloon expanded while being carried up the mountain. Although the amount of air inside the balloon stayed the same, the air pressure pushing in on it from the outside decreased. Consequently, the particles of air inside the balloon were able to spread out further.

Figure 19 Notice how the balloon expands as it is carried up the mountain. The reason is that atmospheric pressure decreases with altitude. With less pressure pushing in on the balloon, the gas particles within the balloon are free to expand.

Air Travel If you travel to higher altitudes, perhaps flying in an airplane or driving up a mountain, you might feel a popping sensation in your ears. As the air pressure drops, the air pressure in your ears becomes greater than the air pressure outside your body. The release of some of the air trapped inside your ears is heard as a pop. Airplanes are pressurized so that the air pressure within the cabin does not change dramatically throughout the course of a flight.

Changes in Gas Pressure

In the same way that atmospheric pressure can vary as conditions change, the pressure of gases in confined containers also can change. The pressure of a gas in a closed container changes with volume and temperature.

Pressure and Volume If you squeeze a portion of a filled balloon, the remaining portion of the balloon becomes more firm. By squeezing it, you decrease the volume of the balloon, forcing the same number of gas particles into a smaller space. As a result, the particles collide with the walls more often, thereby producing greater pressure. This is true as long as the temperature of the gas remains the same. You can see the change in the motion of the particles in **Figure 20.** What will happen if the volume of a gas increases? If you make a container larger without changing its temperature, the gas particles will collide less often and thereby produce a lower pressure.

Predicting a Waterfall

Procedure

1. Fill a **plastic cup** to the brim with **water.**
2. Cover the top of the cup with an **index card.**
3. Predict what will happen if you turn the cup upside down.
4. While holding the index card in place, turn the cup upside down over a sink. Then let go of the card.

Analysis

1. What happened to the water when you turned the cup?
2. How can you explain your observation in terms of the concept of fluid pressure?

Try at Home

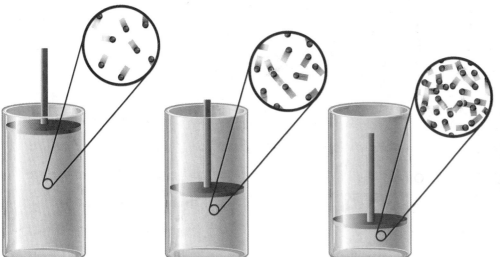

Figure 20 As volume decreases, pressure increases.

As the piston is moved down, the gas particles have less space and collide more often. The pressure increases.

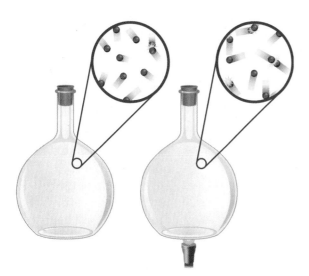

Pressure and Temperature When the volume of a confined gas remains the same, the pressure can change as the temperature of the gas changes. You have learned that temperature rises as the kinetic energy of the particles in a substance increases. The greater the kinetic energy is, the faster the particles move. The faster the speed of the particles is, the more they collide and the greater the pressure is. If the temperature of a confined gas increases, the pressure of the gas will increase, as shown in **Figure 21.**

☑ **Reading Check** *Why would a sealed container of air be crushed after being frozen?*

Figure 21 Even though the volume of this container does not change, the pressure increases as the substance is heated.
Describe *what will happen if the substance is heated too much.*

3.1i: Explain the terms buoyancy and buoyant force in your own words.

Figure 22 The pressure pushing up on an immersed object is greater than the pressure pushing down on it. This difference results in the buoyant force.

Float or Sink

You may have noticed that you feel lighter in water than you do when you climb out of it. While you are under water, you experience water pressure pushing on you in all directions. Just as air pressure increases as you walk down a mountain, water pressure increases as you swim deeper in water. Water pressure increases with depth. As a result, the pressure pushing up on the bottom of an object is greater than the pressure pushing down on it because the bottom of the object is deeper than the top.

The difference in pressure results in an upward force on an object immersed in a fluid, as shown in **Figure 22.** This force is known as the **buoyant force.** If the buoyant force is equal to the weight of an object, the object will float. If the buoyant force is less than the weight of an object, the object will sink.

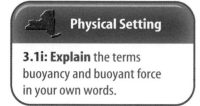

Pressure pushing down

Pressure pushing up

Weight is a force in the downward direction. The buoyant force is in the upward direction. An object will float if the upward force is equal to the downward force.

Weight

Buoyant force

122 CHAPTER 4 States of Matter

Archimedes' Principle

Archimedes' Principle What determines the buoyant force? According to **Archimedes'** (ar kuh MEE deez) **principle,** the buoyant force on an object is equal to the weight of the fluid displaced by the object. In other words, if you place an object in a beaker that already is filled to the brim with water, some water will spill out of the beaker, as in **Figure 23.** If you weigh the spilled water, you will find the buoyant force on the object.

Density Understanding density can help you predict whether an object will float or sink. **Density** is mass divided by volume.

$$\text{density} = \frac{\text{mass}}{\text{volume}}$$

An object will float in a fluid that is more dense than itself and sink in a fluid that is less dense than itself. If an object has the same density, the object will neither sink nor float but instead stay at the same level in the fluid.

Hot Words Hot Topics: Bk 1 pp. 137, 271

Figure 23 When the golf ball was dropped in the large beaker, it displaced some of the water, which was collected and placed into the smaller beaker. **Communicate** *what you know about the weight and the volume of the displaced water.*

Applying Math   Find an Unknown

CALCULATING DENSITY You are given a sample of a solid that has a mass of 10.0 g and a volume of 4.60 cm³. Will it float in liquid water, which has a density of 1.00 g/cm³?

Solution

1 *This is what you know:*
- mass = 10.0 g
- volume = 4.60 cm³
- density of water = 1.00 g/cm³

2 *This is what you need to find:* the density of the sample

3 *This is the procedure you need to use:*
- density = mass/volume
- density = 10.0 g/4.60 cm³ = 2.17 g/cm³
- The density of the sample is greater than the density of water. The sample will sink.

4 *Check your answer:*
- Find the mass of your sample by multiplying the density and the volume.

Practice Problems

1. A 7.40-cm³ sample of mercury has a mass of 102 g. Will it float in water?

2. A 5.0-cm³ sample of aluminum has a mass of 13.5 g. Will it float in water?

For more practice, visit glencoe.com

Pascal's Principle

What happens if you squeeze a plastic container filled with water? If the container is closed, the water has nowhere to go. As a result, the pressure in the water increases by the same amount everywhere in the container—not just where you squeeze or near the top of the container. When a force is applied to a confined fluid, an increase in pressure is transmitted equally to all parts of the fluid. This relationship is known as **Pascal's principle.**

Hydraulic Systems You witness Pascal's principle when a car is lifted up to have its oil changed or if you are in a dentist's chair as it is raised or lowered, as shown in **Figure 24.** These devices, known as hydraulic (hi DRAW lihk) systems, use Pascal's principle to increase force. Look at the tube in **Figure 25.** The force applied to the piston on the left increases the pressure within the fluid. That increase in pressure is transmitted to the piston on the right. Recall that pressure is equal to force divided by area. You can solve for force by multiplying pressure by area.

$$\text{pressure} = \frac{\text{force}}{\text{area}} \quad \text{or} \quad \text{force} = \text{pressure} \times \text{area}$$

If the two pistons on the tube have the same area, the force will be the same on both pistons. If, however, the piston on the right has a greater surface area than the piston on the left, the resulting force will be greater. The same pressure multiplied by a larger area equals a greater force. Hydraulic systems enable people to lift heavy objects using relatively small forces.

Figure 24 A hydraulic lift utilizes Pascal's principle to help lift this car and this dentist's chair.

Physical Setting

3.1h: Define density. Then imagine two similar objects and compare the density of each.

Figure 25 By increasing the area of the piston on the right side of the tube, you can increase the force exerted on the piston. In this way a small force pushing down on the left piston can result in a large force pushing up on the right piston. The force can be great enough to lift a car.

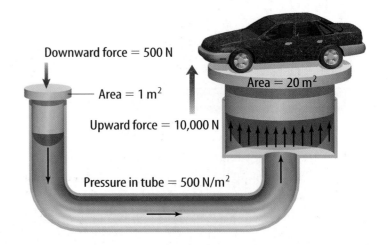

Downward force = 500 N
Area = 1 m²
Upward force = 10,000 N
Area = 20 m²
Pressure in tube = 500 N/m²

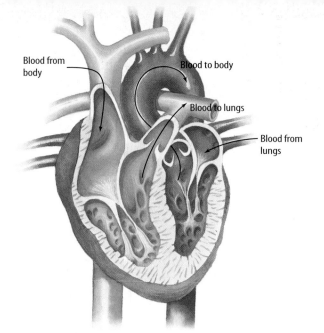

Blood from body
Blood to body
Blood to lungs
Blood from lungs

Figure 26 The heart is responsible for moving blood throughout the body. Two force pumps work together to move blood to and from the lungs and to the rest of the body.

Force Pumps If an otherwise closed container has a hole in it, any fluid in the container will be pushed out the opening when you squeeze it. This arrangement, known as a force pump, makes it possible for you to squeeze toothpaste out of a tube or mustard from a plastic container.

Your heart has two force pumps. One pump pushes blood to the lungs, where it picks up oxygen. The other force pump pushes the oxygen-rich blood to the rest of your body. These pumps are shown in **Figure 26.**

Topic: Blood Pressure
Visit glencoe.com for Web links to information about blood pressure. Find out what the term means, how it changes throughout the human body, and why it is unhealthy to have high blood pressure.

Activity Write a paragraph in your Science Journal that explains why high blood pressure is dangerous.

section 3 review

Summary

Pressure

- Pressure depends on force and area.
- The air around you exerts a pressure.
- The pressure inside your body matches the pressure exerted by air.

Changes in Gas Pressure

- The pressure exerted by a gas depends on its volume and its temperature.

Float or Sink

- Whether an object floats or sinks depends on its density relative to the density of the fluid it's in.

Pascal's Principle

- This principle relates pressure and area to force.

Self Check

1. **Describe** what happens to pressure as the force exerted on a given area increases.
2. **Describe** how atmospheric pressure changes as altitude increases.
3. **State** Pascal's principle in your own words.
4. **Infer** An object floats in a fluid. What can you say about the buoyant force on the object?
5. **Think Critically** All the air is removed from a sealed metal can. After the air has been removed, the can looks as if it were crushed. Why?

Hot Words Hot Topics: BK 1 pp. 274-276

Applying Math

6. **Simple Equations** What pressure is created when 5.0 N of force are applied to an area of 2.0 m^2? How does the pressure change if the force is increased to 10.0 N? What about if instead the area is decreased to 1.0 m^2?

LAB

Design Your Own

Design Your  Own Ship

▶ Real-World Question

It is amazing to watch ships that are taller than buildings float easily on water. Passengers and cargo are carried on these ships in addition to the tremendous weight of the ship itself. How can you determine the size of a ship needed to keep a certain mass of cargo afloat?

▶ Form a Hypothesis

Think about Archimedes' principle and how it relates to buoyant force. Form a hypothesis to explain how the volume of water displaced by a ship relates to the mass of cargo the ship can carry.

▶ Test Your Hypothesis

Make a Plan

1. Obtain a set of marbles or other items from your teacher. This is the cargo that your ship must carry. Think about the type of ship

Cargo ship

Goals

■ **Design** an experiment that uses Archimedes' principle to determine the size of ship needed to carry a given amount of cargo in such a way that the top of the ship is even with the surface of the water.

Possible Materials

balance
small plastic cups (2)
graduated cylinder
metric ruler
scissors
marbles (cupful)
sink
*basin, pan, or bucket
*Alternate materials

Safety Precautions

126

you will design. Consider the types of materials you will use. Decide how your group is going to test your hypothesis.

2. **List** the steps you need to follow to test your hypothesis. Include in your plan how you will measure the mass of your ship and cargo, calculate the volume of water your ship must displace in order to float with its cargo, and measure the volume and mass of the displaced water. Also, explain how you will design your ship so that it will float with the top of the ship even with the surface of the water. Make the ship.

3. **Prepare** a data table in your Science Journal to use as your group collects data. Think about what data you need to collect.

Follow Your Plan

1. Make sure your teacher approves your plan before you start.

2. Perform your experiment as planned. Be sure to follow all proper safety procedures. In particular, clean up any spilled water immediately.

3. Record your observations carefully and complete the data table in your Science Journal.

⊙ *Analyze Your Data*

1. **Write** your calculations showing how you determined the volume of displaced water needed to make your ship and cargo float.

2. Did your ship float at the water's surface, sink, or float above the water's surface? Draw a diagram of your ship in the water.

3. **Explain** how your experimental results agreed or failed to agree with your hypothesis.

⊙ *Conclude and Apply*

1. If your ship sank, how would you change your experiment or calculations to correct the problem? What changes would you make if your ship floated too high in the water?

2. What does the density of a ship's cargo have to do with the volume of cargo the ship can carry? What about the density of the water?

*C*ommunicating
Your Data

Compare your results with other students' data. Prepare a combined data table or summary showing how the calculations affect the success of the ship. **For more help, refer to the** Science Skill Handbook.

Oops! Accidents in SCIENCE

The Incredible Stretching Goo

A serious search turns up a toy

During World War II, when natural resources were scarce and needed for the war effort, the U.S. government asked an engineer to come up with an inexpensive alternative to synthetic rubber. While researching the problem and looking for solutions, the engineer dropped boric acid into silicone oil. The result of these two substances mixing together was—a goo!

Because of its molecular structure, the goo could bounce and stretch in all directions. The engineer also discovered the goo could break into pieces. When strong pressure is applied to the substance, it reacts like a solid and breaks apart. Even though the combination was versatile—and quite amusing, the U.S. government decided the new substance wasn't a good substitute for synthetic rubber.

A few years later, the recipe for the stretch material fell into the hands of a businessperson, who saw the goo's potential—as a toy. The toymaker paid $147 for rights to the boric acid and silicone oil mixture. And in 1949 it was sold at toy stores for the first time. The material was packaged in a plastic egg and it took the U.S. by storm. Today, the acid and oil mixture comes in a multitude of colors and almost every child has played with it at some time.

The substance can be used for more than child's play. Its sticky consistency makes it good for cleaning computer keyboards and removing small specks of lint from fabrics.

People use it to make impressions of newspaper print or comics. Athletes strengthen their grips by grasping it over and over. Astronauts use it to anchor tools on spacecraft in zero gravity. All in all, a most *eggs-cellent* idea!

Research As a group, examine a sample of the colorful, sticky, stretch toy made of boric acid and silicone oil. Then brainstorm some practical—and impractical—uses for the substance.

Science online

For more information, visit glencoe.com

Reviewing Main Ideas

Section 1 Matter

1. All matter is composed of tiny particles that are in constant motion.

2. In the solid state, the attractive force between particles holds them in place to vibrate.

3. Particles in the liquid state have defined volumes and are free to move about within the liquid.

Section 2 Changes of State

1. Thermal energy is the total energy of the particles in a sample of matter. Temperature is the average kinetic energy of the particles in a sample.

2. An object gains thermal energy when it changes from a solid to a liquid, or when it changes from a liquid to a gas.

3. An object loses thermal energy when it changes from a gas to a liquid, or when it changes from a liquid to a solid.

Section 3 Behavior of Fluids

1. Pressure is force divided by area.

2. Fluids exert a buoyant force in the upward direction on objects immersed in them.

3. An object will float in a fluid that is more dense than itself.

4. Pascal's principle states that pressure applied to a liquid is transmitted evenly throughout the liquid.

Visualizing Main Ideas

Copy and complete the following concept map on matter.

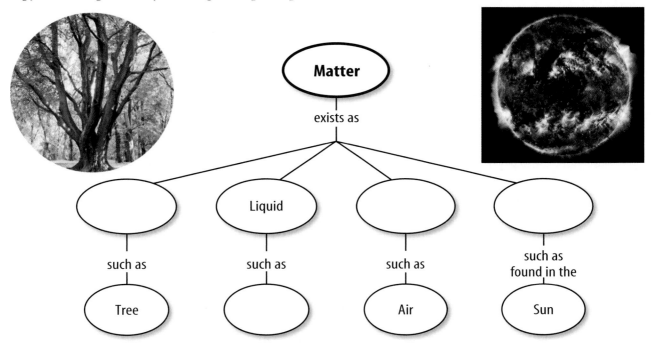

Using Vocabulary

Archimedes'
  principle p. 123
buoyant force p. 127
condensation p. 115
density p. 123
freezing p. 113
gas p. 108
heat p. 110
liquid p. 106
matter p. 104

melting p. 111
Pascal's principle p. 124
pressure p. 114
solid p. 105
surface tension p. 107
temperature p. 110
thermal energy p. 109
vaporization p. 119
viscosity p. 107

Fill in the blanks with the correct vocabulary word.

1. A(n) _____ can change shape and volume.

2. A(n) _____ has a different shape but the same volume in any container.

3. _____ is thermal energy moving from one substance to another.

4. _____ is a measure of the average kinetic energy of the particles of a substance.

5. A substance changes from a gas to a liquid during the process of _____.

6. A liquid becomes a gas during _____.

7. _____ is mass divided by volume.

8. _____ is force divided by area.

9. _____ explains what happens when force is applied to a confined fluid.

Checking Concepts

Choose the word or phrase that best answers the question.

10. Which of these is a crystalline solid?
    A) glass   C) rubber
    B) sugar   D) plastic

11. Which description best describes a solid?
    A) It has a definite shape and volume.
    B) It has a definite shape but not a definite volume.
    C) It adjusts to the shape of its container.
    D) It can flow.

12. What property enables you to float a needle on water?
    A) viscosity   C) surface tension
    B) temperature   D) crystal structure

13. What happens to an object as its kinetic energy increases?
    A) It holds more tightly to nearby objects.
    B) Its mass increases.
    C) Its particles move more slowly.
    D) Its particles move faster.

14. During which process do particles of matter release energy?
    A) melting   C) sublimation
    B) freezing   D) boiling

15. How does water vapor in air form clouds?
    A) melting   C) condensation
    B) evaporation   D) sublimation

16. Which is a unit of pressure?
    A) N   C) g/cm^3
    B) kg   D) N/m^2

17. Which change results in an increase in gas pressure in a balloon?
    A) decrease in temperature
    B) decrease in volume
    C) increase in volume
    D) increase in altitude

18. In which case will an object float on a fluid?
    A) Buoyant force is greater than weight.
    B) Buoyant force is less than weight.
    C) Buoyant force equals weight.
    D) Buoyant force equals zero.

Use the photo below to answer question 19.

19. In the photo above, the water in the small beaker was displaced when the golf ball was added to the large beaker. What principle does this show?
   A) Pascal's principle
   B) the principle of surface tension
   C) Archimedes' principle
   D) the principle of viscosity

20. Which is equal to the buoyant force on an object?
   A) volume of the object
   B) weight of the displaced fluid
   C) weight of object
   D) volume of fluid

Thinking Critically

21. **Explain** why steam causes more severe burns than boiling water.

22. **Explain** why a bathroom mirror becomes fogged while you take a shower.

23. **Form Operational Definitions** Write operational definitions that explain the properties of and differences among solids, liquids, and gases.

24. **Determine** A king's crown has a volume of 110 cm^3 and a mass of 1,800 g. The density of gold is 19.3 g/cm^3. Is the crown pure gold?

25. **Infer** Why do some balloons pop when they are left in sunlight for too long?

Performance Activities

26. **Storyboard** Create a visual-aid storyboard to show ice changing to steam. There should be a minimum of five frames.

Hot Words Hot Topics: Bk 1 (27) p. 195; (28) pp. 195, 283-284

Applying Math

Use the graph below to answer question 27.

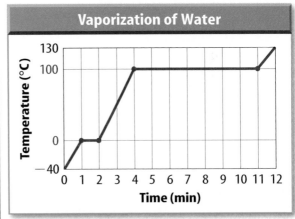

Vaporization of Water

27. **Explain** how this graph would change if a greater volume of water were heated. How would it stay the same?

Use the table below to answer question 28.

Water Pressure			
Depth (m)	Pressure (atm)	Depth (m)	Pressure (atm)
0	1.0	100	11.0
25	3.5	125	13.5
50	6.0	150	16.0
75	8.5	175	18.5

28. **Make and Use Graphs** In July of 2001, Yasemin Dalkilic of Turkey dove to a depth of 105 m without any scuba equipment. Make a depth-pressure graph for the data above. Based on your graph, how does water pressure vary with depth? Note: The pressure at sea level, 101.3 kPa, is called one atmosphere (atm).

Record your answers on the answer sheet provided by your teacher or on a sheet of paper.

1 In which state of matter do particles stay close together, yet are able to move past one another?
(1) solid
(3) liquid
(2) gas
(4) plasma

Use the illustration below to answer questions 2 and 3.

2 Which statement is true about the volume of the water displaced when the golf ball was dropped into the large beaker?
(1) It is equal to the volume of the golf ball.
(2) It is greater than the volume of the golf ball.
(3) It is less than the volume of the golf ball.
(4) It is twice the volume of a golf ball.

3 What do you know about the buoyant force on the golf ball?
(1) It is equal to the density of the water displaced.
(2) It is equal to the volume of the water displaced.
(3) It is less than the weight of the water displaced.
(4) It is equal to the weight of the water displaced.

4 What is the process called when a gas cools to form a liquid?
(1) condensation
(3) boiling
(2) sublimation
(4) freezing

5 Which of the following is an amorphous solid?
(1) diamond
(3) glass
(2) sugar
(4) sand

6 Which description best describes a liquid?
(1) It has a definite shape and volume.
(2) It has a definite volume but not a definite shape.
(3) It expands to fill the shape and volume of its container.
(4) It cannot flow.

7 During which processes do particles of matter absorb energy?
(1) freezing and boiling
(2) condensation and melting
(3) melting and vaporization
(4) sublimation and freezing

Use the illustration below to answer questions 8 and 9.

8 What happens as the piston moves down?
(1) The volume of the gas increases.
(2) The volume of the gas decreases.
(3) The gas particles collide less often.
(4) The pressure of the gas decreases.

9 What relationship between the volume and pressure of a gas does this illustrate?
(1) As volume decreases, pressure decreases.
(2) As volume decreases, pressure increases.
(3) As volume decreases, pressure remains the same.
(4) As the volume increases, pressure remains the same.

Record your answers on the answer sheet provided by your teacher or on a sheet of paper.

Use the illustration below to answer questions 10 and 11.

10 If the force exerted by the dancer is 510 N, what is the pressure she exerts if the area is 335 cm² on the left and 37 cm² on the right?

11 Compare the pressure the dancer would exert on the floor if she were wearing large clown shoes to the photo on the left.

12 Analyze how some insects are able to move around on the surface of a lake or pond.

13 How does the weight of a floating object compare with the buoyant force acting on the object?

14 Compare and contrast evaporation and boiling.

Use the illustration below to answer questions 15 and 16.

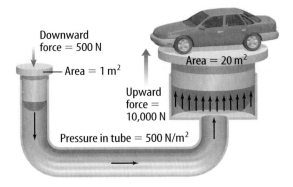

15 Name and explain the principle that is used in lifting the car.

16 Analyze what would happen if you doubled the area of the piston on the right side of the hydraulic system.

17 Compare the arrangement and movement of the particles in a solid, a liquid, and a gas.

PS 3.2a: During a physical change a substance keeps its chemical composition and properties.
4.1d: Different forms of energy include heat, light, electrical, mechanical, sound, nuclear, and chemical. Energy is transformed in many ways. **Also covered:** 4.1e, 4.2a, 4.2b, 4.5a, 5.2c.

chapter

5

Thermal Energy

chapter preview

sections

1 **Temperature and Thermal Energy**

2 **Heat**
   Lab   Heating Up and Cooling Down

3 **Engines and Refrigerators**
   Lab   Comparing Thermal Insulators

   Virtual Lab   How do the insulation properties of various materials compare?

Fastest to the Finish Line

In order to reach an extraordinary speed in a short distance, this dragster depends on more than an aerodynamic design. Its engine must transform the thermal energy produced by burning fuel to mechanical energy, which propels the dragster down the track.

Science Journal   Describe five things that you do to make yourself feel warmer or cooler.

Start-Up Activities

Measuring Temperature

When you leave a glass of ice water on a kitchen table, the ice gradually melts and the temperature of the water increases. What is temperature, and why does the temperature of the ice water increase? In this lab you will explore one way of determining temperature.

1. Obtain three pans. Fill one pan with lukewarm water. Fill a second pan with cold water and crushed ice. Fill a third pan with very warm tap water. Label each pan.

2. Soak one of your hands in the warm water for one minute. Remove your hand from the warm water and put it in the lukewarm water. Does the lukewarm water feel cool or warm?

3. Now soak your hand in the cold water for one minute. Remove your hand from the cold water and place it in the lukewarm water. Does the lukewarm water feel cool or warm?

4. **Think Critically** Write a paragraph in your Science Journal discussing whether your sense of touch would make a useful thermometer.

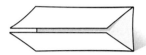

Thermal Energy Make the following Foldable to help you identify how thermal energy, heat, and temperature are related.

STEP 1 Fold a vertical piece of paper into thirds.

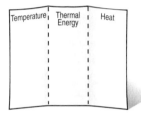

STEP 2 Turn the paper horizontally. Unfold and label the three columns as shown.

Temperature	Thermal Energy	Heat

Read for Main Ideas Before you read the chapter, write down what you know about temperature, thermal energy, and heat on the appropriate tab. As you read, add to and correct what you wrote. Write what you have learned about the relationship between heat and thermal energy on the back of your Foldable.

 Preview this chapter's content and activities at glencoe.com

Temperature and Thermal Energy

What **You'll Learn**

■ **Explain** how temperature is related to kinetic energy.
■ **Describe** three scales used for measuring temperature.
■ **Define** thermal energy.

Why **It's Important**

The movement of thermal energy toward or away from your body determines whether you feel too cold, too hot, or just right.

Review Vocabulary
kinetic energy: energy a moving object has that increases as the speed of the object increases

New Vocabulary
● temperature
● thermal energy

What is temperature?

Imagine it's a hot day and you jump into a swimming pool to cool off. When you first hit the water, you might think it feels cold. Perhaps someone else, who has been swimming for a few minutes, thinks the water feels warm. When you swim in water, touch a hot pan, or swallow a cold drink, your sense of touch tells you whether something is hot or cold. However, the words *cold*, *warm*, and *hot* can mean different things to different people.

Temperature How hot or cold something feels is related to its temperature. To understand temperature, think of a glass of water sitting on a table. The water might seem perfectly still, but water is made of molecules that are in constant, random motion. Because these molecules are always moving, they have energy of motion, or kinetic energy.

However, water molecules in random motion don't all move at the same speed. Some are moving faster and some are moving slower. **Temperature** is a measure of the average value of the kinetic energy of the molecules in random motion. The more kinetic energy the molecules have, the higher the temperature. Molecules have more kinetic energy when they are moving faster. So the higher the temperature, the faster the molecules are moving, as shown in **Figure 1.**

Figure 1 The temperature of a substance depends on how fast its molecules are moving. Water molecules are moving faster in the hot water on the left than in the cold water on the right.

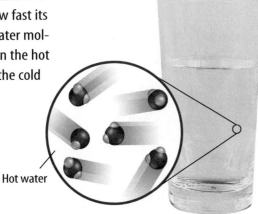

Cold water

Hot water

Thermal Expansion It wasn't an earthquake that caused the sidewalk to buckle in **Figure 2**. Hot weather caused the concrete to expand so much that it cracked, and the pieces squeezed each other upward. When the temperature of an object is increased, its molecules speed up and tend to move farther apart. This causes the object to expand. When the object is cooled, its molecules slow down and move closer together. This causes the object to shrink, or contract.

Almost all substances expand when they are heated and contract when they are cooled. The amount of expansion or contraction depends on the type of material and the change in temperature. For example, liquids usually expand more than solids. Also, the greater the change in temperature, the more an object expands or contracts.

Figure 2 Most objects expand as their temperatures increase. Pieces of this concrete sidewalk forced each other upward when the concrete expanded on a hot day.

 *Why do materials expand when their temperatures increase?*

Measuring Temperature

The temperature of an object depends on the average kinetic energy of all the molecules in an object. However, molecules are so small and objects contain so many of them, that it is impossible to measure the kinetic energy of all the individual molecules.

A more practical way to measure temperature is to use a thermometer. Thermometers usually use the expansion and contraction of materials to measure temperature. One common type of thermometer uses a glass tube containing a liquid. When the temperature of the liquid increases, it expands so that the height of the liquid in the tube depends on the temperature.

Temperature Scales To be able to give a number for the temperature, a thermometer has to have a temperature scale. Two common temperature scales are the Fahrenheit and Celsius scales, shown in **Figure 3**.

On the Fahrenheit scale, the freezing point of water is given the temperature 32°F and the boiling point 212°F. The space between the boiling point and the freezing point is divided into 180 equal degrees. The Fahrenheit scale is used mainly in the United States.

On the Celsius temperature scale, the freezing point of water is given the temperature 0°C and the boiling point is given the temperature 100°C. Because there are only 100 Celsius degrees between the boiling and freezing point of water, Celsius degrees are bigger than Fahrenheit degrees.

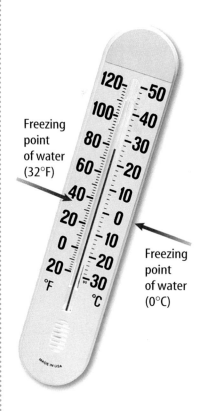

Freezing point of water (32°F)

Freezing point of water (0°C)

Figure 3 The Fahrenheit and Celsius scales are commonly used temperature scales.

Physical Setting

3.3b, 4.1e: Explain how temperature and kinetic energy are related.

Converting Fahrenheit and Celsius You can convert temperatures back and forth between the two temperature scales by using the following equations.

Temperature Conversion Equations

To convert temperature in °F to °C: $°C = (\frac{5}{9})(°F - 32)$

To convert temperature in °C to °F: $°F = (\frac{9}{5})(°C) + 32$

For example, to convert 68°F to degrees Celsius, first subtract 32, multiply by 5, then divide by 9. The result is 20°C.

The Kelvin Scale Another temperature scale that is sometimes used is the Kelvin scale. On this scale, 0 K is the lowest temperature an object can have. This temperature is known as absolute zero. The size of a degree on the Kelvin scale is the same as on the Celsius scale. You can change from Celsius degrees to Kelvin degrees by adding 273 to the Celsius temperature.

$$K = °C + 273$$

Hot Words Hot Topics: Bk 1 pp. 120-122, 271

Applying Math   Solving a Simple Equation

CONVERTING TO CELSIUS On a hot summer day, a Fahrenheit thermometer shows the temperature to be 86°F. What is this temperature on the Celsius scale?

Solution

1 *This is what you know:*   Fahrenheit temperature: °F = 86

2 *This is what you need to find:*   Celsius temperature: °C

3 *This is the procedure you need to use:*   Substitute the Fahrenheit temperature into the equation that converts temperature in °F to °C.

$$°C = (\frac{5}{9})(°F - 32) = \frac{5}{9}(86 - 32) = \frac{5}{9}(54) = 30°C$$

4 *Check the answer:*   Add 32 to your answer and multiply by 9/5. The result should be the given Fahrenheit temperature.

Practice Problems

1. A student's body temperature is 98.6°F. What is this temperature on the Celsius scale?

2. A temperature of 57°C was recorded in 1913 at Death Valley, California. What is this temperature on the Fahrenheit scale?

 For more practice visit glencoe.com

Thermal Energy

The temperature of an object is related to the average kinetic energy of molecules in random motion. But molecules also have potential energy. Potential energy is energy that the molecules have that can be converted into kinetic energy. The sum of the kinetic and potential energy of all the molecules in an object is the **thermal energy** of the object.

The Potential Energy of Molecules When you hold a ball above the ground, it has potential energy. When you drop the ball, its potential energy is converted into kinetic energy as the ball falls toward Earth. It is the attractive force of gravity between Earth and the ball that gives the ball potential energy.

The molecules in a material also exert attractive forces on each other. As a result, the molecules in a material have potential energy. As the molecules get closer together or farther apart, their potential energy changes.

Increasing Thermal Energy Temperature and thermal energy are different. Suppose you have two glasses filled with the same amount of milk, and at the same temperature. If you pour both glasses of milk into a pitcher, as shown in **Figure 4,** the temperature of the milk won't change. However, because there are more molecules of milk in the pitcher than in either glass, the thermal energy of the milk in the pitcher is greater than the thermal energy of the milk in either glass.

Figure 4 At the same temperature, the larger volume of milk in the pitcher has more thermal energy than the smaller volumes of milk in either glass.

---

section ① review

Summary

Temperature

- Temperature is related to the average kinetic energy of the molecules an object contains.
- Most materials expand when their temperatures increase.

Measuring Temperature

- On the Celsius scale the freezing point of water is 0°C and the boiling point is 100°C.
- On the Fahrenheit scale the freezing point of water is 32°F and the boiling point is 212°F.

Thermal Energy

- The thermal energy of an object is the sum of the kinetic and potential energy of all the molecules in an object.

Self Check

1. **Explain** the difference between temperature and thermal energy. How are they related?
2. **Determine** which temperature is always larger—an object's Celsius temperature or its Kelvin temperature.
3. **Explain** how kinetic energy and thermal energy are related.
4. **Describe** how a thermometer uses the thermal expansion of a material to measure temperature.

Hot Words Hot Topics: Bk 1 pp. 120-122, 271

Applying Math

5. **Convert Temperatures** A turkey cooking in an oven will be ready when the internal temperature reaches 180°F. Convert this temperature to °C and K.

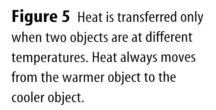

section

2

Heat

as you read

What You'll Learn

- **Explain** the difference between thermal energy and heat.
- **Describe** three ways heat is transferred.
- **Identify** materials that are insulators or conductors.

Why It's Important

To keep you comfortable, the flow of heat into and out of your house must be controlled.

◉ Review Vocabulary

electromagnetic wave: a wave produced by vibrating electric charges that can travel in matter and empty space

New Vocabulary

- heat
- conduction
- radiation
- convection
- conductor
- specific heat
- thermal pollution

Heat and Thermal Energy

It's the heat of the day. Heat the oven to 375°F. A heat wave has hit the Midwest. You've often heard the word *heat*, but what is it? Is it something you can see? Can an object have heat? Is heat anything like thermal energy? **Heat** is thermal energy that is transferred from one object to another when the objects are at different temperatures. The amount of heat that is transferred when two objects are brought into contact depends on the difference in temperature between the objects.

For example, no heat is transferred when two pots of boiling water are touching, because the water in both pots is at the same temperature. However, heat is transferred from the pot of hot water in **Figure 5** that is touching a pot of cold water. The hot water cools down and the cold water gets hotter. Heat continues to be transferred until both objects are the same temperature.

Transfer of Heat When heat is transferred, thermal energy always moves from warmer to cooler objects. Heat never flows from a cooler object to a warmer object. The warmer object loses thermal energy and becomes cooler as the cooler object gains thermal energy and becomes warmer. This process of heat transfer can occur in three ways—by conduction, radiation, or convection.

Figure 5 Heat is transferred only when two objects are at different temperatures. Heat always moves from the warmer object to the cooler object.

Conduction

When you eat hot pizza, you experience conduction. As the hot pizza touches your mouth, heat moves from the pizza to your mouth. This transfer of heat by direct contact is called conduction. **Conduction** occurs when the particles in a material collide with neighboring particles.

Imagine holding an ice cube in your hand, as in **Figure 6.** The faster-moving molecules in your warm hand bump against the slower-moving molecules in the cold ice. In these collisions, energy is passed from molecule to molecule. Heat flows from your warmer hand to the colder ice, and the slow-moving molecules in the ice move faster. As a result, the ice becomes warmer and its temperature increases. Molecules in your hand move more slowly as they lose thermal energy, and your hand becomes cooler.

Conduction usually occurs most easily in solids and liquids, where atoms and molecules are close together. Then atoms and molecules need to move only a short distance before they bump into one another and transfer energy. As a result, heat is transferred more rapidly by conduction in solids and liquids than in gases.

 **Reading Check** *Why does conduction occur more easily in solids and liquids than in gases?*

Radiation

On a beautiful, clear day, you walk outside and notice the warmth of the Sun. You know that the Sun heats Earth, but how does this transfer of thermal energy occur? Heat transfer does not occur by conduction because almost no matter exists between the Sun and Earth. Instead, heat is transferred from the Sun to Earth by radiation. Heat transfer by **radiation** occurs when energy is transferred by electromagnetic waves. These waves carry energy through empty space, as well as through matter. The transfer of thermal energy by radiation can occur in empty space, as well as in solids, liquids, and gases.

The Sun is not the only source of radiation. All objects emit electromagnetic radiation, although warm objects emit more radiation than cool objects. The warmth you feel when you sit next to a fireplace is due to heat transferred by radiation from the fire to your skin.

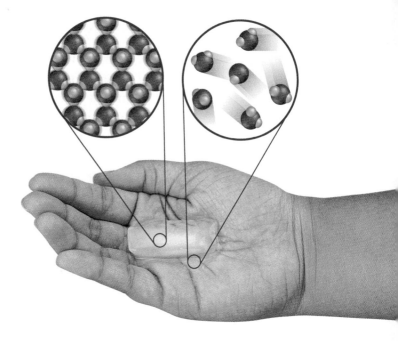

Figure 6 An ice cube in your hand melts because of conduction. The solid ice melts, becoming liquid water. Molecules in the water move faster than molecules in the ice.
Explain *how the thermal energy of the ice cube changes.*

Physical Setting

4.2a, 4.2b: Heat moves in predictable ways, flowing from warmer objects to cooler ones, until both reach the same temperature. **Explain** how this statement is true for conduction, radiation, and convection. Provide examples to support your responses.

Comparing Rates of Melting

Procedure

1. Prepare ice water by filling a **glass** with ice and then adding water. Let the glass sit until all the ice melts.
2. Place an ice cube in a **coffee cup**.
3. Place a similar-sized ice cube in another **coffee cup** and add ice water to a depth of about 1 cm.
4. Time how long it takes both ice cubes to melt.

Analysis

1. Which ice cube melted fastest? Why?
2. Is air or water a better insulator? Explain.

Convection

When you heat a pot of water on a stove, heat can be transferred through the water by a process other than conduction and radiation. In a gas or liquid, molecules can move much more easily than they can in a solid. As a result, the more energetic molecules can travel from one place to another, and carry their energy along with them. This transfer of thermal energy by the movement of molecules from one part of a material to another is called **convection.**

Transferring Heat by Convection As a pot of water is heated, heat is transferred by convection. First, thermal energy is transferred to the water molecules at the bottom of the pot from the stove. These water molecules move faster as their thermal energy increases. The faster-moving molecules tend to be farther apart than the slower-moving molecules in the cooler water above. Because the molecules are farther apart in the warm water, this water is less dense than the cooler water. As a result, the warm water rises and is replaced at the bottom of the pot by cooler water. The cooler water is heated, rises, and the cycle is repeated until all the water in the pan is at the same temperature.

Natural Convection Natural convection occurs when a warmer, less dense fluid is pushed away by a cooler, denser fluid. For example, imagine the shore of a lake. During the day, the water is cooler than the land. As shown in **Figure 7,** air above the warm land is heated by conduction. When the air gets hotter, its particles move faster and get farther from each other, making the air less dense. The cooler, denser air from over the lake flows in over the land, pushing the less dense air upward. You feel this movement of incoming cool air as wind. The cooler air then is heated by the land and also begins to rise.

Figure 7 Wind movement near a lake or ocean can result from natural convection. Air is heated by the land and becomes less dense. Denser cool air rushes in, pushing the warm air up. The cooler air then is heated by the land and the cycle is repeated.

Warm air

Cool air

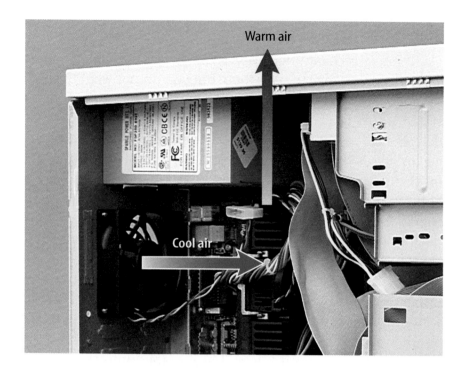

Warm air

Cool air

Figure 8 This computer uses forced convection to keep the electronic components surrounded by cooler air.
Identify *another example of forced convection.*

Forced Convection

Sometimes convection can be forced. Forced convection occurs when an outside force pushes a fluid, such as air or water, to make it move and transfer heat. A fan is one type of device that is used to move air. For example, computers use fans to keep their electronic components from getting too hot, which can damage them. The fan blows cool air onto the hot electronic components, as shown in **Figure 8.** Heat from the electronic components is transferred to the air around them by conduction. The warm air is pushed away as cool air rushes in. The hot components then continue to lose heat as the fan blows cool air over them.

Thermal Conductors

Why are cooking pans usually made of metal? Why does the handle of a metal spoon in a bowl of hot soup become warm? The answer to both questions is that metal is a good conductor. A **conductor** is any material that easily transfers heat. Some materials are good conductors because of the types of atoms or chemical compounds they are made up of.

Reading Check *What is a conductor?*

Remember that an atom has a nucleus surrounded by one or more electrons. Certain materials, such as metals, have some electrons that are not held tightly by the nucleus and are freer to move around. These loosely held electrons can bump into other atoms and help transfer thermal energy. The best conductors of heat are metals such as gold and copper.

Mini LAB

Observing Convection

Procedure

1. Fill a **250-mL beaker** with room-temperature **water** and let it stand undisturbed for at least 1 min.
2. Using a **hot plate**, heat a small amount of water in a **50-mL beaker** until it is almost boiling.
   WARNING: *Do not touch the heated hot plate.*
3. Carefully drop a **penny** into the hot water and let it stand for about 1 min.
4. Take the penny out of the hot water with **metal tongs** and place it on a table. Immediately place the 250-mL beaker on the penny.
5. Using a **dropper,** gently place one drop of **food coloring** on the bottom of the 250-mL beaker of water.
6. Observe what happens in the beaker for several minutes.

Analysis
What happened when you placed the food coloring in the 250-mL beaker? Why?

Animal Insulation
To survive in its arctic environment, a polar bear needs good insulation against the cold. Underneath its fur, a polar bear has 10 cm of insulating blubber. Research how animals in polar regions are able to keep themselves warm. Summarize the different ways in your Science Journal.

Figure 9 The insulation in houses and buildings helps reduce the transfer of heat between the air inside and air outside.

Thermal Insulators

If you're cooking food, you want the pan to conduct heat easily from the stove to your food, but you do not want the heat to move easily to the handle of the pan. An insulator is a material in which heat doesn't flow easily. Most pans have handles that are made from insulators. Liquids and gases are usually better insulators than solids are. Air is a good insulator, and many insulating materials contain air spaces that reduce the transfer of heat by conduction within the material. Materials that are good conductors, such as metals, are poor insulators, and poor conductors are good insulators.

Houses and buildings are made with insulating materials to reduce heat conduction between the inside and outside. Fluffy insulation like that shown in **Figure 9** is put in the walls. Some windows have double layers of glass that sandwich a layer of air or other insulating gas. This reduces the outward flow of heat in the winter and the inward flow of heat in the summer.

Heat Absorption

On a hot day, you can walk barefoot across the lawn, but the asphalt pavement of a street is too hot to walk on. Why is the pavement hotter than the grass? The change in temperature of an object as it absorbs heat depends on the material it is made of.

Specific Heat The amount of heat needed to change the temperature of a substance is related to its specific heat. The **specific heat** of a substance is the amount of heat needed to raise the temperature of 1 kg of that substance by 1°C.

More heat is needed to change the temperature of a material with a high specific heat than one with a low specific heat. For example, the sand on a beach has a lower specific heat than water. When you're at the beach during the day, the sand feels much warmer than the water does. Radiation from the Sun warms the sand and the water. Because of its lower specific heat, the sand heats up faster than the water. At night, however, the sand feels cool and the water feels warmer. The temperature of the water changes more slowly than the temperature of the sand as they both lose thermal energy to the cooler night air.

Thermal Pollution

Some electric power plants and factories that use water for cooling produce hot water as a by-product. If this hot water is released into an ocean, lake, or river, it will raise the temperature of the water nearby. This increase in the temperature of a body of water caused by adding warmer water is called **thermal pollution.** Rainwater that is heated after it falls on warm roads or parking lots also can cause thermal pollution if it runs off into a river or lake.

Effects of Thermal Pollution Increasing the water temperature causes fish and other aquatic organisms to use more oxygen. Because warmer water contains less dissolved oxygen than cooler water, some organisms can die due to a lack of oxygen. Also, in warmer water, many organisms become more sensitive to chemical pollutants, parasites, and diseases.

Reducing Thermal Pollution Thermal pollution can be reduced by cooling the warm water produced by factories, power plants, and runoff before it is released into a body of water. Cooling towers like the ones shown in **Figure 10** are used to cool the water used by some power plants and factories.

Figure 10 This power plant uses cooling towers to cool the warm water produced by the power plant.

section 2 review

Summary

Heat and Thermal Energy

- Heat is the transfer of thermal energy due to a temperature difference.
- Heat always moves from a higher temperature to a lower temperature.

Conduction, Radiation, and Convection

- Conduction is the transfer of thermal energy when substances are in direct contact.
- Radiation is the transfer of thermal energy by electromagnetic waves.
- Convection is the transfer of thermal energy by the movement of matter.

Thermal Conductors and Specific Heat

- A thermal conductor is a material in which heat moves easily.
- The specific heat of a substance is the amount of heat needed to raise the temperature of 1 kg of the substance by 1°C.

Self Check

1. **Explain** why materials such as plastic foam, feathers, and fur are poor conductors of heat.
2. **Explain** why the sand on a beach cools down at night more quickly than the ocean water.
3. **Infer** If a substance can contain thermal energy, can a substance also contain heat?
4. **Describe** how heat is transferred from one place to another by convection.
5. **Explain** why a blanket keeps you warm.
6. **Think Critically** In order to heat a room evenly, should heating vents be placed near the floor or near the ceiling of the room? Explain.

Applying Skills

7. **Design an Experiment** to determine whether wood or iron is a better thermal conductor. Identify the dependent and independent variables in your experiment.

Heating Up and Cooling Down

Do you remember how long it took for a cup of hot chocolate to cool before you could take a sip? The hotter the chocolate, the longer it seemed to take to cool.

▶ *Real-World Question*

How does the temperature of a liquid affect how quickly it warms or cools?

Goals
■ **Measure** the temperature change of water at different temperatures.
■ **Infer** how the rate of heating or cooling depends on the initial water temperature.

Materials
thermometers (5)
400-mL beakers (5)
stopwatch
*watch with second hand
hot plate
*Alternate materials

Safety Precautions

WARNING: *Do not use mercury thermometers. Use caution when heating with a hot plate. Hot and cold glass appears the same.*

▶ *Procedure*

1. Make a data table to record the temperature of water in five beakers every minute from 0 to 10 min.

2. Fill one beaker with 100 mL of water. Place the beaker on a hot plate and bring the water to a boil. Carefully remove the hot beaker from the hot plate.

3. Record the water temperature at minute 0, and then every minute for 10 min.

4. Repeat step 3 starting with hot tap water, cold tap water, refrigerated water, and ice water with the ice removed.

▶ *Conclude and Apply*

1. **Graph** your data. **Plot and label** lines for all five beakers on one graph.

2. **Calculate** the rate of heating or cooling for the water in each beaker by subtracting the initial temperature of the water from the final temperature and then dividing this answer by 10 min.

3. **Infer** from your results how the difference between room temperature and the initial temperature of the water affected the rate at which it heated up or cooled down.

𝒞ommunicating
Your Data

Share your data and graphs with other classmates and explain any differences among your data.

PS 4.1d: Different forms of energy include heat, light, electrical, mechanical, sound, nuclear, and chemical. Energy is transformed in many ways. **4.5a:** Energy cannot be created or destroyed, but only changed from one form into another. **Also covered:** 5.2c.

Engines and Refrigerators

Heat Engines

The engines used in cars, motorcycles, trucks, and other vehicles, like the one shown in **Figure 11,** are heat engines. A **heat engine** is a device that converts thermal energy into mechanical energy. Mechanical energy is the sum of the kinetic and potential energy of an object. The heat engine in a car converts thermal energy into mechanical energy when it makes the car move faster, causing the car's kinetic energy to increase.

Forms of Energy There are other forms of energy besides thermal energy and mechanical energy. For example, chemical energy is energy stored in the chemical bonds between atoms. Radiant energy is the energy carried by electromagnetic waves. Nuclear energy is energy stored in the nuclei of atoms. Electrical energy is the energy carried by electric charges as they move in a circuit. Devices such as heat engines convert one form of energy into other useful forms.

The Law of Conservation of Energy When energy is transformed from one form to another, the total amount of energy doesn't change. According to the law of conservation of energy, energy cannot be created or destroyed. Energy only can be transformed from one form to another. No device, including a heat engine, can produce energy or destroy energy.

as you read

What You'll Learn

- **Describe** what a heat engine does.
- **Explain** that energy can exist in different forms, but is never created or destroyed.
- **Describe** how an internal combustion engine works.
- **Explain** how refrigerators move heat.

Why It's Important

Heat engines enable you to travel long distances.

Review Vocabulary

work: a way of transferring energy by exerting a force over a distance

New Vocabulary

- heat engine
- internal combustion engine

Physical Setting

4.1d: List six forms of energy.

Figure 11 The engine in this earth mover transforms thermal energy into mechanical energy that can perform useful work.

Figure 12 Internal combustion engines are found in many tools and machines.

Science Online

Topic: Automobile Engines

Visit glencoe.com for Web links to information on how internal combustion engines were developed for use in cars.

Activity Make a time line showing the five important events in the development of the automobile engine.

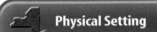

Physical Setting

4.5a: Give an example to show the meaning of the law of conservation of energy.

Internal Combustion Engines The heat engine you are probably most familiar with is the internal combustion engine. In **internal combustion engines,** the fuel burns in a combustion chamber inside the engine. Many machines, including cars, airplanes, buses, boats, trucks, and lawn mowers, use internal combustion engines, as shown in **Figure 12.**

Most cars have an engine with four or more combustion chambers, or cylinders. Usually the more cylinders an engine has, the more power it can produce. Each cylinder contains a piston that can move up and down. A mixture of fuel and air is injected into a combustion chamber and ignited by a spark. When the fuel mixture is ignited, it burns explosively and pushes the piston down. The up-and-down motion of the pistons turns a rod called a crankshaft, which turns the wheels of the car. **Figure 13** shows how an internal combustion engine converts thermal energy to mechanical energy in a process called the four-stroke cycle.

Several kinds of internal combustion engines have been designed. In diesel engines, the air in the cylinder is compressed to such a high pressure that the highly flammable fuel ignites without the need for a spark plug. Many lawn mowers use a two-stroke gasoline engine. The first stroke is a combination of intake and compression. The second stroke is a combination of power and exhaust.

 **Reading Check** *How does the burning of fuel mixture cause a piston to move?*

Figure 13

Most modern cars are powered by fuel-injected internal combustion engines that have a four-stroke combustion cycle. Inside the engine, thermal energy is converted into mechanical energy as gasoline is burned under pressure inside chambers known as cylinders. The steps in the four-stroke cycle are shown here.

EXHAUST STROKE

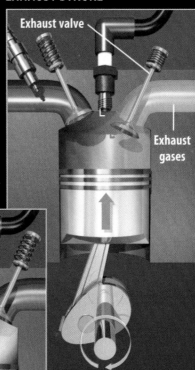

COMPRESSION STROKE

POWER STROKE

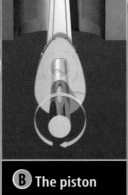

INTAKE STROKE

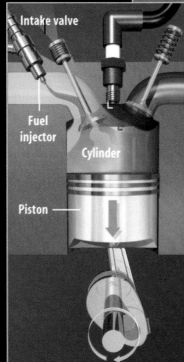

D The exhaust valve opens as the piston moves up, pushing the exhaust gases out of the cylinder.

B The piston moves up, compressing the fuel-air mixture.

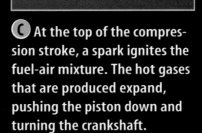

C At the top of the compression stroke, a spark ignites the fuel-air mixture. The hot gases that are produced expand, pushing the piston down and turning the crankshaft.

A During the intake stroke, the piston inside the cylinder moves downward. As it does, air fills the cylinder through the intake valve, and a mist of fuel is injected into the cylinder.

Figure 14 A refrigerator uses a coolant to move thermal energy from inside to outside the refrigerator. The compressor supplies the energy that enables the coolant to transfer thermal energy to the room.
Diagram *how the temperature of the coolant changes as it moves in a refrigerator.*

Refrigerators

If thermal energy will only flow from something that is warm to something that is cool, how can a refrigerator be cooler inside than the air in the kitchen? A refrigerator is a heat mover. It absorbs thermal energy from the food inside the refrigerator. Then it carries the thermal energy to outside the refrigerator, where it is transferred to the surrounding air.

A refrigerator contains a material called a coolant that is pumped through pipes inside and outside the refrigerator. The coolant is the substance that carries thermal energy from the inside to the outside of the refrigerator.

Absorbing Thermal Energy **Figure 14** shows how a refrigerator operates. Liquid coolant is forced up a pipe toward the freezer unit. The liquid passes through an expansion valve where it changes into a gas. When it changes into a gas, it becomes cold. The cold gas passes through pipes around the inside of the refrigerator. Because the coolant gas is so cold, it absorbs thermal energy from inside the refrigerator, and becomes warmer.

Releasing Thermal Energy However, the gas is still colder than the outside air. So, the thermal energy absorbed by the coolant cannot be transferred to the air. The coolant gas then passes through a compressor that compresses the gas. When the gas is compressed, it becomes warmer than room temperature. The gas then flows through the condenser coils, where thermal energy is transferred to the cooler air in the room. As the coolant gas cools, it changes into a liquid. The liquid is pumped through the expansion valve, changes into a gas, and the cycle is repeated.

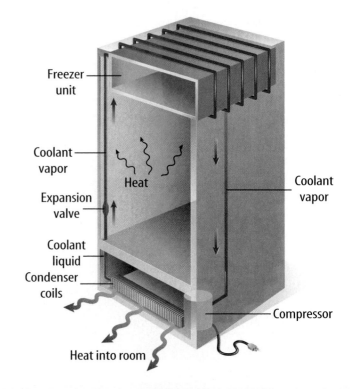

Freezer unit

Coolant vapor

Heat

Expansion valve

Coolant vapor

Coolant liquid

Condenser coils

Compressor

Heat into room

Air Conditioners Most air conditioners cool in the same way that a refrigerator does. You've probably seen air-conditioning units outside of many houses. As in a refrigerator, thermal energy from inside the house is absorbed by the coolant within pipes inside the air conditioner. The coolant then is compressed by a compressor, and becomes warmer. The warmed coolant travels through pipes that are exposed to the outside air. Here the thermal energy is transferred to the outside air.

Heat Pumps Some buildings use a heat pump for heating and cooling. Like an air conditioner or refrigerator, a heat pump moves thermal energy from one place to another. In heating mode, shown in **Figure 15,** the coolant absorbs thermal energy through the outside coils. The coolant is warmed when it is compressed and transfers thermal energy to the house through the inside coils. When a heat pump is used for cooling, it removes thermal energy from the indoor air and transfers it outdoors.

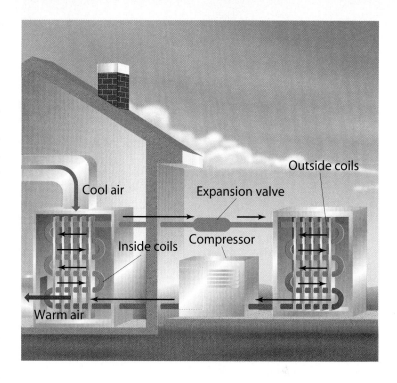
Cool air
Outside coils
Expansion valve
Inside coils
Compressor
Warm air

Figure 15 A heat pump heats a building by absorbing thermal energy from the outside air and transferring thermal energy to the cooler air inside.

---

section 3 review

Summary

Heat Engines and Energy

- A heat engine is a device that converts thermal energy into mechanical energy.
- Energy cannot be created or destroyed. It only can be transformed from one form to another.
- An internal combustion engine is a heat engine that burns fuel in a combustion chamber inside the engine.

Refrigerators and Heat Pumps

- A refrigerator uses a coolant to transfer thermal energy to outside the refrigerator.
- The coolant gas absorbs thermal energy from inside the refrigerator.
- Compressing the coolant makes it warmer than the air outside the refrigerator.
- A heat pump heats by absorbing thermal energy from the air outside, and transferring it inside a building.

Self Check

1. **Diagram** the movement of coolant and the flow of heat when a heat pump is used to cool a building.
2. **Explain** why diesel engines don't use spark plugs.
3. **Identify** the source of thermal energy in an internal combustion engine.
4. **Determine** whether you could cool a kitchen by keeping the refrigerator door open.
5. **Describe** how a refrigerator uses a coolant to keep the food compartment cool.
6. **Think Critically** Explain how an air conditioner could also be used to heat a room.

Applying Skills

7. **Make a Concept Map** Make an events-chain concept map showing the sequence of steps in a four-stroke cycle.

Comparing Thermal Insulators

Goals

■ **Predict** the temperature change of a hot drink in various types of containers over time.

■ **Design** an experiment to test the hypothesis and collect data that can be graphed.

■ **Interpret** the data.

Possible Materials

hot plate
large beaker
water
100-mL graduated cylinder
alcohol thermometers
various beverage
   containers
material to cover the
   containers
stopwatch
tongs
thermal gloves or mitts

Safety Precautions

WARNING: *Use caution when heating liquids. Use tongs or thermal gloves when handling hot materials. Hot and cold glass appear the same. Treat thermometers with care and keep them away from the edges of tables.*

◗ *Real-World Question*

Insulated beverage containers are used to reduce heat transfer. What kinds of containers do you most often drink from? Aluminum soda cans? Paper, plastic, or foam cups? Glass containers? In this investigation, compare how well several different containers block heat transfer. Which types of beverage containers are most effective at blocking heat transfer from a hot drink?

◗ *Form a Hypothesis*

Predict the temperature change of a hot liquid in several containers made of different materials over a time interval.

◗ *Test Your Hypothesis*

Make a Plan

1. **Decide** what types of containers you will test. Design an experiment to test your hypothesis. This is a group activity, so make certain that everyone gets to contribute to the discussion.

2. **List** the materials you will use in your experiment. Describe exactly how you will use these materials. Which liquid will you test? At what temperature will the liquid begin? How will you cover the hot liquids in the container? What material will you use as a cover?

3. **Identify** the variables and controls in your experiment.

4. **Design** a data table in your Science Journal to record the observations you make.

Follow Your Plan

1. Ask your teacher to examine the steps of your experiment and your data table before you start.

2. To see the pattern of how well various containers retain heat, you will need to graph your data. What kind of graph will you use? Make certain you take enough measurements during the experiment to make your graph.

3. The time intervals between measurements should be the same. Be sure to keep track of time as the experiment goes along. For how long will you measure the temperature?

4. Carry out your investigation and record your observations.

◉ *Analyze Your Data*

1. **Graph** your data. Use one graph to show the data collected from all your containers. Label each line on your graph.

2. **Interpret Data** How can you tell by looking at your graphs which containers retain heat best?

3. **Evaluate** Did the water temperature change as you had predicted? Use your data and graph to explain your answers.

◉ *Conclude and Apply*

1. **Explain** why the rate of temperature change varies among the containers. Did the size of the containers affect the rate of cooling?

2. **Conclude** which containers were the best insulators.

*C*ommunicating
Your Data

Compare your data and graphs with other classmates and explain any differences in your results or conclusions.

TIME
SCIENCE AND *Society*

SCIENCE
ISSUES
THAT AFFECT
YOU!

The Heat Is On

You may live far from water, but still live on an island—a heat island

Think about all the things that are made of asphalt and concrete in a city. As far as the eye can see, there are buildings and parking lots, sidewalks and streets. The combined effect of these paved surfaces and towering structures can make a city sizzle in the summer. There's even a name for this effect. It's called the heat island effect.

Hot Times

You can think of a city as an island surrounded by an ocean of green trees and other vegetation. In the midst of those green trees, the air can be up to 8°C cooler than it is downtown. During the day in rural areas, the Sun's energy is absorbed by plants and soil. Some of this energy causes water to evaporate, so less energy is available to heat the surroundings. This keeps the temperature lower.

Higher temperatures aren't the only problems caused by heat islands. People crank up their air conditioners for relief, so the use of energy skyrockets. Also, the added heat speeds up the rates of chemical reactions in the atmosphere. Smog is due to chemical reactions caused by the interaction of sunlight and vehicle emissions. So hotter air means more smog. And more smog means more health problems.

Cool Cures

Several U.S. cities are working with NASA scientists to come up with a cure for the summertime blues. For instance, dark materials absorb heat more efficiently than light materials. So painting buildings, especially roofs, white can reduce heat and save on cooling bills.

Dark materials, such as asphalt, absorb more heat than light materials. In extreme heat, it's even possible to fry an egg on dark pavement!

Design and Research Visit the Web Site to the right to research NASA's Urban Heat Island Project. What actions are cities taking to reduce the heat-island effect? Design a city area that would help reduce this effect.

Science Online

For more information, visit
glencoe.com

Reviewing Main Ideas

Section 1 **Temperature and Thermal Energy**

1. Molecules of matter are moving constantly. Temperature is related to the average value of the kinetic energy of the molecules.

2. Thermometers measure temperature. Three common temperature scales are the Celsius, Fahrenheit, and Kelvin scales.

3. Thermal energy is the total kinetic and potential energy of the particles in matter.

Section 2 **Heat**

1. Heat is thermal energy that is transferred from a warmer object to a colder object.

2. Heat can be transferred by conduction, convection, and radiation.

3. A material that easily transfers heat is called a conductor. A material that resists the flow of heat is an insulator.

4. The specific heat of a substance is the amount of heat needed to change the temperature of 1 kg of the substance 1°C.

5. Thermal pollution occurs when warm water is added to a body of water.

Section 3 **Engines and Refrigerators**

1. A device that converts thermal energy into mechanical energy is an engine.

2. In an internal combustion engine, fuel is burned in combustion chambers inside the engine using a four-stroke cycle.

3. Refrigerators and air conditioners use a coolant to move heat.

Visualizing Main Ideas

Copy and complete the following cycle map about the four-stroke cycle.

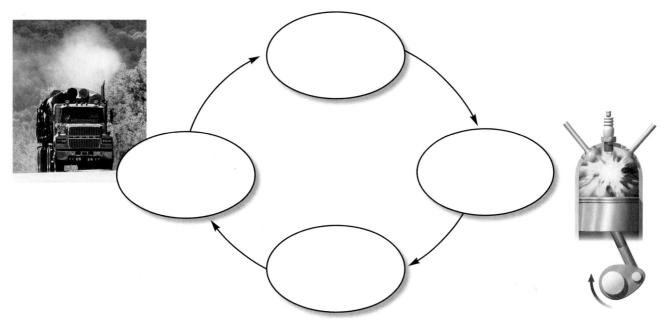

chapter ⑤ Review

Using Vocabulary

conduction p. 141
conductor p. 143
convection p. 142
heat p. 140
heat engine p. 147
internal combustion
    engine p. 148

radiation p. 141
specific heat p. 144
temperature p. 136
thermal energy p. 139
thermal pollution p. 145

Explain the differences in the vocabulary words given below. Then explain how the words are related. Use complete sentences in your answers.

1. internal combustion engine—heat engine

2. temperature—thermal energy

3. thermal energy—thermal pollution

4. conduction—convection

5. conduction—heat

6. heat—specific heat

7. conduction—radiation

8. convection—radiation

9. conductor—heat

Checking Concepts

Choose the word or phrase that best answers the question.

10. What source of thermal energy does an internal combustion engine use?
    A) steam   **C)** burning fuel
    B) hot water   **D)** refrigerant

11. What happens to most materials when they become warmer?
    A) They contract.   **C)** They vaporize.
    B) They float.   **D)** They expand.

12. Which occurs if two objects at different temperatures are in contact?
    A) convection   **C)** condensation
    B) radiation   **D)** conduction

13. Which of the following describes the thermal energy of particles in a substance?
    A) average value of all kinetic energy
    B) total value of all kinetic energy
    C) total value of all kinetic and potential energy
    D) average value of all kinetic and potential energy

14. Heat being transferred from the Sun to Earth is an example of which process?
    A) convection   **C)** radiation
    B) expansion   **D)** conduction

15. Many insulating materials contain spaces filled with air because air is what type of material?
    A) conductor   **C)** radiator
    B) coolant   **D)** insulator

16. A recipe calls for a cake to be baked at a temperature of 350°F. What is this temperature on the Celsius scale?
    A) 162°C   **C)** 194°C
    B) 177°C   **D)** 212°C

17. Which of the following is true?
    A) Warm air is less dense than cool air.
    B) Warm air is as dense as cool air.
    C) Warm air has no density.
    D) Warm air is denser than cool air.

18. Which of these is the name for thermal energy that moves from a warmer object to a cooler one?
    A) kinetic energy   **C)** heat
    B) specific heat   **D)** temperature

19. Which of the following is an example of heat transfer by conduction?
    A) water moving in a pot of boiling water
    B) warm air rising from hot pavement
    C) the warmth you feel sitting near a fire
    D) the warmth you feel holding a cup of hot cocoa

156 CHAPTER REVIEW

Vocabulary Puzzlemaker glencoe.com

Thinking Critically

20. Infer Water is a poor conductor of heat. Yet when you heat water in a pan, the surface gets hot quickly, even though you are applying heat to the bottom of the water. Explain.

21. Explain why several layers of clothing often keep you warmer than a single layer.

22. Identify The phrase "heat rises" is sometimes used to describe the movement of heat. For what type of materials is this phrase correct? Explain.

23. Describe When a lightbulb is turned on, the electric current in the filament causes the filament to become hot and glow. If the filament is surrounded by a gas, describe how thermal energy is transferred from the filament to the air outside the bulb.

24. Design an Experiment Some colors of clothing absorb heat better than other colors. Design an experiment that will test various colors by placing them in the hot Sun for a period of time. Explain your results.

25. Explain Concrete sidewalks usually are made of slabs of concrete. Why do the concrete slabs have a space between them?

26. Concept Map Copy and complete the following concept map on convection in a liquid.

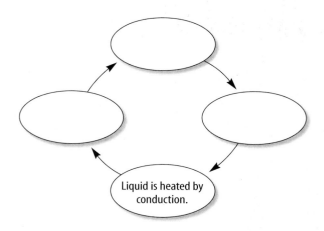

Liquid is heated by conduction.

27. Explain A winter jacket is lined with insulating material that contains air spaces. How would the insulating properties of the jacket change if the insulating material in the jacket becomes wet? Explain.

28. Compare Two glasses of water are poured into a pitcher. If the temperature of the water in both glasses was the same before they were mixed, describe how the temperature and thermal energy of the water in the pitcher compares to the water in the glasses.

Performance Activities

29. Poll In the United States, the Fahrenheit temperature scale is used most often. Some people feel that Americans should switch to the Celsius scale. Take a poll of at least 20 people. Find out if they feel the switch to the Celsius scale should be made. Make a list of reasons people give for or against changing.

Hot Words Hot Topics: Bk 1 pp. 70, 120-122, 271

Applying Math

30. Temperature Order List the following temperatures from coldest to warmest: 80° C, 200 K, 50° F.

31. Temperature Change The high temperature on a summer day is 88°F and the low temperature is 61°F. What is the difference between these two temperatures in degrees Celsius?

32. Global Temperature The average global temperature is 286 K. Convert this temperature to degrees Celsius.

33. Body Temperature A doctor measures a patient's temperature at 38.4°C. Convert this temperature to degrees Fahrenheit.

Part I

Record your answers on the answer sheet provided by your teacher or on a sheet of paper.

Use the photo below to answer questions 1 and 2.

1 The temperatures of the two glasses of water shown in the photograph above are 30°C and 0°C. Which of the following is a correct statement about the two glasses of water?
   (1) The cold water has a higher average kinetic energy.
   (2) The warmer water has lower thermal energy.
   (3) The molecules of the cold water move faster.
   (4) The molecules of the warmer water have more kinetic energy.

2 The difference in temperature of the two glasses of water is 30°C. What is their difference in temperature on the Kelvin scale?
   (1) 30 K   (3) 243 K
   (2) 86 K   (4) 303 K

3 Which of the following describes a refrigerator?
   (1) heat engine   (3) heat mover
   (2) heat pump   (4) conductor

4 Which of the following is not a step in the four-stroke cycle of internal combustion engines?
   (1) compression   (3) idling
   (2) exhaust   (4) power

Use the table below to answer question 5.

Material	Specific Heat (J/kg °C)
aluminum	897
copper	385
lead	129
nickel	444
zinc	388

5 A sample of each of the metals in the table above is formed into a 50-g cube. If 100 J of heat are applied to each of the samples, which metal would change temperature by the greatest amount?
   (1) aluminum   (3) lead
   (2) copper   (4) nickel

6 An internal combustion engine converts thermal energy to which of the following forms of energy?
   (1) chemical   (3) radiant
   (2) mechanical   (4) electrical

7 Which of the following is a statement of the law of conservation of energy?
   (1) Energy never can be created or destroyed.
   (2) Energy can be created, but never destroyed.
   (3) Energy can be destroyed, but never created.
   (4) Energy can be created and destroyed when it changes form.

Record your answers on the answer sheet provided by your teacher or on a sheet of paper.

8 If you add ice to a glass of room-temperature water, does the water warm the ice or does the ice cool the water? Explain.

9 Analyze why cooking pots are often made of metal. Explain why the handle might be made of wood or plastic.

10 When heating water in the pot, electrical energy from the cooking unit is changed to what other type of energy?

Use the illustration below to answer questions 11 and 12.

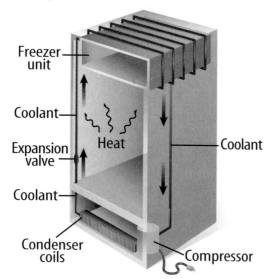

11 The illustration above shows the parts of a refrigerator and how coolant flows through the refrigerator. Explain how thermal energy is transferred to the coolant inside the refrigerator and then transferred from the coolant to the outside air.

12 Explain the functions of the expansion valve, the condenser coils, and the compressor in a refrigerator.

13 Draw a sketch with arrows showing how conduction, convection, and radiation affect the movement and temperature of air near an ocean.

14 Define temperature and explain how it is related to the movement of molecules in a substance.

15 You place a cookie sheet in a hot oven. A few minutes later you hear a sound as the cookie sheet bends slightly. Explain what causes this.

PS 2.1a: Nearly all the atmosphere is confined to a thin shell surrounding Earth. The atmosphere is a mixture of gases. The atmosphere is stratified into layers, each having distinct properties. Nearly all weather occurs in the lowest layer of the atmosphere. **4.1a:** The Sun is a major source of energy for Earth. **Also covered:** 2.1b, 2.1c, 2.1d, 2.1j, 2.2.k, 2.2l, 2.2m, 2.2n, 3.3b, 4.1d, 4.2a, 4.2b.

chapter

6

Atmosphere

chapter preview

sections

1 Earth's Atmosphere
   Lab Evaluating Sunscreens

2 Energy Transfer in the Atmosphere

3 Air Movement
   Lab The Heat is On

⊙ *Virtual Lab What is the structure of Earth's atmosphere?*

Fresh mountain air?

On top of Mt. Everest the air is a bit thin. Without breathing equipment, an average person quickly would become dizzy, then unconscious, and eventually would die. In this chapter you'll learn what makes the atmosphere at high altitudes different from the atmosphere we are used to.

Science Journal Write a short article describing how you might prepare to climb Mt. Everest.

Start-Up Activities

Observe Air Pressure

The air around you is made of billions of molecules. These molecules are constantly moving in all directions and bouncing into every object in the room, including you. Air pressure is the result of the billions of collisions of molecules into these objects. Because you usually do not feel molecules in air hitting you, do the lab below to see the effect of air pressure.

1. Cut out a square of cardboard about 10 cm from the side of a cereal box.
2. Fill a glass to the brim with water.
3. Hold the cardboard firmly over the top of the glass, covering the water, and invert the glass.
4. Slowly remove your hand holding the cardboard in place and observe.
5. **Think Critically** Write a paragraph in your Science Journal describing what happened to the cardboard when you inverted the glass and removed your hand. How does air pressure explain what happened?

FOLDABLES Study Organizer

Earth's Atmospheric Layers
Make the following Foldable to help you visualize the five layers of Earth's atmosphere.

STEP 1 Collect 3 sheets of paper and layer them about 1.25 cm apart vertically. Keep the edges level.

STEP 2 Fold up the bottom edges of the paper to form 6 equal tabs.

STEP 3 Fold the paper and crease well to hold the tabs in place. Staple along the fold. **Label** each tab.

Exosphere
Thermosphere
Mesosphere
Stratosphere
Troposphere
Earth's Atmosphere

Find Main Ideas Label the tabs *Earth's Atmosphere, Troposphere, Stratosphere, Mesosphere, Thermosphere,* and *Exosphere* from bottom to top as shown. As you read the chapter, write information about each layer of Earth's atmosphere under the appropriate tab.

Preview this chapter's content and activities at glencoe.com

PS 2.1a: Nearly all the atmosphere is confined to a thin shell surrounding Earth. The atmosphere is a mixture of gases. The atmosphere is stratified into layers, each having distinct properties. Nearly all weather occurs in the lowest layer of the atmosphere. **Also covered:** 2.1b, 2.1c, 2.1d.

section 1

Earth's Atmosphere

as you read

What You'll Learn

- **Identify** the gases in Earth's atmosphere.
- **Describe** the structure of Earth's atmosphere.
- **Explain** what causes air pressure.

Why It's Important

The atmosphere makes life on Earth possible.

Review Vocabulary

pressure: force exerted on an area

New Vocabulary

- atmosphere
- troposphere
- ionosphere
- ozone layer
- ultraviolet radiation
- chlorofluorocarbon

Importance of the Atmosphere

Earth's **atmosphere,** shown in **Figure 1,** is a thin layer of air that forms a protective covering around the planet. If Earth had no atmosphere, days would be extremely hot and nights would be extremely cold. Earth's atmosphere maintains a balance between the amount of heat absorbed from the Sun and the amount of heat that escapes back into space. It also protects life-forms from some of the Sun's harmful rays.

Makeup of the Atmosphere

Earth's atmosphere is a mixture of gases, solids, and liquids that surrounds the planet. It extends from Earth's surface to outer space. The atmosphere is much different today from what it was when Earth was young.

Earth's early atmosphere, produced by erupting volcanoes, contained nitrogen and carbon dioxide, but little oxygen. Then, more than 2 billon years ago, Earth's early organisms released oxygen into the atmosphere as they made food with the aid of sunlight. These early organisms, however, were limited to layers of ocean water deep enough to be shielded from the Sun's harmful rays, yet close enough to the surface to receive sunlight. Eventually, a layer rich in ozone (O_3) that protects Earth from the Sun's harmful rays formed in the upper atmosphere. This protective layer eventually allowed green plants to flourish all over Earth, releasing even more oxygen. Today, a variety of life forms, including you, depends on a certain amount of oxygen in Earth's atmosphere.

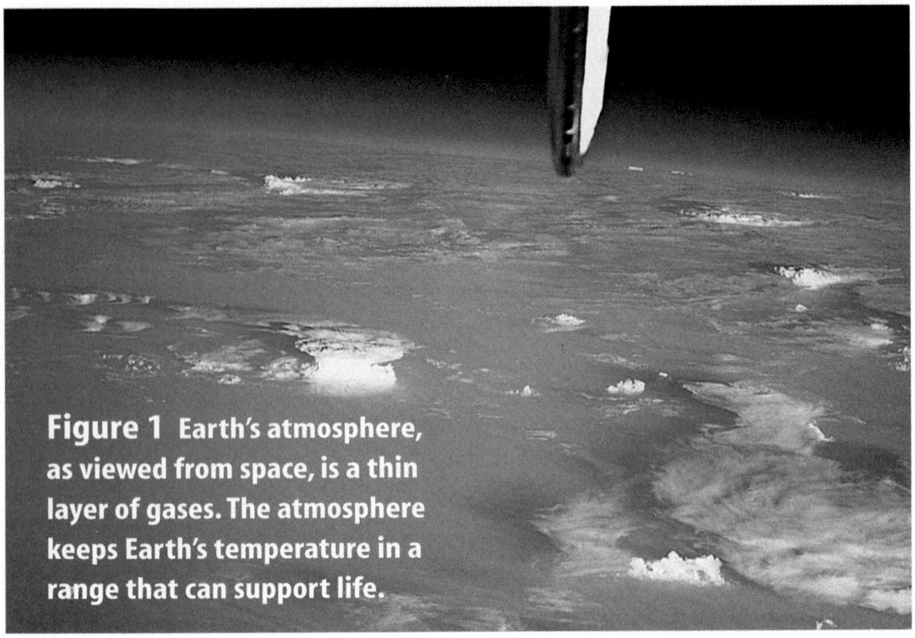

Figure 1 Earth's atmosphere, as viewed from space, is a thin layer of gases. The atmosphere keeps Earth's temperature in a range that can support life.

Gases in the Atmosphere

Today's atmosphere is a mixture of the gases shown in **Figure 2.** Nitrogen is the most abundant gas, making up 78 percent of the atmosphere. Oxygen actually makes up only 21 percent of Earth's atmosphere. As much as four percent of the atmosphere is water vapor. Other gases that make up Earth's atmosphere include argon and carbon dioxide.

The composition of the atmosphere is changing in small but important ways. For example, car exhaust emits gases into the air. These pollutants mix with oxygen and other chemicals in the presence of sunlight and form a brown haze called smog. Humans burn fuel for energy. As fuel is burned, carbon dioxide is released as a by-product into Earth's atmosphere. Increasing energy use may increase the amount of carbon dioxide in the atmosphere.

Solids and Liquids in Earth's Atmosphere

In addition to gases, Earth's atmosphere contains small, solid particles such as dust, salt, and pollen. Dust particles get into the atmosphere when wind picks them up off the ground and carries them along. Salt is picked up from ocean spray. Plants give off pollen that becomes mixed throughout part of the atmosphere.

The atmosphere also contains small liquid droplets other than water droplets in clouds. The atmosphere constantly moves these liquid droplets and solids from one region to another. For example, the atmosphere above you may contain liquid droplets and solids from an erupting volcano thousands of kilometers from your home, as illustrated in **Figure 3.**

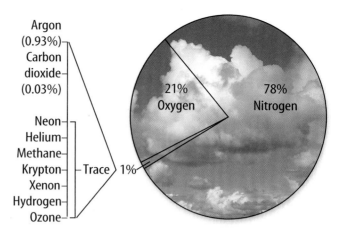

Argon (0.93%)
Carbon dioxide (0.03%)

Neon
Helium
Methane
Krypton ⎬ Trace ⟩ 1%
Xenon
Hydrogen
Ozone

21% Oxygen

78% Nitrogen

Figure 2 This circle graph shows the percentages of the gases, excluding water vapor, that make up Earth's atmosphere.
Determine *Approximately what fraction of Earth's atmosphere is oxygen?*

Physical Setting

2.1a: List the percentages of Earth's atmospheric gases from greatest to least.

Figure 3 Solids and liquids can travel large distances in Earth's atmosphere, affecting regions far from their source.

On June 12, 1991, Mount Pinatubo in the Philippines erupted, causing liquid droplets to form in Earth's atmosphere.

Droplets of sulfuric acid from volcanoes can produce spectacular sunrises.

Topic: Earth's Atmospheric Layers

Visit glencoe.com for Web links to information about layers of Earth's atmosphere.

Activity Locate data on recent ozone layer depletion. Graph your data.

Layers of the Atmosphere

What would happen if you left a glass of chocolate milk on the kitchen counter for a while? Eventually, you would see a lower layer with more chocolate separating from upper layers with less chocolate. Like a glass of chocolate milk, Earth's atmosphere has layers. There are five layers in Earth's atmosphere, each with its own properties, as shown in **Figure 4.** The lower layers include the troposphere and stratosphere. The upper atmospheric layers are the mesosphere, thermosphere, and exosphere. The troposphere and stratosphere contain most of the air.

Lower Layers of the Atmosphere You study, eat, sleep, and play in the **troposphere** which is the lowest of Earth's atmospheric layers. It contains 99 percent of the water vapor and 75 percent of the atmospheric gases. Rain, snow, and clouds occur in the troposphere, which extends up to about 10 km.

The stratosphere, the layer directly above the troposphere, extends from 10 km above Earth's surface to about 50 km. As **Figure 4** shows, a portion of the stratosphere contains higher levels of a gas called ozone. Each molecule of ozone is made up of three oxygen atoms bonded together. Later in this section you will learn how ozone protects Earth from the Sun's harmful rays.

Figure 4 Earth's atmosphere is divided into five layers.
Describe *the layer of the atmosphere in which you live.*

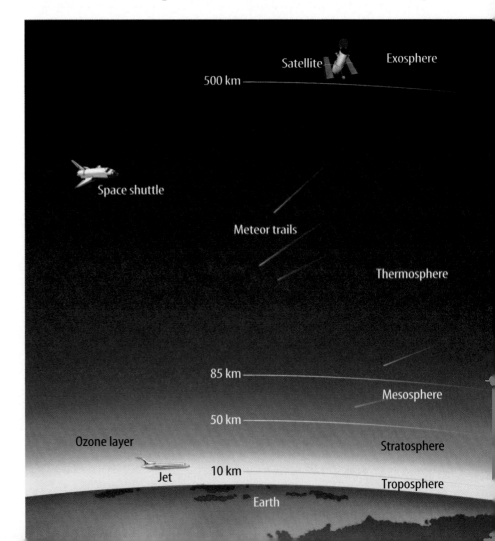

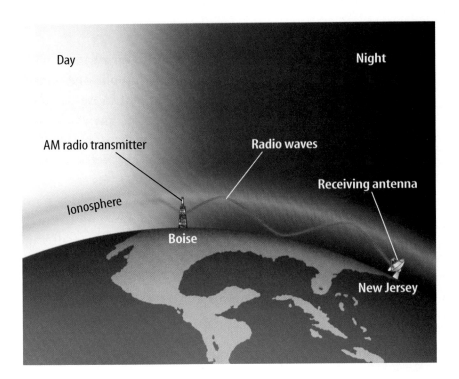

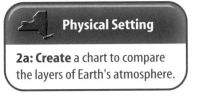

Figure 5 During the day, the ionosphere absorbs radio transmissions. This prevents you from hearing distant radio stations. At night, the ionosphere reflects radio waves. The reflected waves can travel to distant cities.
Describe *what causes the ionosphere to change between day and night.*

Day

Night

AM radio transmitter

Radio waves

Receiving antenna

Ionosphere

Boise

New Jersey

Upper Layers of the Atmosphere

Beyond the stratosphere are the mesosphere, thermosphere, and exosphere. The mesosphere extends from the top of the stratosphere to about 85 km above Earth. If you've ever seen a shooting star, you might have witnessed a meteor in the mesosphere.

The thermosphere is named for its high temperatures. This is the thickest atmospheric layer and is found between 85 km and 500 km above Earth's surface.

Within the mesosphere and thermosphere is a layer of electrically charged particles called the **ionosphere** (i AH nuh sfihr). If you live in New Jersey and listen to the radio at night, you might pick up a station from Boise, Idaho. The ionosphere allows radio waves to travel across the country to another city, as shown in **Figure 5.** During the day, energy from the Sun interacts with the particles in the ionosphere, causing them to absorb AM radio frequencies. At night, without solar energy, AM radio transmissions reflect off the ionosphere, allowing radio transmissions to be received at greater distances.

The space shuttle in **Figure 6** orbits Earth in the exosphere. In contrast to the troposphere, the layer you live in, the exosphere has so few molecules that the wings of the shuttle are useless. In the exosphere, the spacecraft relies on bursts from small rocket thrusters to move around. Beyond the exosphere is outer space.

 *How does the space shuttle maneuver in the exosphere?*

Physical Setting

2a: Create a chart to compare the layers of Earth's atmosphere.

Figure 6 Wings help move aircraft in lower layers of the atmosphere. The space shuttle can't use its wings to maneuver in the exosphere because so few molecules are present.

Atmospheric Pressure

Imagine you're a football player running with the ball. Six players tackle you and pile one on top of the other. Who feels the weight more—you or the player on top? Like molecules anywhere else, atmospheric gases have mass. Atmospheric gases extend hundreds of kilometers above Earth's surface. As Earth's gravity pulls the gases toward its surface, the weight of these gases presses down on the air below. As a result, the molecules nearer Earth's surface are closer together. This dense air exerts more force than the less dense air near the top of the atmosphere. Force exerted on an area is known as pressure.

Like the pile of football players, air pressure is greater near Earth's surface and decreases higher in the atmosphere, as shown in **Figure 7.** People find it difficult to breathe in high mountains because fewer molecules of air exist there. Jets that fly in the stratosphere must maintain pressurized cabins so that people can breathe.

Figure 7 Air pressure decreases as you go higher in Earth's atmosphere.

 **Reading Check** *Where is air pressure greater—in the exosphere or in the troposphere?*

Applying Science

How does altitude affect air pressure?

Atmospheric gases extend hundreds of kilometers above Earth's surface, but the molecules that make up these gases are fewer and fewer in number as you go higher. This means that air pressure decreases with altitude.

Identifying the Problem

The graph on the right shows these changes in air pressure. Note that altitude on the graph goes up only to 50 km. The troposphere and the stratosphere are represented on the graph, but other layers of the atmosphere are not. By examining the graph, can you understand the relationship between altitude and pressure?

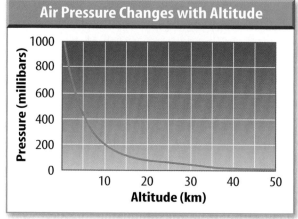

Solving the Problem

1. Estimate the air pressure at an altitude of 5 km.
2. Does air pressure change more quickly at higher altitudes or at lower altitudes?

Temperature in Atmospheric Layers

The Sun is the source of most of the energy on Earth. Before it reaches Earth's surface, energy from the Sun must pass through the atmosphere. Because some layers contain gases that easily absorb the Sun's energy while other layers do not, the various layers have different temperatures, illustrated by the red line in **Figure 8.**

Molecules that make up air in the troposphere are warmed mostly by heat from Earth's surface. The Sun warms Earth's surface, which then warms the air above it. When you climb a mountain, the air at the top is usually cooler than the air at the bottom. Every kilometer you climb, the air temperature decreases about 6.5°C.

Molecules of ozone in the stratosphere absorb some of the Sun's energy. Energy absorbed by ozone molecules raises the temperature. Because more ozone molecules are in the upper portion of the stratosphere, the temperature in this layer rises with increasing altitude.

Like the troposphere, the temperature in the mesosphere decreases with altitude. The thermosphere and exosphere are the first layers to receive the Sun's rays. Few molecules are in these layers, but each molecule has a great deal of energy. Temperatures here are high.

Mini LAB

Determining if Air Has Mass

Procedure
1. On a **pan balance,** find the mass of an **inflatable ball** that is completely deflated.
2. Hypothesize about the change in the mass of the ball when it is inflated.
3. Inflate the ball to its maximum recommended inflation pressure.
4. Determine the mass of the fully inflated ball.

Analysis
1. What change occurs in the mass of the ball when it is inflated?
2. Infer from your data whether air has mass.

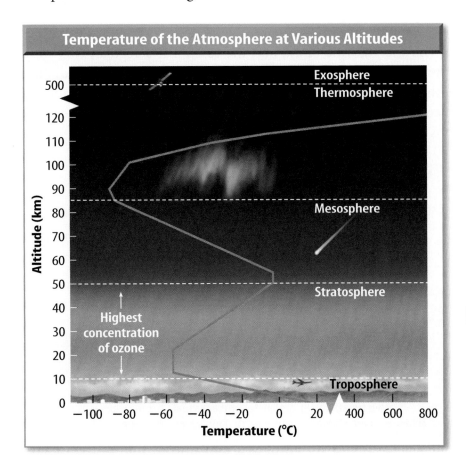

Temperature of the Atmosphere at Various Altitudes

Figure 8 The division of the atmosphere into layers is based mainly on differences in temperature.
Determine *Does the temperature increase or decrease with altitude in the mesosphere?*

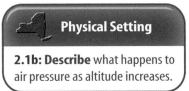

Physical Setting

2.1b: Describe what happens to air pressure as altitude increases.

Effects of UV Light on Algae Algae are organisms that use sunlight to make their own food. This process releases oxygen to Earth's atmosphere. Some scientists suggest that growth is reduced when algae are exposed to ultraviolet radiation. Infer what might happen to the oxygen level of the atmosphere if increased ultraviolet radiation damages some algae.

Figure 9 Chlorofluorocarbon (CFC) molecules once were used in refrigerators and air conditioners. Each CFC molecule has three chlorine atoms. One atom of chlorine can destroy approximately 100,000 ozone molecules.

The Ozone Layer

Within the stratosphere, about 19 km to 48 km above your head, lies an atmospheric layer called the **ozone layer.** Ozone is made of oxygen. Although you cannot see the ozone layer, your life depends on it.

The oxygen you breathe has two atoms per molecule, but an ozone molecule is made up of three oxygen atoms bound together. The ozone layer contains a high concentration of ozone and shields you from the Sun's harmful energy. Ozone absorbs most of the ultraviolet radiation that enters the atmosphere. **Ultraviolet radiation** is one of the many types of energy that come to Earth from the Sun. Too much exposure to ultraviolet radiation can damage your skin and cause cancer.

CFCs Evidence exists that some air pollutants are destroying the ozone layer. Blame has fallen on **chlorofluorocarbons** (CFCs), chemical compounds used in some refrigerators, air conditioners, and aerosol sprays, and in the production of some foam packaging. CFCs can enter the atmosphere if these appliances leak or if they and other products containing CFCs are improperly discarded.

Recall that an ozone molecule is made of three oxygen atoms bonded together. Chlorofluorocarbon molecules, shown in **Figure 9,** destroy ozone. When a chlorine atom from a chlorofluorocarbon molecule comes near a molecule of ozone, the ozone molecule breaks apart. One of the oxygen atoms combines with the chlorine atom, and the rest form a regular, two-atom molecule. These compounds don't absorb ultraviolet radiation the way ozone can. In addition, the original chlorine atom can continue to break apart thousands of ozone molecules. The result is that more ultraviolet radiation reaches Earth's surface.

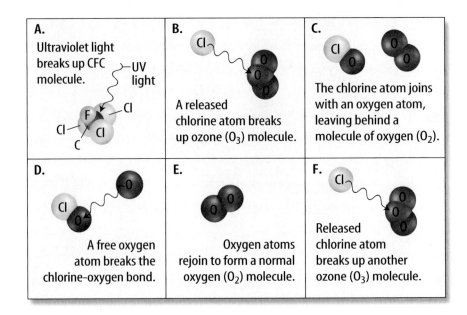

A. Ultraviolet light breaks up CFC molecule. — UV light

B. A released chlorine atom breaks up ozone (O_3) molecule.

C. The chlorine atom joins with an oxygen atom, leaving behind a molecule of oxygen (O_2).

D. A free oxygen atom breaks the chlorine-oxygen bond.

E. Oxygen atoms rejoin to form a normal oxygen (O_2) molecule.

F. Released chlorine atom breaks up another ozone (O_3) molecule.

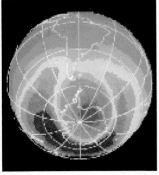
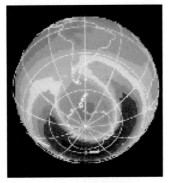
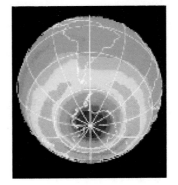
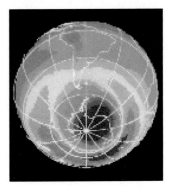

| October 1980 | October 1988 | October 1990 | September 1999 |

The Ozone Hole The destruction of ozone molecules by CFCs seems to cause a seasonal reduction in ozone over Antarctica called the ozone hole. Every year beginning in late August or early September the amount of ozone in the atmosphere over Antarctica begins to decrease. By October, the ozone concentration reaches its lowest values and then begins to increase again. By December, the ozone hole disappears. **Figure 10** shows how the ozone hole over Antarctica has changed. In the mid-1990s, many governments banned the production and use of CFCs. Since then, the concentration of CFCs in the atmosphere has started to decrease.

Figure 10 These images of Antarctica were produced using data from a NASA satellite. The lowest values of ozone concentration are shown in dark blue and purple. These data show that the size of the seasonal ozone hole over Antarctica has grown larger over time.

section 1 review

Summary

Layers of the Atmosphere

- The atmosphere is a mixture of gases, solids, and liquids.
- The atmosphere has five layers—troposphere, stratosphere, mesosphere, thermosphere, and exosphere.
- The ionosphere is made up of electrically charged particles.

Atmospheric Pressure and Temperature

- Atmospheric pressure decreases with distance from Earth.
- Because some layers absorb the Sun's energy more easily than others, the various layers have different temperatures.

Ozone Layer

- The ozone layer absorbs most UV light.
- Chlorofluorocarbons (CFCs) break down the ozone layer.

Self Check

1. **Describe** How did oxygen come to make up 21 percent of Earth's present atmosphere?
2. **Infer** While hiking in the mountains, you notice that it is harder to breathe as you climb higher. Explain.
3. **State** some effects of a thinning ozone layer.
4. **Think Critically** Explain why, during the day, the radio only receives AM stations from a nearby city, while at night, you're able to hear a distant city's stations.

Applying Skills

5. **Interpret Scientific Illustrations** Using **Figure 2,** determine the total percentage of nitrogen and oxygen in the atmosphere. What is the total percentage of argon and carbon dioxide?
6. **Communicate** The names of the atmospheric layers end with the suffix *-sphere,* a word that means "ball." Find out what *tropo-, meso-, thermo-,* and *exo-* mean. Write their meanings in your Science Journal and explain if the layers are appropriately named.

Evaluating Sunscreens

Without protection, sun exposure can damage your health. Sunscreens protect your skin from UV radiation. In this lab, you will draw inferences using different sunscreen labels.

◉ Real-World Question

How effective are various brands of sunscreens?

Goals
- **Draw inferences** based on labels on sunscreen brands.
- **Compare** the effectiveness of different sunscreen brands for protection against the Sun.
- **Compare** the cost of several sunscreen brands.

Materials
variety of sunscreens of different brand names

Safety Precautions

◉ Procedure

1. Make a data table in your Science Journal using the following headings: *Brand Name, SPF, Cost per Milliliter,* and *Misleading Terms.*
2. The Sun Protection Factor (SPF) tells you how long the sunscreen will protect you. For example, an SPF of 4 allows you to stay in the Sun four times longer than if you did not use sunscreen. Record the SPF of each sunscreen on your data table.
3. **Calculate** the cost per milliliter of each sunscreen brand.
4. Government guidelines say that terms like *sunblock* and *waterproof* are misleading because sunscreens can't block the Sun's rays, and they do wash off in water. List misleading terms in your data table for each brand.

Sunscreen Assessment			
Brand Name			
SPF			
Cost per Milliliter	Do not write in this book.		
Misleading Terms			

◉ Conclude and Apply

1. **Explain** why you need to use sunscreen.
2. **Evaluate** A minimum of SPF 15 is considered adequate protection for a sunscreen. An SPF greater than 30 is considered by government guidelines to be misleading because sunscreens wash or wear off. Evaluate the SPF of each sunscreen brand.
3. **Discuss** Considering the cost and effectiveness of all the sunscreen brands, discuss which you consider to be the best buy.

*C*ommunicating Your Data

Create a poster on the proper use of sunscreens, and provide guidelines for selecting the safest product.

section 2

PS 4.1a: The Sun is a major source of energy for Earth. **4.2b:** Heat can be transferred through matter by the collisions of atoms and/or molecules (conduction) or through space (radiation). In a liquid or gas, currents will facilitate the transfer of heat (convection). **Also covered:** 2.1j, 3.3b, 4.1d, 4.2a.

Energy Transfer in the Atmosphere

Energy from the Sun

The Sun provides most of Earth's energy. This energy drives winds and ocean currents and allows plants to grow and produce food, providing nutrition for many animals. When Earth receives energy from the Sun, three different things can happen to that energy, as shown in **Figure 11.** Some energy is reflected back into space by clouds, particles, and Earth's surface. Some is absorbed by the atmosphere or by land and water on Earth's surface.

Heat

Heat is energy that flows from an object with a higher temperature to an object with a lower temperature. Energy from the Sun reaches Earth's surface and heats it. Heat then is transferred through the atmosphere in three ways—radiation, conduction, and convection, as shown in **Figure 12.**

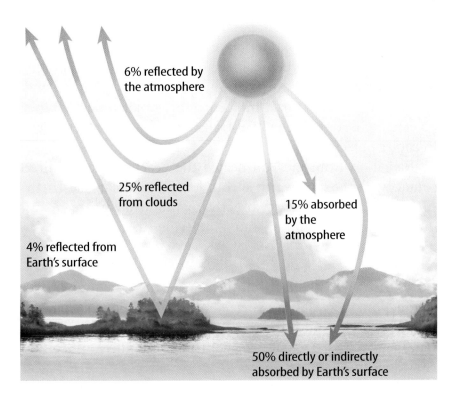

6% reflected by the atmosphere

25% reflected from clouds

15% absorbed by the atmosphere

4% reflected from Earth's surface

50% directly or indirectly absorbed by Earth's surface

as you read

***What* You'll Learn**
- **Describe** what happens to the energy Earth receives from the Sun.
- **Compare and contrast** radiation, conduction, and convection.
- **Explain** the water cycle and its effect on weather patterns and climate.

***Why* It's Important**
The Sun provides energy to Earth's atmosphere, allowing life to exist.

Review Vocabulary
evaporation: when a liquid changes to a gas at a temperature below the liquid's boiling point

New Vocabulary
- radiation
- conduction
- convection
- hydrosphere
- condensation

Figure 11 The Sun is the source of energy for Earth's atmosphere. Thirty-five percent of incoming solar radiation is reflected back into space.
Infer *how much is absorbed by Earth's surface and atmosphere.*

Radiation warms the surface.

The air near Earth's surface is heated by conduction.

Cooler air pushes warm air upward, creating a convection current.

Figure 12 Heat is transferred within Earth's atmosphere by radiation, conduction, and convection.

Physical Setting

4.1a, 4.2b: Describe how the Sun is a major source of energy for Earth.

Specific Heat Specific heat is the amount of heat required to raise the temperature of one kilogram of a substance one degree Celsius. Substances with high specific heat absorb a lot of heat for a small increase in temperature. Land warms faster than water does. Infer whether soil or water has a higher specific heat value.

Radiation Sitting on the beach, you feel the Sun's warmth on your face. How can you feel the Sun's heat even though you aren't in direct contact with it? Energy from the Sun reaches Earth in the form of radiant energy, or radiation. **Radiation** is energy that is transferred in the form of rays or waves. Earth radiates some of the energy it absorbs from the Sun back toward space. Radiant energy from the Sun warms your face.

✔ **Reading Check** *How does the Sun warm your skin?*

Conduction If you walk barefoot on a hot beach, your feet heat up because of conduction. **Conduction** is the transfer of energy that occurs when molecules bump into one another. Molecules are always in motion, but molecules in warmer objects move faster than molecules in cooler objects. When objects are in contact, energy is transferred from warmer objects to cooler objects.

Radiation from the Sun heated the beach sand, but direct contact with the sand warmed your feet. In a similar way, Earth's surface conducts energy directly to the atmosphere. As air moves over warm land or water, molecules in air are heated by direct contact.

Convection After the atmosphere is warmed by radiation or conduction, the heat is transferred by a third process called convection. **Convection** is the transfer of heat by the flow of material. Convection circulates heat throughout the atmosphere. How does this happen?

When air is warmed, the molecules in it move apart and the air becomes less dense. Air pressure decreases because fewer molecules are in the same space. In cold air, molecules move closer together. The air becomes more dense and air pressure increases. Cooler, denser air sinks while warmer, less dense air rises, forming a convection current. As **Figure 12** shows, radiation, conduction, and convection together distribute the Sun's heat throughout Earth's atmosphere.

The Water Cycle

Hydrosphere is a term that describes all the waters of Earth. The constant cycling of water within the atmosphere and the hydrosphere, as shown in **Figure 13,** plays an important role in determining weather patterns and climate types.

Energy from the Sun causes water to change from a liquid to a gas by a process called evaporation. Water that evaporates from lakes, streams, and oceans enters Earth's atmosphere. If water vapor in the atmosphere cools enough, it changes back into a liquid. This process of water vapor changing to a liquid is called **condensation.**

Clouds form when condensation occurs high in the atmosphere. Clouds are made up of tiny water droplets that can collide to form larger drops. As the drops grow, they fall to Earth as precipitation. This completes the water cycle within the hydrosphere. Classification of world climates is commonly based on annual and monthly averages of temperature and precipitation that are strongly affected by the water cycle.

Modeling Heat Transfer

Procedure
1. Cover the outside of an empty **soup can,** with **black construction paper.**
2. Fill the can with **cold water** and feel it with your fingers.
3. Place the can in sunlight for 1 h, then pour the water over your fingers.

Analysis
1. Does the water in the can feel warmer or cooler after placing the can in sunlight?
2. What types of heat transfer did you model?

Try at Home

Figure 13 In the water cycle, water moves from Earth to the atmosphere and back to Earth again.

Precipitation

Condensation

Evaporation

Runoff

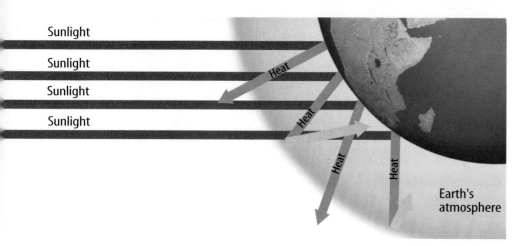

Sunlight
Sunlight
Sunlight
Sunlight

Heat
Heat
Heat
Heat

Earth's atmosphere

Earth's Atmosphere is Unique

On Earth, radiation from the Sun can be reflected into space, absorbed by the atmosphere, or absorbed by land and water. Once it is absorbed, heat can be transferred by radiation, conduction, or convection. Earth's atmosphere, shown in **Figure 14,** helps control how much of the Sun's radiation is absorbed or lost.

Figure 14 Earth's atmosphere creates a delicate balance between energy received and energy lost. **Infer** *What could happen if the balance is tipped toward receiving more energy than it does now?*

Physical Setting

4.1b: Analyze the importance of the hydrosphere.

✔ **Reading Check** *What helps control how much of the Sun's radiation is absorbed on Earth?*

Why doesn't life exist on Mars or Venus? Mars is a cold, lifeless world because its atmosphere is too thin to support life or to hold much of the Sun's heat. Temperatures on the surface of Mars range from 35°C to −170°C. On the other hand, gases in Venus's dense atmosphere trap heat coming from the Sun. The temperature on the surface of Venus is 470°C. Living things would burn instantly if they were placed on Venus's surface. Life on Earth exists because the atmosphere holds just the right amount of the Sun's energy.

section ② review

Summary

Energy From the Sun

- The Sun's radiation is either absorbed or reflected by Earth.
- Heat is transferred by radiation (waves), conduction (contact), or convection (flow).

The Water Cycle

- The water cycle affects climate.
- Water moves between the hydrosphere and the atmosphere through a continual process of evaporation and condensation.

Earth's Atmosphere is Unique

- Earth's atmosphere controls the amount of solar radiation that reaches Earth's surface.

Self Check

1. **State** how the Sun transfers energy to Earth.
2. **Contrast** the atmospheres of Earth and Mars.
3. **Describe** briefly the steps included in the water cycle.
4. **Explain** how the water cycle is related to weather patterns and climate.
5. **Think Critically** What would happen to temperatures on Earth if the Sun's heat were not distributed throughout the atmosphere?

Hot Words Hot Topics: Bk 1 pp. 90, 271

Applying Math

6. **Solve One-Step Equations** Earth is about 150 million km from the Sun. The radiation coming from the Sun travels at 300,000 km/s. How long does it take for radiation from the Sun to reach Earth?

section 3

Air Movement

Forming Wind

Earth is mostly rock or land, with three-fourths of its surface covered by a relatively thin layer of water, the oceans. These two areas strongly influence global wind systems. Uneven heating of Earth's surface by the Sun causes some areas to be warmer than others. Recall that warmer air expands, becoming lower in density than the colder air. This causes air pressure to be generally lower where air is heated. Wind is the movement of air from an area of higher pressure to an area of lower pressure.

Heated Air Areas of Earth receive different amounts of radiation from the Sun because Earth is curved. **Figure 15** illustrates why the equator receives more radiation than areas to the north or south. The heated air at the equator is less dense, so it is displaced by denser, colder air, creating convection currents.

This cold, denser air comes from the poles, which receive less radiation from the Sun, making air at the poles much cooler. The resulting dense, high-pressure air sinks and moves along Earth's surface. However, dense air sinking as less-dense air rises does not explain everything about wind.

as you read

What You'll Learn

- **Explain** why different latitudes on Earth receive different amounts of solar energy.
- **Describe** the Coriolis effect.
- **Explain** how land and water surfaces affect the overlying air.

Why It's Important

Wind systems determine major weather patterns on Earth.

Review Vocabulary
density: mass per unit volume

New Vocabulary
- Coriolis effect
- jet stream
- sea breeze
- land breeze

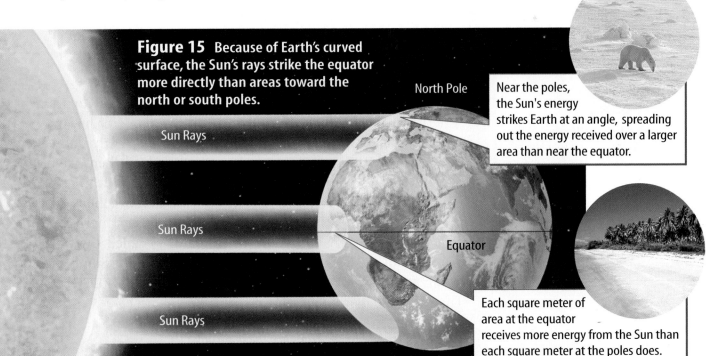

Figure 15 Because of Earth's curved surface, the Sun's rays strike the equator more directly than areas toward the north or south poles.

Sun Rays

Sun Rays

Sun Rays

North Pole

Equator

South Pole

Near the poles, the Sun's energy strikes Earth at an angle, spreading out the energy received over a larger area than near the equator.

Each square meter of area at the equator receives more energy from the Sun than each square meter at the poles does.

Figure 16 The Coriolis effect causes moving air to turn to the right in the northern hemisphere and to the left in the southern hemisphere.
Explain *What causes this to happen?*

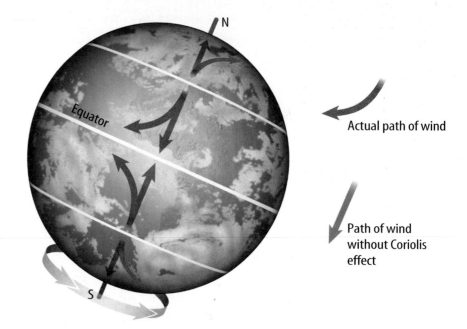

Actual path of wind

Path of wind without Coriolis effect

Physical Setting

2.2k: Explain how the uneven heating of Earth's surface by the Sun is the cause of weather.

Science nline

Topic: Global Winds
Visit glencoe.com for Web links to information about global winds.

Activity Make a model of Earth showing the locations of global wind patterns.

The Coriolis Effect What would happen if you threw a ball to someone sitting directly across from you on a moving merry-go-round? Would the ball go to your friend? By the time the ball got to the opposite side, your friend would have moved and the ball would appear to have curved.

Like the merry-go-round, the rotation of Earth causes moving air and water to appear to turn to the right north of the equator and to the left south of the equator. This is called the **Coriolis** (kohr ee OH lus) **effect.** It is illustrated in **Figure 16.** The flow of air caused by differences in the amount of solar radiation received on Earth's surface and by the Coriolis effect creates distinct wind patterns on Earth's surface. These wind systems not only influence the weather, they also determine when and where ships and planes travel most efficiently.

Global Winds

How did Christopher Columbus get from Spain to the Americas? The *Nina,* the *Pinta,* and the *Santa Maria* had no source of power other than the wind in their sails. Early sailors discovered that the wind patterns on Earth helped them navigate the oceans. These wind systems are shown in **Figure 17.**

Sometimes sailors found little or no wind to move their sailing ships near the equator. It also rained nearly every afternoon. This windless, rainy zone near the equator is called the doldrums. Look again at **Figure 17.** Near the equator, the Sun heats the air and causes it to rise, creating low pressure and little wind. The rising air then cools, causing rain.

✔ **Reading Check** *What are the doldrums?*

Figure 17

The Sun's uneven heating of Earth's surface forms giant loops, or cells, of moving air. The Coriolis effect deflects the surface winds to the west or east, setting up belts of prevailing winds that distribute heat and moisture around the globe.

A WESTERLIES Near 30° north and south latitude, Earth's rotation deflects air from west to east as air moves toward the polar regions. In the United States, the westerlies move weather systems, such as this one along the Oklahoma-Texas border, from west to east.

B DOLDRUMS Along the equator, heating causes air to expand, creating a zone of low pressure. Cloudy, rainy weather, as shown here, develops almost every afternoon.

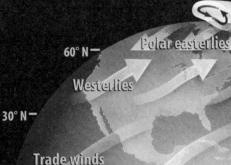

60° N — Polar easterlies

Westerlies

30° N —

Trade winds

0° — Equatorial doldrums

Trade winds

30° S —

Westerlies

60° S — Polar easterlies

C TRADE WINDS Air warmed near the equator travels toward the poles but gradually cools and sinks. As the air flows back toward the low pressure of the doldrums, the Coriolis effect deflects the surface wind to the west. Early sailors, in ships like the one above, relied on these winds to navigate global trade routes.

D POLAR EASTERLIES In the polar regions, cold, dense air sinks and moves away from the poles. Earth's rotation deflects this wind from east to west.

Surface Winds Air descending to Earth's surface near 30° north and south latitude creates steady winds that blow in tropical regions. These are called trade winds because early sailors used their dependability to establish trade routes.

Between 30° and 60° latitude, winds called the prevailing westerlies blow in the opposite direction from the trade winds. Prevailing westerlies are responsible for much of the movement of weather across North America.

Polar easterlies are found near the poles. Near the north pole, easterlies blow from northeast to southwest. Near the south pole, polar easterlies blow from the southeast to the northwest.

Winds in the Upper Troposphere Narrow belts of strong winds, called **jet streams,** blow near the top of the troposphere. The polar jet stream forms at the boundary of cold, dry polar air to the north and warmer, more moist air to the south, as shown in **Figure 18.** The jet stream moves faster in the winter because the difference between cold air and warm air is greater. The jet stream helps move storms across the country.

Jet pilots take advantage of the jet streams. When flying eastward, planes save time and fuel. Going west, planes fly at different altitudes to avoid the jet streams.

Local Wind Systems

Global wind systems determine the major weather patterns for the entire planet. Smaller wind systems affect local weather. If you live near a large body of water, you're familiar with two such wind systems—sea breezes and land breezes.

Figure 18 The polar jet stream affecting North America forms along a boundary where colder air lies to the north and warmer air lies to the south. It is a swiftly flowing current of air that moves in a wavy west-to-east direction and is usually found between 10 km and 15 km above Earth's surface.

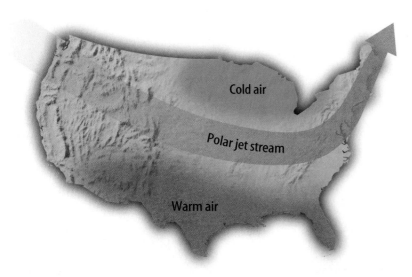

Cold air

Polar jet stream

Warm air

Flying from Boston to Seattle may take 30 min longer than flying from Seattle to Boston.
Think Critically *Why would it take longer to fly from east to west than it would from west to east?*

A

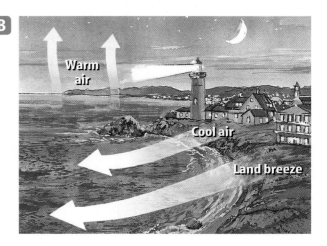
B

Sea and Land Breezes Convection currents over areas where the land meets the sea can cause wind. A **sea breeze,** shown in **Figure 19,** is created during the day because solar radiation warms the land more than the water. Air over the land is heated by conduction. This heated air is less dense and has lower pressure. Cooler, denser air over the water has higher pressure and flows toward the warmer, less dense air. A convection current results, and wind blows from the sea toward the land. The reverse occurs at night, when land cools much more rapidly than ocean water. Air over the land becomes cooler than air over the ocean. Cooler, denser air above the land moves over the water, as the warm air over the water rises. Movement of air toward the water from the land is called a **land breeze.**

Figure 19 These daily winds occur because land heats up and cools off faster than water does. **A** During the day, cool air from the water moves over the land, creating a sea breeze. **B** At night, cool air over the land moves toward the warmer air over the water, creating a land breeze.

✔ **Reading Check** *How does a sea breeze form?*

section **3** review

Summary

Forming Wind

- Warm air is less dense than cool air.
- Differences in density and pressure cause air movement and wind.
- The Coriolis effect causes moving air to appear to turn right north of the equator and left south of the equator.

Wind Systems

- Wind patterns are affected by latitude.
- High-altitude belts of wind, called jet streams, can be found near the top of the troposphere.
- Sea breezes blow from large bodies of water toward land, while land breezes blow from land toward water.

Self Check

1. **Conclude** why some parts of Earth's surface, such as the equator, receive more of the Sun's heat than other regions.
2. **Explain** how the Coriolis effect influences winds.
3. **Analyze** why little wind and much afternoon rain occur in the doldrums.
4. **Infer** which wind system helped early sailors navigate Earth's oceans.
5. **Think Critically** How does the jet stream help move storms across North America?

Applying Skills

6. **Compare and contrast** sea breezes and land breezes.

Design Your Own

The Heat Is On

● Real-World Question

Sometimes, a plunge in a pool or lake on a hot summer day feels cool and refreshing. Why does the beach sand get so hot when the water remains cool? A few hours later, the water feels warmer than the land does. How do soil and water compare in their abilities to absorb and emit heat?

● Form a Hypothesis

Form a hypothesis about how soil and water compare in their abilities to absorb and release heat. Write another hypothesis about how air temperatures above soil and above water differ during the day and night.

Goals

■ **Design** an experiment to compare heat absorption and release for soil and water.
■ **Observe** how heat release affects the air above soil and above water.

Possible Materials

ring stand
soil
metric ruler
water
masking tape
clear-plastic boxes (2)
overhead light
   with reflector
thermometers (4)
colored pencils (4)

Safety Precautions

WARNING: *Be careful when handling the hot overhead light. Do not let the light or its cord make contact with water.*

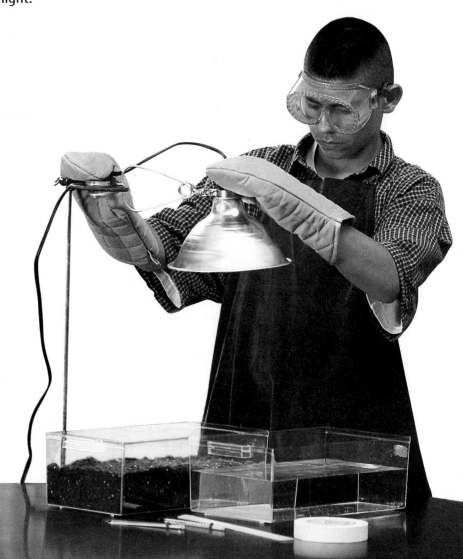

⊙ Test Your Hypothesis

Make a Plan

1. As a group, agree upon and write your hypothesis.
2. **List** the steps that you need to take to test your hypothesis. Include in your plan a description of how you will use your equipment to compare heat absorption and release for water and soil.
3. **Design** a data table in your Science Journal for both parts of your experiment—when the light is on and energy can be absorbed and when the light is off and energy is released to the environment.

Follow Your Plan

1. Make sure your teacher approves your plan and your data table before you start.
2. Carry out the experiment as planned.
3. During the experiment, record your observations and complete the data table in your Science Journal.
4. Include the temperatures of the soil and the water in your measurements. Also compare heat release for water and soil. Include the temperatures of the air immediately above both of the substances. Allow 15 min for each test.

⊙ Analyze Your Data

1. Use your colored pencils and the information in your data tables to make line graphs. Show the rate of temperature increase for soil and water. Graph the rate of temperature decrease for soil and water after you turn the light off.
2. **Analyze** your graphs. When the light was on, which heated up faster—the soil or the water?
3. **Compare** how fast the air temperature over the water changed with how fast the temperature over the land changed after the light was turned off.

⊙ Conclude and Apply

1. Were your hypotheses supported or not? Explain.
2. **Infer** from your graphs which cooled faster—the water or the soil.
3. **Compare** the temperatures of the air above the water and above the soil 15 minutes after the light was turned off. How do water and soil compare in their abilities to absorb and release heat?

Communicating Your Data

Make a poster showing the steps you followed for your experiment. Include graphs of your data. Display your poster in the classroom.

Science and Language Arts

Song of the Sky Loom[1]

Brian Swann, ed.

This Native American prayer probably comes from the Tewa-speaking Pueblo village of San Juan, New Mexico. The poem is actually a chanted prayer used in ceremonial rituals.

Mother Earth   Father Sky

we are your children
With tired backs we bring you gifts you love
Then weave for us a garment of brightness
its warp[2] the white light of morning,
weft[3] the red light of evening,
fringes the falling rain,
its border the standing rainbow.
Thus weave for us a garment of brightness
So we may walk fittingly where birds sing,
So we may walk fittingly where grass is green.

Mother Earth   Father Sky

1 a machine or device from which cloth is produced

2 threads that run lengthwise in a piece of cloth

3 horizontal threads interlaced through the warp in a piece of cloth

Understanding Literature

Metaphor A metaphor is a figure of speech that compares seemingly unlike things. Unlike a simile, a metaphor does not use the connecting words *like* or *as*. Why does the song use the image of a garment to describe Earth's atmosphere?

Respond to Reading

1. What metaphor does the song use to describe Earth's atmosphere?
2. Why do the words *Mother Earth* and *Father Sky* appear on either side and above and below the rest of the words?
3. **Linking Science and Writing** Write a four-line poem that uses a metaphor to describe rain.

In this chapter, you learned about the composition of Earth's atmosphere. The atmosphere maintains the proper balance between the amount of heat absorbed from the Sun and the amount of heat that escapes back into space. The water cycle explains how water evaporates from Earth's surface back into the atmosphere. Using metaphor instead of scientific facts, the Tewa song conveys to the reader how the relationship between Earth and its atmosphere is important to all living things.

Reviewing Main Ideas

Section 1 Earth's Atmosphere

1. Earth's atmosphere is made up mostly of gases, with some suspended solids and liquids. The unique atmosphere allows life on Earth to exist.

2. The atmosphere is divided into five layers with different characteristics.

3. The ozone layer protects Earth from too much ultraviolet radiation, which can be harmful.

Section 2 Energy Transfer in the Atmosphere

1. Earth receives its energy from the Sun. Some of this energy is reflected back into space, and some is absorbed.

2. Heat is distributed in Earth's atmosphere by radiation, conduction, and convection.

3. Energy from the Sun powers the water cycle between the atmosphere and Earth's surface.

4. Unlike the atmosphere on Mars or Venus, Earth's unique atmosphere maintains a balance between energy received and energy lost that keeps temperatures mild. This delicate balance allows life on Earth to exist.

Section 3 Air Movement

1. Because Earth's surface is curved, not all areas receive the same amount of solar radiation. This uneven heating causes temperature differences at Earth's surface.

2. Convection currents modified by the Coriolis effect produce Earth's global winds.

3. The polar jet stream is a strong current of wind found in the upper troposphere. It forms at the boundary between cold, polar air and warm, tropical air.

4. Land breezes and sea breezes occur near the ocean.

Visualizing Main Ideas

Copy and complete the following cycle map on the water cycle.

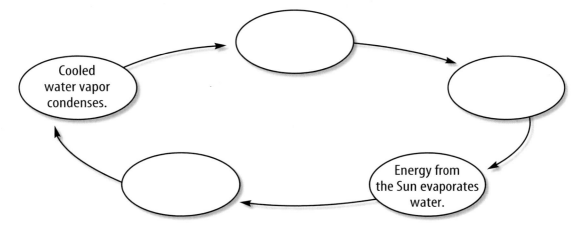

Using Vocabulary

atmosphere p. 162
chlorofluorocarbon p. 168
condensation p. 173
conduction p. 172
convection p. 172
Coriolis effect p. 176
hydrosphere p. 173
ionosphere p. 165

jet stream p. 178
land breeze p. 179
ozone layer p. 168
radiation p. 172
sea breeze p. 179
troposphere p. 164
ultraviolet radiation p. 168

Fill in the blanks below with the correct vocabulary word or words.

1. Chlorofluorocarbons are dangerous because they destroy the _____.

2. Narrow belts of strong winds called _____ blow near the top of the troposphere.

3. The thin layer of air that surrounds Earth is called the _____.

4. Heat energy transferred in the form of waves is called _____.

5. The ozone layer helps protect us from _____.

Checking Concepts

Choose the word or phrase that best answers the question.

6. Nitrogen makes up what percentage of the atmosphere?
   A) 21%   C) 78%
   B) 1%   D) 90%

7. What causes a brown haze near cities?
   A) conduction
   B) mud
   C) car exhaust
   D) wind

8. Which is the uppermost layer of the atmosphere?
   A) troposphere   C) exosphere
   B) stratosphere   D) thermosphere

9. What layer of the atmosphere has the most water?
   A) troposphere   C) mesosphere
   B) stratosphere   D) exosphere

10. What protects living things from too much ultraviolet radiation?
    A) the ozone layer   C) nitrogen
    B) oxygen   D) argon

11. Where is air pressure least?
    A) troposphere   C) exosphere
    B) stratosphere   D) thermosphere

12. How is energy transferred when objects are in contact?
    A) trade winds   C) radiation
    B) convection   D) conduction

13. Which surface winds are responsible for most of the weather movement across the United States?
    A) polar easterlies
    B) sea breeze
    C) prevailing westerlies
    D) trade winds

14. What type of wind is a movement of air toward water?
    A) sea breeze
    B) polar easterlies
    C) land breeze
    D) trade winds

15. What are narrow belts of strong winds near the top of the troposphere called?
    A) doldrums
    B) jet streams
    C) polar easterlies
    D) trade winds

Thinking Critically

16. **Explain** why there are few or no clouds in the stratosphere.

17. **Describe** It is thought that life could not have existed on land until the ozone layer formed about 2 billion years ago. Why does life on land require an ozone layer?

18. **Diagram** Why do sea breezes occur during the day but not at night?

19. **Describe** what happens when water vapor rises and cools.

20. **Explain** why air pressure decreases with an increase in altitude.

21. **Concept Map** Copy and complete the cycle concept map below using the following phrases to explain how air moves to form a convection current: *Cool air moves toward warm air, warm air is lifted and cools, and cool air sinks.*

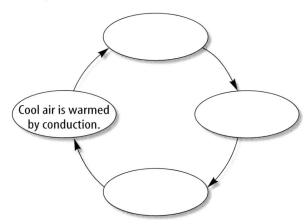

Cool air is warmed by conduction.

22. **Form Hypotheses** Carbon dioxide in the atmosphere prevents some radiation from Earth's surface from escaping to space. Hypothesize how the temperature on Earth might change if more carbon dioxide were released from burning fossil fuels.

23. **Identify and Manipulate Variables and Controls** Design an experiment to find out how plants are affected by differing amounts of ultraviolet radiation. In the design, use filtering film made for car windows. What is the variable you are testing? What are your constants? Your controls?

24. **Recognize Cause and Effect** Why is the inside of a car hotter than the outdoor temperature on a sunny summer day?

Performance Activities

25. **Make a Poster** Find newspaper and magazine photos that illustrate how the water cycle affects weather patterns and climate around the world.

26. **Experiment** Design and conduct an experiment to find out how different surfaces such as asphalt, soil, sand, and grass absorb and reflect solar energy. Share the results with your class.

Hot Words Hot Topics: Bk 1 (27) p. 195; (28) p. 90

Applying Math

Use the graph below to answer questions 27–28.

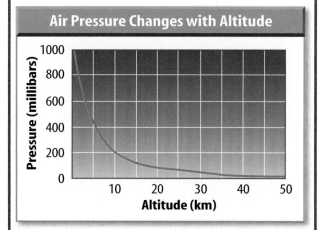

Air Pressure Changes with Altitude

27. **Altitude and Air Pressure** What is the altitude at which air pressure is about 1,000 millibars? What is it at 200 millibars?

28. **Mt. Everest** Assume the altitude on Mt. Everest is about 10 km high. How many times greater is air pressure at sea level than on top of Mt. Everest?

Record your answers on the answer sheet provided by your teacher or on a sheet of paper.

Use the illustration below to answer questions 1–3.

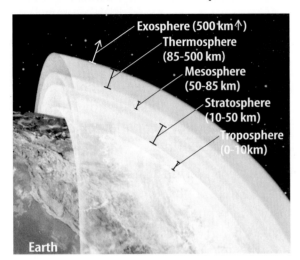

Earth

1 Which layer of the atmosphere contains the ozone layer?
(1) exosphere
(2) mesosphere
(3) stratosphere
(4) troposphere

2 Which atmospheric layer contains weather?
(1) mesosphere
(2) stratosphere
(3) thermosphere
(4) troposphere

3 Which atmospheric layer contains electrically charged particles?
(1) stratosphere
(2) ionosphere
(3) exosphere
(4) troposphere

4 What process changes water vapor to a liquid?
(1) condensation
(2) evaporation
(3) infiltration
(4) precipitation

5 Which process transfers heat by contact?
(1) conduction
(2) convection
(3) evaporation
(4) radiation

6 Which global wind affects weather in the U.S.?
(1) doldrums   (3) trade winds
(2) easterlies   (4) westerlies

Use the illustration below to answer question 7.

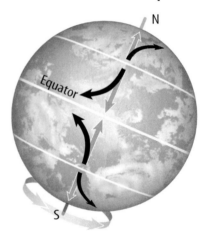

7 Which deflects winds to the west or east?
(1) convection
(2) Coriolis effect
(3) jet stream
(4) radiation

8 Which forms during the day because water heats slower than land?
(1) easterlies   (3) land breeze
(2) westerlies   (4) sea breeze

9 Which is the most abundant gas in Earth's atmosphere?
(1) carbon dioxide
(2) nitrogen
(3) oxygen
(4) water vapor

Part II

Record your answers on the answer sheet provided by your teacher or on a sheet of paper.

10 Why does a land breeze form at night?

Use the illustration below to answer questions 11–13.

11 Identify the process illustrated

12 Explain how this cycle affects weather patterns and climate.

13 Analyze what happens to water that falls as precipitation and does not runoff and flow into streams.

14 Why can flying from Seattle to Boston take less time than flying from Boston to Seattle in the same aircraft?

15 Draw three diagrams to demonstrate radiation, convection, and conduction.

Use the graph below to answer question 16.

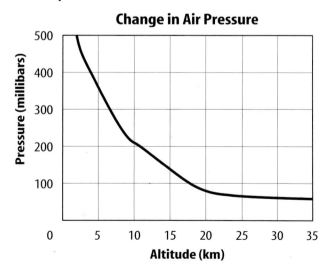

Change in Air Pressure

16 Analyze what happens to the air pressure as you increase in altitude. How might this affect athletes who compete at higher altitudes?

PS 2.2i: Weather describes the conditions of the atmosphere at a given location for a short period of time. **2.2j:** Climate is the characteristic weather that prevails from season to season and year to year. **2.2k:** The uneven heating of Earth's surface is the cause of weather.
Also covered: 2.2l, 2.2m, 2.2n, 2.2o, 2.2p.

Weather

chapter preview

sections

1 **What is weather?**

2 **Weather Patterns**

3 **Weather Forecasts**

   Lab Reading a Weather Map
   Lab Measuring Wind Speed

   ⊙ *Virtual Lab How do meteorologists predict the weather?*

To play or not to play?

Will this approaching storm be over before the game begins? New weather technology can provide information that allows us to make plans based on predicted weather conditions, such as whether or not to delay the start of a baseball game.

Science Journal   Write three questions you would ask a meteorologist about weather.

Start-Up Activities

What causes rain?

How can it rain one day and be sunny the next? Powered by heat from the Sun, the air that surrounds you stirs and swirls. This constant mixing produces storms, calm weather, and everything in between. What causes rain and where does the water come from? Do the lab below to find out. **WARNING:** *Boiling water and steam can cause burns.*

1. Bring a pan of water to a boil on a hot plate.
2. Carefully hold another pan containing ice cubes about 20 cm above the boiling water. Be sure to keep your hands and face away from the steam.
3. Keep the pan with the ice cubes in place until you see drops of water dripping from the bottom.
4. **Think Critically** In your Science Journal, describe how the droplets formed. Infer where the water on the bottom of the pan came from.

Weather When information is grouped into clear categories, it is easier to make sense of what you are learning. Make the following Foldable to help you organize your thoughts about weather.

STEP 1 Collect 2 sheets of paper and layer them about 1.25 cm apart vertically. Keep the edges level.

STEP 2 Fold up the bottom edges of the paper to form 4 equal tabs.

STEP 3 Fold the papers and crease well to hold the tabs in place. Staple along the fold.

STEP 4 Label the tabs *Weather, What is weather?, Weather Patterns,* and *Forecasting Weather* as shown.

Summarize As you read the chapter, summarize what you learn under the appropriate tabs.

Preview this chapter's content and activities at glencoe.com

189

section

1

What is weather?

What You'll Learn

- **Explain** how solar heating and water vapor in the atmosphere affect weather.
- **Discuss** how clouds form and how they are classified.
- **Describe** how rain, hail, sleet, and snow develop.

Why It's Important

Weather changes affect your daily activities.

🔍 Review Vocabulary

factor: something that influences a result

New Vocabulary

- weather
- humidity
- relative humidity
- dew point
- fog
- precipitation

Weather Factors

It might seem like small talk to you, but for farmers, truck drivers, pilots, and construction workers, the weather can have a huge impact on their livelihoods. Even professional athletes, especially golfers, follow weather patterns closely. You can describe what happens in different kinds of weather, but can you explain how it happens?

Weather refers to the state of the atmosphere at a specific time and place. Weather describes conditions such as air pressure, wind, temperature, and the amount of moisture in the air.

The Sun provides almost all of Earth's energy. Energy from the Sun evaporates water into the atmosphere where it forms clouds. Eventually, the water falls back to Earth as rain or snow. However, the Sun does more than evaporate water. It is also a source of heat energy. Heat from the Sun is absorbed by Earth's surface, which then heats the air above it. Differences in Earth's surface lead to uneven heating of Earth's atmosphere. Heat is eventually redistributed by air and water currents. Weather, as shown in **Figure 1,** is the result of heat and Earth's air and water.

Figure 1 The Sun provides the energy that drives Earth's weather.
Identify *storms in this image.*

Molecules in air

Wind

Molecules in air

Temperature Pressure

Temperature Pressure

When air is heated, it expands and becomes less dense. This creates lower pressure.

Molecules making up air are closer together in cooler temperatures, creating high pressure. Wind blows from higher pressure toward lower pressure.

Air Temperature During the summer when the Sun is hot and the air is still, a swim can be refreshing. But would a swim seem refreshing on a cold, winter day? The temperature of air influences your daily activities.

Air is made up of molecules that are always moving randomly, even when there's no wind. Temperature is a measure of the average amount of motion of molecules. When the temperature is high, molecules in air move rapidly and it feels warm. When the temperature is low, molecules in air move less rapidly, and it feels cold.

Wind Why can you fly a kite on some days but not others? Kites fly because air is moving. Air moving in a specific direction is called wind. As the Sun warms the air, the air expands and becomes less dense. Warm, expanding air has low atmospheric pressure. Cooler air is denser and tends to sink, bringing about high atmospheric pressure. Wind results because air moves from regions of high pressure to regions of low pressure. You may have experienced this on a small scale if you've ever spent time along a beach, as in **Figure 2.**

Many instruments are used to measure wind direction and speed. Wind direction can be measured using a wind vane. A wind vane has an arrow that points in the direction from which the wind is blowing. A wind sock has one open end that catches the wind, causing the sock to point in the direction toward which the wind is blowing. Wind speed can be measured using an anemometer (a nuh MAH muh tur). Anemometers have rotating cups that spin faster when the wind is strong.

Figure 2 The temperature of air can affect air pressure. Wind is air moving from high pressure to low pressure.
Infer *In the above picture, which way would the wind move at night if the land cooled?*

INTEGRATE
Life Science

Body Temperature Birds and mammals maintain a fairly constant internal temperature, even when the temperature outside their bodies changes. On the other hand, the internal temperature of fish and reptiles changes when the temperature around them changes. Infer from this which group is more likely to survive a quick change in the weather.

Figure 3 Warmer air can have more water vapor than cooler air can because water vapor doesn't easily condense in warm air.

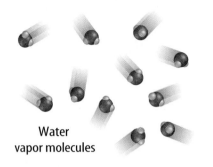 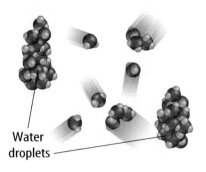

Water vapor molecules

Water droplets

Water vapor molecules in warm air move rapidly. The molecules can't easily come together and condense.

As air cools, water molecules in air move closer together. Some of them collide, allowing condensation to take place.

Determining Dew Point

Procedure

1. Partially fill a **metal can** with **room-temperature water**. Dry the outer surface of the can.
2. Place a **stirring rod** in the water.
3. Slowly stir the water and add small amounts of **ice**.
4. Make a data table in your **Science Journal**. With a **thermometer**, note the exact water temperature at which a thin film of moisture first begins to form on the outside of the metal can.
5. Repeat steps 1 through 4 two more times.
6. The average of the three temperatures at which the moisture begins to appear is the dew point temperature of the air surrounding the metal container.

Analysis

1. What determines the dew point temperature?
2. Will the dew point change with increasing temperature if the amount of moisture in the air doesn't change? Explain.

Humidity Heat evaporates water into the atmosphere. Where does the water go? Water vapor molecules fit into spaces among the molecules that make up air. The amount of water vapor present in the air is called **humidity.**

Air doesn't always contain the same amount of water vapor. As you can see in **Figure 3,** more water vapor can be present when the air is warm than when it is cool. At warmer temperatures, the molecules of water vapor in air move quickly and don't easily come together. At cooler temperatures, molecules in air move more slowly. The slower movement allows water vapor molecules to stick together and form droplets of liquid water. The formation of liquid water from water vapor is called condensation. When enough water vapor is present in air for condensation to take place, the air is saturated.

☑ Reading Check *Why can more water vapor be present in warm air than in cold air?*

Relative Humidity On a hot, sticky afternoon, the weather forecaster reports that the humidity is 50 percent. How can the humidity be low when it feels so humid? Weather forecasters report the amount of moisture in the air as relative humidity. **Relative humidity** is a measure of the amount of water vapor present in the air compared to the amount needed for saturation at a specific temperature.

If you hear a weather forecaster say that the relative humidity is 50 percent, it means that the air contains 50 percent of the water needed for the air to be saturated.

As shown in **Figure 4,** air at 25°C is saturated when it contains 22 g of water vapor per cubic meter of air. The relative humidity is 100 percent. If air at 25°C contains 11 g of water vapor per cubic meter, the relative humidity is 50 percent.

Dew Point

When the temperature drops, less water vapor can be present in air. The water vapor in air will condense to a liquid or form ice crystals. The temperature at which air is saturated and condensation forms is the dew point. The **dew point** changes with the amount of water vapor in the air.

You've probably seen water droplets form on the outside of a glass of cold milk. The cold glass cooled the air next to it to its dew point. The water vapor in the surrounding air condensed and formed water droplets on the glass. In a similar way, when air near the ground cools to its dew point, water vapor condenses and forms dew. Frost may form when temperatures are near 0°C.

Hot Words Hot Topics: Bk 1 pp. 134, 278

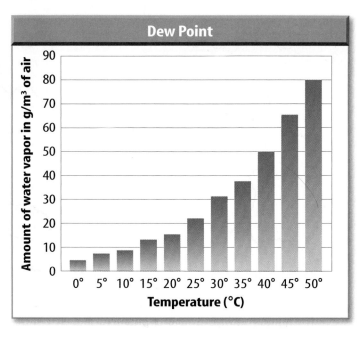

Figure 4 This graph shows that as the temperature of air increases, more water vapor can be present in the air.

Applying Math   Calculate Percent

DEW POINT One summer day, the relative humidity is 80 percent and the temperature is 35°C. Use **Figure 4** to find the dew point reached if the temperature falls to 25°C?

Solution

1 *This is what you know:*

Air Temperature (°C)	Amount of Water Vapor Needed for Saturation (g/m³)
35	37
25	22
15	14

2 *This is what you need to find out:* x = amount of water vapor in 35°C air at 80 percent relative humidity. Is $x > 22$ g/m³ or is $x < 22$ g/m³?

3 *This is how you solve the problem:* $x = .80 \, (37 \text{ g/m}^3)$
$x = 29.6$ g/m³ of water vapor
29.6 g/m³ > 22 g/m³, so the dew point is reached and dew will form.

Practice Problems

1. If the relative humidity is 50 percent and the air temperature is 35°C, will the dew point be reached if the temperature falls to 20°C?

2. If the air temperature is 25°C and the relative humidity is 30 percent, will the dew point be reached if the temperature drops to 15°C?

 | **For more practice, visit** glencoe.com

Physical Setting

2.2i, 2.2l: Define weather. Identify the four factors that determine weather.

Forming Clouds

Why are there clouds in the sky? Clouds form as warm air is forced upward, expands, and cools. **Figure 5** shows several ways that warm, moist air forms clouds. As the air cools, the amount of water vapor needed for saturation decreases and the relative humidity increases. When the relative humidity reaches 100 percent, the air is saturated. Water vapor soon begins to condense in tiny droplets around small particles such as dust and salt. These droplets of water are so small that they remain suspended in the air. Billions of these droplets form a cloud.

Classifying Clouds

Clouds are classified mainly by shape and height. Some clouds extend high into the sky, and others are low and flat. Some dense clouds bring rain or snow, while thin, wispy clouds appear on mostly sunny days. The shape and height of clouds vary with temperature, pressure, and the amount of water vapor in the atmosphere.

Figure 5 Clouds form when moist air is lifted and cools. This occurs where air is heated, at mountain ranges, and where cold air meets warm air.

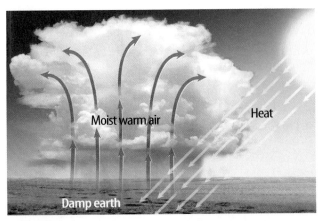

Rays from the Sun heat the ground and the air next to it. The warm air rises and cools. If the air is moist, some water vapor condenses and forms clouds.

As moist air moves over mountains, it is lifted and cools. Clouds formed in this way can cover mountains for long periods of time.

When cool air meets warm, moist air, the warm air is lifted and cools.
Explain what happens to the water vapor when the dew point is reached.

Shape The three main cloud types are stratus, cumulus, and cirrus. Stratus clouds form layers, or smooth, even sheets in the sky. Stratus clouds usually form at low altitudes and may be associated with fair weather or rain or snow. When air is cooled to its dew point near the ground, it forms a stratus cloud called **fog,** as shown in **Figure 6.**

Cumulus (KYEW myuh lus) clouds are masses of puffy, white clouds, often with flat bases. They sometimes tower to great heights and can be associated with fair weather or thunderstorms.

Cirrus (SIHR us) clouds appear fibrous or curly. They are high, thin, white, feathery clouds made of ice crystals. Cirrus clouds are associated with fair weather, but they can indicate approaching storms.

Height Some prefixes of cloud names describe the height of the cloud base. The prefix *cirro-* describes high clouds, *alto-* describes middle-elevation clouds, and *strato-* refers to clouds at low elevations. Some clouds' names combine the altitude prefix with the term *stratus* or *cumulus.*

Cirrostratus clouds are high clouds, like those in **Figure 7.** Usually, cirrostratus clouds indicate fair weather, but they also can signal an approaching storm. Altostratus clouds form at middle levels. If the clouds are not too thick, sunlight can filter through them.

Figure 6 Fog surrounds the Golden Gate Bridge, San Francisco. Fog is a stratus cloud near the ground.
Think Critically *Why do you think fog is found in San Francisco Bay?*

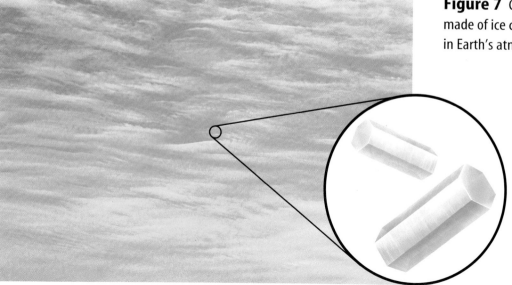

Figure 7 Cirrostratus clouds are made of ice crystals and form high in Earth's atmosphere.

Figure 8 Water vapor in air collects on particles to form water droplets or ice crystals. The type of precipitation that is received on the ground depends on the temperature of the air.

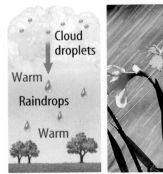 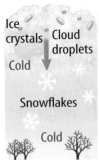

When the air is warm, water vapor forms raindrops that fall as rain.

When the air is cold, water vapor forms snowflakes.

Physical Setting

2.2o: Design a chart to compare the four main types of precipitation and the effect of air temperature.

Rain- or Snow-Producing Clouds Clouds associated with rain or snow often have the word nimbus attached to them. The term *nimbus* is Latin for "dark rain cloud" and this is a good description, because the water content of these clouds is so high that little sunlight can pass through them. When a cumulus cloud grows into a thunderstorm, it is called a cumulonimbus (kyew myuh loh NIHM bus) cloud. These clouds can tower to nearly 18 km. Nimbostratus clouds are layered clouds that can bring long, steady rain or snowfall.

Precipitation

Water falling from clouds is called **precipitation.** Precipitation occurs when cloud droplets combine and grow large enough to fall to Earth. The cloud droplets form around small particles, such as salt and dust. These particles are so small that a puff of smoke can contain millions of them.

You might have noticed that raindrops are not all the same size. The size of raindrops depends on several factors. One factor is the strength of updrafts in a cloud. Strong updrafts can keep drops suspended in the air where they can combine with other drops and grow larger. The rate of evaporation as a drop falls to Earth also can affect its size. If the air is dry, the size of raindrops can be reduced or they can completely evaporate before reaching the ground.

Air temperature determines whether water forms rain, snow, sleet, or hail—the four main types of precipitation. **Figure 8** shows these different types of precipitation. Drops of water falling in temperatures above freezing fall as rain. Snow forms when the air temperature is so cold that water vapor changes directly to a solid. Sleet forms when raindrops pass through a layer of freezing air near Earth's surface, forming ice pellets.

 **Reading Check** *What are the four main types of precipitation?*

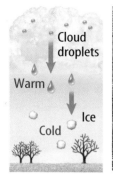

When the air near the ground is cold, sleet, which is made up of many small ice pellets, falls.

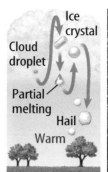

Hailstones are pellets of ice that form inside a cloud.

Hail Hail is precipitation in the form of lumps of ice. Hail forms in cumulonimbus clouds of a thunderstorm when water freezes in layers around a small nucleus of ice. Hailstones grow larger as they're tossed up and down by rising and falling air. Most hailstones are smaller than 2.5 cm but can grow larger than a softball. Of all forms of precipitation, hail produces the most damage immediately, especially if winds blow during a hailstorm. Falling hailstones can break windows and destroy crops.

If you understand the role of water vapor in the atmosphere, you can begin to understand weather. The relative humidity of the air helps determine whether a location will have a dry day or experience some form of precipitation. The temperature of the atmosphere determines the form of precipitation. Studying clouds can add to your ability to forecast weather.

section 1 review

Summary

Weather Factors

- Weather is the state of the atmosphere at a specific time and place.
- Temperature, wind, air pressure, dew point, and humidity describe weather.

Clouds

- Warm, moist air rises, forming clouds.
- The main types of clouds are stratus, cumulus, and cirrus.

Precipitation

- Water falling from clouds is called precipitation.
- Air temperature determines whether water forms rain, snow, sleet, or hail.

Self Check

1. **Explain** When does water vapor in air condense?
2. **Compare and contrast** humidity and relative humidity.
3. **Summarize** how clouds form.
4. **Describe** How does precipitation occur and what determines the type of precipitation that falls to Earth?
5. **Think Critically** Cumulonimbus clouds form when warm, moist air is suddenly lifted. How can the same cumulonimbus cloud produce rain and hail?

Hot Words Hot Topics: Bk 1 pp. 134, 278

Applying Math

6. **Use Graphs** If the air temperature is 30°C and the relative humidity is 60 percent, will the dew point be reached if the temperature drops to 25°C? Use the graph in **Figure 4** to explain your answer.

PS 2.2l: Air masses form when air remains nearly stationary over a large section of Earth's surface and takes on the conditions of temperature and humidity from that location. 2.2o: Fronts are boundaries between air masses. Also covered: 2.2m, 2.2n, 2.2p.

section 2

Weather Patterns

as you read

What You'll Learn

■ **Describe** how weather is associated with fronts and high- and low-pressure areas.
■ **Explain** how tornadoes develop from thunderstorms.
■ **Discuss** the dangers of severe weather.

Why It's Important

Air masses, pressure systems, and fronts cause weather to change.

⊙ Review Vocabulary

barometer: instrument used to measure atmospheric pressure

New Vocabulary

● air mass   ● hurricane
● front   ● blizzard
● tornado

Weather Changes

When you leave for school in the morning, the weather might be different from what it is when you head home in the afternoon. Because of the movement of air and moisture in the atmosphere, weather constantly changes.

Air Masses An **air mass** is a large body of air that has properties similar to the part of Earth's surface over which it develops. For example, an air mass that develops over land is dry compared with one that develops over water. An air mass that develops in the tropics is warmer than one that develops over northern regions. An air mass can cover thousands of square kilometers. When you observe a change in the weather from one day to the next, it is due to the movement of air masses. **Figure 9** shows air masses that affect the United States.

Figure 9 Six major air masses affect weather in the United States. Each air mass has the same characteristics of temperature and moisture content as the area over which it formed.

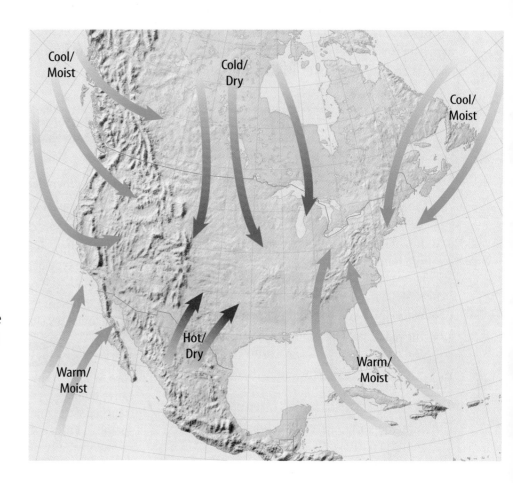

Cool/Moist

Cold/Dry

Cool/Moist

Cool/Moist

Hot/Dry

Warm/Moist

Warm/Moist

Highs and Lows Atmospheric pressure varies over Earth's surface. Anyone who has watched a weather report on television has heard about high- and low-pressure systems. Recall that winds blow from areas of high pressure to areas of low pressure. As winds blow into a low-pressure area in the northern hemisphere, Earth's rotation causes these winds to swirl in a counterclockwise direction. Large, swirling areas of low pressure are called cyclones and are associated with stormy weather.

✓ Reading Check *How do winds move in a cyclone?*

Winds blow away from a center of high pressure. Earth's rotation causes these winds to spiral clockwise in the northern hemisphere. High-pressure areas are associated with fair weather and are called anticyclones. Air pressure is measured using a barometer, like the one shown in **Figure 10.**

Variation in atmospheric pressure affects the weather. Low pressure systems at Earth's surface are regions of rising air. Clouds form when air is lifted and cools. Areas of low pressure usually have cloudy weather. Sinking motion in high-pressure air masses makes it difficult for air to rise and clouds to form. That's why high pressure usually means good weather.

Fronts

A boundary between two air masses of different density, moisture, or temperature is called a **front.** If you've seen a weather map in the newspaper or on the evening news, you've seen fronts represented by various types of curving lines.

Cloudiness, precipitation, and storms sometimes occur at frontal boundaries. Four types of fronts include cold, warm, occluded, and stationary.

Cold and Warm Fronts A cold front, shown on a map as a blue line with triangles , occurs when colder air advances toward warm air. The cold air wedges under the warm air like a plow. As the warm air is lifted, it cools and water vapor condenses, forming clouds. When the temperature difference between the cold and warm air is large, thunderstorms and even tornadoes may form.

Warm fronts form when lighter, warmer air advances over heavier, colder air. A warm front is drawn on weather maps as a red line with red semicircles .

Figure 10 A barometer measures atmospheric pressure. The red pointer points to the current pressure. Watch how atmospheric pressure changes over time when you line up the white pointer to the one indicating the current pressure each day.

Physical Setting

2.2o: Analyze why precipitation is most likely to occur at frontal boundaries.

Science Online

Topic: Atmospheric Pressure

Visit glencoe.com for Web links to information about the current atmospheric pressure of your town or nearest city.

Activity Look up the pressure of a city west of your town and the pressure of a city to the east. Compare the pressures to local weather conditions. Share your information with the class.

Occluded and Stationary Fronts An occluded front involves three air masses of different temperatures—colder air, cool air, and warm air. An occluded front may form when a cold air mass moves toward cool air with warm air between the two. The colder air forces the warm air upward, closing off the warm air from the surface. Occluded fronts are shown on maps as purple lines with triangles and semicircles ▲●▲.

A stationary front occurs when a boundary between air masses stops advancing. Stationary fronts may remain in the same place for several days, producing light wind and precipitation. A stationary front is drawn on a weather map as an alternating red and blue line. Red semicircles point toward the cold air and blue triangles point toward the warm air ➤▼➤. **Figure 11** summarizes the four types of fronts.

Figure 11 Cold, warm, occluded, and stationary fronts occur at the boundaries of air masses.

Describe *what type of weather occurs at front boundaries.*

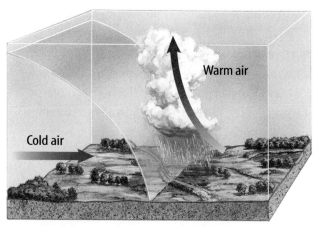

A cold front can advance rapidly. Thunderstorms often form as warm air is suddenly lifted up over the cold air.

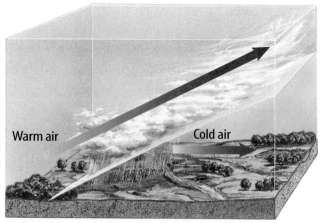

Warm air slides over colder air along a warm front, forming a boundary with a gentle slope. This can lead to hours, if not days, of wet weather.

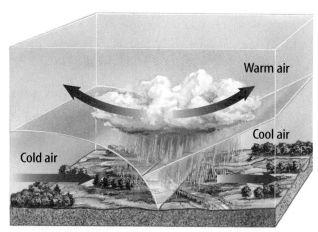

The term *occlusion* means "closure." Colder air forces warm air upward, forming an occluded front that closes off the warm air from the surface.

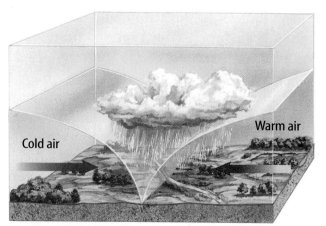

A stationary front results when neither cold air nor warm air advances.

Severe Weather

Despite the weather, you usually can do your daily activities. If it's raining, you still go to school. You can still get there even if it snows a little. However, some weather conditions, such as those caused by thunderstorms, tornadoes, and blizzards, prevent you from going about your normal routine. Severe weather poses danger to people, structures, and animals.

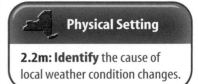
Thunderstorms In a thunderstorm, heavy rain falls, lightning flashes, thunder roars, and hail might fall. What forces cause such extreme weather conditions?

Thunderstorms occur in warm, moist air masses and along fronts. Warm, moist air can be forced upward where it cools and condensation occurs, forming cumulonimbus clouds that can reach heights of 18 km, like the one in **Figure 12.** When rising air cools, water vapor condenses into water droplets or ice crystals. Smaller droplets collide to form larger ones, and the droplets fall through the cloud toward Earth's surface. The falling droplets collide with still more droplets and grow larger. Raindrops cool the air around them. This cool, dense air then sinks and spreads over Earth's surface. Sinking, rain-cooled air and strong updrafts of warmer air cause the strong winds associated with thunderstorms. Hail also may form as ice crystals alternately fall to warmer layers and are lifted into colder layers by the strong updrafts inside cumulonimbus clouds.

Thunderstorm Damage Sometimes thunderstorms can stall over a region, causing rain to fall heavily for a period of time. When streams cannot contain all the water running into them, flash flooding can occur. Flash floods can be dangerous because they occur with little warning.

Strong winds generated by thunderstorms also can cause damage. If a thunderstorm is accompanied by winds traveling faster than 89 km/h, it is classified as a severe thunderstorm. Hail from a thunderstorm can dent cars and the aluminum siding on houses. Although rain from thunderstorms helps crops grow, hail has been known to flatten and destroy entire crops in a matter of minutes.

Figure 12 Tall cumulonimbus clouds may form quickly as warm, moist air rapidly rises.
Identify *some things these clouds are known to produce.*

Lightning and Thunder

What are lightning and thunder? Inside a storm cloud, warm air is lifted rapidly as cooler air sinks. This movement of air can cause different parts of a cloud to become oppositely charged. When current flows between regions of opposite electrical charge, lightning flashes. Lightning, as shown in **Figure 13,** can occur within a cloud, between clouds, or between a cloud and the ground.

Thunder results from the rapid heating of air around a bolt of lightning. Lightning can reach temperatures of about 30,000°C, which is more than five times the temperature of the surface of the Sun. This extreme heat causes air around the lightning to expand rapidly. Then it cools quickly and contracts. The rapid movement of the molecules forms sound waves heard as thunder.

Figure 13 This time-elapsed photo shows a thunderstorm over Arizona.

Tornadoes Some of the most severe thunderstorms produce tornadoes. A **tornado** is a violently rotating column of air in contact with the ground. In severe thunderstorms, wind at different heights blows in different directions and at different speeds. This difference in wind speed and direction, called wind shear, creates a rotating column parallel to the ground. A thunderstorm's updraft can tilt the rotating column upward into the thunderstorm creating a funnel cloud. If the funnel comes into contact with Earth's surface, it is called a tornado.

Reading Check *What causes a tornado to form?*

A tornado's destructive winds can rip apart buildings and uproot trees. High winds can blow through broken windows. When winds blow inside a house, they can lift off the roof and blow out the walls, making it look as though the building exploded. The updraft in the center of a powerful tornado can lift animals, cars, and even houses into the air. Although tornadoes rarely exceed 200 m in diameter and usually last only a few minutes, they often are extremely destructive. In May 1999, multiple thunderstorms produced more than 70 tornadoes in Kansas, Oklahoma, and Texas. This severe tornado outbreak caused 40 deaths, 100 injuries, and more than $1.2 billion in property damage.

Physical Setting

2.2n, 2.2p: Determine the direction high and low pressure systems travel across the United States. Hypothesize how this happens.

Topic: Lightning
Visit glencoe.com for Web links to research the number of lightning strikes in your state during the last year.

Activity Compare your findings with data from previous years. Communicate to your class what you learn.

Figure 14

Tornadoes are extremely rapid, rotating winds that form at the base of cumulonimbus clouds. Smaller tornadoes may even form inside larger ones. Luckily, most tornadoes remain on the ground for just a few minutes. During that time, however, they can cause considerable—and sometimes strange— damage, such as driving a fork into a tree.

Tornadoes often form from a type of cumulonimbus cloud called a wall cloud. Strong, spiraling updrafts of warm, moist air may form in these clouds. As air spins upward, a low-pressure area forms, and the cloud descends to the ground in a funnel. The tornado sucks up debris as it moves along the ground, forming a dust envelope.

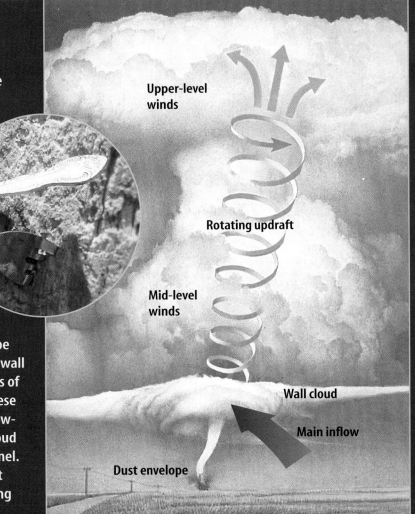

Upper-level winds

Rotating updraft

Mid-level winds

Wall cloud

Main inflow

Dust envelope

The Fujita Scale

	Wind speed (km/h)	Damage
F0	<116	Light: broken branches and chimneys
F1	116–180	Moderate: roofs damaged, mobile homes upturned
F2	181–253	Considerable: roofs torn off homes, large trees uprooted
F3	254–332	Severe: trains overturned, roofs and walls torn off
F4	333–419	Devastating: houses completely destroyed, cars picked up and carried elsewhere
F5	420–512	Incredible: total demolition

The Fujita scale, named after tornado expert Theodore Fujita, ranks tornadoes according to how much damage they cause. Fortunately, only one percent of tornadoes are classified as violent (F4 and F5).

Global Warming Some scientists hypothesize that Earth's ocean temperatures are increasing due to global warming. In your Science Journal, predict what might happen to the strength of hurricanes if Earth's oceans become warmer.

Figure 15 In this hurricane cross section, the small, red arrows indicate rising, warm, moist air. This air forms cumulus and cumulonimbus clouds in bands around the eye. The green arrows indicate cool, dry air sinking in the eye and between the cloud bands.

Hurricanes The most powerful storm is the hurricane. A **hurricane,** illustrated in **Figure 15,** is a large, swirling, low-pressure system that forms over the warm Atlantic Ocean. It is like a machine that turns heat energy from the ocean into wind. A storm must have winds of at least 119 km/h to be called a hurricane. Similar storms are called typhoons in the Pacific Ocean and cyclones in the Indian Ocean.

Hurricanes are similar to low-pressure systems on land, but they are much stronger. In the Atlantic and Pacific Oceans, low pressure sometimes develops near the equator. In the northern hemisphere, winds around this low pressure begin rotating counterclockwise. The strongest hurricanes affecting North America usually begin as a low-pressure system west of Africa. Steered by surface winds, these storms can travel west, gaining strength from the heat and moisture of warm ocean water.

When a hurricane strikes land, high winds, tornadoes, heavy rains, and high waves can cause a lot of damage. Floods from the heavy rains can cause additional damage. Hurricane weather can destroy crops, demolish buildings, and kill people and other animals. As long as a hurricane is over water, the warm, moist air rises and provides energy for the storm. When a hurricane reaches land, however, its supply of energy disappears and the storm loses power.

Blizzards Severe storms also can occur in winter. If you live in the northern United States, you may have awakened from a winter night's sleep to a cold, howling wind and blowing snow, like the storm in **Figure 16.** The National Weather Service classifies a winter storm as a **blizzard** if the winds are 56 km/h, the temperature is low, the visibility is less than 400 m in falling or blowing snow, and if these conditions persist for three hours or more.

Severe Weather Safety When severe weather threatens, the National Weather Service issues a watch or warning. Watches are issued when conditions are favorable for severe thunderstorms, tornadoes, floods, blizzards, and hurricanes. During a watch, stay tuned to a radio or television station reporting the weather. When a warning is issued, severe weather conditions already exist. You should take immediate action. During a severe thunderstorm or tornado warning, take shelter in the basement or a room in the middle of the house away from windows. When a hurricane or flood watch is issued, be prepared to leave your home and move farther inland.

Blizzards can be blinding and have dangerously low temperatures with high winds. During a blizzard, stay indoors. Spending too much time outside can result in severe frostbite.

Figure 16 Blizzards can be extremely dangerous because of their high winds, low temperatures, and poor visibility.

---

section 2 review

Summary

Weather Changes

- Air masses tend to have temperature and moisture properties similar to Earth's surface.
- Winds blow from areas of high pressure to areas of lower pressure.

Fronts

- A boundary between different air masses is called a front.

Severe Weather

- The National Weather Service issues watches or warnings, depending on the severity of the storm, for people's safety.

Self Check

1. **Draw Conclusions** Why is fair weather common during periods of high pressure?
2. **Describe** how a cold front affects weather.
3. **Explain** what causes lightning and thunder.
4. **Compare and contrast** a watch and a warning. How can you keep safe during a tornado warning?
5. **Think Critically** Explain why some fronts produce stronger storms than others.

Applying Skills

6. **Recognize Cause and Effect** Describe how an occluded front may form over your city and what effects it can have on the weather.

Weather Forecasts

as you read

What You'll Learn

- **Explain** how data are collected for weather maps and forecasts.
- **Identify** the symbols used in a weather station model.

Why It's Important

Weather observations help you predict future weather events.

🔎 Review Vocabulary

forecast: to predict a condition or event on the basis of observations

New Vocabulary

- meteorologist
- station model
- isotherm
- isobar

Figure 17 A meteorologist uses Doppler radar to track a tornado. Since the nineteenth century, technology has greatly improved weather forecasting.

Weather Observations

You can determine current weather conditions by checking the thermometer and looking to see whether clouds are in the sky. You know when it's raining. You have a general idea of the weather because you are familiar with the typical weather where you live. If you live in Florida, you don't expect snow in the forecast. If you live in Maine, you assume it will snow every winter. What weather concerns do you have in your region?

A **meteorologist** (mee tee uh RAH luh jist) is a person who studies the weather. Meteorologists take measurements of temperature, air pressure, winds, humidity, and precipitation. Computers, weather satellites, Doppler radar shown in **Figure 17,** and instruments attached to balloons are used to gather data. Such instruments improve meteorologists' ability to predict the weather. Meteorologists use the information provided by weather instruments to make weather maps. These maps are used to make weather forecasts.

Forecasting Weather

Meteorologists gather information about current weather and use computers to make predictions about future weather patterns. Because storms can be dangerous, you do not want to be unprepared for threatening weather. However, meteorologists cannot always predict the weather exactly because conditions can change rapidly.

The National Weather Service depends on two sources for its information—data collected from the upper atmosphere and data collected on Earth's surface. Meteorologists of the National Weather Service collect information recorded by satellites, instruments attached to weather balloons, and from radar. This information is used to describe weather conditions in the atmosphere above Earth's surface.

Station Models When meteorologists gather data from Earth's surface, it is recorded on a map using a combination of symbols, forming a **station model.** A station model, like the one in **Figure 18,** shows the weather conditions at a specific location on Earth's surface. Information provided by station models and instruments in the upper atmosphere is entered into computers and used to forecast weather.

Temperature and Pressure In addition to station models, weather maps have lines that connect locations of equal temperature or pressure. A line that connects points of equal temperature is called an **isotherm** (I suh thurm). *Iso* means "same" and *therm* means "temperature." You probably have seen isotherms on weather maps on TV or in the newspaper.

An **isobar** is a line drawn to connect points of equal atmospheric pressure. You can tell how fast wind is blowing in an area by noting how closely isobars are spaced. Isobars that are close together indicate a large pressure difference over a small area. A large pressure difference causes strong winds. Isobars that are spread apart indicate a smaller difference in pressure. Winds in this area are gentler. Isobars also indicate the locations of high- and low-pressure areas.

Reading Check *How do isobars indicate wind speed?*

Mini LAB

Measuring Rain

Procedure
1. You will need a **straight-sided container,** such as a soup or coffee can, **duct tape,** and a **ruler.**
2. Tape the ruler to the inner wall of your container.
3. Place the container on a level surface outdoors, away from buildings or plants.
4. Measure the amount of water in your container after it rains. Continue to take measurements for a week.

Analysis
1. What was the average daily rainfall?
2. Why is it necessary to use containers with straight sides?

Try at Home

Figure 18 A station model shows the weather conditions at one specific location.

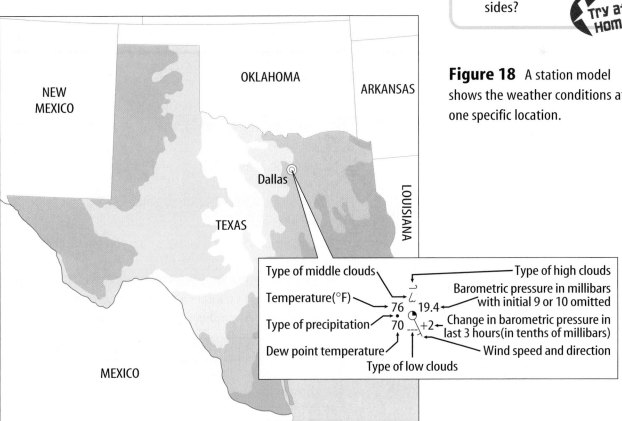

NEW MEXICO

OKLAHOMA

ARKANSAS

Dallas

TEXAS

LOUISIANA

MEXICO

Type of middle clouds

Temperature(°F)

Type of precipitation

Dew point temperature

76

70

Type of high clouds

19.4 — Barometric pressure in millibars with initial 9 or 10 omitted

+2 — Change in barometric pressure in last 3 hours(in tenths of millibars)

Wind speed and direction

Type of low clouds

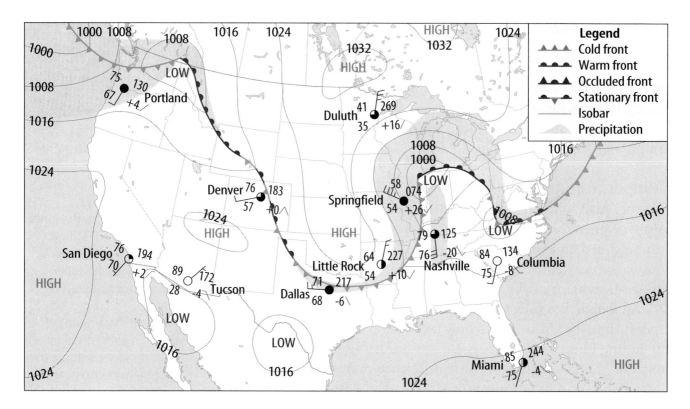

Figure 19 Highs, lows, isobars, and fronts on this weather map help meteorologists forecast the weather.

Weather Maps On a weather map like the one in **Figure 19,** pressure areas are drawn as circles with the word High or Low in the middle of the circle. Fronts are drawn as lines and symbols. When you watch weather forecasts on television, notice how weather fronts move from west to east. This is a pattern that meteorologists depend on to forecast weather.

section 3 review

Summary

Weather Observations

- Meteorologists are people who study the weather and make weather maps.

Forecasting Weather

- Meteorologists gather information about current weather and make predictions about future weather patterns.

- A station model shows weather conditions at a specific location on Earth's surface by using symbols to record meteorological data.

- On weather maps, isotherms are lines that connect points of equal temperature.

- An isobar is a line drawn on a weather map that connects points of equal atmospheric pressure.

Self Check

1. **List** some instruments that are used to collect weather data.

2. **Describe** at least six items of data that might be recorded in a station model.

3. **Explain** how the National Weather Service makes weather maps.

4. **Explain** what closely spaced isobars on a weather map indicate.

5. **Think Critically** In the morning you hear a meteorologist forecast today's weather as sunny and warm. After school, it is raining. Why is the weather so hard to predict?

Applying Skills

6. **Concept Map** Using a computer, make an events-chain concept map for how a weather forecast is made.

Reading a Weather Map

Meteorologists use a series of symbols to provide a picture of local and national weather conditions. With what you know, can you interpret weather information from weather map symbols?

◉ Real-World Question

How do you read a weather map?

Materials
magnifying lens
Weather Map Symbols Appendix
Figure 19 (Weather Map)

Goals
- ■ **Learn** how to read a weather map.
- ■ **Use** information from a station model and a weather map to forecast weather.

◉ Procedure

Use the information provided in the questions below and the Weather Map Symbols Appendix to learn how to read a weather map.

1. Find the station models on the map for Portland, Oregon, and Miami, Florida. Find the dew point, wind direction, barometric pressure, and temperature at each location.

2. Looking at the placement of the isobars, determine whether the wind would be stronger at Springfield, Illinois, or at San Diego, California. Record your answer. What is another way to determine the wind speed at these locations?

3. **Determine** the type of front near Dallas, Texas. Record your answer.

4. The triangles or half-circles are on the side of the line toward the direction the front is moving. In which direction is the cold front located over Washington state moving?

◉ Conclude and Apply

1. Locate the pressure system over southeast Kansas. Predict what will happen to the weather of Nashville, Tennessee, if this pressure system moves there.

2. Prevailing westerlies are winds responsible for the movement of much of the weather across the United States. Based on this, would you expect Columbia, South Carolina, to continue to have clear skies? Explain.

3. The direction line on the station model indicates the direction from which the wind blows. The wind is named for that direction. Infer from this the name of the wind blowing at Little Rock, Arkansas.

𝒞ommunicating Your Data

Pretend you are a meteorologist for a local TV news station. Make a poster of your weather data and present a weather forecast to your class.

Model and Invent

Measuring Wind Speed

Goals

■ **Invent** an instrument or devise a system for measuring wind speeds using common materials.

■ **Devise** a method for using your invention or system to compare different wind speeds.

Possible Materials

paper
scissors
confetti
grass clippings
meterstick
*measuring tape
*Alternate materials

Safety Precautions

Data Source

Refer to Section 1 for more information about anemometers and other wind speed instruments. Consult the data table for information about Beaufort's wind speed scale.

⊙ *Real-World Question*

When you watch a gust of wind blow leaves down the street, do you wonder how fast the wind is moving? For centuries, people could only guess at wind speeds, but in 1805, Admiral Beaufort of the British navy invented a method for estimating wind speeds based on their effect on sails. Later, Beaufort's system was modified for use on land. Meteorologists use a simple instrument called an anemometer to measure wind speeds, and they still use Beaufort's system to estimate the speed of the wind. What type of instrument or system can you invent to measure wind speed? How could you use simple materials to invent an instrument or system for measuring wind speeds? What observations do you use to estimate the speed of the wind?

⊙ *Make a Model*

1. Scan the list of possible materials and choose the materials you will need to devise your system.

2. **Devise** a system to measure different wind speeds. Be certain the materials you use are light enough to be moved by slight breezes.

Check the Model Plans

1. **Describe** your plan to your teacher. Provide a sketch of your instrument or system and ask your teacher how you might improve its design.
2. Present your idea for measuring wind speed to the class in the form of a diagram or poster. Ask your classmates to suggest improvements in your design that will make your system more accurate or easier to use.

Test Your Model

1. Confetti or grass clippings that are all the same size can be used to measure wind speed by dropping them from a specific height. Measuring the distances they travel in different strength winds will provide data for devising a wind speed scale.
2. Different sizes and shapes of paper also could be dropped into the wind, and the strength of the wind would be determined by measuring the distances traveled by these different types of paper.

Analyze Your Data

1. **Develop** a scale for your method.
2. **Compare** your results with Beaufort's wind speed scale.
3. **Analyze** what problems may exist in the design of your system and suggest steps you could take to improve your design.

Conclude and Apply

1. **Explain** why it is important for meteorologists to measure wind speeds.
2. **Evaluate** how well your system worked in gentle breezes and strong winds.

Beaufort's Wind Speed Scale

Description	Wind Speed (km/h)
calm—smoke drifts up	less than 1
light air—smoke drifts with wind	1–5
light breeze—leaves rustle	6–11
gentle breeze—leaves move constantly	12–19
moderate breeze—branches move	20–29
fresh breeze—small trees sway	30–39
strong breeze—large branches move	40–50
moderate gale—whole trees move	51–61
fresh gale—twigs break	62–74
strong gale—slight damage to houses	75–87
whole gale—much damage to houses	88–101
storm—extensive damage	102–120
hurricane—extreme damage	more than 120

Communicating Your Data

Demonstrate your system for the class. Compare your results and measurements with the results of other classmates.

Rainmakers

Cloud seeding is an inexact science

You listen to a meteorologist give the long-term weather forecast. Another week with no rain in sight. As a farmer, you are concerned that your crops are withering in the fields. Home owners' lawns are turning brown. Wildfires are possible. Cattle are starving. And, if farmers' crops die, there could be a shortage of food and prices will go up for consumers.

Meanwhile, several states away, another farmer is listening to the weather report calling for another week of rain. Her crops are getting so water soaked that they are beginning to rot.

Weather. Can't scientists find a way to better control it? The answer is...not exactly. Scientists have been experimenting with methods to control our weather since the 1940s. And nothing really works.

Cloud seeding is one such attempt. It uses technology to enhance the natural rainfall process. The idea has been used to create rain where it is needed or to reduce hail damage. Government officials also use cloud seeding or weather modification to try to reduce the force of a severe storm.

Some people seed a cloud by flying a plane above it and releasing highway-type flares with chemicals, such as silver iodide. Another method is to fly beneath the cloud and spray a chemical that can be carried into the cloud by air currents.

Cloud seeding doesn't work with clouds that have little water vapor or are not near the dew point. Seeding chemicals must be released into potential rain clouds. The chemicals provide nuclei for water molecules to cluster around. Water then falls to Earth as precipitation.

Cloud seeding does have its critics. If you seed clouds and cause rain for your area, aren't you preventing rain from falling in another area? Would that be considered "rain theft" by people who live in places where the cloudburst would naturally occur? What about those cloud-seeding agents? Could the cloud-seeding chemicals, such as silver iodide and acetone, affect the environment in a harmful way? Are humans meddling with nature and creating problems in ways that haven't been determined?

Flares are lodged under a plane. The pilot will drop them into potential rain clouds.

Debate Learn more about cloud seeding and other methods of changing weather. Then debate whether or not cloud seeding can be considered "rain theft."

Science Online

For more information, visit glencoe.com

Reviewing Main Ideas

Section 1 What is weather?

1. Factors that determine weather include air pressure, wind, temperature, and the amount of moisture in the air.

2. More water vapor can be present in warm air than in cold air. Water vapor condenses when the dew point is reached. Clouds are formed when warm, moist air rises and cools to its dew point.

3. Rain, hail, sleet, and snow are types of precipitation.

Section 2 Weather Patterns

1. Fronts form when air masses with different characteristics meet. Types of fronts include cold, warm, occluded, and stationary fronts.

2. High atmospheric pressure at Earth's surface usually means good weather. Cloudy and stormy weather occurs under low pressure.

3. Tornadoes, thunderstorms, hurricanes, and blizzards are examples of severe weather.

Section 3 Weather Forecasts

1. Meteorologists use information from radar, satellites, computers, and other weather instruments to forecast the weather.

2. Weather maps include information about temperature and air pressure. Station models indicate weather at a particular location.

Visualizing Main Ideas

Copy and complete the following concept map about air temperature, water vapor, and pressure.

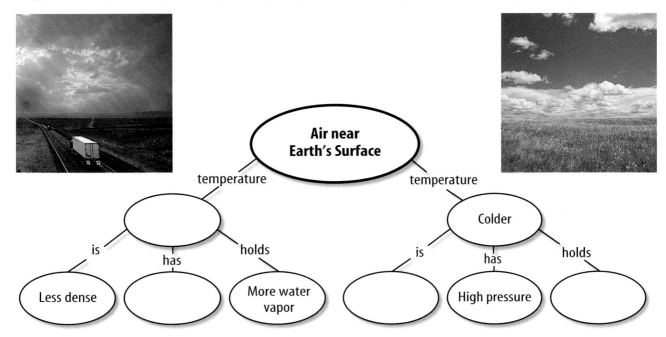

Using Vocabulary

air mass p. 198	isotherm p. 207
blizzard p. 205	meteorologist p. 206
dew point p. 193	precipitation p. 196
fog p. 195	relative humidity p. 192
front p. 199	station model p. 207
humidity p. 192	tornado p. 202
hurricane p. 204	weather p. 190
isobar p. 207	

Explain the differences between the vocabulary words in each of the following sets.

1. air mass—front
2. humidity—relative humidity
3. relative humidity—dew point
4. dew point—precipitation
5. hurricane—tornado
6. blizzard—fog
7. meteorologist—station model
8. precipitation—fog
9. isobar—isotherm
10. isobar—front

Checking Concepts

Choose the word or phrase that best answers the question.

11. Which term refers to the amount of water vapor in the air?
    A) dew point
    C) humidity
    B) precipitation
    D) relative humidity

12. What does an anemometer measure?
    A) wind speed
    C) air pressure
    B) precipitation
    D) relative humidity

13. Which type of air has a relative humidity of 100 percent?
    A) humid
    C) dry
    B) temperate
    D) saturated

Use the photo below to answer question 14.

14. Which type of the following clouds are high feathery clouds made of ice crystals?
    A) cirrus
    C) cumulus
    B) nimbus
    D) stratus

15. What is a large body of air that has the same properties as the area over which it formed called?
    A) air mass
    C) front
    B) station model
    D) isotherm

16. At what temperature does water vapor in air condense?
    A) dew point
    C) front
    B) station model
    D) isobar

17. Which type of precipitation forms when water vapor changes directly into a solid?
    A) rain
    C) sleet
    B) hail
    D) snow

18. Which type of front may form when cool air, cold air, and warm air meet?
    A) warm
    C) stationary
    B) cold
    D) occluded

19. Which is issued when severe weather conditions exist and immediate action should be taken?
    A) front
    C) station model
    B) watch
    D) warning

20. What is a large, swirling storm that forms over warm, tropical water called?
    A) hurricane
    C) blizzard
    B) tornado
    D) hailstorm

Vocabulary Puzzlemaker glencoe.com

Thinking Critically

21. Explain the relationship between temperature and relative humidity.

22. Describe how air, water, and the Sun interact to cause weather.

23. Explain why northwest Washington often has rainy weather and southwest Texas is dry.

24. Determine What does it mean if the relative humidity is 79 percent?

25. Infer Why don't hurricanes form in Earth's polar regions?

26. Compare and contrast the weather at a cold front and the weather at a warm front.

27. Interpret Scientific Illustrations Use the cloud descriptions in this chapter to describe the weather at your location today. Then try to predict tomorrow's weather.

28. Compare and contrast tornadoes and thunderstorms. Include information about wind location and direction.

29. Concept Map Copy and complete the sequence map below showing how precipitation forms.

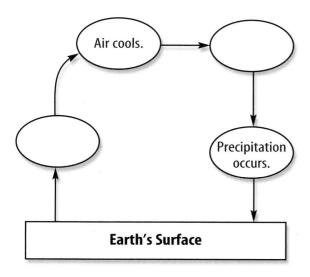

30. Observe and Infer You take a hot shower. The mirror in the bathroom fogs up. Infer from this information what has happened.

Performance Activities

31. Board Game Make a board game using weather terms. You could make cards to advance or retreat a token.

32. Design your own weather station. Record temperature, precipitation, and wind speed for one week.

Hot Words Hot Topics: Bk 1 pp. 134, 278

Applying Math

Use the table below to answer question 33.

Air Temperature (°C)	Amount of Water Vapor Needed for Saturation (g/m³)
25	22
20	15

33. Dew Point If the air temperature is 25°C and the relative humidity is 55 percent, will the dew point be reached if the temperature drops to 20°C?

34. Rising Temperature If the air temperature is 30°C and the relative humidity is 60 percent, will the dew point be reached if the temperature rises to 35°C? Use the graph in **Figure 4** to explain your answer.

Record your answers on the answer sheet provided by your teacher or on a sheet of paper.

Use the table and paragraph below to answer questions 1 and 2.

Hurricanes are rated on a scale based on their wind speed and barometric pressure. The table below lists hurricane categories.

Hurricane Rating Scale		
Category	Wind Speed (km/h)	Barometric Pressure (millibars)
1	119–154	>980
2	155–178	965–980
3	179–210	945–964
4	211–250	920–944
5	>250	<920

1 Hurricane Mitch, with winds of 313 km/h and a pressure of 907 mb, struck the east coast of Central America in 1998. What category was Hurricane Mitch?
(1) 2
(2) 3
(3) 4
(4) 5

2 Which of the following is true when categorizing a hurricane?
(1) Storm category increases as wind increases and pressure decreases.
(2) Storm category increases as wind decreases and pressure increases.
(3) Storm category increases as wind and pressure increase.
(4) Storm category decreases as wind and pressure decrease.

3 Which of the following instruments is used to measure air pressure?
(1) anemometer   (3) barometer
(2) thermometer   (4) rain gauge

4 Which of the following is a description of a tornado?
(1) a large, swirling, low-pressure system that forms over the warm Atlantic Ocean
(2) a winter storm with winds at least 56 km/h and low visibility
(3) a violently rotating column of air in contact with the ground
(4) a boundary between two air masses of different density, moisture, or temperature

Use the figure below to answer questions 5 and 6.

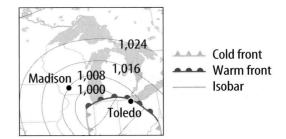

5 What is the atmospheric pressure in the city of Madison, Wisconsin?
(1) 1024 mb   (3) 1008 mb
(2) 1016 mb   (4) 1000 mb

6 What type of front is near Toledo, Ohio?
(1) cold front
(2) warm front
(3) stationary front
(4) occluded front

7 Which of the following terms is used to describe a person studies the weather?
(1) meteorologist
(2) geologist
(3) biologist
(4) paleontologist

Record your answer on the answer sheet provided by your teacher or on a sheet of paper.

8 Describe weather conditions during which hailstones form and the process by which they form.

9 What effects do high-pressure systems have on air circulation and weather? What effects do low-pressure systems have on weather?

10 Explain the relationship between lightning and thunder.

Use the figure below to answer question 11.

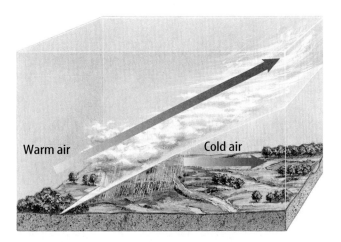

11 What type of front is shown? How does this type of front form?

12 Explain what type of weather occurs at front boundaries.

13 Explain how the Sun's heat energy creates Earth's weather.

14 What are the four main types of precipitation? Describe the differences between each type.

15 Describe how a hurricane in the Northern Hemisphere forms.

16 Explain why hurricanes lose power once they reach land.

Student Resources

Student Resources

CONTENTS

Science Skill Handbook 342

Scientific Methods 342
- Identify a Question 342
- Gather and
  - Organize Information 342
- Form a Hypothesis 345
- Test the Hypothesis 346
- Collect Data 346
- Analyze the Data 349
- Draw Conclusions 350
- Communicate 350

Safety Symbols 351

Safety in the Science Laboratory 352
- General Safety Rules 352
- Prevent Accidents 352
- Laboratory Work 352
- Laboratory Cleanup 353
- Emergencies 353

Extra Try at Home Labs 354

1. Testing Horoscopes 354
2. The Heat is On 354
3. Simple Machines 355
4. Microscopic Crystals 355
5. Estimate Temperature 356
6. The Pressure's On 356
7. Bottling a Tornado 357
8. Classification Poster 357
9. Rock Creatures 358
10. A Light in the Forest 358
11. Echinoderm Hold 359

Technology Skill Handbook ... 360

- Hardware Basics 360
- Storing Your Data 360
- Getting Started with
  - Word Processing Programs 361
- Getting Started with
  - Spreadsheet Programs 361
- Getting Started with
  - Presentation Programs 362
- Doing Research with the
  - World Wide Web 363

Math Skill Handbook 364

Math Review 364
- Use Fractions 364
- Use Ratios 367
- Use Decimals 367
- Use Proportions 368
- Use Percentages 369
- Solve One-Step Equations 369
- Use Statistics 370
- Use Geometry 371

Science Applications 374
- Measure in SI 374
- Dimensional Analysis 374
- Precision and Significant Digits ... 376
- Scientific Notation 376
- Make and Use Graphs 377

Reference Handbooks 379

Use and Care of a Microscope 379
Topographic Map Symbols 380
Weather Map Symbols 381
Classification of Living Organisms ... 382
Periodic Table of Elements 386

English/Spanish Glossary 388

Index 402

Credits 413

Scientific Methods

Scientists use an orderly approach called the scientific method to solve problems. This includes organizing and recording data so others can understand them. Scientists use many variations in this method when they solve problems.

Identify a Question

The first step in a scientific investigation or experiment is to identify a question to be answered or a problem to be solved. For example, you might ask which gasoline is the most efficient.

Gather and Organize Information

After you have identified your question, begin gathering and organizing information. There are many ways to gather information, such as researching in a library, interviewing those knowledgeable about the subject, testing and working in the laboratory and field. Fieldwork is investigations and observations done outside of a laboratory.

Researching Information Before moving in a new direction, it is important to gather the information that already is known about the subject. Start by asking yourself questions to determine exactly what you need to know. Then you will look for the information in various reference sources, like the student is doing in **Figure 1.** Some sources may include textbooks, encyclopedias, government documents, professional journals, science magazines, and the Internet. Always list the sources of your information.

Figure 1 The Internet can be a valuable research tool.

Evaluate Sources of Information Not all sources of information are reliable. You should evaluate all of your sources of information, and use only those you know to be dependable. For example, if you are researching ways to make homes more energy efficient, a site written by the U.S. Department of Energy would be more reliable than a site written by a company that is trying to sell a new type of weatherproofing material. Also, remember that research always is changing. Consult the most current resources available to you. For example, a 1985 resource about saving energy would not reflect the most recent findings.

Sometimes scientists use data that they did not collect themselves, or conclusions drawn by other researchers. This data must be evaluated carefully. Ask questions about how the data were obtained, if the investigation was carried out properly, and if it has been duplicated exactly with the same results. Would you reach the same conclusion from the data? Only when you have confidence in the data can you believe it is true and feel comfortable using it.

Interpret Scientific Illustrations As you research a topic in science, you will see drawings, diagrams, and photographs to help you understand what you read. Some illustrations are included to help you understand an idea that you can't see easily by yourself, like the tiny particles in an atom in **Figure 2.** A drawing helps many people to remember details more easily and provides examples that clarify difficult concepts or give additional information about the topic you are studying. Most illustrations have labels or a caption to identify or to provide more information.

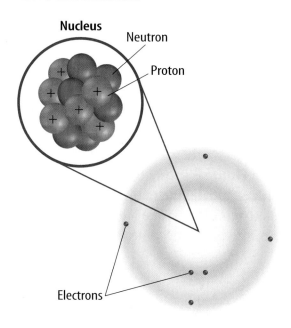

Figure 2 This drawing shows an atom of carbon with its six protons, six neutrons, and six electrons.

Concept Maps One way to organize data is to draw a diagram that shows relationships among ideas (or concepts). A concept map can help make the meanings of ideas and terms more clear, and help you understand and remember what you are studying. Concept maps are useful for breaking large concepts down into smaller parts, making learning easier.

Network Tree A type of concept map that not only shows a relationship, but how the concepts are related is a network tree, shown in **Figure 3.** In a network tree, the words are written in the ovals, while the description of the type of relationship is written across the connecting lines.

When constructing a network tree, write down the topic and all major topics on separate pieces of paper or notecards. Then arrange them in order from general to specific. Branch the related concepts from the major concept and describe the relationship on the connecting line. Continue to more specific concepts until finished.

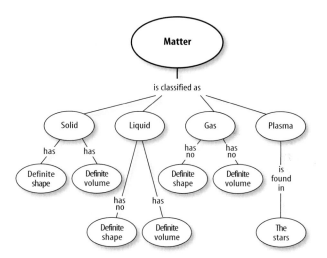

Figure 3 A network tree shows how concepts or objects are related.

Events Chain Another type of concept map is an events chain. Sometimes called a flow chart, it models the order or sequence of items. An events chain can be used to describe a sequence of events, the steps in a procedure, or the stages of a process.

When making an events chain, first find the one event that starts the chain. This event is called the initiating event. Then, find the next event and continue until the outcome is reached, as shown in **Figure 4.**

Initiating Event

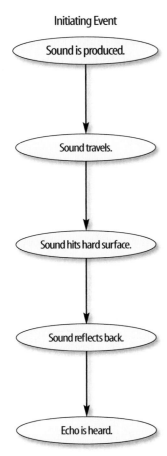

Figure 4 Events-chain concept maps show the order of steps in a process or event. This concept map shows how a sound makes an echo.

Cycle Map A specific type of events chain is a cycle map. It is used when the series of events do not produce a final outcome, but instead relate back to the beginning event, such as in **Figure 5.** Therefore, the cycle repeats itself.

To make a cycle map, first decide what event is the beginning event. This is also called the initiating event. Then list the next events in the order that they occur, with the last event relating back to the initiating event. Words can be written between the events that describe what happens from one event to the next. The number of events in a cycle map can vary, but usually contain three or more events.

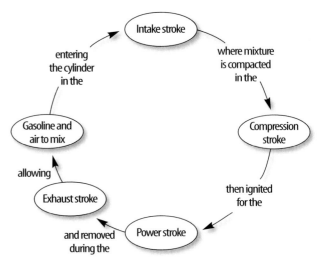

Figure 5 A cycle map shows events that occur in a cycle.

Spider Map A type of concept map that you can use for brainstorming is the spider map. When you have a central idea, you might find that you have a jumble of ideas that relate to it but are not necessarily clearly related to each other. The spider map on sound in **Figure 6** shows that if you write these ideas outside the main concept, then you can begin to separate and group unrelated terms so they become more useful.

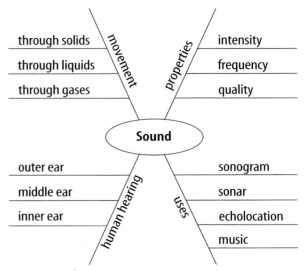

Figure 6 A spider map allows you to list ideas that relate to a central topic but not necessarily to one another.

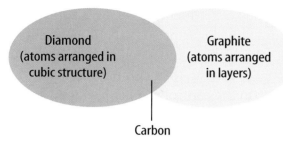

Figure 7 This Venn diagram compares and contrasts two substances made from carbon.

Venn Diagram To illustrate how two subjects compare and contrast you can use a Venn diagram. You can see the characteristics that the subjects have in common and those that they do not, shown in **Figure 7.**

To create a Venn diagram, draw two overlapping ovals that that are big enough to write in. List the characteristics unique to one subject in one oval, and the characteristics of the other subject in the other oval. The characteristics in common are listed in the overlapping section.

Make and Use Tables One way to organize information so it is easier to understand is to use a table. Tables can contain numbers, words, or both.

To make a table, list the items to be compared in the first column and the characteristics to be compared in the first row. The title should clearly indicate the content of the table, and the column or row heads should be clear. Notice that in **Table 1** the units are included.

Table 1 Recyclables Collected During Week			
Day of Week	**Paper (kg)**	**Aluminum (kg)**	**Glass (kg)**
Monday	5.0	4.0	12.0
Wednesday	4.0	1.0	10.0
Friday	2.5	2.0	10.0

Make a Model One way to help you better understand the parts of a structure, the way a process works, or to show things too large or small for viewing is to make a model. For example, an atomic model made of a plastic-ball nucleus and pipe-cleaner electron shells can help you visualize how the parts of an atom relate to each other. Other types of models can by devised on a computer or represented by equations.

Form a Hypothesis

A possible explanation based on previous knowledge and observations is called a hypothesis. After researching gasoline types and recalling previous experiences in your family's car you form a hypothesis—our car runs more efficiently because we use premium gasoline. To be valid, a hypothesis has to be something you can test by using an investigation.

Predict When you apply a hypothesis to a specific situation, you predict something about that situation. A prediction makes a statement in advance, based on prior observation, experience, or scientific reasoning. People use predictions to make everyday decisions. Scientists test predictions by performing investigations. Based on previous observations and experiences, you might form a prediction that cars are more efficient with premium gasoline. The prediction can be tested in an investigation.

Design an Experiment A scientist needs to make many decisions before beginning an investigation. Some of these include: how to carry out the investigation, what steps to follow, how to record the data, and how the investigation will answer the question. It also is important to address any safety concerns.

Test the Hypothesis

Now that you have formed your hypothesis, you need to test it. Using an investigation, you will make observations and collect data, or information. This data might either support or not support your hypothesis. Scientists collect and organize data as numbers and descriptions.

Follow a Procedure In order to know what materials to use, as well as how and in what order to use them, you must follow a procedure. **Figure 8** shows a procedure you might follow to test your hypothesis.

Procedure
1. Use regular gasoline for two weeks.
2. Record the number of kilometers between fill-ups and the amount of gasoline used.
3. Switch to premium gasoline for two weeks.
4. Record the number of kilometers between fill-ups and the amount of gasoline used.

Figure 8 A procedure tells you what to do step by step.

Identify and Manipulate Variables and Controls In any experiment, it is important to keep everything the same except for the item you are testing. The one factor you change is called the independent variable. The change that results is the dependent variable. Make sure you have only one independent variable, to assure yourself of the cause of the changes you observe in the dependent variable. For example, in your gasoline experiment the type of fuel is the independent variable. The dependent variable is the efficiency.

Many experiments also have a control—an individual instance or experimental subject for which the independent variable is not changed. You can then compare the test results to the control results. To design a control you can have two cars of the same type. The control car uses regular gasoline for four weeks. After you are done with the test, you can compare the experimental results to the control results.

Collect Data

Whether you are carrying out an investigation or a short observational experiment, you will collect data, as shown in **Figure 9.** Scientists collect data as numbers and descriptions and organize it in specific ways.

Observe Scientists observe items and events, then record what they see. When they use only words to describe an observation, it is called qualitative data. Scientists' observations also can describe how much there is of something. These observations use numbers, as well as words, in the description and are called quantitative data. For example, if a sample of the element gold is described as being "shiny and very dense" the data are qualitative. Quantitative data on this sample of gold might include "a mass of 30 g and a density of 19.3 g/cm^3."

Figure 9 Collecting data is one way to gather information directly.

Figure 10 Record data neatly and clearly so it is easy to understand.

When you make observations you should examine the entire object or situation first, and then look carefully for details. It is important to record observations accurately and completely. Always record your notes immediately as you make them, so you do not miss details or make a mistake when recording results from memory. Never put unidentified observations on scraps of paper. Instead they should be recorded in a notebook, like the one in **Figure 10.** Write your data neatly so you can easily read it later. At each point in the experiment, record your observations and label them. That way, you will not have to determine what the figures mean when you look at your notes later. Set up any tables that you will need to use ahead of time, so you can record any observations right away. Remember to avoid bias when collecting data by not including personal thoughts when you record observations. Record only what you observe.

Estimate Scientific work also involves estimating. To estimate is to make a judgment about the size or the number of something without measuring or counting. This is important when the number or size of an object or population is too large or too difficult to accurately count or measure.

Sample Scientists may use a sample or a portion of the total number as a type of estimation. To sample is to take a small, representative portion of the objects or organisms of a population for research. By making careful observations or manipulating variables within that portion of the group, information is discovered and conclusions are drawn that might apply to the whole population. A poorly chosen sample can be unrepresentative of the whole. If you were trying to determine the rainfall in an area, it would not be best to take a rainfall sample from under a tree.

Measure You use measurements everyday. Scientists also take measurements when collecting data. When taking measurements, it is important to know how to use measuring tools properly. Accuracy also is important.

Length To measure length, the distance between two points, scientists use meters. Smaller measurements might be measured in centimeters or millimeters.

Length is measured using a metric ruler or meter stick. When using a metric ruler, line up the 0-cm mark with the end of the object being measured and read the number of the unit where the object ends. Look at the metric ruler shown in **Figure 11.** The centimeter lines are the long, numbered lines, and the shorter lines are millimeter lines. In this instance, the length would be 4.50 cm.

Figure 11 This metric ruler has centimeter and millimeter divisions.

Mass The SI unit for mass is the kilogram (kg). Scientists can measure mass using units formed by adding metric prefixes to the unit gram (g), such as milligram (mg). To measure mass, you might use a triple-beam balance similar to the one shown in **Figure 12.** The balance has a pan on one side and a set of beams on the other side. Each beam has a rider that slides on the beam.

When using a triple-beam balance, place an object on the pan. Slide the largest rider along its beam until the pointer drops below zero. Then move it back one notch. Repeat the process for each rider proceeding from the larger to smaller until the pointer swings an equal distance above and below the zero point. Sum the masses on each beam to find the mass of the object. Move all riders back to zero when finished.

Instead of putting materials directly on the balance, scientists often take a tare of a container. A tare is the mass of a container into which objects or substances are placed for measuring their masses. To mass objects or substances, find the mass of a clean container. Remove the container from the pan, and place the object or substances in the container. Find the mass of the container with the materials in it. Subtract the mass of the empty container from the mass of the filled container to find the mass of the materials you are using.

Figure 12 A triple-beam balance is used to determine the mass of an object.

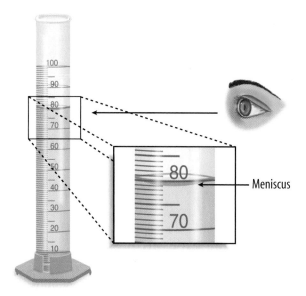

Figure 13 Graduated cylinders measure liquid volume.

Liquid Volume To measure liquids, the unit used is the liter. When a smaller unit is needed, scientists might use a milliliter. Because a milliliter takes up the volume of a cube measuring 1 cm on each side it also can be called a cubic centimeter (cm^3 = cm × cm × cm).

You can use beakers and graduated cylinders to measure liquid volume. A graduated cylinder, shown in **Figure 13,** is marked from bottom to top in milliliters. In lab, you might use a 10-mL graduated cylinder or a 100-mL graduated cylinder. When measuring liquids, notice that the liquid has a curved surface. Look at the surface at eye level, and measure the bottom of the curve. This is called the meniscus. The graduated cylinder in **Figure 13** contains 79.0 mL, or 79.0 cm^3, of a liquid.

Temperature Scientists often measure temperature using the Celsius scale. Pure water has a freezing point of 0°C and boiling point of 100°C. The unit of measurement is degrees Celsius. Two other scales often used are the Fahrenheit and Kelvin scales.

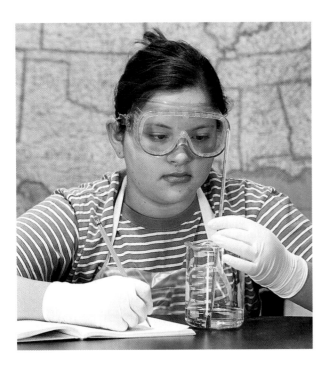

Figure 14 A thermometer measures the temperature of an object.

Scientists use a thermometer to measure temperature. Most thermometers in a laboratory are glass tubes with a bulb at the bottom end containing a liquid such as colored alcohol. The liquid rises or falls with a change in temperature. To read a glass thermometer like the thermometer in **Figure 14,** rotate it slowly until a red line appears. Read the temperature where the red line ends.

Form Operational Definitions An operational definition defines an object by how it functions, works, or behaves. For example, when you are playing hide and seek and a tree is home base, you have created an operational definition for a tree.

Objects can have more than one operational definition. For example, a ruler can be defined as a tool that measures the length of an object (how it is used). It can also be a tool with a series of marks used as a standard when measuring (how it works).

Analyze the Data

To determine the meaning of your observations and investigation results, you will need to look for patterns in the data. Then you must think critically to determine what the data mean. Scientists use several approaches when they analyze the data they have collected and recorded. Each approach is useful for identifying specific patterns.

Interpret Data The word *interpret* means "to explain the meaning of something." When analyzing data from an experiment, try to find out what the data show. Identify the control group and the test group to see whether or not changes in the independent variable have had an effect. Look for differences in the dependent variable between the control and test groups.

Classify Sorting objects or events into groups based on common features is called classifying. When classifying, first observe the objects or events to be classified. Then select one feature that is shared by some members in the group, but not by all. Place those members that share that feature in a subgroup. You can classify members into smaller and smaller subgroups based on characteristics. Remember that when you classify, you are grouping objects or events for a purpose. Keep your purpose in mind as you select the features to form groups and subgroups.

Compare and Contrast Observations can be analyzed by noting the similarities and differences between two more objects or events that you observe. When you look at objects or events to see how they are similar, you are comparing them. Contrasting is looking for differences in objects or events.

Recognize Cause and Effect A cause is a reason for an action or condition. The effect is that action or condition. When two events happen together, it is not necessarily true that one event caused the other. Scientists must design a controlled investigation to recognize the exact cause and effect.

Draw Conclusions

When scientists have analyzed the data they collected, they proceed to draw conclusions about the data. These conclusions are sometimes stated in words similar to the hypothesis that you formed earlier. They may confirm a hypothesis, or lead you to a new hypothesis.

Infer Scientists often make inferences based on their observations. An inference is an attempt to explain observations or to indicate a cause. An inference is not a fact, but a logical conclusion that needs further investigation. For example, you may infer that a fire has caused smoke. Until you investigate, however, you do not know for sure.

Apply When you draw a conclusion, you must apply those conclusions to determine whether the data supports the hypothesis. If your data do not support your hypothesis, it does not mean that the hypothesis is wrong. It means only that the result of the investigation did not support the hypothesis. Maybe the experiment needs to be redesigned, or some of the initial observations on which the hypothesis was based were incomplete or biased. Perhaps more observation or research is needed to refine your hypothesis. A successful investigation does not always come out the way you originally predicted.

Avoid Bias Sometimes a scientific investigation involves making judgments. When you make a judgment, you form an opinion. It is important to be honest and not to allow any expectations of results to bias your judgments. This is important throughout the entire investigation, from researching to collecting data to drawing conclusions.

Communicate

The communication of ideas is an important part of the work of scientists. A discovery that is not reported will not advance the scientific community's understanding or knowledge. Communication among scientists also is important as a way of improving their investigations.

Scientists communicate in many ways, from writing articles in journals and magazines that explain their investigations and experiments, to announcing important discoveries on television and radio. Scientists also share ideas with colleagues on the Internet or present them as lectures, like the student is doing in **Figure 15.**

Figure 15 A student communicates to his peers about his investigation.

SAFETY SYMBOLS

SAFETY SYMBOLS	HAZARD	EXAMPLES	PRECAUTION	REMEDY
DISPOSAL	Special disposal procedures need to be followed.	certain chemicals, living organisms	Do not dispose of these materials in the sink or trash can.	Dispose of wastes as directed by your teacher.
BIOLOGICAL	Organisms or other biological materials that might be harmful to humans	bacteria, fungi, blood, unpreserved tissues, plant materials	Avoid skin contact with these materials. Wear mask or gloves.	Notify your teacher if you suspect contact with material. Wash hands thoroughly.
EXTREME TEMPERATURE	Objects that can burn skin by being too cold or too hot	boiling liquids, hot plates, dry ice, liquid nitrogen	Use proper protection when handling.	Go to your teacher for first aid.
SHARP OBJECT	Use of tools or glassware that can easily puncture or slice skin	razor blades, pins, scalpels, pointed tools, dissecting probes, broken glass	Practice common-sense behavior and follow guidelines for use of the tool.	Go to your teacher for first aid.
FUME	Possible danger to respiratory tract from fumes	ammonia, acetone, nail polish remover, heated sulfur, moth balls	Make sure there is good ventilation. Never smell fumes directly. Wear a mask.	Leave foul area and notify your teacher immediately.
ELECTRICAL	Possible danger from electrical shock or burn	improper grounding, liquid spills, short circuits, exposed wires	Double-check setup with teacher. Check condition of wires and apparatus.	Do not attempt to fix electrical problems. Notify your teacher immediately.
IRRITANT	Substances that can irritate the skin or mucous membranes of the respiratory tract	pollen, moth balls, steel wool, fiberglass, potassium permanganate	Wear dust mask and gloves. Practice extra care when handling these materials.	Go to your teacher for first aid.
CHEMICAL	Chemicals can react with and destroy tissue and other materials	bleaches such as hydrogen peroxide; acids such as sulfuric acid, hydrochloric acid; bases such as ammonia, sodium hydroxide	Wear goggles, gloves, and an apron.	Immediately flush the affected area with water and notify your teacher.
TOXIC	Substance may be poisonous if touched, inhaled, or swallowed.	mercury, many metal compounds, iodine, poinsettia plant parts	Follow your teacher's instructions.	Always wash hands thoroughly after use. Go to your teacher for first aid.
FLAMMABLE	Flammable chemicals may be ignited by open flame, spark, or exposed heat.	alcohol, kerosene, potassium permanganate	Avoid open flames and heat when using flammable chemicals.	Notify your teacher immediately. Use fire safety equipment if applicable.
OPEN FLAME	Open flame in use, may cause fire.	hair, clothing, paper, synthetic materials	Tie back hair and loose clothing. Follow teacher's instruction on lighting and extinguishing flames.	Notify your teacher immediately. Use fire safety equipment if applicable.

 Eye Safety Proper eye protection should be worn at all times by anyone performing or observing science activities.

 Clothing Protection This symbol appears when substances could stain or burn clothing.

 Animal Safety This symbol appears when safety of animals and students must be ensured.

 Handwashing After the lab, wash hands with soap and water before removing goggles.

Safety in the Science Laboratory

The science laboratory is a safe place to work if you follow standard safety procedures. Being responsible for your own safety helps to make the entire laboratory a safer place for everyone. When performing any lab, read and apply the caution statements and safety symbol listed at the beginning of the lab.

General Safety Rules

1. Obtain your teacher's permission to begin all investigations and use laboratory equipment.

2. Study the procedure. Ask your teacher any questions. Be sure you understand safety symbols shown on the page.

3. Notify your teacher about allergies or other health conditions which can affect your participation in a lab.

4. Learn and follow use and safety procedures for your equipment. If unsure, ask your teacher.

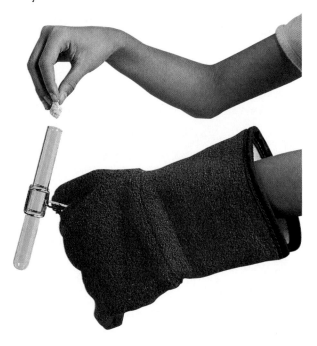

5. Never eat, drink, chew gum, apply cosmetics, or do any personal grooming in the lab. Never use lab glassware as food or drink containers. Keep your hands away from your face and mouth.

6. Know the location and proper use of the safety shower, eye wash, fire blanket, and fire alarm.

Prevent Accidents

1. Use the safety equipment provided to you. Goggles and a safety apron should be worn during investigations.

2. Do NOT use hair spray, mousse, or other flammable hair products. Tie back long hair and tie down loose clothing.

3. Do NOT wear sandals or other open-toed shoes in the lab.

4. Remove jewelry on hands and wrists. Loose jewelry, such as chains and long necklaces, should be removed to prevent them from getting caught in equipment.

5. Do not taste any substances or draw any material into a tube with your mouth.

6. Proper behavior is expected in the lab. Practical jokes and fooling around can lead to accidents and injury.

7. Keep your work area uncluttered.

Laboratory Work

1. Collect and carry all equipment and materials to your work area before beginning a lab.

2. Remain in your own work area unless given permission by your teacher to leave it.

3. Always slant test tubes away from yourself and others when heating them, adding substances to them, or rinsing them.

4. If instructed to smell a substance in a container, hold the container a short distance away and fan vapors towards your nose.

5. Do NOT substitute other chemicals/substances for those in the materials list unless instructed to do so by your teacher.

6. Do NOT take any materials or chemicals outside of the laboratory.

7. Stay out of storage areas unless instructed to be there and supervised by your teacher.

Laboratory Cleanup

1. Turn off all burners, water, and gas, and disconnect all electrical devices.

2. Clean all pieces of equipment and return all materials to their proper places.

3. Dispose of chemicals and other materials as directed by your teacher. Place broken glass and solid substances in the proper containers. Never discard materials in the sink.

4. Clean your work area.

5. Wash your hands with soap and water thoroughly BEFORE removing your goggles.

Emergencies

1. Report any fire, electrical shock, glassware breakage, spill, or injury, no matter how small, to your teacher immediately. Follow his or her instructions.

2. If your clothing should catch fire, STOP, DROP, and ROLL. If possible, smother it with the fire blanket or get under a safety shower. NEVER RUN.

3. If a fire should occur, turn off all gas and leave the room according to established procedures.

4. In most instances, your teacher will clean up spills. Do NOT attempt to clean up spills unless you are given permission and instructions to do so.

5. If chemicals come into contact with your eyes or skin, notify your teacher immediately. Use the eyewash or flush your skin or eyes with large quantities of water.

6. The fire extinguisher and first-aid kit should only be used by your teacher unless it is an extreme emergency and you have been given permission.

7. If someone is injured or becomes ill, only a professional medical provider or someone certified in first aid should perform first-aid procedures.

EXTRA  Labs

From Your Kitchen, Junk Drawer, or Yard

1 Testing Horoscopes

▶ *Real-World Question*
How can horoscopes be tested scientifically?

Possible Materials
- horoscope from previous week
- scissors
- transparent tape
- white paper
- correction fluid

▶ *Procedure*
1. Obtain a horoscope from last week and cut out the predictions for each sign. Do not cut out the zodiac signs or birth dates accompanying each prediction.
2. As you cut out a horoscope prediction, write the correct zodiac sign on the back of each prediction.
3. Develop a code for the predictions to allow you to identify them. Keep your code list in your Science Journal.
4. Scramble your predictions and tape them to a sheet of white paper. Write each prediction's code above it.
5. Ask your friends and family members to read all the predictions and choose the one that best matched their life events from the previous week. Interview at least 20 people.

▶ *Conclude and Apply*
1. Calculate the percentage of people who chose the correct sign.
2. Calculate the chances of a person choosing their correct sign randomly.

2 The Heat is On

▶ *Real-World Question*
How can different types of energy be transformed into thermal energy?

Possible Materials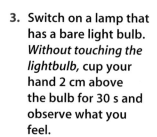
- lamp
- incandescent light bulb
- black construction paper or cloth

▶ *Procedure*
1. Feel the temperature of a black sheet of paper. Lay the paper in direct sunlight, wait 10 min, and observe how it feels.
2. Rub the palms of your hands together quickly for 10 s and observe how they feel.
3. Switch on a lamp that has a bare light bulb. *Without touching the lightbulb,* cup your hand 2 cm above the bulb for 30 s and observe what you feel.

▶ *Conclude and Apply*
1. Infer the type of energy transformation that happened on the paper.
2. Infer the type of energy transformation that happened between the palms of your hands.
3. Infer the type of energy transformation that happened to the lightbulb.

Adult supervision required for all labs.

3 Simple Machines

▶ Real-World Question

What types of simple machines are found in a toolbox?

Possible Materials
- box of tools

▶ Procedure

1. Obtain a box of tools and lay all the tools and other hardware from the box on a table.
2. Carefully examine all the tools and hardware, and separate all the items that are a type of inclined plane.
3. Carefully examine all the tools and hardware, and separate all the items that are a type of lever.
4. Identify and separate all the items that are a wheel and axle.
5. Identify any pulleys in the toolbox.
6. Identify any tools that are a combination of two or more simple machines.

▶ Conclude and Apply

1. List all the tools you found that were a type of inclined plane, lever, wheel and axle, or pulley.
2. List all the tools that were a combination of two or more simple machines.
3. Infer how a hammer could be used as both a first class lever and a third class lever.

4 Microscopic Crystals

▶ Real-World Question

What do crystalline and non-crystalline solids look like under a magnifying lens?

Possible Materials
- salt or sugar
- pepper
- magnifying lens
- paper
- bowl
- spoon
- measuring cup

▶ Procedure

1. Pour 10 mL of salt into a bowl and grind the salt into small, powdery pieces with the back of the spoon.
2. Sprinkle a few grains of salt from the bowl onto a piece of paper and view the salt grains with the magnifying lens.
3. Clean out the bowl.
4. Pour 10 mL of pepper into the bowl and grind it into powder with the spoon.
5. Sprinkle a few grains of pepper from the bowl onto the paper and view the grains with the magnifying lens.

▶ Conclude and Apply

1. Compare the difference between the salt and pepper grains under the magnifying lens.
2. Describe what a crystal is.

5 Estimate Temperature

▶ Real-World Question
How can we learn to estimate temperatures?

Possible Materials
- thermometer
- water
- bowl
- ice

▶ Procedure
1. If you have a dual-scale weather thermometer, you can learn twice as much by trying to do your estimation in degrees Fahrenheit and Celsius each time.
2. Fill a bowl with ice water. Submerge your fingers in the water and estimate the water temperature.
3. Place the thermometer in the bowl and observe the temperature.
4. Place a bowl of warm water in direct sunlight for 20 min. Submerge your fingers in the water and estimate the water temperature.
5. Place the thermometer in the bowl and observe the temperature.
6. Place the thermometer outside in a location where you can see it each day.
7. Each day for a month, step outside and estimate the temperature. Check the accuracy of your estimates with the thermometer. Record the weather conditions as well.

▶ Conclude and Apply
1. Describe how well you can estimate air temperatures after estimating the temperature each day for a month. Did the cloudiness of the day affect your estimation skills?
2. Infer why understanding the Celsius scale might be helpful to you in the future.

6 The Pressure's On

▶ Real-World Question
How can atmospheric air pressure changes be modeled?

Possible Materials
- large pot
- stove or hotplate
- tongs
- oven mitt
- empty aluminum soda can
- water
- cold water
- small aquarium or large bowl
- large jar
- measuring cup

▶ Procedure
1. Fill a small aquarium or large bowl with cold water.
2. Pour water into a large pot and boil it.
3. Pour 25 mL of water into an empty aluminum can.
4. Using an oven mitt and tongs, hold the bottom of the can in the boiling water for 1 min.
5. Remove the can from the pot and immediately submerge it upside-down in the cold water in the aquarium or large bowl.

▶ Conclude and Apply
1. Describe what happened to the can in the cold water.
2. Infer why the can changed in the cold water.

Adult supervision required for all labs.

7 Bottling a Tornado

▶ Real-World Question
How can you model a tornado?

Possible Materials
- 2-L soda bottles (2)
- dish soap
- masking tape
- duct tape
- measuring cup
- towel

▶ Procedure
1. Remove the labels from two 2-L soda bottles.
2. Fill one bottle with 1.5 L of water.
3. Add two drops of dish soap to the bottle with the water.
4. Invert the second bottle and connect the openings of the bottles.
5. Attach the two bottles together with duct tape.
6. Flip the bottles upside-down and quickly swirl the top bottle with a smooth motion. Observe the tornado pattern made in the water.

▶ Conclude and Apply
1. Describe how you modeled a tornado.
2. Research how a real tornado forms.

8 Classification Poster

▶ Real-World Question
How can you classify organisms?

Possible Materials
- old magazines or other resources with organism pictures
- poster board
- scissors
- glue
- colored pencils, markers, or crayons

▶ Procedure
1. Search for pictures and photographs of a wide variety of organisms. Try to find organisms from all kingdoms.
2. Organize your pictures into a classification system you have researched or one you have made up.
3. Cut out the photographs and glue them to your poster.
4. Present your classification system to the class.

▶ Conclude and Apply
1. Infer why you found more animal photographs than any other type of organism.
2. Infer why you found few protist photographs in the magazines.

9 Rock Creatures

▶ Real-World Question
What types of organisms live under stream rocks?

Possible Materials 🔖 📰 📄 📋

- waterproof boots
- ice cube tray (white)
- aquarium net
- bucket
- collecting jars
- guidebook to pond life

▶ Procedure
1. With permission, search under the rocks of a local stream. Look for aquatic organisms under the rocks and leaves of the stream. Compare what you find in fast- and slow-moving water.
2. With permission, carefully pull organisms you find off the rocks and put them into separate compartments of your ice cube tray. Take care not to injure the creatures you find.
3. Use your net and bucket to collect larger organisms.
4. Use your guidebook to pond life to identify the organisms you find.
5. Release the organisms back into the stream once you identify them.

▶ Conclude and Apply
1. Identify and list the organisms you found under the stream rocks.
2. Infer why so many aquatic organisms make their habitats beneath stream rocks.

10 A Light in the Forest

▶ Real-World Question
Does the amount of sunlight vary in a forest?

Possible Materials 📋

- empty toilet paper or paper towel roll
- Science Journal

▶ Procedure
1. Copy the data table into your Science Journal.
2. Go with an adult to a nearby forest or large grove of trees.
3. Stand near the edge of the forest and look straight up through your cardboard tube. Estimate the percentage of blue sky and clouds you can see in the circle. This percentage is the amount of sunlight reaching the forest floor.
4. Record your location and estimated percentage of sunlight in your data table.
5. Test several other locations in the forest. Choose places where the trees completely cover the forest floor and where sunlight is partially coming through.

Data Table

Location	% of Sunlight

▶ Conclude and Apply
1. Explain how the amount of sunlight reaching the forest floor changed from place to place.
2. Infer why it is important for leaves and branches to stop sunlight from reaching much of the forest floor.

Adult supervision required for all labs.

11 Echinoderm Hold

▶ Real-World Question
How do echinoderms living in intertidal ecosystems hold on to rocks?

Possible Materials
- plastic suction cup
- water
- paper towel or sponge

▶ Procedure
1. Moisten a paper towel or sponge with water.
2. Press a plastic suction cup on the moist towel or sponge until the entire bottom surface of the cup is wet.
3. Firmly press the suction cup down on a kitchen counter for 10 s.
4. Grab the top handle of the suction cup and try removing the cup from the counter by pulling it straight up.

▶ Conclude and Apply
1. Describe what happened when you tried to remove the cup from the counter.
2. Infer how echinoderms living in intertidal ecosystems withstand the constant pull of ocean waves and currents.

Computer Skills

People who study science rely on computer technology to do research, record experimental data, analyze results from investigations, and communicate with other scientists. Whether you work in a laboratory or just need to write a lab report, good computer skills are necessary.

Figure 16 Students and scientists rely on computers to gather data and communicate ideas.

Hardware Basics

Your personal computer is a system consisting of many components. The parts you can see and touch are called hardware.

Figure 17 Most desktop computers consist of the components shown above. Notebook computers have the same components in a compact unit.

Desktop systems, like the one shown in **Figure 17,** typically have most of these components. Notebook and tablet computers have most of the same components as a desktop computer, but the components are integrated into a single, book-sized portable unit.

Storing Your Data

When you save documents created on computers at your school, they probably are stored in a directory on your school's network. However, if you want to take the documents you have created home, you need to save them on something portable. Removable media, like those shown in **Figure 18,** are disks and drives that are designed to be moved from one computer to another.

Figure 18 Removable data storage is a convenient way to carry your documents from place to place.

Removable media vary from floppy disks and recordable CDs and DVDs to small solid-state storage. Tiny USB "keychain" drives have become popular because they can store large amounts of data and plug into any computer with a USB port. Each of these types of media stores different amounts of data. Be sure that you save your data to a medium that is compatible with your computer.

Getting Started with Word Processing Programs

A word processor is used for the composition, editing, and formatting of written material. Word processors vary from program to program, but most have the basic functions shown in **Figure 19.** Most word processors also can be used to make simple tables and graphics.

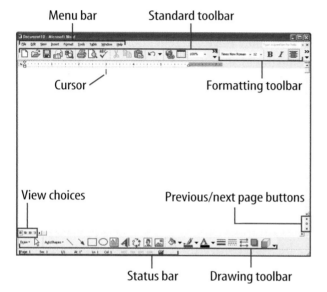

Figure 19 Word processors have functions that easily allow you to edit, format, view, and save text, tables, and images, making them useful for writing lab reports and research papers.

Word Processor Tips

- As you type, text will automatically wrap to the next line. Press *Enter* on your keyboard if you wish to start a new paragraph.
- You can move multiple lines of text around by using the *cut* and *paste* functions on the toolbar.
- If you make a typing or formatting error, use the *undo* function on the toolbar.
- Be sure to save your document early and often. This will prevent you from losing your work if your computer turns off unexpectedly.

- Use the *spell-check* function to check your spelling and grammar. Remember that *spell-check* will not catch words that are misspelled to look like other words, such as *cold* instead of *gold*. Reread your document to look for spelling and grammar mistakes.
- Graphics and spreadsheets can be added to your document by copying them from other programs and pasting them into your document.
- If you have questions about using your word processor, ask your teacher or use the program's *help* menu.

Getting Started with Spreadsheet Programs

A spreadsheet, like the one shown in **Figure 20,** helps you organize information into columns and rows. Spreadsheets are particularly useful for making data tables. Spreadsheets also can be used to perform mathematical calculations with your data. Then, you can use the spreadsheet to generate graphs and charts displaying your results.

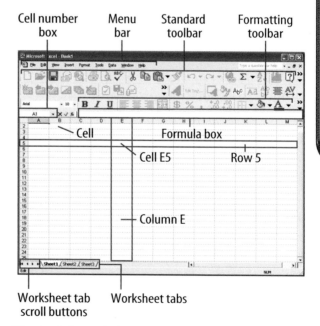

Figure 20 With formulas and graphs, spreadsheets help you organize and analyze your data.

Spreadsheet Tips

- Think about how to organize your data before you begin entering data.
- Each column (vertical) is assigned a letter and each row (horizontal) is assigned a number. Each point where a row and column intersect is called a cell, and is labeled according to where it is located. For example: column A, row 1 is cell A1.
- To edit the information in a cell, you must first activate the cell by clicking on it.
- When using a spreadsheet to generate a graph, make sure you use the type of graph that best represents the data. Review the *Science Skill Handbook* in this book for help with graphs.
- To learn more about using your spreadsheet program ask your teacher or use the program's Help menu.

Getting Started with Presentation Programs

There are many programs that help you orally communicate results of your research in an organized and interesting way. Many of these are slideshow programs, which allow you to organize text, graphs, digital photographs, sound, animations, and digital video into one multimedia presentation. Presentations can be printed onto paper or displayed on-screen. Slideshow programs are particularly effective when used with video projectors and interactive whiteboards, like the one shown in **Figure 21.** Although presentation programs are not the only way to communicate information publicly, they are an effective way to organize your presentation and remind your audience of major points.

Figure 21 Video projectors and interactive whiteboards allow you to present information stored on a computer to an entire classroom. They are becoming increasingly common in the classrooms.

Presentation Program Tips

- Often, color and strong images will convey a point better than words alone. But, be sure to organize your presentation clearly. Don't let the graphics confuse the message.
- Most presentation programs will let you copy and paste text, spreadsheets, art and graphs from other programs.
- Most presentation programs have built-in templates that help you organize text and graphics.
- As with any kind of presentation, familiarize yourself with the equipment and practice your presentation before you present it to an audience.
- Most presentation programs will allow you to save your document in html format so that you can publish your document on a Web site.
- If you have questions about using your presentation software or hardware, ask your teacher or use the program's Help menu.

Doing Research with the World Wide Web

The Internet is a global network of computers where information can be stored and shared by anyone with an internet connection. One of the easiest ways to find information on the internet is by using the World Wide Web, a vast graphical system of documents written in the computer language, html (hypertext markup language). Web pages are arranged in collections of related material called "Web sites." The content on a Web site is viewed using a program called a Web browser. Web browsers, like the one shown in **Figure 22,** allow you to browse or surf the Web by clicking on highlighted hyperlinks, which move you from Web page to Web page. Web content can be searched by topic using a search engine. Search engines are located on Web sites which catalog key words on Web pages all over the World Wide Web.

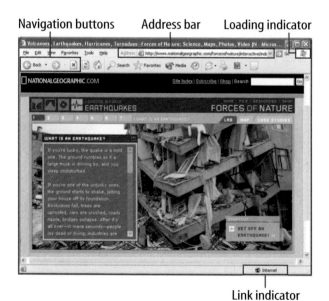

Navigation buttons   Address bar   Loading indicator

Link indicator

Figure 22 Web browsers have all the tools you need to navigate and view information on the Web.

World Wide Web Tips

- Search the Web using specific keywords. For example, if you want to research the element gold don't type *elements* into the search engine.

- When performing a Web search, enclose multiple keywords with quotes to narrow your results to the most relevant pages.

- The first hit your Web search results in is not always the best. Search results are arranged by popularity, not by relevance to your topic. Be patient and look at many links in your search results to find the best information.

- Think critically when you do science research on the Web. Compared to a traditional library, finding accurate information on the Web is not always easy because anyone can create a Web site. Some of the best places to start your research are websites for major newspapers and magazines, as well as U.S. government (*.gov*) and university (*.edu*) Web sites.

- Security is a major concern when browsing the Web. Your computer can be exposed to advertising software and computer viruses, which can hurt your computer's data and performance. *Do not download software at your school unless your teacher tells you to do so.*

- Cite information you find on the Web just as you would books and journals. An example of proper Web citation is the following:
  Menk, Amy J. (2004). *Urban Ecology*. Retrieved January 21, 2005, from McGraw-Hill Web site: http://www.mcgraw-hill.com/papers/urban.html

- The World Wide Web is a great resource for information, but don't forget to utilize local libraries, including your school library.

Math Review

Use Fractions

A fraction compares a part to a whole. In the fraction $\frac{2}{3}$, the 2 represents the part and is the numerator. The 3 represents the whole and is the denominator.

Reduce Fractions To reduce a fraction, you must find the largest factor that is common to both the numerator and the denominator, the greatest common factor (GCF). Divide both numbers by the GCF. The fraction has then been reduced, or it is in its simplest form.

Example Twelve of the 20 chemicals in the science lab are in powder form. What fraction of the chemicals used in the lab are in powder form?

Step 1 Write the fraction.
$$\frac{part}{whole} = \frac{12}{20}$$

Step 2 To find the GCF of the numerator and denominator, list all of the factors of each number.
Factors of 12: 1, 2, 3, 4, 6, 12 (the numbers that divide evenly into 12)
Factors of 20: 1, 2, 4, 5, 10, 20 (the numbers that divide evenly into 20)

Step 3 List the common factors.
1, 2, 4.

Step 4 Choose the greatest factor in the list.
The GCF of 12 and 20 is 4.

Step 5 Divide the numerator and denominator by the GCF.
$$\frac{12 \div 4}{20 \div 4} = \frac{3}{5}$$

In the lab, $\frac{3}{5}$ of the chemicals are in powder form.

Practice Problem At an amusement park, 66 of 90 rides have a height restriction. What fraction of the rides, in its simplest form, has a height restriction?

Add and Subtract Fractions To add or subtract fractions with the same denominator, add or subtract the numerators and write the sum or difference over the denominator. After finding the sum or difference, find the simplest form for your fraction.

Example 1 In the forest outside your house, $\frac{1}{8}$ of the animals are rabbits, $\frac{3}{8}$ are squirrels, and the remainder are birds and insects. How many are mammals?

Step 1 Add the numerators.
$$\frac{1}{8} + \frac{3}{8} = \frac{(1 + 3)}{8} = \frac{4}{8}$$

Step 2 Find the GCF.
$$\frac{4}{8} \quad (GCF, 4)$$

Step 3 Divide the numerator and denominator by the GCF.
$$\frac{4}{4} = 1, \; \frac{8}{4} = 2$$

$\frac{1}{2}$ of the animals are mammals.

Example 2 If $\frac{7}{16}$ of the Earth is covered by freshwater, and $\frac{1}{16}$ of that is in glaciers, how much freshwater is not frozen?

Step 1 Subtract the numerators.
$$\frac{7}{16} - \frac{1}{16} = \frac{(7 - 1)}{16} = \frac{6}{16}$$

Step 2 Find the GCF.
$$\frac{6}{16} \quad (GCF, 2)$$

Step 3 Divide the numerator and denominator by the GCF.
$$\frac{6}{2} = 3, \; \frac{16}{2} = 8$$

$\frac{3}{8}$ of the freshwater is not frozen.

Practice Problem A bicycle rider is going 15 km/h for $\frac{4}{9}$ of his ride, 10 km/h for $\frac{2}{9}$ of his ride, and 8 km/h for the remainder of the ride. How much of his ride is he going over 8 km/h?

Unlike Denominators To add or subtract fractions with unlike denominators, first find the least common denominator (LCD). This is the smallest number that is a common multiple of both denominators. Rename each fraction with the LCD, and then add or subtract. Find the simplest form if necessary.

Example 1 A chemist makes a paste that is $\frac{1}{2}$ table salt (NaCl), $\frac{1}{3}$ sugar ($C_6H_{12}O_6$), and the rest water (H_2O). How much of the paste is a solid?

Step 1 Find the LCD of the fractions.

$\frac{1}{2} + \frac{1}{3}$ (LCD, 6)

Step 2 Rename each numerator and each denominator with the LCD.

$1 \times 3 = 3, \ 2 \times 3 = 6$
$1 \times 2 = 2, \ 3 \times 2 = 6$

Step 3 Add the numerators.

$\frac{3}{6} + \frac{2}{6} = \frac{(3+2)}{6} = \frac{5}{6}$

$\frac{5}{6}$ of the paste is a solid.

Example 2 The average precipitation in Grand Junction, CO, is $\frac{7}{10}$ inch in November, and $\frac{3}{5}$ inch in December. What is the total average precipitation?

Step 1 Find the LCD of the fractions.

$\frac{7}{10} + \frac{3}{5}$ (LCD, 10)

Step 2 Rename each numerator and each denominator with the LCD.

$7 \times 1 = 7, \ 10 \times 1 = 10$
$3 \times 2 = 6, \ 5 \times 2 = 10$

Step 3 Add the numerators.

$\frac{7}{10} + \frac{6}{10} = \frac{(7+6)}{10} = \frac{13}{10}$

$\frac{13}{10}$ inches total precipitation, or $1\frac{3}{10}$ inches.

Practice Problem On an electric bill, about $\frac{1}{8}$ of the energy is from solar energy and about $\frac{1}{10}$ is from wind power. How much of the total bill is from solar energy and wind power combined?

Example 3 In your body, $\frac{7}{10}$ of your muscle contractions are involuntary (cardiac and smooth muscle tissue). Smooth muscle makes $\frac{3}{15}$ of your muscle contractions. How many of your muscle contractions are made by cardiac muscle?

Step 1 Find the LCD of the fractions.

$\frac{7}{10} - \frac{3}{15}$ (LCD, 30)

Step 2 Rename each numerator and each denominator with the LCD.

$7 \times 3 = 21, \ 10 \times 3 = 30$
$3 \times 2 = 6, \ 15 \times 2 = 30$

Step 3 Subtract the numerators.

$\frac{21}{30} - \frac{6}{30} = \frac{(21-6)}{30} = \frac{15}{30}$

Step 4 Find the GCF.

$\frac{15}{30}$ (GCF, 15)

$\frac{1}{2}$

$\frac{1}{2}$ of all muscle contractions are cardiac muscle.

Example 4 Tony wants to make cookies that call for $\frac{3}{4}$ of a cup of flour, but he only has $\frac{1}{3}$ of a cup. How much more flour does he need?

Step 1 Find the LCD of the fractions.

$\frac{3}{4} - \frac{1}{3}$ (LCD, 12)

Step 2 Rename each numerator and each denominator with the LCD.

$3 \times 3 = 9, \ 4 \times 3 = 12$
$1 \times 4 = 4, \ 3 \times 4 = 12$

Step 3 Subtract the numerators.

$\frac{9}{12} - \frac{4}{12} = \frac{(9-4)}{12} = \frac{5}{12}$

$\frac{5}{12}$ of a cup of flour.

Practice Problem Using the information provided to you in Example 3 above, determine how many muscle contractions are voluntary (skeletal muscle).

Multiply Fractions To multiply with fractions, multiply the numerators and multiply the denominators. Find the simplest form if necessary.

Example Multiply $\frac{3}{5}$ by $\frac{1}{3}$.

Step 1 Multiply the numerators and denominators.

$$\frac{3}{5} \times \frac{1}{3} = \frac{(3 \times 1)}{(5 \times 3)} = \frac{3}{15}$$

Step 2 Find the GCF.

$$\frac{3}{15} \quad (\text{GCF, } 3)$$

Step 3 Divide the numerator and denominator by the GCF.

$$\frac{3}{3} = 1, \quad \frac{15}{3} = 5$$

$$\frac{1}{5}$$

$\frac{3}{5}$ multiplied by $\frac{1}{3}$ is $\frac{1}{5}$.

Practice Problem Multiply $\frac{3}{14}$ by $\frac{5}{16}$.

Find a Reciprocal Two numbers whose product is 1 are called multiplicative inverses, or reciprocals.

Example Find the reciprocal of $\frac{3}{8}$.

Step 1 Inverse the fraction by putting the denominator on top and the numerator on the bottom.

$$\frac{8}{3}$$

The reciprocal of $\frac{3}{8}$ is $\frac{8}{3}$.

Practice Problem Find the reciprocal of $\frac{4}{9}$.

Divide Fractions To divide one fraction by another fraction, multiply the dividend by the reciprocal of the divisor. Find the simplest form if necessary.

Example 1 Divide $\frac{1}{9}$ by $\frac{1}{3}$.

Step 1 Find the reciprocal of the divisor.

The reciprocal of $\frac{1}{3}$ is $\frac{3}{1}$.

Step 2 Multiply the dividend by the reciprocal of the divisor.

$$\frac{\frac{1}{9}}{\frac{1}{3}} = \frac{1}{9} \times \frac{3}{1} = \frac{(1 \times 3)}{(9 \times 1)} = \frac{3}{9}$$

Step 3 Find the GCF.

$$\frac{3}{9} \quad (\text{GCF, } 3)$$

Step 4 Divide the numerator and denominator by the GCF.

$$\frac{3}{3} = 1, \quad \frac{9}{3} = 3$$

$$\frac{1}{3}$$

$\frac{1}{9}$ divided by $\frac{1}{3}$ is $\frac{1}{3}$.

Example 2 Divide $\frac{3}{5}$ by $\frac{1}{4}$.

Step 1 Find the reciprocal of the divisor.

The reciprocal of $\frac{1}{4}$ is $\frac{4}{1}$.

Step 2 Multiply the dividend by the reciprocal of the divisor.

$$\frac{\frac{3}{5}}{\frac{1}{4}} = \frac{3}{5} \times \frac{4}{1} = \frac{(3 \times 4)}{(5 \times 1)} = \frac{12}{5}$$

$\frac{3}{5}$ divided by $\frac{1}{4}$ is $\frac{12}{5}$ or $2\frac{2}{5}$.

Practice Problem Divide $\frac{3}{11}$ by $\frac{7}{10}$.

Use Ratios

When you compare two numbers by division, you are using a ratio. Ratios can be written 3 to 5, 3:5, or $\frac{3}{5}$. Ratios, like fractions, also can be written in simplest form.

Ratios can represent probabilities, also called odds. This is a ratio that compares the number of ways a certain outcome occurs to the number of outcomes. For example, if you flip a coin 100 times, what are the odds that it will come up heads? There are two possible outcomes, heads or tails, so the odds of coming up heads are 50:100. Another way to say this is that 50 out of 100 times the coin will come up heads. In its simplest form, the ratio is 1:2.

Example 1 A chemical solution contains 40 g of salt and 64 g of baking soda. What is the ratio of salt to baking soda as a fraction in simplest form?

Step 1 Write the ratio as a fraction.
$$\frac{salt}{baking\ soda} = \frac{40}{64}$$

Step 2 Express the fraction in simplest form.
The GCF of 40 and 64 is 8.
$$\frac{40}{64} = \frac{40 \div 8}{64 \div 8} = \frac{5}{8}$$

The ratio of salt to baking soda in the sample is 5:8.

Example 2 Sean rolls a 6-sided die 6 times. What are the odds that the side with a 3 will show?

Step 1 Write the ratio as a fraction.
$$\frac{number\ of\ sides\ with\ a\ 3}{number\ of\ sides} = \frac{1}{6}$$

Step 2 Multiply by the number of attempts.
$$\frac{1}{6} \times 6\ attempts = \frac{6}{6}\ attempts = 1\ attempt$$

1 attempt out of 6 will show a 3.

Practice Problem Two metal rods measure 100 cm and 144 cm in length. What is the ratio of their lengths in simplest form?

Use Decimals

A fraction with a denominator that is a power of ten can be written as a decimal. For example, 0.27 means $\frac{27}{100}$. The decimal point separates the ones place from the tenths place.

Any fraction can be written as a decimal using division. For example, the fraction $\frac{5}{8}$ can be written as a decimal by dividing 5 by 8. Written as a decimal, it is 0.625.

Add or Subtract Decimals When adding and subtracting decimals, line up the decimal points before carrying out the operation.

Example 1 Find the sum of 47.68 and 7.80.

Step 1 Line up the decimal places when you write the numbers.
$$\begin{array}{r} 47.68 \\ +\ 7.80 \\ \end{array}$$

Step 2 Add the decimals.
$$\begin{array}{r} 47.68 \\ +\ 7.80 \\ \hline 55.48 \\ \end{array}$$

The sum of 47.68 and 7.80 is 55.48.

Example 2 Find the difference of 42.17 and 15.85.

Step 1 Line up the decimal places when you write the number.
$$\begin{array}{r} 42.17 \\ -15.85 \\ \end{array}$$

Step 2 Subtract the decimals.
$$\begin{array}{r} 42.17 \\ -15.85 \\ \hline 26.32 \\ \end{array}$$

The difference of 42.17 and 15.85 is 26.32.

Practice Problem Find the sum of 1.245 and 3.842.

Multiply Decimals To multiply decimals, multiply the numbers like any other number, ignoring the decimal point. Count the decimal places in each factor. The product will have the same number of decimal places as the sum of the decimal places in the factors.

Example Multiply 2.4 by 5.9.

Step 1 Multiply the factors like two whole numbers.

$24 \times 59 = 1416$

Step 2 Find the sum of the number of decimal places in the factors. Each factor has one decimal place, for a sum of two decimal places.

Step 3 The product will have two decimal places.

14.16

The product of 2.4 and 5.9 is 14.16.

Practice Problem Multiply 4.6 by 2.2.

Divide Decimals When dividing decimals, change the divisor to a whole number. To do this, multiply both the divisor and the dividend by the same power of ten. Then place the decimal point in the quotient directly above the decimal point in the dividend. Then divide as you do with whole numbers.

Example Divide 8.84 by 3.4.

Step 1 Multiply both factors by 10.

$3.4 \times 10 = 34, 8.84 \times 10 = 88.4$

Step 2 Divide 88.4 by 34.

$$
\begin{array}{r}
2.6 \\
34\overline{)88.4} \\
-68 \\
\hline
204 \\
-204 \\
\hline
0
\end{array}
$$

8.84 divided by 3.4 is 2.6.

Practice Problem Divide 75.6 by 3.6.

Use Proportions

An equation that shows that two ratios are equivalent is a proportion. The ratios $\frac{2}{4}$ and $\frac{5}{10}$ are equivalent, so they can be written as $\frac{2}{4} = \frac{5}{10}$. This equation is a proportion.

When two ratios form a proportion, the cross products are equal. To find the cross products in the proportion $\frac{2}{4} = \frac{5}{10}$, multiply the 2 and the 10, and the 4 and the 5. Therefore $2 \times 10 = 4 \times 5$, or $20 = 20$.

Because you know that both proportions are equal, you can use cross products to find a missing term in a proportion. This is known as solving the proportion.

Example The heights of a tree and a pole are proportional to the lengths of their shadows. The tree casts a shadow of 24 m when a 6-m pole casts a shadow of 4 m. What is the height of the tree?

Step 1 Write a proportion.

$$\frac{\text{height of tree}}{\text{height of pole}} = \frac{\text{length of tree's shadow}}{\text{length of pole's shadow}}$$

Step 2 Substitute the known values into the proportion. Let h represent the unknown value, the height of the tree.

$$\frac{h}{6} = \frac{24}{4}$$

Step 3 Find the cross products.

$$h \times 4 = 6 \times 24$$

Step 4 Simplify the equation.

$$4h = 144$$

Step 5 Divide each side by 4.

$$\frac{4h}{4} = \frac{144}{4}$$
$$h = 36$$

The height of the tree is 36 m.

Practice Problem The ratios of the weights of two objects on the Moon and on Earth are in proportion. A rock weighing 3 N on the Moon weighs 18 N on Earth. How much would a rock that weighs 5 N on the Moon weigh on Earth?

Use Percentages

The word *percent* means "out of one hundred." It is a ratio that compares a number to 100. Suppose you read that 77 percent of the Earth's surface is covered by water. That is the same as reading that the fraction of the Earth's surface covered by water is $\frac{77}{100}$. To express a fraction as a percent, first find the equivalent decimal for the fraction. Then, multiply the decimal by 100 and add the percent symbol.

Example Express $\frac{13}{20}$ as a percent.

Step 1 Find the equivalent decimal for the fraction.

$$
\begin{array}{r}
0.65 \\
20\overline{)13.00} \\
12\ 0 \\
\hline
1\ 00 \\
1\ 00 \\
\hline
0
\end{array}
$$

Step 2 Rewrite the fraction $\frac{13}{20}$ as 0.65.

Step 3 Multiply 0.65 by 100 and add the % sign.
$$0.65 \times 100 = 65 = 65\%$$

So, $\frac{13}{20} = 65\%$.

This also can be solved as a proportion.

Example Express $\frac{13}{20}$ as a percent.

Step 1 Write a proportion.
$$\frac{13}{20} = \frac{x}{100}$$

Step 2 Find the cross products.
$$1300 = 20x$$

Step 3 Divide each side by 20.
$$\frac{1300}{20} = \frac{20x}{20}$$
$$65\% = x$$

Practice Problem In one year, 73 of 365 days were rainy in one city. What percent of the days in that city were rainy?

Solve One-Step Equations

A statement that two things are equal is an equation. For example, $A = B$ is an equation that states that A is equal to B.

An equation is solved when a variable is replaced with a value that makes both sides of the equation equal. To make both sides equal the inverse operation is used. Addition and subtraction are inverses, and multiplication and division are inverses.

Example 1 Solve the equation $x - 10 = 35$.

Step 1 Find the solution by adding 10 to each side of the equation.
$$x - 10 = 35$$
$$x - 10 + 10 = 35 + 10$$
$$x = 45$$

Step 2 Check the solution.
$$x - 10 = 35$$
$$45 - 10 = 35$$
$$35 = 35$$

Both sides of the equation are equal, so $x = 45$.

Example 2 In the formula $a = bc$, find the value of c if $a = 20$ and $b = 2$.

Step 1 Rearrange the formula so the unknown value is by itself on one side of the equation by dividing both sides by b.
$$a = bc$$
$$\frac{a}{b} = \frac{bc}{b}$$
$$\frac{a}{b} = c$$

Step 2 Replace the variables a and b with the values that are given.
$$\frac{a}{b} = c$$
$$\frac{20}{2} = c$$
$$10 = c$$

Step 3 Check the solution.
$$a = bc$$
$$20 = 2 \times 10$$
$$20 = 20$$

Both sides of the equation are equal, so $c = 10$ is the solution when $a = 20$ and $b = 2$.

Practice Problem In the formula $h = gd$, find the value of d if $g = 12.3$ and $h = 17.4$.

Math Skill Handbook

Use Statistics

The branch of mathematics that deals with collecting, analyzing, and presenting data is statistics. In statistics, there are three common ways to summarize data with a single number—the mean, the median, and the mode.

The **mean** of a set of data is the arithmetic average. It is found by adding the numbers in the data set and dividing by the number of items in the set.

The **median** is the middle number in a set of data when the data are arranged in numerical order. If there were an even number of data points, the median would be the mean of the two middle numbers.

The **mode** of a set of data is the number or item that appears most often.

Another number that often is used to describe a set of data is the range. The **range** is the difference between the largest number and the smallest number in a set of data.

A **frequency table** shows how many times each piece of data occurs, usually in a survey. **Table 2** below shows the results of a student survey on favorite color.

Table 2 Student Color Choice

Color	Tally	Frequency
red	||||	4
blue	₩	5
black	||	2
green	|||	3
purple	₩ ||	7
yellow	₩ |	6

Based on the frequency table data, which color is the favorite?

Example The speeds (in m/s) for a race car during five different time trials are 39, 37, 44, 36, and 44.

To find the mean:

Step 1 Find the sum of the numbers.
$$39 + 37 + 44 + 36 + 44 = 200$$

Step 2 Divide the sum by the number of items, which is 5.
$$200 \div 5 = 40$$

The mean is 40 m/s.

To find the median:

Step 1 Arrange the measures from least to greatest.
36, 37, 39, 44, 44

Step 2 Determine the middle measure.
36, 37, 39, 44, 44

The median is 39 m/s.

To find the mode:

Step 1 Group the numbers that are the same together.
44, 44, 36, 37, 39

Step 2 Determine the number that occurs most in the set.
44, 44, 36, 37, 39

The mode is 44 m/s.

To find the range:

Step 1 Arrange the measures from largest to smallest.
44, 44, 39, 37, 36

Step 2 Determine the largest and smallest measures in the set.
44, 44, 39, 37, 36

Step 3 Find the difference between the largest and smallest measures.
$$44 - 36 = 8$$

The range is 8 m/s.

Practice Problem Find the mean, median, mode, and range for the data set 8, 4, 12, 8, 11, 14, 16.

Use Geometry

The branch of mathematics that deals with the measurement, properties, and relationships of points, lines, angles, surfaces, and solids is called geometry.

Perimeter The **perimeter** (P) is the distance around a geometric figure. To find the perimeter of a rectangle, add the length and width and multiply that sum by two, or $2(l + w)$. To find perimeters of irregular figures, add the length of the sides.

Example 1 Find the perimeter of a rectangle that is 3 m long and 5 m wide.

Step 1 You know that the perimeter is 2 times the sum of the width and length.
$$P = 2(3\text{ m} + 5\text{ m})$$

Step 2 Find the sum of the width and length.
$$P = 2(8\text{ m})$$

Step 3 Multiply by 2.
$$P = 16\text{ m}$$

The perimeter is 16 m.

Example 2 Find the perimeter of a shape with sides measuring 2 cm, 5 cm, 6 cm, 3 cm.

Step 1 You know that the perimeter is the sum of all the sides.
$$P = 2 + 5 + 6 + 3$$

Step 2 Find the sum of the sides.
$$P = 2 + 5 + 6 + 3$$
$$P = 16$$

The perimeter is 16 cm.

Practice Problem Find the perimeter of a rectangle with a length of 18 m and a width of 7 m.

Practice Problem Find the perimeter of a triangle measuring 1.6 cm by 2.4 cm by 2.4 cm.

Area of a Rectangle The **area** (A) is the number of square units needed to cover a surface. To find the area of a rectangle, multiply the length times the width, or $l \times w$. When finding area, the units also are multiplied. Area is given in square units.

Example Find the area of a rectangle with a length of 1 cm and a width of 10 cm.

Step 1 You know that the area is the length multiplied by the width.
$$A = (1\text{ cm} \times 10\text{ cm})$$

Step 2 Multiply the length by the width. Also multiply the units.
$$A = 10\text{ cm}^2$$

The area is 10 cm^2.

Practice Problem Find the area of a square whose sides measure 4 m.

Area of a Triangle To find the area of a triangle, use the formula:

$$A = \frac{1}{2}(\text{base} \times \text{height})$$

The base of a triangle can be any of its sides. The height is the perpendicular distance from a base to the opposite endpoint, or vertex.

Example Find the area of a triangle with a base of 18 m and a height of 7 m.

Step 1 You know that the area is $\frac{1}{2}$ the base times the height.
$$A = \frac{1}{2}(18\text{ m} \times 7\text{ m})$$

Step 2 Multiply $\frac{1}{2}$ by the product of 18×7. Multiply the units.
$$A = \frac{1}{2}(126\text{ m}^2)$$
$$A = 63\text{ m}^2$$

The area is 63 m^2.

Practice Problem Find the area of a triangle with a base of 27 cm and a height of 17 cm.

Circumference of a Circle The **diameter** (d) of a circle is the distance across the circle through its center, and the **radius** (r) is the distance from the center to any point on the circle. The radius is half of the diameter. The distance around the circle is called the **circumference** (C). The formula for finding the circumference is:

$$C = 2\pi r \ \ or \ \ C = \pi d$$

The circumference divided by the diameter is always equal to 3.1415926... This nonterminating and nonrepeating number is represented by the Greek letter π (pi). An approximation often used for π is 3.14.

Example 1 Find the circumference of a circle with a radius of 3 m.

Step 1 You know the formula for the circumference is 2 times the radius times π.
$$C = 2\pi(3)$$

Step 2 Multiply 2 times the radius.
$$C = 6\pi$$

Step 3 Multiply by π.
$$C = 19 \text{ m}$$

The circumference is 19 m.

Example 2 Find the circumference of a circle with a diameter of 24.0 cm.

Step 1 You know the formula for the circumference is the diameter times π.
$$C = \pi(24.0)$$

Step 2 Multiply the diameter by π.
$$C = 75.4 \text{ cm}$$

The circumference is 75.4 cm.

Practice Problem Find the circumference of a circle with a radius of 19 cm.

Area of a Circle The formula for the area of a circle is:
$$A = \pi r^2$$

Example 1 Find the area of a circle with a radius of 4.0 cm.

Step 1 $A = \pi(4.0)^2$

Step 2 Find the square of the radius.
$$A = 16\pi$$

Step 3 Multiply the square of the radius by π.
$$A = 50 \text{ cm}^2$$

The area of the circle is 50 cm².

Example 2 Find the area of a circle with a radius of 225 m.

Step 1 $A = \pi(225)^2$

Step 2 Find the square of the radius.
$$A = 50625\pi$$

Step 3 Multiply the square of the radius by π.
$$A = 158962.5$$

The area of the circle is 158,962 m².

Example 3 Find the area of a circle whose diameter is 20.0 mm.

Step 1 You know the formula for the area of a circle is the square of the radius times π, and that the radius is half of the diameter.
$$A = \pi\left(\frac{20.0}{2}\right)^2$$

Step 2 Find the radius.
$$A = \pi(10.0)^2$$

Step 3 Find the square of the radius.
$$A = 100\pi$$

Step 4 Multiply the square of the radius by π.
$$A = 314 \text{ mm}^2$$

The area is 314 mm².

Practice Problem Find the area of a circle with a radius of 16 m.

Volume The measure of space occupied by a solid is the **volume** (V). To find the volume of a rectangular solid multiply the length times width times height, or $V = l \times w \times h$. It is measured in cubic units, such as cubic centimeters (cm^3).

Example Find the volume of a rectangular solid with a length of 2.0 m, a width of 4.0 m, and a height of 3.0 m.

Step 1 You know the formula for volume is the length times the width times the height.
$$V = 2.0 \text{ m} \times 4.0 \text{ m} \times 3.0 \text{ m}$$

Step 2 Multiply the length times the width times the height.
$$V = 24 \text{ m}^3$$

The volume is 24 m^3.

Practice Problem Find the volume of a rectangular solid that is 8 m long, 4 m wide, and 4 m high.

To find the volume of other solids, multiply the area of the base times the height.

Example 1 Find the volume of a solid that has a triangular base with a length of 8.0 m and a height of 7.0 m. The height of the entire solid is 15.0 m.

Step 1 You know that the base is a triangle, and the area of a triangle is $\frac{1}{2}$ the base times the height, and the volume is the area of the base times the height.
$$V = \left[\frac{1}{2}(b \times h)\right] \times 15$$

Step 2 Find the area of the base.
$$V = \left[\frac{1}{2}(8 \times 7)\right] \times 15$$
$$V = \left(\frac{1}{2} \times 56\right) \times 15$$

Step 3 Multiply the area of the base by the height of the solid.
$$V = 28 \times 15$$
$$V = 420 \text{ m}^3$$

The volume is 420 m^3.

Example 2 Find the volume of a cylinder that has a base with a radius of 12.0 cm, and a height of 21.0 cm.

Step 1 You know that the base is a circle, and the area of a circle is the square of the radius times π, and the volume is the area of the base times the height.
$$V = (\pi r^2) \times 21$$
$$V = (\pi 12^2) \times 21$$

Step 2 Find the area of the base.
$$V = 144\pi \times 21$$
$$V = 452 \times 21$$

Step 3 Multiply the area of the base by the height of the solid.
$$V = 9490 \text{ cm}^3$$

The volume is 9490 cm^3.

Example 3 Find the volume of a cylinder that has a diameter of 15 mm and a height of 4.8 mm.

Step 1 You know that the base is a circle with an area equal to the square of the radius times π. The radius is one-half the diameter. The volume is the area of the base times the height.
$$V = (\pi r^2) \times 4.8$$
$$V = \left[\pi\left(\frac{1}{2} \times 15\right)^2\right] \times 4.8$$
$$V = (\pi 7.5^2) \times 4.8$$

Step 2 Find the area of the base.
$$V = 56.25\pi \times 4.8$$
$$V = 176.63 \times 4.8$$

Step 3 Multiply the area of the base by the height of the solid.
$$V = 847.8$$

The volume is 847.8 mm^3.

Practice Problem Find the volume of a cylinder with a diameter of 7 cm in the base and a height of 16 cm.

Science Applications

Measure in SI

The metric system of measurement was developed in 1795. A modern form of the metric system, called the International System (SI), was adopted in 1960 and provides the standard measurements that all scientists around the world can understand.

The SI system is convenient because unit sizes vary by powers of 10. Prefixes are used to name units. Look at **Table 3** for some common SI prefixes and their meanings.

Table 3 Common SI Prefixes			
Prefix	**Symbol**	**Meaning**	
kilo-	k	1,000	thousand
hecto-	h	100	hundred
deka-	da	10	ten
deci-	d	0.1	tenth
centi-	c	0.01	hundredth
milli-	m	0.001	thousandth

Example   How many grams equal one kilogram?

Step 1   Find the prefix *kilo* in **Table 3.**

Step 2   Using **Table 3,** determine the meaning of *kilo.* According to the table, it means 1,000. When the prefix *kilo* is added to a unit, it means that there are 1,000 of the units in a "*kilo*unit."

Step 3   Apply the prefix to the units in the question. The units in the question are grams. There are 1,000 grams in a kilogram.

Practice Problem   Is a milligram larger or smaller than a gram? How many of the smaller units equal one larger unit? What fraction of the larger unit does one smaller unit represent?

Dimensional Analysis

Convert SI Units   In science, quantities such as length, mass, and time sometimes are measured using different units. A process called dimensional analysis can be used to change one unit of measure to another. This process involves multiplying your starting quantity and units by one or more conversion factors. A conversion factor is a ratio equal to one and can be made from any two equal quantities with different units. If 1,000 mL equal 1 L then two ratios can be made.

$$\frac{1,000 \text{ mL}}{1 \text{ L}} = \frac{1 \text{ L}}{1,000 \text{ mL}} = 1$$

One can covert between units in the SI system by using the equivalents in **Table 3** to make conversion factors.

Example 1   How many cm are in 4 m?

Step 1   Write conversion factors for the units given. From **Table 3,** you know that 100 cm = 1 m. The conversion factors are

$$\frac{100 \text{ cm}}{1 \text{ m}} \quad and \quad \frac{1 \text{ m}}{100 \text{ cm}}$$

Step 2   Decide which conversion factor to use. Select the factor that has the units you are converting from (m) in the denominator and the units you are converting to (cm) in the numerator.

$$\frac{100 \text{ cm}}{1 \text{ m}}$$

Step 3   Multiply the starting quantity and units by the conversion factor. Cancel the starting units with the units in the denominator. There are 400 cm in 4 m.

$$4 \text{ m} \times \frac{100 \text{ cm}}{1 \text{ m}} = 400 \text{ cm}$$

Practice Problem   How many milligrams are in one kilogram? (Hint: You will need to use two conversion factors from **Table 3.**)

Table 4 Unit System Equivalents

Type of Measurement	Equivalent
Length	1 in = 2.54 cm
	1 yd = 0.91 m
	1 mi = 1.61 km
Mass and Weight*	1 oz = 28.35 g
	1 lb = 0.45 kg
	1 ton (short) = 0.91 tonnes (metric tons)
	1 lb = 4.45 N
Volume	$1\ in^3 = 16.39\ cm^3$
	1 qt = 0.95 L
	1 gal = 3.78 L
Area	$1\ in^2 = 6.45\ cm^2$
	$1\ yd^2 = 0.83\ m^2$
	$1\ mi^2 = 2.59\ km^2$
	1 acre = 0.40 hectares
Temperature	$°C = \dfrac{(°F - 32)}{1.8}$
	$K = °C + 273$

*Weight is measured in standard Earth gravity.

Convert Between Unit Systems Table 4 gives a list of equivalents that can be used to convert between English and SI units.

Example If a meterstick has a length of 100 cm, how long is the meterstick in inches?

Step 1 Write the conversion factors for the units given. From **Table 4,** 1 in = 2.54 cm.

$$\frac{1\ in}{2.54\ cm} \quad and \quad \frac{2.54\ cm}{1\ in}$$

Step 2 Determine which conversion factor to use. You are converting from cm to in. Use the conversion factor with cm on the bottom.

$$\frac{1\ in}{2.54\ cm}$$

Step 3 Multiply the starting quantity and units by the conversion factor. Cancel the starting units with the units in the denominator. Round your answer based on the number of significant figures in the conversion factor.

$$100\ cm \times \frac{1\ in}{2.54\ cm} = 39.37\ in$$

The meterstick is 39.4 in long.

Practice Problem A book has a mass of 5 lbs. What is the mass of the book in kg?

Practice Problem Use the equivalent for in and cm (1 in = 2.54 cm) to show how $1\ in^3 = 16.39\ cm^3$.

Math Skill Handbook

Precision and Significant Digits

When you make a measurement, the value you record depends on the precision of the measuring instrument. This precision is represented by the number of significant digits recorded in the measurement. When counting the number of significant digits, all digits are counted except zeros at the end of a number with no decimal point such as 2,050, and zeros at the beginning of a decimal such as 0.03020. When adding or subtracting numbers with different precision, round the answer to the smallest number of decimal places of any number in the sum or difference. When multiplying or dividing, the answer is rounded to the smallest number of significant digits of any number being multiplied or divided.

Example The lengths 5.28 and 5.2 are measured in meters. Find the sum of these lengths and record your answer using the correct number of significant digits.

Step 1 Find the sum.

5.28 m	2 digits after the decimal
+ 5.2 m	1 digit after the decimal
10.48 m	

Step 2 Round to one digit after the decimal because the least number of digits after the decimal of the numbers being added is 1.

The sum is 10.5 m.

Practice Problem How many significant digits are in the measurement 7,071,301 m? How many significant digits are in the measurement 0.003010 g?

Practice Problem Multiply 5.28 and 5.2 using the rule for multiplying and dividing. Record the answer using the correct number of significant digits.

Scientific Notation

Many times numbers used in science are very small or very large. Because these numbers are difficult to work with scientists use scientific notation. To write numbers in scientific notation, move the decimal point until only one non-zero digit remains on the left. Then count the number of places you moved the decimal point and use that number as a power of ten. For example, the average distance from the Sun to Mars is 227,800,000,000 m. In scientific notation, this distance is 2.278×10^{11} m. Because you moved the decimal point to the left, the number is a positive power of ten.

The mass of an electron is about 0.000 000 000 000 000 000 000 000 000 000 911 kg. Expressed in scientific notation, this mass is 9.11×10^{-31} kg. Because the decimal point was moved to the right, the number is a negative power of ten.

Example Earth is 149,600,000 km from the Sun. Express this in scientific notation.

Step 1 Move the decimal point until one non-zero digit remains on the left.
1.496 000 00

Step 2 Count the number of decimal places you have moved. In this case, eight.

Step 3 Show that number as a power of ten, 10^8.

The Earth is 1.496×10^8 km from the Sun.

Practice Problem How many significant digits are in 149,600,000 km? How many significant digits are in 1.496×10^8 km?

Practice Problem Parts used in a high performance car must be measured to 7×10^{-6} m. Express this number as a decimal.

Practice Problem A CD is spinning at 539 revolutions per minute. Express this number in scientific notation.

Make and Use Graphs

Data in tables can be displayed in a graph—a visual representation of data. Common graph types include line graphs, bar graphs, and circle graphs.

Line Graph A line graph shows a relationship between two variables that change continuously. The independent variable is changed and is plotted on the *x*-axis. The dependent variable is observed, and is plotted on the *y*-axis.

Example Draw a line graph of the data below from a cyclist in a long-distance race.

Table 5 Bicycle Race Data	
Time (h)	Distance (km)
0	0
1	8
2	16
3	24
4	32
5	40

Step 1 Determine the *x*-axis and *y*-axis variables. Time varies independently of distance and is plotted on the *x*-axis. Distance is dependent on time and is plotted on the *y*-axis.

Step 2 Determine the scale of each axis. The *x*-axis data ranges from 0 to 5. The *y*-axis data ranges from 0 to 40.

Step 3 Using graph paper, draw and label the axes. Include units in the labels.

Step 4 Draw a point at the intersection of the time value on the *x*-axis and corresponding distance value on the *y*-axis. Connect the points and label the graph with a title, as shown in **Figure 20.**

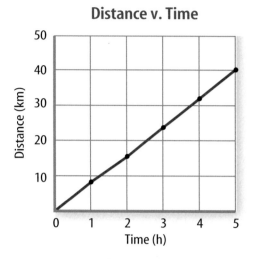

Figure 20 This line graph shows the relationship between distance and time during a bicycle ride.

Practice Problem A puppy's shoulder height is measured during the first year of her life. The following measurements were collected: (3 mo, 52 cm), (6 mo, 72 cm), (9 mo, 83 cm), (12 mo, 86 cm). Graph this data.

Find a Slope The slope of a straight line is the ratio of the vertical change, rise, to the horizontal change, run.

$$\text{Slope} = \frac{\text{vertical change (rise)}}{\text{horizontal change (run)}} = \frac{\text{change in } y}{\text{change in } x}$$

Example Find the slope of the graph in **Figure 20.**

Step 1 You know that the slope is the change in *y* divided by the change in *x*.
$$\text{Slope} = \frac{\text{change in } y}{\text{change in } x}$$

Step 2 Determine the data points you will be using. For a straight line, choose the two sets of points that are the farthest apart.
$$\text{Slope} = \frac{(40-0) \text{ km}}{(5-0) \text{ hr}}$$

Step 3 Find the change in *y* and *x*.
$$\text{Slope} = \frac{40 \text{ km}}{5 \text{h}}$$

Step 4 Divide the change in *y* by the change in *x*.
$$\text{Slope} = \frac{8 \text{ km}}{\text{h}}$$

The slope of the graph is 8 km/h.

Bar Graph To compare data that does not change continuously you might choose a bar graph. A bar graph uses bars to show the relationships between variables. The *x*-axis variable is divided into parts. The parts can be numbers such as years, or a category such as a type of animal. The *y*-axis is a number and increases continuously along the axis.

Example A recycling center collects 4.0 kg of aluminum on Monday, 1.0 kg on Wednesday, and 2.0 kg on Friday. Create a bar graph of this data.

Step 1 Select the *x*-axis and *y*-axis variables. The measured numbers (the masses of aluminum) should be placed on the *y*-axis. The variable divided into parts (collection days) is placed on the *x*-axis.

Step 2 Create a graph grid like you would for a line graph. Include labels and units.

Step 3 For each measured number, draw a vertical bar above the *x*-axis value up to the *y*-axis value. For the first data point, draw a vertical bar above Monday up to 4.0 kg.

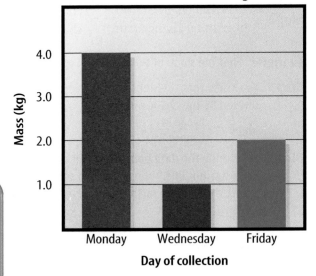

Aluminum Collected During Week

Practice Problem Draw a bar graph of the gases in air: 78% nitrogen, 21% oxygen, 1% other gases.

Circle Graph To display data as parts of a whole, you might use a circle graph. A circle graph is a circle divided into sections that represent the relative size of each piece of data. The entire circle represents 100%, half represents 50%, and so on.

Example Air is made up of 78% nitrogen, 21% oxygen, and 1% other gases. Display the composition of air in a circle graph.

Step 1 Multiply each percent by 360° and divide by 100 to find the angle of each section in the circle.

$$78\% \times \frac{360°}{100} = 280.8°$$

$$21\% \times \frac{360°}{100} = 75.6°$$

$$1\% \times \frac{360°}{100} = 3.6°$$

Step 2 Use a compass to draw a circle and to mark the center of the circle. Draw a straight line from the center to the edge of the circle.

Step 3 Use a protractor and the angles you calculated to divide the circle into parts. Place the center of the protractor over the center of the circle and line the base of the protractor over the straight line.

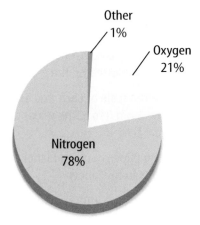

Other
1%

Oxygen
21%

Nitrogen
78%

Practice Problem Draw a circle graph to represent the amount of aluminum collected during the week shown in the bar graph to the left.

Use and Care of a Microscope

Eyepiece Contains magnifying lenses you look through.

Arm Supports the body tube.

Low-power objective Contains the lens with the lowest power magnification.

Stage clips Hold the microscope slide in place.

Coarse adjustment Focuses the image under low power.

Fine adjustment Sharpens the image under high magnification.

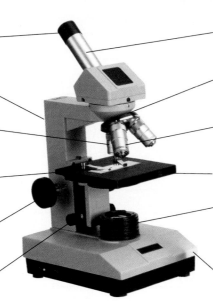

Body tube Connects the eyepiece to the revolving nosepiece.

Revolving nosepiece Holds and turns the objectives into viewing position.

High-power objective Contains the lens with the highest magnification.

Stage Supports the microscope slide.

Light source Provides light that passes upward through the diaphragm, the specimen, and the lenses.

Base Provides support for the microscope.

Caring for a Microscope

1. Always carry the microscope holding the arm with one hand and supporting the base with the other hand.

2. Don't touch the lenses with your fingers.

3. The coarse adjustment knob is used only when looking through the lowest-power objective lens. The fine adjustment knob is used when the high-power objective is in place.

4. Cover the microscope when you store it.

Using a Microscope

1. Place the microscope on a flat surface that is clear of objects. The arm should be toward you.

2. Look through the eyepiece. Adjust the diaphragm so light comes through the opening in the stage.

3. Place a slide on the stage so the specimen is in the field of view. Hold it firmly in place by using the stage clips.

4. Always focus with the coarse adjustment and the low-power objective lens first. After the object is in focus on low power, turn the nosepiece until the high-power objective is in place. Use ONLY the fine adjustment to focus with the high-power objective lens.

Making a Wet-Mount Slide

1. Carefully place the item you want to look at in the center of a clean, glass slide. Make sure the sample is thin enough for light to pass through.

2. Use a dropper to place one or two drops of water on the sample.

3. Hold a clean coverslip by the edges and place it at one edge of the water. Slowly lower the coverslip onto the water until it lies flat.

4. If you have too much water or a lot of air bubbles, touch the edge of a paper towel to the edge of the coverslip to draw off extra water and draw out unwanted air.

Topographic Map Symbols

Topographic Map Symbols

———————	Primary highway, hard surface	~~~~~~	Index contour
═══•═══	Secondary highway, hard surface	··········	Supplementary contour
═══════	Light-duty road, hard or improved surface	~~~~~~	Intermediate contour
========	Unimproved road	⬭	Depression contours
+——+——+	Railroad: single track		
═╪═╪═╪═	Railroad: multiple track	— — — —	Boundaries: national
+++++++	Railroads in juxtaposition	— — —	State
		— — — ··	County, parish, municipal
▪▫▪■▨	Buildings	— — —	Civil township, precinct, town, barrio
⋮ ⊞ cem	Schools, church, and cemetery	— · — · —	Incorporated city, village, town, hamlet
▫▭▨▨	Buildings (barn, warehouse, etc.)	· — · — ··	Reservation, national or state
○ ○	Wells other than water (labeled as to type)	— — — —	Small park, cemetery, airport, etc.
●●●⊘	Tanks: oil, water, etc. (labeled only if water)	— ·· — ··	Land grant
⊙ ⚐	Located or landmark object; windmill	———————	Township or range line, U.S. land survey
⤬ ✕	Open pit, mine, or quarry; prospect	— — — — —	Township or range line, approximate location
Marsh (swamp)			
	Marsh (swamp)		
	Wooded marsh	∿∿∿	Perennial streams
	Woods or brushwood	→——←	Elevated aqueduct
	Vineyard	○ ⌒	Water well and spring
	Land subject to controlled inundation	∿⊬	Small rapids
	Submerged marsh	∿∿	Large rapids
	Mangrove	≋≋≋	Intermittent lake
	Orchard	∿∿	Intermittent stream
	Scrub	→====←	Aqueduct tunnel
	Urban area	≈≈≈	Glacier
		⤙⤚	Small falls
x7369	Spot elevation	▨▨	Large falls
670	Water elevation	⠿⠿	Dry lake bed

Weather Map Symbols

Sample Station Model

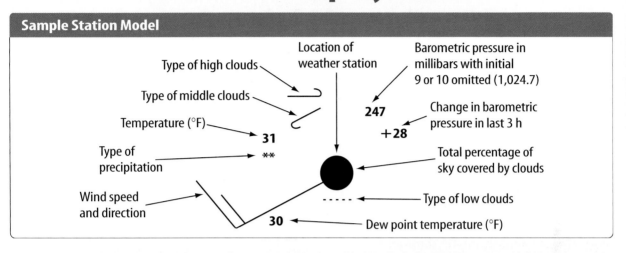

Type of high clouds
Type of middle clouds
Temperature (°F)
Type of precipitation
Wind speed and direction

Location of weather station
Barometric pressure in millibars with initial 9 or 10 omitted (1,024.7)
Change in barometric pressure in last 3 h
Total percentage of sky covered by clouds
Type of low clouds
Dew point temperature (°F)

247
+28
31
30

Sample Plotted Report at Each Station

Precipitation	Wind Speed and Direction	Sky Coverage	Some Types of High Clouds
≡ Fog	○ 0 calm	○ No cover	⌐⊃ Scattered cirrus
★ Snow	╱ 1–2 knots	◍ 1/10 or less	⌐⊃⊃ Dense cirrus in patches
● Rain	╲ 3–7 knots	◕ 2/10 to 3/10	⌐⌐⊂ Veil of cirrus covering entire sky
Thunderstorm	╲ 8–12 knots	◑ 4/10	⌐⊂ Cirrus not covering entire sky
, Drizzle	╲ 13–17 knots	◑ –	
▽ Showers	╲ 18–22 knots	◕ 6/10	
	╲ 23–27 knots	◕ 7/10	
	╲ 48–52 knots	◖ Overcast with openings	
	1 knot = 1.852 km/h	● Completely overcast	

Some Types of Middle Clouds		Some Types of Low Clouds		Fronts and Pressure Systems	
╱	Thin altostratus layer	⌒	Cumulus of fair weather	(H) or High (L) or Low	Center of high- or low-pressure system
╱╱	Thick altostratus layer	⌣	Stratocumulus	▲▲▲▲	Cold front
╱	Thin altostratus in patches	- - - - -	Fractocumulus of bad weather	●●●●	Warm front
╱	Thin altostratus in bands	——	Stratus of fair weather	▲●▲●	Occluded front
				●—▲—●—▼	Stationary front

Diversity of Life: Classification of Living Organisms

A six-kingdom system of classification of organisms is used today. Two kingdoms—Kingdom Archaebacteria and Kingdom Eubacteria—contain organisms that do not have a nucleus and that lack membrane-bound structures in the cytoplasm of their cells. The members of the other four kingdoms have a cell or cells that contain a nucleus and structures in the cytoplasm, some of which are surrounded by membranes. These kingdoms are Kingdom Protista, Kingdom Fungi, Kingdom Plantae, and Kingdom Animalia.

Kingdom Archaebacteria

one-celled; some absorb food from their surroundings; some are photosynthetic; some are chemosynthetic; many are found in extremely harsh environments including salt ponds, hot springs, swamps, and deep-sea hydrothermal vents

Kingdom Eubacteria

one-celled; most absorb food from their surroundings; some are photosynthetic; some are chemosynthetic; many are parasites; many are round, spiral, or rod-shaped; some form colonies

Kingdom Protista

Phylum Euglenophyta   one-celled; photosynthetic or take in food; most have one flagellum; euglenoids

Phylum Bacillariophyta   one-celled; photosynthetic; have unique double shells made of silica; diatoms

Phylum Dinoflagellata   one-celled; photosynthetic; contain red pigments; have two flagella; dinoflagellates

Phylum Chlorophyta   one-celled, many-celled, or colonies; photosynthetic; contain chlorophyll; live on land, in freshwater, or salt water; green algae

Phylum Rhodophyta   most are many-celled; photosynthetic; contain red pigments; most live in deep, saltwater environments; red algae

Phylum Phaeophyta   most are many-celled; photosynthetic; contain brown pigments; most live in saltwater environments; brown algae

Phylum Rhizopoda   one-celled; take in food; are free-living or parasitic; move by means of pseudopods; amoebas

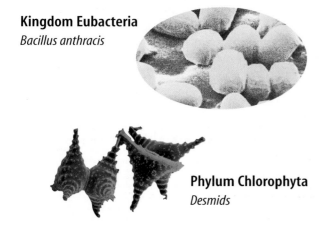

Kingdom Eubacteria
Bacillus anthracis

Phylum Chlorophyta
Desmids

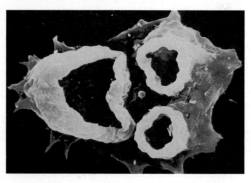

Amoeba

Phylum Zoomastigina one-celled; take in food; free-living or parasitic; have one or more flagella; zoomastigotes

Phylum Ciliophora one-celled; take in food; have large numbers of cilia; ciliates

Phylum Sporozoa one-celled; take in food; have no means of movement; are parasites in animals; sporozoans

Phyla Myxomycota and Acrasiomycota one- or many-celled; absorb food; change form during life cycle; cellular and plasmodial slime molds

Phylum Oomycota many-celled; are either parasites or decomposers; live in freshwater or salt water; water molds, rusts and downy mildews

Kingdom Fungi

Phylum Zygomycota many-celled; absorb food; spores are produced in sporangia; zygote fungi; bread mold

Phylum Ascomycota one- and many-celled; absorb food; spores produced in asci; sac fungi; yeast

Phylum Basidiomycota many-celled; absorb food; spores produced in basidia; club fungi; mushrooms

Phylum Deuteromycota members with unknown reproductive structures; imperfect fungi; *Penicillium*

Phylum Mycophycota organisms formed by symbiotic relationship between an ascomycote or a basidiomycote and green alga or cyanobacterium; lichens

Phylum Myxomycota
Slime mold

Phylum Oomycota
Phytophthora infestans

Lichens

Kingdom Plantae

Divisions Bryophyta (mosses), **Anthocerophyta** (hornworts), **Hepaticophyta** (liverworts), **Psilophyta** (whisk ferns) many-celled nonvascular plants; reproduce by spores produced in capsules; green; grow in moist, land environments

Division Lycophyta many-celled vascular plants; spores are produced in conelike structures; live on land; are photosynthetic; club mosses

Division Arthrophyta vascular plants; ribbed and jointed stems; scalelike leaves; spores produced in conelike structures; horsetails

Division Pterophyta vascular plants; leaves called fronds; spores produced in clusters of sporangia called sori; live on land or in water; ferns

Division Ginkgophyta deciduous trees; only one living species; have fan-shaped leaves with branching veins and fleshy cones with seeds; ginkgoes

Division Cycadophyta palmlike plants; have large, featherlike leaves; produces seeds in cones; cycads

Division Coniferophyta deciduous or evergreen; trees or shrubs; have needlelike or scalelike leaves; seeds produced in cones; conifers

Division Gnetophyta shrubs or woody vines; seeds are produced in cones; division contains only three genera; gnetum

Division Anthophyta dominant group of plants; flowering plants; have fruits with seeds

Kingdom Animalia

Phylum Porifera aquatic organisms that lack true tissues and organs; are asymmetrical and sessile; sponges

Phylum Cnidaria radially symmetrical organisms; have a digestive cavity with one opening; most have tentacles armed with stinging cells; live in aquatic environments singly or in colonies; includes jellyfish, corals, hydra, and sea anemones

Phylum Platyhelminthes bilaterally symmetrical worms; have flattened bodies; digestive system has one opening; parasitic and free-living species; flatworms

Division Bryophyta
Liverwort

Division Anthophyta
Tomato plant

Phylum Platyhelminthes
Flatworm

Phylum Chordata

Phylum Nematoda round, bilaterally symmetrical body; have digestive system with two openings; free-living forms and parasitic forms; roundworms

Phylum Mollusca soft-bodied animals, many with a hard shell and soft foot or footlike appendage; a mantle covers the soft body; aquatic and terrestrial species; includes clams, snails, squid, and octopuses

Phylum Annelida bilaterally symmetrical worms; have round, segmented bodies; terrestrial and aquatic species; includes earthworms, leeches, and marine polychaetes

Phylum Arthropoda largest animal group; have hard exoskeletons, segmented bodies, and pairs of jointed appendages; land and aquatic species; includes insects, crustaceans, and spiders

Phylum Echinodermata marine organisms; have spiny or leathery skin and a water-vascular system with tube feet; are radially symmetrical; includes sea stars, sand dollars, and sea urchins

Phylum Chordata organisms with internal skeletons and specialized body systems; most have paired appendages; all at some time have a notochord, nerve cord, gill slits, and a post-anal tail; include fish, amphibians, reptiles, birds, and mammals

PERIODIC TABLE OF THE ELEMENTS

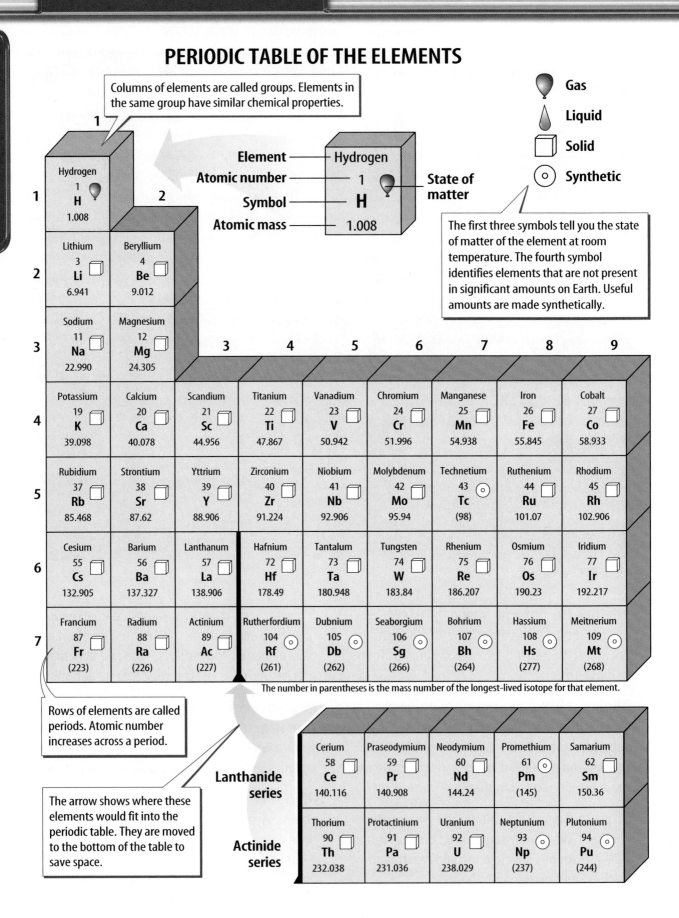

Columns of elements are called groups. Elements in the same group have similar chemical properties.

Gas
Liquid
Solid
Synthetic

Element — Hydrogen
Atomic number — 1
Symbol — H
Atomic mass — 1.008
State of matter

The first three symbols tell you the state of matter of the element at room temperature. The fourth symbol identifies elements that are not present in significant amounts on Earth. Useful amounts are made synthetically.

	1	2	3	4	5	6	7	8	9
1	Hydrogen 1 H 1.008								
2	Lithium 3 Li 6.941	Beryllium 4 Be 9.012							
3	Sodium 11 Na 22.990	Magnesium 12 Mg 24.305							
4	Potassium 19 K 39.098	Calcium 20 Ca 40.078	Scandium 21 Sc 44.956	Titanium 22 Ti 47.867	Vanadium 23 V 50.942	Chromium 24 Cr 51.996	Manganese 25 Mn 54.938	Iron 26 Fe 55.845	Cobalt 27 Co 58.933
5	Rubidium 37 Rb 85.468	Strontium 38 Sr 87.62	Yttrium 39 Y 88.906	Zirconium 40 Zr 91.224	Niobium 41 Nb 92.906	Molybdenum 42 Mo 95.94	Technetium 43 Tc (98)	Ruthenium 44 Ru 101.07	Rhodium 45 Rh 102.906
6	Cesium 55 Cs 132.905	Barium 56 Ba 137.327	Lanthanum 57 La 138.906	Hafnium 72 Hf 178.49	Tantalum 73 Ta 180.948	Tungsten 74 W 183.84	Rhenium 75 Re 186.207	Osmium 76 Os 190.23	Iridium 77 Ir 192.217
7	Francium 87 Fr (223)	Radium 88 Ra (226)	Actinium 89 Ac (227)	Rutherfordium 104 Rf (261)	Dubnium 105 Db (262)	Seaborgium 106 Sg (266)	Bohrium 107 Bh (264)	Hassium 108 Hs (277)	Meitnerium 109 Mt (268)

Rows of elements are called periods. Atomic number increases across a period.

The number in parentheses is the mass number of the longest-lived isotope for that element.

The arrow shows where these elements would fit into the periodic table. They are moved to the bottom of the table to save space.

Lanthanide series	Cerium 58 Ce 140.116	Praseodymium 59 Pr 140.908	Neodymium 60 Nd 144.24	Promethium 61 Pm (145)	Samarium 62 Sm 150.36
Actinide series	Thorium 90 Th 232.038	Protactinium 91 Pa 231.036	Uranium 92 U 238.029	Neptunium 93 Np (237)	Plutonium 94 Pu (244)

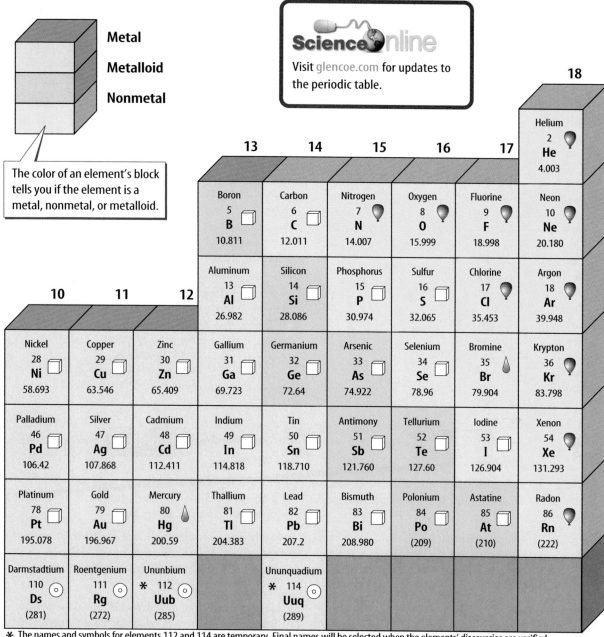

Metal

Metalloid

Nonmetal

The color of an element's block tells you if the element is a metal, nonmetal, or metalloid.

Science Online
Visit glencoe.com for updates to the periodic table.

13	14	15	16	17	18
					Helium 2 He 4.003
Boron 5 B 10.811	Carbon 6 C 12.011	Nitrogen 7 N 14.007	Oxygen 8 O 15.999	Fluorine 9 F 18.998	Neon 10 Ne 20.180

10	11	12	Aluminum 13 Al 26.982	Silicon 14 Si 28.086	Phosphorus 15 P 30.974	Sulfur 16 S 32.065	Chlorine 17 Cl 35.453	Argon 18 Ar 39.948
Nickel 28 Ni 58.693	Copper 29 Cu 63.546	Zinc 30 Zn 65.409	Gallium 31 Ga 69.723	Germanium 32 Ge 72.64	Arsenic 33 As 74.922	Selenium 34 Se 78.96	Bromine 35 Br 79.904	Krypton 36 Kr 83.798
Palladium 46 Pd 106.42	Silver 47 Ag 107.868	Cadmium 48 Cd 112.411	Indium 49 In 114.818	Tin 50 Sn 118.710	Antimony 51 Sb 121.760	Tellurium 52 Te 127.60	Iodine 53 I 126.904	Xenon 54 Xe 131.293
Platinum 78 Pt 195.078	Gold 79 Au 196.967	Mercury 80 Hg 200.59	Thallium 81 Tl 204.383	Lead 82 Pb 207.2	Bismuth 83 Bi 208.980	Polonium 84 Po (209)	Astatine 85 At (210)	Radon 86 Rn (222)
Darmstadtium 110 Ds (281)	Roentgenium 111 Rg (272)	Ununbium * 112 Uub (285)		Ununquadium * 114 Uuq (289)				

* The names and symbols for elements 112 and 114 are temporary. Final names will be selected when the elements' discoveries are verified.

Europium 63 Eu 151.964	Gadolinium 64 Gd 157.25	Terbium 65 Tb 158.925	Dysprosium 66 Dy 162.500	Holmium 67 Ho 164.930	Erbium 68 Er 167.259	Thulium 69 Tm 168.934	Ytterbium 70 Yb 173.04	Lutetium 71 Lu 174.967
Americium 95 Am (243)	Curium 96 Cm (247)	Berkelium 97 Bk (247)	Californium 98 Cf (251)	Einsteinium 99 Es (252)	Fermium 100 Fm (257)	Mendelevium 101 Md (258)	Nobelium 102 No (259)	Lawrencium 103 Lr (262)

Glossary/Glosario

A science multilingual glossary is available at
www.glencoe.com
The glossary includes the following languages.

Arabic	Haitian Creole	Portuguese	Tagalog
Bengali	Hmong	Russian	Urdu
Chinese	Korean	Spanish	Vietnamese
English			

Cómo usar el glosario en español:
1. Busca el término en inglés que desees encontrar.
2. El término en español, junto con la definición, se encuentran en la columna de la derecha.

Pronunciation Key

Use the following key to help you sound out words in the glossary.

a.............back (BAK)		ew...........food (FEWD)
ay............day (DAY)		yoo..........pure (PYOOR)
ah............father (FAH thur)		yew..........few (FYEW)
ow...........flower (FLOW ur)		uh...........comma (CAH muh)
ar............car (CAR)		u (+ con)......rub (RUB)
e.............less (LES)		sh............shelf (SHELF)
ee............leaf (LEEF)		ch...........nature (NAY chur)
ih............trip (TRIHP)		g.............gift (GIHFT)
i (i + con + e)..idea (i DEE uh)		j.............gem (JEM)
oh............go (GOH)		ing...........sing (SING)
aw...........soft (SAWFT)		zh............vision (VIH zhun)
or............orbit (OR buht)		k.............cake (KAYK)
oy............coin (COYN)		s.............seed, cent (SEED, SENT)
oo............foot (FOOT)		z.............zone, raise (ZOHN, RAYZ)

English — A — Español

abiotic: nonliving, physical features of the environment, including air, water, sunlight, soil, temperature, and climate.

abiótico: características inertes y físicas del medio ambiente, incluyendo el aire, el agua, la luz solar, el suelo, la temperatura y el clima.

air mass: large body of air that has the same characteristics of temperature and moisture content as the part of Earth's surface over which it formed. (p. 198)

masa de aire: gran cuerpo de aire que tiene las mismas características de temperatura y contenido de humedad que la parte de la superficie terrestre sobre la cual se formó. (p. 198)

alternative resource: new renewable or inexhaustible energy source; includes solar energy, wind, and geothermal energy. (p. 59)

recurso alternativo: nueva fuente de energía renovable o inagotable; incluye energía solar, eólica y geotérmica. (p. 59)

Archimedes' (ar kuh MEE deez) principle: states that the buoyant force on an object is equal to the weight of the fluid displaced by the object. (p. 123)

principio de Arquímedes: establece que la fuerza de empuje ejercida sobre un objeto es igual al peso del fluido desplazado por dicho objeto. (p. 123)

atmosphere: Earth's air, which is made up of a thin layer of gases, solids, and liquids; forms a protective layer around the planet and is divided into five distinct layers. (p. 162)

atmósfera: el aire de la Tierra; está compuesta por una capa fina de gases, sólidos y líquidos, forma una capa protectora alrededor del planeta y está dividida en cinco capas distintas. (p. 162)

Glossary/Glosario

binomial nomenclature (bi NOH mee ul · NOH mun klay chur): two-word naming system that gives all organisms their scientific name.

biomes (BI ohmz): large geographic areas with similar climates and ecosystems; includes tundra, taiga, desert, temperate deciduous forest, temperate rain forest, tropical rain forest, and grassland.

biosphere: part of Earth that supports life, including the top portion of Earth's crust, the atmosphere, and all the water on Earth's surface.

biotic (bi AHT ik): features of the environment that are alive or were once alive.

blizzard: winter storm that lasts at least three hours with temperatures of −12°C or below, poor visibility, and winds of at least 51 km/h. (p. 205)

buoyant force: upward force exerted on an object immersed in a fluid. (p. 122)

nomenclatura binaria: sistema de dos palabras que da a todos los organismos su nombre científico.

biomas: grandes áreas geográficas con climas y ecosistemas similares; incluyen la tundra, la taiga, el desierto, el bosque caducifolio templado, el bosque lluvioso templado, la selva húmeda tropical y los pastizales.

biosfera: capa de la Tierra que alberga la vida, incluyendo la porción superior de la corteza terrestre, la atmósfera y toda el agua de la superficie terrestre.

biótico: características del ambiente que tienen o alguna vez tuvieron vida.

nevasca: tormenta invernal que dura por lo menos tres horas con temperaturas de −12°C o menores, escasa visibilidad y vientos de por lo menos 51 km/h. (p. 205)

fuerza de empuje: fuerza ascendente ejercida sobre un objeto inmerso en un fluido. (p. 122)

carbon cycle: model describing how carbon molecules move between the living and nonliving world.

carrying capacity: largest number of individuals of a particular species that an ecosystem can support over time.

cell: smallest unit of an organism that can carry on life functions.

cell membrane: protective outer covering of all cells that regulates the interaction between the cell and the environment.

cell theory: states that all organisms are made up of one or more cells, the cell is the basic unit of life, and all cells come from other cells.

cell wall: rigid structure that encloses, supports, and protects the cells of plants, algae, fungi, and most bacteria.

chemical energy: energy stored in chemical bonds. (p. 45)

ciclo del carbono: modelo que describe cómo se mueven las moléculas de carbono entre el mundo vivo y el mundo inerte.

capacidad de carga: el mayor número de individuos de una especie en particular que un ecosistema puede albergar en un periodo de tiempo.

célula: la unidad más pequeña de un organismo que puede llevar a cabo funciones biológicas.

membrana celular: cubierta externa protectora de todas las células que regula la interacción entre la célula y su medio ambiente.

teoría celular: establece que todos los organismos están formados por una o más células, que las células son la unidad básica de la vida y que las células provienen de otras células.

pared celular: estructura rígida que rodea, mantiene y protege las células de las plantas, algas, hongos y la mayoría de las bacterias.

energía química: energía almacenada en enlaces químicos. (p. 45)

chemosynthesis (kee moh SIN thuh sus): process in which producers make energy-rich nutrient molecules from chemicals.

chlorofluorocarbons (CFCs): group of chemical compounds used in refrigerators, air conditioners, foam packaging, and aerosol sprays that may enter the atmosphere and destroy ozone. (p. 168)

chloroplast: green, chlorophyll-containing, plant-cell organelle that captures light energy, which is used to make sugar.

climate: average weather conditions of an area over time, including wind, temperature, and rainfall or other types of precipitation such as snow or sleet.

climax community: stable, end stage of ecological succession in which balance is in the absence of disturbance.

commensalism: a type of symbiotic relationship in which one organism benefits and the other organism is not affected.

community: all the populations of different species that live in an ecosystem.

compound machine: machine made up of a combination of two or more simple machines. (p. 85)

condensation: change of matter from a gas to a liquid state. (pp. 115, 173)

conduction: transfer of thermal energy by direct contact; occurs when energy is transferred by collisions between particles. (pp. 141, 172)

conductor: material that transfers heat easily. (p. 143)

constant: variable that is not changed in an experiment. (p. 18)

consumer: organism that cannot create energy-rich molecules but obtains its food by eating other organisms.

controlled experiment: involves changing one factor and observing its effect on one thing while keeping all other things constant. (p. 18)

convection: transfer of thermal energy by the movement of particles from one place to another in a gas or liquid. (p. 142)

convection: transfer of heat by the flow of material. (p. 172)

quimiosíntesis: proceso a través del cual los productores fabrican moléculas ricas en energía a partir de agentes químicos.

clorofluorocarbonos (CFCs): grupo de compuestos químicos usados en refrigeradores, acondicionadores de aire, espumas de empaque y aerosoles; pueden entrar en la atmósfera y destruir el ozono. (p. 168)

cloroplasto: organelo verde de las células vegetales que contiene clorofila y utiliza la energía de la luz para producir azúcar.

clima: condiciones meteorológicas promedio de un área durante un periodo de tiempo; incluye viento, temperatura y precipitación pluvial u otros tipos de precipitación como la nieve o el granizo.

clímax comunitario: etapa final estable de la sucesión ecológica en la cual se da un equilibrio en ausencia de alteraciones.

comensalismo: tipo de relación simbiótica en la que un organismo se beneficia sin afectar al otro.

comunidad: todas las poblaciones de diferentes especies que viven en un mismo ecosistema.

máquina compuesta: máquina compuesta por la combinación de dos o más máquinas. (p. 85)

condensación: cambio de estado de la materia de gas a líquido. (pp. 115, 173)

conducción: transferencia de energía térmica por contacto directo; se produce cuando la energía se transfiere mediante colisiones entre las partículas. (pp. 141, 172)

conductor: material que transfiere calor fácilmente. (p. 143)

constante: variable que no cambia en un experimento. (p. 18)

consumidor: organismo que no puede fabricar moléculas ricas en energía por lo que debe obtener su alimento ingiriendo otros organismos.

experimento controlado: consiste en cambiar un factor y observar su efecto sobre algo mientras el resto de las cosas se mantiene constante. (p. 18)

convección: transferencia de energía térmica por el movimiento de partículas de un sitio a otro en un líquido o un gas. (p. 142)

convección: transferencia de calor mediante flujo de material. (p. 172)

coral reef: diverse ecosystem formed from the calcium carbonate shells secreted by corals.

arrecife de coral: ecosistema diverso conformado de caparazones de carbonato de calcio secretados por los corales.

Coriolis (kor ee OH lus) effect: causes moving air and water to turn left in the southern hemisphere and turn right in the northern hemisphere due to Earth's rotation. (p. 176)

efecto de Coriolis: causa el movimiento del aire y agua hacia la izquierda en el hemisferio sur y hacia la derecha en el hemisferio norte; este efecto es debido a la rotación de la Tierra. (p. 176)

critical thinking: involves using knowledge and thinking skills to evaluate evidence and explanations. (p. 27)

pensamiento crítico: consiste en utilizar los conocimientos y habilidades del pensamiento para evaluar evidencias y explicaciones. (p. 27)

cytoplasm: constantly moving gelatinlike mixture inside the cell membrane that contains heredity material and is the location of most of a cell's life processes.

citoplasma: mezcla de apariencia gelatinosa que se mueve constantemente en el interior de las membranas de las células y contienen material hereditario; es donde se realizan la mayoría de los procesos biológicos de una célula.

D

data: information gathered during an investigation; recorded in the form of descriptions, tables, graphs, or drawings. (p. 28)

datos: información recopilada durante una investigación y archivada en forma de descripciones, tablas, gráficas o planos. (p. 28)

density: mass of an object divided by its volume. (p. 123)

densidad: masa de un objeto dividida por su volumen. (p. 123)

dependent variable: variable that changes as a result of a change in the independent variable. (p. 18)

variable dependiente: variable que cambia como resultado de un cambio en la variable independiente. (p. 18)

desert: driest biome on Earth with less than 25 cm of rain each year; has dunes or thin soil with little organic matter, where plants and animals are adapted to survive extreme conditions.

desierto: el bioma más seco sobre la Tierra con menos de 25 centímetros cúbicos de lluvia al año; tiene dunas o un suelo delgado con muy poca materia orgánica y aquí las plantas y animales están adaptados para sobrevivir en condiciones extremosas.

dew point: temperature at which air is saturated and condensation forms. (p. 193)

punto de condensación: temperatura a la que el aire se satura y se genera la condensación. (p. 193)

E

Earth science: study of Earth systems and systems in space, including weather and climate systems, and the study of nonliving things such as rocks, oceans, and planets. (p. 10)

ciencias de la Tierra: estudio del sistema de la Tierra y de los sistemas en el espacio, incluyendo el clima y los sistemas climáticos y el estudio de los seres inanimados como las rocas, los océanos y los planetas. (p. 10)

ecology: study of the interactions that take place among organisms and their environment.

ecología: estudio de las interacciones que se dan entre los organismos y su medio ambiente.

Glossary/Glosario

ecosystem: all the living organisms that live in an area and the nonliving features of their environment.

efficiency: equals the output work divided by the input work; expressed as a percentage. (p. 83)

electrical energy: energy carried by electric current. (p. 46)

endoplasmic reticulum (ER): cytoplasmic organelle that moves materials around in a cell and is made up of a complex series of folded membranes; can be rough (with attached ribosomes) or smooth (without attached ribosomes).

energy: the ability to cause change. (p. 42)

energy pyramid: model that shows the amount of energy available at each feeding level in an ecosystem.

estuary: extremely fertile area where a river meets an ocean; contains a mixture of freshwater and saltwater and serves as a nursery for many species of fish.

evaporation: process that takes place when a liquid changes to a gas.

ecosistema: conjunto de organismos vivos que habitan en un área y las características de su medio ambiente.

eficiencia: equivale al trabajo aplicado dividido el trabajo generado y se expresa en porcentaje. (p. 83)

energía eléctrica: energía transportada por corriente eléctrica. (p. 46)

retículo endoplásmico (RE): organelo citoplásmico que mueve los materiales en el interior de una célula y está compuesto por una serie compleja de membranas plegadas; puede ser áspero (con ribosomas incorporados) o liso (sin ribosomas incorporados).

energía: capacidad de producir cambios. (p. 42)

pirámide de energía: modelo que muestra la cantidad de energía disponible en cada nivel alimenticio de un ecosistema.

estuario: área extremadamente fértil donde un río desemboca en el océano; contiene una mezcla de agua dulce y salada y sirve como vivero para muchas especies de peces.

evaporación: proceso que tiene lugar cuando un líquido cambia a estado gaseoso.

F

fog: a stratus cloud that forms when air is cooled to its dew point near the ground. (p. 195)

food web: model that shows the complex feeding relationships among organisms in a community.

freezing: change of matter from a liquid state to a solid state. (p. 113)

front: boundary between two air masses with different temperatures, density, or moisture; can be cold, warm, occluded, and stationary. (p. 199)

niebla: nube de estrato que se forma cuando el aire se enfría a su punto de condensación cerca del suelo. (p. 195)

cadena alimenticia: modelo que muestra las complejas relaciones alimenticias entre los organismos de una comunidad.

congelación: cambio de la materia de estado líquido a sólido. (p. 113)

frente: límite entre dos masas de aire con temperatura, densidad o humedad diferentes; puede ser frío, caliente, ocluido o estacionario. (p. 199)

G

gas: matter that does not have a definite shape or volume; has particles that move at high speeds in all directions. (p. 108)

gas: materia que no tiene ni forma ni volumen definidos; tiene partículas que se mueven a altas velocidades y en todas las direcciones. (p. 108)

generator: device that transforms kinetic energy into electrical energy. (p. 52)

genus: first word of the two-word scientific name used to identify a group of similar species.

Golgi bodies: organelles that sort and package cellular materials and transport them within the cell or out of the cell.

grasslands: temperate and tropical regions with 25 cm to 75 cm of precipitation each year that are dominated by climax communities of grasses; ideal for growing crops and raising cattle and sheep.

generador: dispositivo que transforma la energía cinética en energía eléctrica. (p. 52)

género: primera palabra del nombre científico de dos palabras usado para identificar un grupo de especies similares.

aparato de Golgi: organelos que clasifican y recogen materiales celulares y los transportan hacia dentro o hacia afuera de la célula.

pastizales: regiones tropicales y templadas con 25 a 75 centímetros cúbicos de lluvia al año; son dominadas por el clímax comunitario de los pastos e ideales para la cría de ganado y ovejas.

habitat: place where an organism lives and that provides the types of food, shelter, moisture, and temperature needed for survival.

heat: movement of thermal energy from a substance at a higher temperature to a substance at a lower temperature. (p. 110, 140)

heat engine: device that converts thermal energy into mechanical energy. (p. 147)

homeostasis: ability of an organism to keep proper internal conditions no matter what external stimuli are occurring.

host cell: living cell in which a virus can actively multiply or in which a virus can hide until activated by environmental stimuli.

humidity: amount of water vapor held in the air. (p. 192)

hurricane: large, severe storm that forms over tropical oceans, has winds of at least 120 km/h, and loses power when it reaches land. (p. 204)

hydrosphere: all the water on Earth's surface. (p. 173)

hypothesis: reasonable guess that can be tested and is based on what is known and what is observed. (p. 14)

hábitat: lugar donde vive un organismo y que le proporciona los tipos de alimento, refugio, humedad y temperatura necesarios para su supervivencia.

calor: movimiento de energía térmica de una sustancia que se encuentra a una alta temperatura hacia una sustancia a una baja temperatura. (p. 110, 140)

motor de calor: motor que transforma la energía térmica en energía mecánica. (p. 147)

homeostasis: capacidad de un organismo para mantener las condiciones internas apropiadas, sin tener en cuenta los estímulos externos que ocurran.

célula huésped: célula viva en la cual un virus se puede multiplicar intensamente o en la que se puede ocultar hasta ser activado por un estímulo del medio ambiente.

humedad: cantidad de vapor de agua suspendido en el aire. (p. 192)

huracán: tormenta grande y severa que se forma sobre los océanos tropicales, tiene vientos de por lo menos 120 km/h y pierde su fuerza cuando alcanza la costa. (p. 204)

hidrosfera: toda el agua en la superficie terrestre. (p. 173)

hipótesis: suposición razonable que puede ser probada y que está basada en lo que se sabe y en lo que ha sido observado. (p. 14)

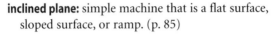
Glossary/Glosario

I

inclined plane: simple machine that is a flat surface, sloped surface, or ramp. (p. 85)

independent variable: variable that is changed in an experiment. (p. 18)

inexhaustible resource: energy source that can't be used up by humans. (p. 59)

infer: to draw a conclusion based on observation. (p. 16)

input force: force exerted on a machine. (p. 80)

internal combustion engine: heat engine in which fuel is burned in a combustion chamber inside the engine. (p. 148)

intertidal zone: part of the shoreline that is under water at high tide and exposed to the air at low tide.

ionosphere: layer of electrically charged particles in the thermosphere that absorbs AM radio waves during the day and reflects them back at night. (p. 165)

isobars: lines drawn on a weather map that connect points having equal atmospheric pressure; also indicate the location of high- and low-pressure areas and can show wind speed. (p. 207)

isotherm (I suh thurm): line drawn on a weather map that connects points having equal temperature. (p. 207)

plano inclinado: máquina simple que consiste en una superficie plana, inclinada, o una rampa. (p. 85)

variable independiente: variable que cambia en un experimento. (p. 18)

recurso inagotable: fuente de energía que no puede ser agotada por los seres humanos. (p. 59)

deducción: sacar una conclusión con base en una observación. (p. 16)

fuerza aplicada: fuerza que se ejerce sobre una máquina. (p. 80)

motor de combustión interna: motor de calor en el cual el combustible es quemado en una cámara de combustión dentro del motor. (p. 148)

zona litoral: parte de la línea costera que está bajo el agua durante la marea alta y expuesta al aire durante la marea baja.

ionosfera: capa de partículas con carga eléctrica presentes en la termosfera, la cual absorbe las ondas de radio AM durante el día y las refleja durante la noche. (p. 165)

isobaras: líneas dibujadas en un mapa meteorológico que conectan los puntos que tienen una presión atmosférica similar; también indican la ubicación de las áreas de baja y alta presión y pueden mostrar la velocidad del viento. (p. 207)

isoterma: línea dibujada en un mapa meteorológico que conecta los puntos que tienen la misma temperatura. (p. 207)

J

jet stream: narrow belt of strong winds that blows near the top of the troposphere. (p. 178)

corriente de chorro: faja angosta de vientos fuertes que soplan cerca de la parte superior de la troposfera. (p. 178)

K

kinetic energy: energy an object has due to its motion. (p. 43)

energía cinética: energía que posee un objeto debido a su movimiento. (p. 43)

kingdom: first and largest category used to classify organisms.

reino: la primera y más grande categoría usada para clasificar a los organismos.

land breeze: movement of air from land to sea at night, created when cooler, denser air from the land forces up warmer air over the sea. (p. 179)

brisa terrestre: movimiento de aire nocturno de la tierra al mar, generado cuando el aire denso y frío proveniente de la tierra empuja hacia arriba al aire caliente que está sobre el mar. (p. 179)

law of conservation of energy: states that energy can change its form but is never created or destroyed. (p. 48)

ley de la conservación de la energía: establece que la energía puede cambiar de forma pero nunca puede ser creada ni destruida. (p. 48)

lever: simple machine consisting of a rigid rod or plank that pivots or rotates about a fixed point called the fulcrum. (p. 88)

palanca: máquina simple que consiste en una barra rígida que puede girar sobre un punto fijo llamado punto de apoyo. (p. 88)

life science: study of living systems and how they interact. (p. 9)

ciencias de la vida: estudio de los sistemas vivos y de la forma como interactúan. (p. 9)

limiting factor: anything that can restrict the size of a population, including living and nonliving features of an ecosystem, such as predators or drought.

factor limitante: cualquier factor que pueda restringir el tamaño de una población, incluyendo las características biológicas y no biológicas de un ecosistema, tales como los depredadores o las sequías.

liquid: matter with a definite volume but no definite shape that can flow from one place to another. (p. 106)

líquido: materia con volumen definido pero no con forma definida que puede fluir de un sitio a otro. (p. 106)

matter: anything that takes up space and has mass. (p. 104)

materia: cualquier cosa que ocupe espacio y tenga masa. (p. 104)

mechanical advantage: number of times the input force is multiplied by a machine; equal to the output force divided by the input force. (p. 81)

ventaja mecánica: número de veces que la fuerza aplicada es multiplicada por una máquina; equivale a la fuerza producida dividida por la fuerza aplicada. (p. 81)

melting: change of matter from a solid state to a liquid state. (p. 111)

fusión: cambio de la materia de estado sólido a líquido. (p. 111)

meteorologist (meet ee uh RAHL uh just): studies weather and uses information from Doppler radar, weather satellites, computers and other instruments to make weather maps and provide forecasts. (p. 206)

meteorólogo: persona que estudia el clima y usa información del radar Doppler, satélites meteorológicos, computadoras y otros instrumentos para elaborar mapas del estado del tiempo y hacer pronósticos. (p. 206)

mitochondrion: cell organelle where food is broken down, which releases energy.

mitocondria: organelo celular en donde se desdoblan los alimentos, los cuales liberan energía.

model: any representation of an object or an event that is used as a tool for understanding the natural world; can communicate observations and ideas, test predictions, and save time, money, and lives. (p. 21)

mutualism: a type of symbiotic relationship in which both organisms benefit.

modelo: cualquier representación de un objeto o evento utilizada como herramienta para entender el mundo natural; puede comunicar observaciones e ideas, predicciones de las pruebas y ahorrar tiempo, dinero y salvar vidas. (p. 21)

mutualismo: tipo de relación simbiótica en la que ambos organismos se benefician.

N

niche: in an ecosystem, refers to the unique ways an organism survives, obtains food and shelter, and avoids danger.

nitrogen cycle: model describing how nitrogen moves from the atmosphere to the soil, to living organisms, and then back to the atmosphere.

nitrogen fixation: process in which some types of bacteria in the soil change nitrogen gas into a form of nitrogen that plants can use.

nonrenewable resource: energy resource that is used up much faster than it can be replaced. (p. 56)

nuclear energy: energy contained in atomic nuclei. (p. 46)

nucleus: organelle that controls all the activities of a cell and contains hereditary material made of DNA.

nicho: en un ecosistema, se refiere a las formas únicas en las que un organismo sobrevive, obtiene alimento, refugio y evita el peligro.

ciclo del nitrógeno: modelo que describe cómo se mueve el nitrógeno de la atmósfera al suelo, a los organismos vivos y de nuevo a la atmósfera.

fijación del nitrógeno: proceso en el cual algunos tipos de bacterias en el suelo transforman el nitrógeno gaseoso en una forma de nitrógeno que las plantas pueden usar.

recurso no renovable: recurso energético que se agota mucho más rápidamente de lo que puede ser reemplazado. (p. 56)

energía nuclear: energía contenida en los núcleos de los átomos. (p. 46)

núcleo: organelo que controla todas las actividades celulares y que contiene el material genético compuesto de ADN.

O

organ: structure, such as the heart, made up of different types of tissues that all work together.

organ system: a group of organs working together to perform a certain function.

organelle: structure in the cytoplasm of a eukaryotic cell that can act as a storage site, process energy, move materials, or manufacture substances.

organism: any living thing.

órgano: estructura, como el corazón, formada por diferentes tipos de tejidos que funcionan en conjunto.

sistema de órganos: grupo de órganos que funcionan conjuntamente para llevar a cabo una función determinada.

organelo: estructura citoplásmica de las células eucarióticas que puede servir para el almacenamiento, procesar energía, movilizar materiales o producir sustancias.

organismo: todo ser viviente.

output force: force exerted by a machine. (p. 80)

ozone layer: layer of the stratosphere with a high concentration of ozone; absorbs most of the Sun's harmful ultraviolet radiation. (p. 168)

fuerza generada: fuerza producida por una máquina. (p. 80)

capa de ozono: capa de la estratosfera con una concentración alta de ozono y que absorbe la mayor parte de la radiación ultravioleta dañina del sol. (p. 168)

parasitism: a type of symbiotic relationship in which one organism benefits and the other organism is harmed.

Pascal's principle: states that when a force is applied to a confined fluid, an increase in pressure is transmitted equally to all parts of the fluid. (p. 124)

photovoltaic: device that transforms radiant energy directly into electrical energy. (p. 60)

phylogeny (fi LAH juh nee): evolutionary history of an organism; used today to group organisms into six kingdoms.

physical science: study of matter, which is anything that takes up space and has mass, and the study of energy, which is the ability to cause change. (p. 10)

pioneer species: first organisms to grow in new or disturbed areas.

population: all the organisms that belong to the same species living in a community.

potential energy: energy stored in an object due to its position. (p. 44)

power: rate at which work is done; equal to the work done divided by the time it takes to do the work; measured in watts (W). (p. 77)

precipitation: water falling from clouds—including rain, snow, sleet, and hail—whose form is determined by air temperature. (p. 196)

pressure: force exerted on a surface divided by the total area over which the force is exerted. (p. 118)

producer: organism, such as a green plant or alga, that uses an outside source of energy like the Sun to create energy-rich food molecules.

parasitismo: tipo de relación simbiótica en la que un organismo se beneficia y el otro es perjudicado.

principio de Pascal: establece que cuando se ejerce una fuerza sobre un fluido encerrado, se transmite un incremento de presión uniforme a todas las partes del fluido. (p. 124)

fotovoltaico: dispositivo que transforma la energía radiante directamente en energía eléctrica. (p. 60)

filogenia: historia evolutiva de los organismos utilizada en la actualidad para agruparlos en seis reinos.

ciencias física: estudio de la materia, lo cual es todo lo que ocupe espacio y tenga masa, y el estudio de la energía, que es la habilidad de producir cambios. (p. 10)

especies pioneras: primeros organismos que crecen en áreas nuevas o alteradas.

población: todos los organismos que pertenecen a la misma especie dentro de una comunidad.

energía potencial: energía almacenada en un objeto debido a su posición. (p. 44)

potencia: velocidad a la que se realiza un trabajo y que equivale al trabajo realizado dividido por el tiempo que toma realizar el trabajo; se mide en vatios (W). (p. 77)

precipitación: agua que cae de las nubes—incluyendo lluvia, nieve, aguanieve y granizo—cuya forma está determinada por la temperatura del aire. (p. 196)

presión: fuerza ejercida sobre una superficie dividida por el área total sobre la cual se ejerce dicha fuerza. (p. 118)

productor: organismo, como una planta o un alga verde, que utiliza una fuente externa de energía, como la luz solar, para producir moléculas de nutrientes ricas en energía.

Glossary/Glosario

pulley: simple machine made from a grooved wheel with a rope or cable wrapped around the groove. (p. 90)

polea: máquina simple que consiste en una rueda acanalada con una cuerda o cable que corre alrededor del canal. (p. 90)

R

radiant energy: energy carried by light. (p. 45)

energía radiante: energía transportada por la luz. (p. 45)

radiation: energy transferred by waves or rays. (pp. 141, 172)

radiación: energía transmitida por ondas o rayos. (pp. 141, 172)

relative humidity: measure of the amount of moisture held in the air compared with the amount it can hold at a given temperature; can range from 0 percent to 100 percent. (p. 192)

humedad relativa: medida de la cantidad de humedad suspendida en el aire en comparación con la cantidad que puede contener a una temperatura determinada; puede variar del cero al cien por ciento. (p. 192)

renewable resource: energy resource that is replenished continually. (p. 58)

recurso renovable: recurso energético regenerado continuamente. (p. 58)

ribosome: small structure on which cells make their own proteins.

ribosoma: pequeña estructura en la que las células producen sus propias proteínas.

S

science: way of learning more about the natural world that provides possible explanations to questions and involves using a collection of skills. (p. 6)

ciencia: mecanismo para aprender más acerca del mundo natural, que da respuestas posibles a los interrogantes e implica hacer uso de numerosas habilidades. (p. 6)

scientific law: a rule that describes a pattern in nature but does not try to explain why something happens. (p. 7)

ley científica: regla que describe un modelo en la naturaleza pero que no intenta explicar por qué suceden las cosas. (p. 7)

scientific theory: a possible explanation for repeatedly observed patterns in nature supported by observations and results from many investigations. (p. 7)

teoría científica: posible explicación para patrones observados repetidamente en la naturaleza y apoyada en observaciones y resultados de muchas investigaciones. (p. 7)

screw: simple machine that is an inclined plane wrapped around a cylinder or post. (p. 87)

tornillo: máquina simple que consiste en un plano inclinado envuelto en espiral alrededor de un cilindro o poste. (p. 87)

sea breeze: movement of air from sea to land during the day when cooler air from above the water moves over the land, forcing the heated, less dense air above the land to rise. (p. 179)

brisa marina: movimiento de aire del mar a la tierra durante el día, cuando el aire frío que está sobre el mar empuja al aire caliente y menos denso que está sobre la tierra. (p. 179)

simple machine: a machine that does work with only one movement; includes the inclined plane, wedge, screw, lever, wheel and axle, and pulley. (p. 85)

máquina simple: máquina que ejecuta el trabajo con un solo movimiento; incluye el plano inclinado, la palanca, el tornillo, la rueda y el eje y la polea. (p. 85)

Glossary/Glosario

soil: mixture of mineral and rock particles, the remains of dead organisms, air, and water that forms the topmost layer of Earth's crust and supports plant growth.

solid: matter with a definite shape and volume; has tightly packed particles that move mainly by vibrating. (p. 105)

specific heat: amount of heat needed to raise the temperature of 1 kg of a substance by 1°C. (p. 144)

station model: indicates weather conditions at a specific location, using a combination of symbols on a map. (p. 207)

succession: natural, gradual changes in the types of species that live in an area; can be primary or secondary.

surface tension: the uneven forces acting on the particles on the surface of a liquid. (p. 107)

symbiosis: any close relationship between species, including mutualism, commensalism, and parasitism.

system: collection of structures, cycles, and processes that relate to and interact with each other. (p. 8)

suelo: mezcla de partículas minerales y rocas, restos de organismos muertos, aire y del agua que forma la capa superior de la corteza terrestre y favorece el crecimiento de las plantas.

sólido: materia con forma y volumen definidos; tiene partículas fuertemente compactadas que se mueven principalmente por vibración. (p. 105)

calor específico: cantidad de calor necesario para elevar la temperatura de 1 kilogramo de una sustancia en 1 grado centígrado. (p. 144)

modelo estacional: indica las condiciones del estado del tiempo en una ubicación específica, utilizando una combinación de símbolos en un mapa. (p. 207)

sucesión: cambios graduales y naturales en los tipos de especies que viven en un área; puede ser primaria o secundaria.

tensión superficial: fuerzas desiguales que actúan sobre las partículas que se encuentran en la superficie de un líquido. (p. 107)

simbiosis: cualquier relación estrecha entre especies, incluyendo mutualismo, comensalismo y parasitismo.

sistema: colección de estructuras, ciclos y procesos relacionados que interactúan entre sí. (p. 8)

taiga (TI guh): world's largest biome, located south of the tundra between 50° N and 60° N latitude; has long, cold winters, precipitation between 35 cm and 100 cm each year, cone-bearing evergreen trees, and dense forests.

technology: use of science to help people in some way. (p. 11)

temperate deciduous forest: biome usually having four distinct seasons, annual precipitation between 75 cm and 150 cm, and climax communities of deciduous trees.

temperate rain forest: biome with 200 cm to 400 cm of precipitation each year, average temperatures between 9°C and 12°C, and forests dominated by trees with needlelike leaves.

temperature: measure of the average kinetic energy of the individual particles of a substance. (pp. 110, 136)

taiga: el bioma más grande del mundo, localizado al sur de la tundra entre 50° y 60° de latitud norte; tiene inviernos prolongados y fríos, una precipitación que alcanza entre 35 y 100 centímetros cúbicos al año, coníferas perennifolias y bosques espesos.

tecnología: uso de la ciencia para ayudar en alguna forma a las personas. (p.11)

bosque caducifolio templado: bioma que generalmente tiene cuatro estaciones distintas, con una precipitación anual entre 75 y 150 centímetros cúbicos y un clímax comunitario de árboles caducifolios.

bosque lluvioso templado: bioma con 200 a 400 centímetros cúbicos de precipitación al año; tiene una temperatura promedio entre 9 y 12°C y bosques dominados por árboles de hojas aciculares.

temperatura: medida de la energía cinética promedio de las partículas individuales de una sustancia. (pp. 110, 136)

thermal energy: the sum of the kinetic and potential energy of the particles in a material. (pp. 44, 139)

thermal pollution: increase in temperature of a natural body of water; caused by adding warmer water. (p. 145)

tissue: group of similar cells that work together to do one job.

tornado: violent, whirling windstorm that crosses land in a narrow path and can result from wind shears inside a thunderhead. (p. 202)

tropical rain forest: most biologically diverse biome; has an average temperature of 25°C and receives between 200 cm and 600 cm of precipitation each year.

troposphere: layer of Earth's atmosphere that is closest to the ground, contains 99 percent of the water vapor and 75 percent of the atmospheric gases, and is where clouds and weather occur. (p. 164)

tundra: cold, dry, treeless biome with less than 25 cm of precipitation each year, a short growing season, permafrost, and winters that can be six to nine months long. Tundra is separated into two types arctic tundra and alpine tundra.

turbine: set of steam-powered fan blades that spins a generator at a power plant. (p. 52)

energía térmica: la suma de la energía cinética y potencial de las partículas en un material. (pp. 44, 139)

polución térmica: incremento de la temperatura de una masa natural de agua producido al agregarle agua a mayor temperatura. (p. 145)

tejido: grupo de células similares que funcionan conjuntamente para llevar a cabo una función.

tornado: tormenta de viento en forma de remolino que cruza la tierra en un curso estrecho y puede resultar de vientos que se entrecruzan en direcciones opuestas dentro del frente de una tormenta. (p. 202)

selva húmeda tropical: el bioma más diverso biológicamente; tiene una temperatura promedio de 25°C y recibe entre 200 y 600 centímetros cúbicos de precipitación al año.

troposfera: capa de la atmósfera terrestre que se encuentra cerca del suelo, contiene el 99 por ciento del vapor de agua y el 75 por ciento de los gases atmosféricos; es donde se forman las nubes y las condiciones meteorológicas. (p. 164)

tundra: bioma sin árboles, frío y seco, con menos de 25 centímetros cúbicos de precipitación al año; tiene una estación corta de crecimiento y permafrost e inviernos que pueden durar entre 6 y 9 meses. La tundra se divide en dos tipos tundra ártica y tundra alpina.

turbina: conjunto de aspas de ventilador impulsadas por vapor que hacen girar a un generador en una planta de energía eléctrica. (p. 52)

ultraviolet radiation: a type of energy that comes to Earth from the Sun, can damage skin and cause cancer, and is mostly absorbed by the ozone layer. (p. 168)

radiación ultravioleta: tipo de energía que llega a la Tierra desde el sol y que puede dañar la piel y causar cáncer; la mayor parte de esta radiación es absorbida por la capa de ozono. (p. 168)

vaporization: change of matter from a liquid state to a gas. (p. 114)

variable: factor that can be changed in an experiment. (p. 18)

aporización: cambio de estado de la materia de líquido a gas. (p. 114)

variable: factor que puede cambiar en un experimento. (p. 14)

virus: a strand of hereditary material surrounded by a protein coating.

viscosity: a liquid's resistance to flow. (p. 107)

virus: cadena de material genético rodeada de una capa proteica.

viscosidad: resistencia de un líquido al flujo. (p. 107)

water cycle: model describing how water moves from Earth's surface to the atmosphere and back to the surface again through evaporation, condensation, and precipitation.

weather: state of the atmosphere at a specific time and place, determined by factors including air pressure, amount of moisture in the air, temperature, wind, and precipitation. (p. 190)

wedge: simple machine consisting of an inclined plane that moves; can have one or two sloping sides. (p. 86)

wetland: a land region that is wet most or all of the year.

wheel and axle: simple machine made from two circular objects of different sizes that are attached and rotate together. (p. 88)

work: is done when a force exerted on an object causes that object to move some distance; equal to force times distance; measured in joules (J). (p. 74)

ciclo del agua: modelo que describe cómo se mueve el agua de la superficie de la Tierra hacia la atmósfera y nuevamente hacia la superficie terrestre a través de la evaporación, la condensación y la precipitación.

estado del tiempo: estado de la atmósfera en un momento y lugar específicos, determinado por factores que incluyen la presión del aire, cantidad de humedad en el aire, temperatura, viento y precipitación. (p. 190)

cuña: máquina simple que consiste en un plano inclinado que se mueve; puede tener uno o dos lados inclinados. (p. 86)

zona húmeda: región lluviosa la mayor parte del año.

rueda y eje: máquina simple compuesta por dos objetos circulares de diferentes tamaños que están interconectados y giran. (p. 88)

trabajo: se realiza cuando la fuerza ejercida sobre un objeto hace que el objeto se mueva determinada distancia; es igual a la fuerza multiplicada por la distancia y se mide en julios (J). (p. 74)

Glossary/Glosario

Italic numbers = illustration/photo   **Bold numbers = vocabulary term**
lab = indicates a page on which the entry is used in a lab
act = indicates a page on which the entry is used in an activity

A

Accelerating, gravity, 5

Activities, Applying Math, 17, 26, 37, 53, 63, 66, 76, 77, 78, 81, 83, 84, 91, 97, 123, 138, 139, 174, 193, 197; Applying Science, 58, 113, 166; Applying Skills, 11, 20, 30, 46, 169, 179, 205, 208; detailed observation, 29

Advertising, evaluating, 30

Air, heated, 175, *175*; mass of, *lab* 167; movement of, 175–179, *176, 177*; oxygen in, 162, 163, *163*

Air conditioner, 151

Air current, computer model predicting weather, 22

Air mass, 198, *198*

Air pollution, ozone depletion, *168*, 168–169, *169*; smog, 163

Air temperature, 191, *191*, 193, *193*, 207

Algae, oxygen production in, 168

Alternative resource, 59

Altitude, and atmospheric pressure, 166, *166*, *act* 166

Altostratus cloud, 195

Amorphous solid, 106, 111, *111*

Analyzing, energy transformation, *lab* 49

Anemometer, 191

Animal, insulation of, 134

Antarctica, ozone hole in, 169, *169*

Anticyclone, 199

Apple, creating energy, 66

Applying, science, 11

Applying Math, 26, 37, 53, 63, 66, 69; Chapter Review, 97; find an unknown, 123; Make a Data Table, 17; Section Review, 78, 84, 91, 139, 197; solving a one-step equation, 76, 77, 81, 83, 174; solving a simple equation, 138; using percentages, 193

Applying Science, How can ice save oranges?, 113; How does altitude affect air pressure?, 166; Is energy consumption outpacing production?, 58

Applying Skills, 11, 20, 30, 46, 108, 145, 151, 169, 179, 205, 208

Aquatic animal, hydroelectricity disrupting life cycle, 58

Archimedes' principle, 123, *123*, *lab* 126–127

Area, and pressure, 119, *119*

Artificial body parts, 94, *94*

Astronaut, training, 25, *25*

Atmosphere, 160–181, *162*, **162**, *174*; carbon dioxide in, 163; energy transfer in, 171–174, *172*, *lab* 180–181; gas in, 163, *163*; heated air in, 175, *175*; heat transfer in, 171–172, *172*, *lab* 180–181; importance of, 162; layers, *164*, 164–165, *act* 164, *165*; makeup of, 162–163, *163*; oxygen in, 162, 163, *163*; ozone layer in, *168*, 168–169, *169*; temperature in, 162, *162*, 167, *167*; uniqueness of, 174, *174*

Atmospheric pressure, 119, 119–121, *120*, *lab* 161, 166, *166*, *act* 166, 199, *act* 199, 207, 208

Atom, nucleus, 46, *46*

Automobile, hybrid, *49*; internal combustion engine, 148, *148*, *act* 148, *149*

Axle. *See* Wheel and axle

B

Balance, laboratory, 15, *15*

Balanced pressure, 120, *120*

Barometer, 199, *199*

Battery, electrical current, 46

Behavior, learning, 9, *9*

Bicycle, 85, *85*

Biologist, 13

Biomass, containing chemical energy, 49

Bionics, 94

Blizzard, 205, *205*

Blood pressure, *act* 125

Body part, artificial, 94, *94*

Body temperature, 83, 191; controlling, 51

Boiling point, 114, *114*

Boiling water, creating steam, 40

Bowling ball, differing from volleyball, 43, *43*

Building material, insulator, 144, *144*

Buoyant force, *122*, 122–123, *123*, *lab* 126–127

C

Calculating, number of power plants, 69; ratio of energy, 69

Calculator, using photovoltaic, 60

Calorie, creating energy, 66

Car, hybrid, *49*

Carbon dioxide, in atmosphere, 163; from fossil fuel, 56

Carnivore, 87

Cell model, *21*

Celsius scale, *137*, 137–138, *act* 138

Chart, observation, 15

Checking Concepts, 36, 68

Index

Chemical compound, 22

Chemical energy, 45, *45*; changing to thermal energy, 48, 49; molecule releasing, 56; transforming, 49; transforming to electrical energy, *52*

Chemical reaction, 83; energy causing, 44

Chemist, 10, *10*, 11

Chemistry, 10

Chlorofluorocarbon (CFC), *168*

Cirrostratus cloud, 195, *195*

Cirrus cloud, 195

City, heat, 154, *154*

Classifying, cloud, 194–196

Cloud, 173, *173*, *194*, 194–196, *195*, 201, *201*, 203

Cloud seedling, 212, *212*

Coal, energy contained within, 40; forming, 56, *56*; making plastic, 63; transforming chemical energy to electrical energy, *52*

Cold front, 199, 200

Columbus, Christopher, 176

Communicating, Science Journal, *act* 46; scientific finding, 17, *17*; through model, 25

Communicating Data, 117, 127

Communicating Your Data, 31, 33, 54, 65, 79, 93, 146, 153, 170, 181, 209, 211

Complex chemical, *45*

Compound chemical, 22

Compound machine, 85, *85*

Compressor, 150, *150*

Computer model, 22, *22*

Concept map, 35

Concept Map, 67, 69

Conclusion, drawing, 16; evaluating, 29

Condensation, 112, **115**, *115*, *act* 115, **173**, *173*, 192, *192*

Conduction, 141, *141*, **172**, *172*

Conductor, 143

Conservation, energy law of, **48**; of energy, 147

Constant, 18

Controlled experiment, 18; 400-m race, *18*

Convection, *142*, 142–143, *143*, *lab* 143, *172*, **172**–173

Coolant, 150, *150*, 151, *151*

Cooling, *lab* 146

Coriolis effect, 176, *176*, *177*

Crankshaft, 148

Crash-test dummy, testing effect of automobile accident, 25, *25*

Critical thinking, 11, 20, 26, 27, 30, 37, 46, 53, 63, 69

Crystal, 105, *105*

Crystalline solid, 105, *105*, 111

Cumulonimbus cloud, 196, 201, *201*, *203*

Cumulus cloud, 195

Cycle, in a system, 8, *8*; water, *lab* 117, 173, *173*

Cyclone, 199

Cylinder, 148, 149

Data, 28. *See also* Communicating Your Data

Density, 123, *act* 123

Dependent variable, 18

Desert ecosystem, studying, 4

Design Your Own, comparing thermal insulators, 152–153; Design your own ship, 126–127; heat is on, 180–181; pulley power, 92–93

Dew point, 192, *lab* 192, **193**, *act* 193

Dinosaur model, *21*

Direction, changing, 82, *82*; force, 75, *75*, 82, *82*

Distance, changing, 82, *82*; and work, 76, 82, *82*

Doldrum, *177*

Doppler radar, 206, *206*

Dry ice, 116, *116*

Earth, producing heat, 60. *See also* Atmosphere

Earth science, 10; solar energy, 66. *See also* Integrate Earth Science

Ecosystem, studying desert, 4

Efficiency, 83–84, *84*; calculating, *act* 84; equation for, 84; and friction, 85

Einstein, Albert, theory of relativity, 23

Electrical current, 46

Electrical energy, 40, *45*, **46**, 147; generating, 52; source of, *53*; transforming, 51

Electricity, generating from nuclear energy, 57, *57*

Energy, 42, 147, 149, *lab* 180–181; alternative resource, 59–61; to Burn, 66; from calorie intake, 66; causing change, *42*; causing chemical reaction, 44; changing form, 47, 49; changing mass, 23; chemical, 45, *45*; conserving, 63; consumption, *act* 58; electrical, 40; geothermal, 60; kinetic, **43**, *43*; law of conservation, **48**; and Marbles, *lab* 41; nuclear, **46**; from ocean, 62; potential, 44, *44*; and power, 78; powering life, *lab* 64–65; radiant, 45, *45*; Science Online, *act* 48; solar, 44, 55, *55*, 59, 171, *171*; source of, 55–63; source of electrical, *53*; studying, 10; sunlight, 11; thermal, 44, *44*, *109*, 109–110; tidal, 62; transfer of, 171–174, *172*; transferring, 42; type of, 110; and work, 78. *See also* Thermal energy

Energy transformation, 47, *47*; analyzing, *lab* 49, 53; chemical energy, 48, 49; electricity from nuclear energy, 57, *57*; hybrid car, *49*; kinetic to potential energy, 48, *48*; listening to radio, 51, *51*; within muscle, 50; National Geographic Visualizing, 50; tracking, 47

Index

Engine, *147,* 147–149, *148, act* 148, *act* 149

Engineer, 11

Environment, dry, 4

Equation, for efficiency, 83; for mechanical advantage, 81; one-step, *act* 76, *act* 77, *act* 81, *act* 83; for power, 77; simple, 138; for work, 76

Eruption, volcanic, 163, *163*

Evaluating, advertising claim, 30

Evaporation, 112, *114,* 114–115, *lab* 114

Examination Practice, 38–39; Intermediate-Level Science, 70–71

Exhaust valve, 149

Exosphere, 164, *164,* 165, *167*

Expansion, thermal, 137, *137*

Experiment, 18

Explanation, modifying, *7;* of observation, 12; scientific, 7

Fahrenheit scale, *137,* 137–138, *act* 138

Favorite food, *tab* 28

Fiber-optic wire, 11

First-class lever, 89, *89*

Fixed pulley, 90, *91*

Flooding, 204

Flower, producing in desert, 4

Fluid, 118–125; and Archimedes' principle, 123, *123, lab* 126–127; and buoyant force, *122,* 122–123, *123, lab* 126–127; and density, 123, *act* 123; and Pascal's principle, *124,* 124–125, *125;* and pressure, 118–122. *See also* Gas; Liquid

Fog, 195, *195*

Foldables, 5, 41, 73, 103, 135, 161, 189

Food, favorite, *tab* 28; as thermal energy, 44

Force, 118; and area, 119, *119;*

buoyant, *122,* **122**–123, *123, lab* 126–127; changing, 81; comparing, *lab* 73; computer model predicting, 22; direction of, 75, *75,* 87, *87;* input, 80, *80;* measurement of, 118; output, 80, *80;* and pressure, 118–122; and work, *lab* 73, 75, *75, lab* 79, *lab* 81

Force pump, 125, *125*

Forecasting weather, *206,* 206–209, *207, 208, lab* 209

Fossey, Dian, 9, *9*

Fossil fuel, decreasing supply, 59; making plastic, 63; as nonrenewable resource, 56; polluting air, 56; power plant, 52

Four-stroke cycle, 148, 149

Freezing, *lab* 103, *112,* **113**

Freezing point, 113, *act* 113

Frequency table, 28

Friction, 84, *84*

Front, 199–200, *200*

Fuel, mining, 59. *See also* fossil fuel

Fujita scale, *203*

Fulcrum, 88, 89

Gas, 108, *108;* in atmosphere, 163, *163;* condensation of, *112,* 115, *115, act* 115; natural, 56; pressure of, *121,* 121–122, *122. See also* Fluid

Generator, 52

Geologist, 10

Geothermal energy, 60

Geothermal power plant, 61, *61*

Geothermal reservoir, 60, 61, *61*

Glass, 111, *111*

Global warming, 204

Global wind, *176,* 176–178, *act* 176, *177*

Gorilla, observing, 9, *9*

Graph, source of electrical energy, 53; temperature change of solar collector, *act* 59

Graphing, data, *lab* 32–33

Gravity, accelerating object, *lab* 5; explaining, 7

Gumdrop-toothpick model, 22

Hail, 197, *197,* 201

Heart, 125, *125*

Heat, 110, **140**–146; conduction of, 141, *141;* convection of, *142,* 142–143, *143, lab* 143; radiation of, 141; specific, 111, *111,* 144, 172; and temperature, 110–111; and thermal energy, 140–143; transfer, 140, *140*

Heated air, 175, *175*

Heat engine, *147,* 147–149, *148, act* 148, *act* 149

Heating, *lab* 146

Heat island, 154, *154*

Heat pump, 61, 151, *151*

Heat transfer, in atmosphere, 171–172, *172, lab* 180–181; modeling, *lab* 172

Height, plant, *tab* 33

Herbivore, 87

High pressure area, 199, 207, *209*

History and Science, Women in Science, 34

Human body, system, 9

Humidity, 192, *192, act* 193; relative, **192,** *act* 193, 198

Hurricane, 204, *204,* 205; releasing energy, 66

Hybrid car, energy transformation, *49*

Hydraulic system, 124, *124*

Hydroelectricity, as renewable source of energy, 58; Science Online, *act* 58

Hydroelectric power plant, 53

Hydrosphere, 173, *173*

Hypothesis, 14; forming, *lab* 14, *lab* 64; testing, 15, 65; using a model to test, 21

Ice, dry, 116, *116*
Idea model, 22, 23
Incline plane, 85–87, *86*
Independent variable, 18
Inexhaustible resource, 59; tidal energy, 62; wind, 63
Infer, 16
Inference, accuracy, 27, *27*
Input force, 80, *80*
Insulator, 144, *144, lab* 152–153
Integrate Career, biologist, 13
Integrate Earth Science, 182; Energy Source Origin, 56
Integrate Environment, global warming, 204
Integrate Health, Health Integration System, 9; ozone hole, 169
Integrate History, 106; James Prescott Joule, 76
Integrate Life Science, animal insulation, 144; body temperature, 83, 191; Controlling Body Temperature, 51; effects of ultraviolet light on algae, 168; thermal pollution, 145; Transforming Chemical Energy, 49; wedges in your body, 87
Integrate Physics, highs and lows, 199; specific heat, 172; type of energy, 110
Intermediate-Level Science Examination Practice, 38–39, 70–71, 98–99, 132–133, 158–159, 186–187
Internal combustion engine, 148, *148, act* 148, *149*
International Space Station, using photovoltaic, 60
Investigating, identifying parts, *lab* 32–33; question and observation, 13, *13*
Ionosphere, 165, 165, *167*
Isobar, 207, *208*
Isotherm, 207

Jaw, hearing with, *lab* 54
Jet stream, 178, *178*
Joule, James Prescott, 76
Journal, 72, 102, 134, 160, 188. *See also* Science Journal

K

Kelvin scale, 138
Kilopascal (kPa), 118
Kinetic energy, 43, *43;* changing to potential energy, 48, *48;* positioning, 44, *44;* producing from steam, 51

Lab, building the pyramids, 79; Design Your Own: Comparing thermal insulators, 152–153; Design Your Own: Design your own ship, 126–127; Design Your Own: Heat is on, 180–181; Design Your Own: Pulley Power, 92–93; evaluating sunscreens, 170; Hearing with Your Jaw, 54; heating up and cooling down, 146; Identifying Parts of an Investigation, 32–33; Launch Lab, 5, 41, 73, 103, 135, 161, 189; Mini Lab, 23, 59, 114, 167, 202; Model and Invent: Measuring wind speed, 202; reading a weather map, 209; Try at Home Mini Lab, *lab* 8, *lab* 14, 49, 77, 121, 173, 207; Use the Internet, 64–65; Water Cycle, 117; What is the right answer?, 31
Laboratory, safety, 19, *19,* 20, *20*
Laboratory balance, 15, *15*
Land breeze, 179, *179*
Launch Lab, 135; compare forces, 73; Experiment with a freezing point, 103; Marbles and Energy, 41; observe air pressure, 161; Observe How Gravity

Accelerates Objects, *lab* 5; What causes rain?, 189
Law, conservation of energy, 147; scientific, **7**
Law of conservation of energy, 48
Lever, 88, *88,* 89, *89*
Levi-Montalcini, Rita, 34
Life cycle, hydroelectricity disrupting, 58
Life science, 9
Life Science, Integrate. *See* Integrate Life Science
Light, studying, *10;* study of behavior, 11; ultraviolet, 168, *lab* 170
Light energy, 45
Lightning, 202, *202, act* 202
Liquid, *106,* **106**–107, *107;* freezing, *lab* 103, 112, 123; and surface tension, 107, *107;* vaporization of, *112, 114,* 114–115, *lab* 114; viscosity of, 107. *See also* Fluid
Living organisms, biomass, 49
Living system, 10
Low pressure area, 199, 207, *208*

M

Machine, 80–93; compound, **85,** *85;* and efficiency, 83–84, *84;* and friction, 84, *84;* and mechanical advantage, *80,* 80–82, 88, *88. See also* Simple machine
Magma, volcanic eruption, 60
Map, *lab* 209; concept, 35, 67; topographic, *act* 22; weather, *22,* 208, *208*
Marbles, and Energy, *lab* 41
Mass, 10, **42;** changing to energy, 23; and kinetic energy, 43, *43*
Math Review, 364–373
Math Skill Handbook, 364–378
Matter, 10, **104.** *See also* States of Matter
Mayer, Maria Goeppert, 34
Measurement, *lab* 210–211; of force, 118; of rain, *lab* 207;

Index

temperature, *137*, 137–138; unit of, 77; wind speed, 191; of work, 78

Mechanical advantage, *80*, 80–82, **81**, 88, *88*

Mechanical energy, 147, *147*, 148

Melting, 111, *111*, *112*; comparing rate of, *lab* 142

Melting point, *111*

Mesosphere, 164, *164*, 165, 167, *167*

Meteorologist, 10, **206**

Method, using scientific, *lab* 65

Mini Lab, 143; Analyzing Energy Transformation, 49; Building a Solar Collector, 59; Classifying Parts of a System, 8; determining dew point, 192; determining if air has mass, 167; Forming a Hypothesis, 14; observing convection, 143; observing pulleys, 90; observing vaporization, 114; Thinking Like a Scientist, 23

Model, 21; communicating observation and idea, 25; creating, 23, *23*; limitation, 26; scientific, 23; type of, *21*, 22

Model and Invent, measuring wind speed, 210–211

Molten rock, 60

Motion, and kinetic energy, 43, *43*; and work, 74, *74*–75, *75*

Movable pulleys, 91, *91*

National Geographic Chapter Opener, 160; States of matter, 102; thermal energy, 134; weather, 188; work and simple machines, 72

National Geographic Visualizing, Energy Transformation, 50; four-stroke cycle, 149; global winds, 177; levers, 89; Modeling of King Tut, 24; states of matter, 112; tornadoes, 203

National Weather Service, 206

Natural gas, as fossil fuel, 56

Nature, studying, *lab* 5, 8

Newton (unit of force), 118

Nimbostratus cloud, 196

Nimbus cloud, 196

Nitrogen, 163, *163*

Nonliving system, 10

Nonrenewable resource, 56

Nuclear energy, 46, 147; generating electricity, 57, *57*

Nuclear power plant., energy transformation, 53

Nuclear waste, 57

Observation, 12; accuracy, 27, *27*; detailed, *act* 29; explaining, 12; gorilla, 9, *9*; gravity accelerating object, *lab* 5; investigating, 13, *13*; model communicating, 25; scientific law, 7; skill of biologist, 13; summarizing, 15; writing down, 28, *28*

Observation chart, 15

Occluded front, 200, *200*

Ocean, energy from, 62

Oil, as fossil fuel, 56; making plastic, 63

One-step equations, *act* 76, *act* 77, *act* 81, *act* 83

Online. *See* Science Online

Oops! Accidents in Science, Incredible Stretching Goo, 128

Optical fiber, 11

Output force, 80, *80*

Oxygen, in atmosphere, 162, 163, *163*; production of, 168

Ozone, 164, 167

Ozone depletion, 168, 168–169, *169*

Ozone layer, *168*, **168**–169, *169*

Pascal (Pa), 118

Pascal's principle, *124*, **124**–125, *125*

Percentage, *act* 203; using energy, 69

Periodic Table of the Elements, 379–380

Photovoltaic, 60

Physical model, 22

Physical science, 10

Physicist, 10, *10*

Physics, 10

Pinatubo volcano (Philippines), 163

Piston, 124, *124*, 148, *149*

Plant, height, *tab* 33

Plasma, *act* 107

Polar bear, 144

Polar easterlies, *177*, 178

Pollution, of air, 163, *168*, 168–169; hydroelectricity, 58; thermal, **145,** *145*

Potential energy, 44, *44*; from kinetic energy, 48, *48*

Power, *77*–78; calculating, 77, *act* 77; and energy, 78; equation for, 77; geothermal, 61; of pulley, *lab* 92–93

Power plant, generating electrical energy, 52, 53; obtaining useful energy, 46, *46*; type of, 53

Precipitation, 196–197, *196*–*197*; snow, *196*–*197*. *See also* Rain

Prediction, 27; making, **14**; model testing, 25

Presentation Skills, 362–363

Pressure, *118*, **118**–122; and area, 119, *119*; atmospheric, *119*, 119–121, *120*, *lab* 161, 166, *166*, *act* 166; balanced, 120, *120*; and force, 118–120; of gas, *121*, 121–122, *122*; and temperature, 122, *122*; and volume, 121, *121*

Prevailing westerlies, *177*, 178

Process, in a system, 8, *8*

Index

Promotional material, evaluating, 30

Prostheses, 94, *94*

Prototype model, *21*

Pulley, 90–93, *lab* 90; fixed, 90, *91*; movable, 91, *91*; power of, *lab* 92–93

Pulley system, 91, *91*, *lab* 92–93

Pyramid, building, *lab* 73, *lab* 79

Question, answering, 6, *7*; investigating, 13, *13*; scientific method, 12; scientist asking, 5, 6

Radiant energy, 45, *45*, 147; from sun, 55

Radiation, 141, **172,** *172*

Radioactive atom, energy from, 55, *55*; producing heat, 60

Radioactivity, from nuclear waste, 57

Radio Wave, 165, *165*

Rain, 196, *196*; and clouds, 196, 212, *212*; formation of, *lab* 189; measuring, *lab* 207; thunderstorm, 196, 199, *211*, 211–212, *212*

Ratio, calculating energy, 69; Earth's temperature, 63; producing electrical energy, 53

Reaction, chemical, 83

Reading Check, 7, 8, 17, 22, 23, 43, 45, 48, 52, 59, 74, 87, 90, 104, 105, 106, 110, 115, 119, 122, 137, 141, 143, 148, 165, 166, 172, 174, 176, 179, 192, 196, 199, 202, 207

Real-World Question, *lab* 31, *lab* 32–33, 54, 64, 79, 90, 117, 126, 146, 152, 170, 180, 209, 210

Refrigerator, 150, *150*

Relative humidity, 202, *act* 203, 207

Relativity, theory of, *23*

Renewable resource, 58

Reservoir, geothermal, 60

Resource, 55; of energy, 55

Reviewing Main Ideas, 67

Rock, molten, 60

Rocket, 165

Safety, laboratory, 19, *19*, 20, *20*; in severe weather, 205; symbol, 19, *19*, 351

Salt, crystal structure of, 105, *105*

Satellite, using photovoltaic, 60

Science, 6; applying, 11, *11*; Earth, **10**; and the heat is on, 154; life, **9**; physical, **10**; women in, 34

Science and History, Women in Science, 34

Science and Language Arts, "Song of the Sky Loom", 182

Science and Society, Bionic People, 94

Science Journal, 0, 4, 40, 160; charting observation, 15; flower growing in desert, 4; recording how energy is used, *act* 46; recording observation, 13, *lab* 14, 29

Science Online, 5, 17, 34, 41, 64, 65, 73, 76, 77, 83, 94; atmospheric pressure, 199; automobile engine, 148; blood pressure, 125; condensation, 115; Earth's atmospheric layers, 164; Energy, 48; freezing point study, 113; global winds, 176; historical tools, 81; Hydroelectricity, 58; James Watt, 78; lightning, 202; plasma, 107; Scientific method, 18; Topographic Map, 22

Science Skill Handbook, 342–352

Science Stats, Energy to Burn, 66

Scientific data, evaluating, 29

Scientific law, 7

Scientific Methods, 21, 79, 92–93, 117, 126–127, 146, 152–153, 170, 180–181, 209, 210–211; Analyze Your Data, 93, 127, 153, 181, 211; Conclude and Apply, 79, 93, 117, 127, 146, 153, 170, 181, 209, 211; Following a Pattern, 12, *12*; Follow Your Plan, 93, 127, 153; Form a Hypothesis, 92, 126, 152, 180; Make a Plan, 92, 126, 152; Make the Model, 210; Test Your Hypothesis, 126, 152, 181; Test Your Model, 211; using, *lab* 65

Scientific model, 23

Scientific theory, 7

Scientist, collection of skills, 12; thinking like, *lab* 23

Screw, 87, *87*

Sea breeze, 179, *179*

Seasonal temperature, *act* 17

Second-class lever, 89, *89*

Section Review, 11, 20, 26, 30, 46, 53, 63

Shark, repelling water, 11

Ship, designing, 126–127

Simple machine, 85–93; incline plane, **85**–87, *86*; lever, 88, *88*, 89, *89*; pulley, 90, *lab* 90, *lab* 90–91, *91*, 93; screw, 87, *87*; wedge, 86, 86–87, *87*; wheel and axle, 88, *88*, 90, *90*

Sleet, 206, *207*

Smog, 163

Snow, 196, *196*, 205, *205*

Sodium chloride, 105, *105*

Solar collector, building, *lab* 59

Solar energy, 171, *171*; as inexhaustible resource, 59

Solar-powered car, *11*

Solar system, model, 26, *26*

Solid, 105, **105**–106; amorphous, 106, 111, *111*; crystalline, 105, *105*, 111; melting, 111, *111*, *112*; sublimation, 116, *116*

Space shuttle, 165, *165*

Specific heat, 111, *111*, 144, 172

Speed, of heating and cooling, *lab* 146; and kinetic energy, 43, *43*

States of matter, 102–127, 104; changes of, 109–117, *lab* 117;

and condensation, *112*, 115, *115, act* 115; and evaporation, *102, 114*, 114–115, *lab* 114; fluid, 118–125, *122, 123, 124, 125, act* 125, *lab* 126–127; and freezing, *lab* 102, *lab* 123; gas, 108, *108*; liquid, *105, 106*, 106–107; and melting, 111, *111, 112*; and pressure, 118–122; solid, *105*, 105–106; and sublimation, 116, *116*; and vaporization, *112, 114*, 114–115, *lab* 114

Stationary front, 200, *200*

Station model, 207, *207*

Steam, creating, 40; heat pump, 61, *61*; producing electrical energy, 52; producing kinetic energy, 51

Stratosphere, 164, 165, 167, *167*

Stratus cloud, 195

Structure, in a system, 8, *8*

Study Guide, 35, 67, 95, 129, 155, 183, 213

Sublimation, 116, *116*

Sugar, 45, *45*

Sun, weather, 190

Sunlight, collecting energy from, 60; energy, 11; energy from, 55, *55*; as thermal energy, 44

Sunscreen, *lab* 170

Surface tension, 107, 107

Swimsuit, repelling water, 11, *11*

System, 8; combining, 9; computer model predicting, 22; health integration, 9; living and nonliving, 10; scientific, 8

Table, Favorite Food, 28; frequency, 28; Observation chart, 15

Technician, ultrasound and x-ray, 11

Technology, air conditioner, 151; anemometer, 191; barometer, 199, *199*; bicycle, 85, *85*; chlorofluorocarbon, 168, *168*; Doppler radar, 206, *206*; heat pump, 151, *151*; internal

combustion engine, 148, *148, act* 148, 149; pyramid, *lab* 73, *lab* 79; refrigerator, 150, *150*; rocket, 165; space shuttle, 165, *165*; thermometer, 137, *137*; using science, **11**; wind sock, 191; wind vane, 191

Technology Skill Handbook, 360–363

Teeth, herbivore and carnivore, 87, *87*

Temperature, 110, *110, lab* 135, *136,* **136**–138; of air, 191, *191*, 193, *193*, 207; in atmosphere, 162, *162*, 167, *167*; body, 83; of body, 191; controlling body, 51; and heat, 110–111; measuring, *137,* 137–138; and pressure, 122, *122*; seasonal, *act* 17; and thermal energy, 139, *139*

Temperature scale, Celsius, *137,* 137–138, *act* 138; converting, 138, *act* 138; Fahrenheit, *137,* 137–138, *act* 138; Kelvin, 138

Theory, 6; relativity, 23; scientific, 7

Thermal collector, 60

Thermal conductor, 143

Thermal energy, 44, *44*, 109, **109**–110, 134–154, **139,** *139, 147, 147, 149*; from chemical energy, 48; moving, 52, *52*; radioactive atom, 55; and temperature, 149, *149*; transfer of, 140–142, *141, 142*; transforming, 51

Thermal expansion, 137, *137*

Thermal insulator, 140, *140, lab* 152–153

Thermal pollution, 145, *145*

Thermometer, 137, *137*

Thermosphere, 164, *164*, 165, 167

Think Critically, 11, 20, 26, 27, 30, 37, 46, 53, 63, 69

Thinking, like a scientist, *lab* 23

Third-class lever, 89, *89*

Thunderstorm, 196, 199, 201, 201–202, *202*

Tidal energy, 62

Tidal power plant, 62, *62*

TIME, Science and History, 34; Science and Language Arts, 182; Science and Society, 94, 154

Tools, historical, *act* 81

Topographic Map, *act* 22

Tornadoes, 202, *203, 206*

Trade wind, 177, 178

Transformation, 47. *See also* Energy transformation

Troposphere, 164, 164, 167, *167*, 178, *178*

Try at Home Mini Lab, 142, 354–359; Analyzing Energy Transformation, 49; Classifying Parts of a System, 8; comparing rates of melting, 142; Forming a Hypothesis, 14; measuring rain, 207; modeling heat transfer, 173; predicting a waterfall, 121; work and power, 77

Tunnel, wind, 25, *25*

Turbine, 52

Ultrasound technician, 11

Ultraviolet radiation, 168, *lab* 170

Unknown, finding, *act* 123

Use and Care of a Microscope, 387

Use the Internet, Energy to Power Your Life, *lab* 64–65

Using Scientific Methods, *lab* 65

Vapor, 108

Vaporization, *112, 114,* **114**–115, *lab* 114

Variable, 18

Viscosity, 107

Volcano, eruption, 163, *163*

Volcanologist, 10, *10*

Volleyball, differing from bowling ball, 43

Volume, and pressure, 121, *121*

Wall cloud, *203*

Wall socket, electrical current, 46

Warm front, 199, *200*

Waste, nuclear, 57

Water, boiling creating steam, 40; boiling point, 114, *114*; freshwater, 106; melting point, 111

Water cycle, *lab* 117, 173, *173*

Waterfall, *lab* 121

Water vapor, in atmosphere, 163; and humidity, 202, *202*, *act* 203; and temperature, 203, *203*

Watt, James, 77, *act* 78

Watt (W), 77

Wave, radio, 165, *165*

Weather, 188, *188*, **190**–212; changes, 198–199, *199*; and clouds, *194*, 194–196, *195*, 201, *201*, *203*; forecasting, *206*, 206–209, *207*, *208*, *lab* 209; and fronts, 199–200, *200*, 208, *208*; measuring wind speed, 201, *lab* 210–211; and precipitation, 196–197, *196–197*; and safety, 205; severe, 201–205, *202*, *203*, *204*, *205*; and sun, 190, *190*

Weather map, 22, 208, *208*, *lab* 209; symbols, 381

Weather pattern, computer model predicting, 22, *22*

Wedge, *86*, **86**–87, *87*

Wheel and axle, **88**, *88*, 90, *90*

Wind, 175–179, 201, *201*; and Coriolis effect, 176, *176*, *177*; global, *176*, 176–178, *act* 176, *177*; inexhaustible energy source, 63; jet stream, 178, *178*; as kinetic energy, 44; land breeze, 179, *179*; local, 178–179, *179*; polar easterlies, *177*, 178; prevailing westerlies, *177*, 178; sea breeze, 179, *179*; surface, 178; trade, *177*, 178

Windmill, producing electrical energy, 63, *63*

Wind shear, 202

Wind sock, 201

Wind speed, 201, *lab* 210–211

Wind tunnel, testing airplane design, 25, *25*

Wind vane, 191

Women in Science, 34

Wood, chemical energy, 46

Work, 74–76; calculating, 76, *act* 76; and distance, 76, 82, *82*; and energy, 78; equation for, 76; and force, *lab* 73, 75, *75*, *lab* 79, 81; measuring, 78; and mechanical advantage, *80*, 80–82; and motion, *74*, 74–75, *75*; and power, *lab* 77

X-ray technician, 11

Yalow, Rosalyn Sussman, 34

Credits

Photo Credits

Cover (t)Silvia Otte/Getty Images, (bl)Bob Krist/CORBIS, (br)Kevin Schafer/CORBIS; **iii** (tl)Roy Johnson/Tom Stack & Assoc., (tr)Rich Iwasaki/Getty Images, (bl) Lynn M. Stone/DRK Photo, (br)Wyman P. Meinzer; **viii** AFP/CORBIS; **ix** Howard Bluestein/Photo Researchers; **x** Marian Bacon/Animals Animals; **xi** John Kaprielian/Photo Researchers; **xii** Ed Reschke/Peter Arnold, Inc.; **xiii** Peter Veit/National Geographic Image Collection; **xiv** Philip Bailey/The Stock Market/CORBIS; **xv** Bob Daemmrich; **xvi** Aaron Haupt; **xvii** Dominic Oldershaw; **xviii** James L. Amos/Peter Arnold, Inc.; **xix** Tess & David Young/Tom Stack & Assoc.; **2–3** Douglas Peebles/CORBIS; **3** Henry Ford Museum & Greenfield Village; **4–5** David Keaton/CORBIS; **6** (l)Jack Star/Photolink/PhotoDisc, (c)Rudi Von Briel, (r)Richard T. Nowitz/CORBIS; **7** (l)Phil Schermeister/CORBIS; **8** Mary Kate Denny/PhotoEdit; **9** Peter Veit/National Geographic Image Collection; **10** (t)G. Brad Lewis/Stone, (c)Roger Ball/The Stock Market, (b)Will & Deni McIntyre/Photo Researchers; **11** (t)AFP/CORBIS, (b)Reuters NewMedia, Inc./CORBIS; **13–14** Richard Hutchings; **15** Matt Meadows; **16** Icon Images; **17** Richard Hutchings/PhotoEdit/PictureQuest; **18** Rudi Von Briel; **19** Bob Daemmrich; **20** Glasheen Graphics/Index Stock; **21** (t)David Young-Wolff/PhotoEdit, (bl)A. Ramey/PhotoEdit, (bc)John Bavosi/Science Photo Library/Photo Researchers, (br)Donald C. Johnson/The Stock Market; **22** CORBIS/PictureQuest; **23** Todd Gipstein/CORBIS; **24** (tl cl r)Betty Pat Gatliff, (tr)Richard Nowitz/Words & Pictures/PictureQuest, (bl)Michael O'Brian/Mud Island, Inc.; **25** (l)Carol Anne Petrachenko/CORBIS, (c)Jim Sugar Photography/CORBIS, (r)Tom Wurl/Stock Boston/PictureQuest; **26** (t)Stock Montage, (b)North Wind Picture Archives; **27** Digital Art/CORBIS; **28** SuperStock; **29** (t)Lester V. Bergman/CORBIS, (b)Bob Handelman/Stone; **31** Amanita Pictures; **32** (t)Aaron Haupt, (b)Matt Meadows, **34** (t)Reuters/CORBIS, (bl)UPI/Bettmann/CORBIS, (br)credit unknown; **37** Tim Courlas; **38** Peter Veit/National Geographic Image Collection; **39** Tim Courlas/Horizons; **40–41** Chris Knapton/Science Photo Library/Photo Researchers; **41** Matt Meadows; **42** (l c)file photo, (r)Mark Burnett; **43** (t)Bob Daemmrich, (c)Al Tielemans/Duomo, (b)Bob Daemmrich; **44** KS Studios, **45** (l)Bob Daemmrich, (r)Andrew McClenaghan/Science Photo Library/Photo Researchers; **46** Mark Burnett/Photo Researchers; **47** Lori Adamski Peek/Stone/Getty Images; **48** Richard Hutchings; **49** (l)Ron Kimball/Ron Kimball Photography; **50** (t)Judy Lutz, (b)Lennart Nilsson; **50** Stephen R. Wagner; **52–54** KS Studios; **60** (t)Dr. Jeremy Burgess/Science Photo Library/Photo Researchers, (b)John Keating/Photo Researchers; **61** Geothermal Education Office; **62** Carsand-Mosher; **63** Billy Hustace/Stone/Getty Images; **64** SuperStock; **65** Roger Ressmeyer/CORBIS; **66** (t)Reuters NewMedia, Inc./CORBIS, (c)PhotoDisc, (b)Dominic Oldershaw; **67** (l)Lowell Georgia/CORBIS, (r)Mark Richards/PhotoEdit; **72–73** Rich Iwasaki/Getty Images; **73** Mark Burnett; **74** Mary Kate Denny/PhotoEdit; **75** (t)Richard Hutchings, (b)Tony Freeman/PhotoEdit; **82** (tl)David Young-Wolff/PhotoEdit, (tr)Tom McHugh/Photo Researchers, (bl)Frank Siteman/Stock Boston, (br)Amanita Pictures; **85** Duomo; **86** Robert Brenner/PhotoEdit; **88** Amanita Pictures;

89 (t)Dorling Kindersley, (c b)Bob Daemmrich; **90** (l)Wernher Krutein/Liaison Agency/Getty Images, (r)Siegfried Layda/Stone/Getty Images; **92** Tony Freeman/PhotoEdit; **93** Aaron Haupt; **94** (t)Ed Kashi/CORBIS, (b)James Balog/Contact; **95** (l)Janeart/The Image Bank/Getty Images, (r)Ryan McVay/PhotoDisc; **99** (t)Comstock Images, (b)PhotoDisc; **100** Stephen Dalton/Animals Animals; **100–101** A.T. Willett/Image Bank/Getty Images; **102–103** Roger Ressmeyer/CORBIS; **104** Layne Kennedy/CORBIS; **105** (t)Telegraph Colour Library/FPG/Getty Images, (b)Paul Silverman/Fundamental Photographs; **106** Bill Aron/PhotoEdit; **107** (l)John Serrao/Photo Researchers; (r)H. Richard Johnston; **108** Tom Tracy/Photo Network/PictureQuest; **109** Annie Griffiths Belt/CORBIS; **110** Amanita Pictures; **111** (t)David Weintraub/Stock Boston, (b)James L. Amos/Peter Arnold, Inc.; **112** (l)Dave King/DK Images; **113** Joseph Sohm/ChromoSohm, Inc./CORBIS; **114** Michael Dalton/Fundamental Photographs; **115** Swarthout & Associates/The Stock Market/CORBIS; **116** Tony Freeman/PhotoEdit; **118** David Young-Wolff/PhotoEdit; **119** (t)Joshua Ets-Hokin/PhotoDisc, (b)Richard Hutchings; **120** Robbie Jack/CORBIS; **122** A. Ramey/Stock Boston; **123** Mark Burnett; **124** (t)Tony Freeman/PhotoEdit, (b)Stephen Simpson/FPG/Getty Images; **126** (t)Lester Lefkowitz/The Stock Market/CORBIS, (b)Bob Daemmrich; **127** Bob Daemmrich; **128** Daniel Belknap; **129** (l)Andrew Ward/Life File/PhotoDisc, (r)NASA/TRACE; **131** Mark Burnett; **134–135** Peter Walton/Index Stock; **136** John Evans; **137** (t)Nancy P. Alexander/Visuals Unlimited, (b)Morton & White; **139** Tom Stack; **140** Doug Martin; **141** Matt Meadows; **142** Jeremy Hoare/PhotoDisc; **143** Donnie Kamin/PhotoEdit; **144** SuperStock; **145** Colin Raw/Stone/Getty Images; **146** Aaron Haupt; **147** PhotoDisc; **148** (t)Doug Menuez/PhotoDisc, (bl)Barbara Stitzer/PhotoEdit, (br)Addison Geary/Stock Boston; **150** C. Squared Studios/PhotoDisc; **152–153** Morton & White; **154** Chip Simons/FPG; **155** Slim Films; **160–161** S.P. Gillette/CORBIS; **162** NASA; **163** (l)Frank Rossotto/The Stock Market/CORBIS, (r)Larry Lee/CORBIS; **166** Laurence Fordyce/CORBIS; **168** Doug Martin; **170** Michael Newman/PhotoEdit; **175** (t)Dan Guravich/Photo Researchers, (b)Bill Brooks/Masterfile; **177** (bkgd)Stephen R. Wagner, (tl)Gene Moore/PhotoTake NYC/PictureQuest, (tr)Phil Schermeister/CORBIS, (bl)Joel W. Rogers, (br)Kevin Schafer/CORBIS; **178** Bill Brooks/Masterfile; **180–181** David Young-Wolff/PhotoEdit; **182** Bob Rowan/CORBIS; **188–189** Reuters NewMedia, Inc/CORBIS; **189** KS Studios; **190** Kevin Horgan/Stone/Getty Images; **191** Fabio Colombini/Earth Scenes; **195** (t)Charles O'Rear/CORBIS, (b)Joyce Photographics/Photo Researchers; **196** (l)Roy Morsch/The Stock Market/CORBIS, (r)Mark McDermott; **197** (l)Mark E. Gibson/Visuals Unlimited, (r)EPI Nancy Adams/Tom Stack & Assoc.; **199** Van Bucher/Science Source/Photo Researchers; **201** Jeffrey Howe/Visuals Unlimited; **202** Roy Johnson/Tom Stack & Assoc.; **203** (l)Warren Faidley/Weatherstock, (r)Robert Hynes; **204** NASA/Science Photo Library/Photo Researchers; **205** Fritz Pölking/Peter Arnold, Inc; **206** Howard Bluestein/Science Source/Photo Researchers; **209** Mark Burnett; **210** (t)Marc Epstein/DRK Photo, (b)Timothy Fuller; **212** (t)Erik Rank/Photonica, (c b)courtesy Weather Modification Inc.; **213** (l)George D. Lepp/Photo Researchers, (r)Janet Foster/Masterfile; **214** Ruth Dixon; **215** Bob

Daemmrich; **342** Tom Pantages; **346** Michell D. Bridwell/PhotoEdit; **347** (t)Mark Burnett, (b)Dominic Oldershaw; **348** StudiOhio; **349** Timothy Fuller; **350** Aaron Haupt; **352** KS Studios; **353** Matt Meadows; **354** John Evans; **355** Mark Burnett; **356** Matt Meadows; **357** Mary Lou Uttermohlen; **358** Rod Planck/Photo Researchers; **360** (l)Brad Armstrong/AP/Wide World Photos, (r)file photo; **362** Stuart Ramson/AP/Wide World Photos; **379** Matt Meadows; **382** (tl)NIBSC/Science Photo Library/Photo Researchers, (bl)Dr. Richard Kessel, (r)David John/Visuals Unlimited; **383** (tl)Runk/Schoenberger from Grant Heilman, (bl)Andrew Syred/Science Photo Library/Photo Researchers, (r)Rich Brommer; **384** (tl)Ralph Reinhold/Earth Scenes, (bl)Scott Johnson/Animals Animals, (r)G.R. Roberts; **385** Martin Harvey/DRK Photo.

PERIODIC TABLE OF THE ELEMENTS

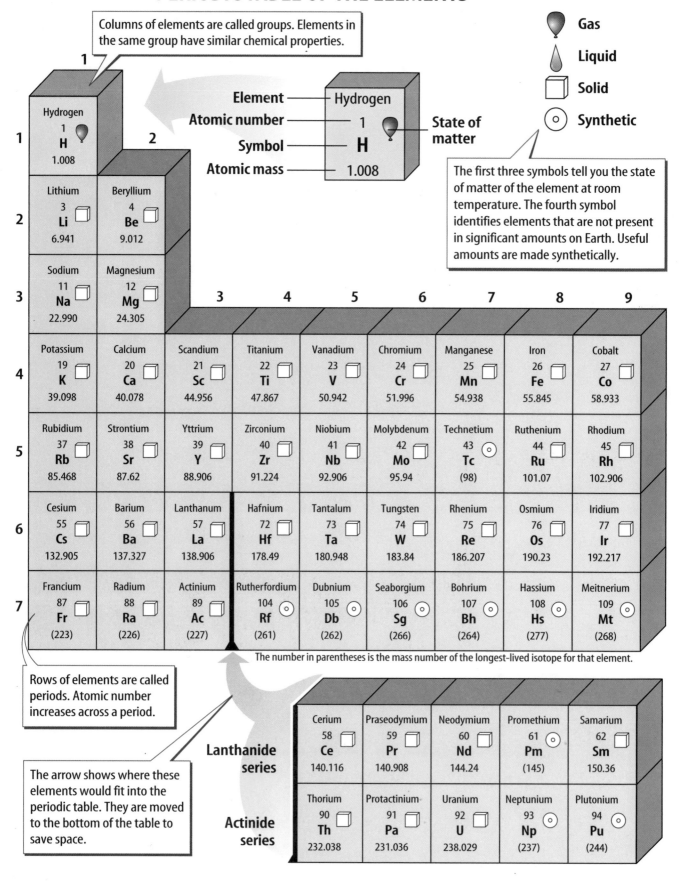

Columns of elements are called groups. Elements in the same group have similar chemical properties.

Element — Hydrogen
Atomic number — 1
Symbol — H
Atomic mass — 1.008

State of matter

Gas
Liquid
Solid
Synthetic

The first three symbols tell you the state of matter of the element at room temperature. The fourth symbol identifies elements that are not present in significant amounts on Earth. Useful amounts are made synthetically.

1	2	3	4	5	6	7	8	9
1 Hydrogen 1 **H** 1.008								
2 Lithium 3 **Li** 6.941	Beryllium 4 **Be** 9.012							
3 Sodium 11 **Na** 22.990	Magnesium 12 **Mg** 24.305							
4 Potassium 19 **K** 39.098	Calcium 20 **Ca** 40.078	Scandium 21 **Sc** 44.956	Titanium 22 **Ti** 47.867	Vanadium 23 **V** 50.942	Chromium 24 **Cr** 51.996	Manganese 25 **Mn** 54.938	Iron 26 **Fe** 55.845	Cobalt 27 **Co** 58.933
5 Rubidium 37 **Rb** 85.468	Strontium 38 **Sr** 87.62	Yttrium 39 **Y** 88.906	Zirconium 40 **Zr** 91.224	Niobium 41 **Nb** 92.906	Molybdenum 42 **Mo** 95.94	Technetium 43 **Tc** (98)	Ruthenium 44 **Ru** 101.07	Rhodium 45 **Rh** 102.906
6 Cesium 55 **Cs** 132.905	Barium 56 **Ba** 137.327	Lanthanum 57 **La** 138.906	Hafnium 72 **Hf** 178.49	Tantalum 73 **Ta** 180.948	Tungsten 74 **W** 183.84	Rhenium 75 **Re** 186.207	Osmium 76 **Os** 190.23	Iridium 77 **Ir** 192.217
7 Francium 87 **Fr** (223)	Radium 88 **Ra** (226)	Actinium 89 **Ac** (227)	Rutherfordium 104 **Rf** (261)	Dubnium 105 **Db** (262)	Seaborgium 106 **Sg** (266)	Bohrium 107 **Bh** (264)	Hassium 108 **Hs** (277)	Meitnerium 109 **Mt** (268)

The number in parentheses is the mass number of the longest-lived isotope for that element.

Rows of elements are called periods. Atomic number increases across a period.

The arrow shows where these elements would fit into the periodic table. They are moved to the bottom of the table to save space.

Lanthanide series

Cerium 58 **Ce** 140.116	Praseodymium 59 **Pr** 140.908	Neodymium 60 **Nd** 144.24	Promethium 61 **Pm** (145)	Samarium 62 **Sm** 150.36

Actinide series

Thorium 90 **Th** 232.038	Protactinium 91 **Pa** 231.036	Uranium 92 **U** 238.029	Neptunium 93 **Np** (237)	Plutonium 94 **Pu** (244)